Conversations with Tennessee Williams

Literary Conversations Series

Peggy Whitman Prenshaw
General Editor

Conversations
with Tennessee Williams

Edited by
Albert J. Devlin

University Press of Mississippi
Jackson and London

Books by Tennessee Williams

27 Wagons Full of Cotton and Other One-Act Plays. Norfolk, CT: New Directions, 1945.

American Blues: Five Short Plays. New York: Dramatists Play Service, 1948.

One Arm and Other Stories. New York: New Directions, 1948.

The Roman Spring of Mrs. Stone. New York: New Directions, 1950.

Hard Candy: A Book of Stories. New York: New Directions, 1954.

In the Winter of Cities: Poems. Norfolk, CT: New Directions, 1956.

The Knightly Quest: A Novella and Four Short Stories. New York: New Directions, 1966.

Dragon Country: A Book of Plays. New York: New Directions, 1969.

The Theatre of Tennessee Williams. 7 vols. New York: New Directions, 1971-1981.

Eight Mortal Ladies Possessed: A Book of Stories. New York: New Directions, 1974.

Moise and the World of Reason. New York: Simon, 1975.

Memoirs. Garden City, NY: Doubleday, 1975.

Tennessee Williams' Letters to Donald Windham, 1940-1965. Ed. Donald Windham. Verona, Italy: Sandy M. Campbell, 1976; New York: Holt, 1977.

Androgyne, Mon Amour: Poems. New York: New Directions, 1977.

Where I Live: Selected Essays. Ed. Christine R. Day and Bob Woods. New York: New Directions, 1978.

Stopped Rocking and Other Screenplays. Intro. Richard Gilman. New York: New Directions, 1984.

Tennessee Williams: Collected Stories. Intro. Gore Vidal. New York: New Directions, 1985.

Copyright © 1986 by the University Press of Mississippi
All rights reserved
Manufactured in the United States of America
90 89 88 87   4 3 2 1

The paper in this book meets the guidelines for permanence and durability
of the Committee on Production Guidelines for Book Longevity
of the Council on Library Resources.

Library of Congress Cataloging-in-Publication Data

Williams, Tennessee, 1911-
  Conversations with Tennessee Williams.

  (Literary conversations series)
  Interviews originally published 1940-1981; some
translated into English for this collection.
  "Works by Tennessee Williams": p.
  Includes index.
  1. Williams, Tennessee, 1911-   —Interviews.
2. Dramatists, American—20th century—Interviews.
I. Devlin, Albert J. II. Title. III. Series.
PS3545.I5365Z463   1986   812'.54   86-9180
ISBN 0-87805-262-3 (alk. paper)
ISBN 0-87805-263-1 (pbk. : alk. paper)

Contents

Introduction   vii

Chronology   xv

Newest Find on Broadway   *Mark Barron*   3

"Tennessee" Williams, Playwright, Author   *William Inge*   6

Playwright with "A Good Conceit"   *Robert Van Gelder*   9

The Life and Ideas of Tennessee Williams   *Jean Evans*   12

The Role of Poetry in the Modern Theatre   *George Freedley*   20

A Playwright Named Tennessee   *R. C. Lewis*   25

Tennessee Williams—Last of Our Solid Gold Bohemians
    Henry Hewes   30

Tennessee Williams: Ten Years Later   *Arthur B. Waters*   34

Williams in Art and Morals: An Anxious Foe of Untruth   *Don Ross*   38

That Baby Doll Man: Part 1   *Louise Davis*   43

Williams on a Hot Tin Roof   *Don Ross*   50

Tennessee Williams   *Mike Wallace*   54

Lonely in Uptown New York   *W. J. Weatherby*   59

Williams and Kazan and the Big Walk-Out   *Arthur Gelb*   64

Interview with Tennessee Williams, Yukio Mishima,
    and Dilys Powell   *Edward R. Murrow*   69

Studs Terkel Talks with Tennessee Williams   *Studs Terkel*   78

Williams on Williams   *Lewis Funke and John E. Booth*   97

Williams: Twenty Years after *Glass Menagerie*   *Joanne Stang*   107

Tennessee Williams   *John Gruen*   112

Tennessee Williams   *Walter Wager*   124

Talking with Tennessee Williams   *Dan Isaac*   134

Will God Talk Back to a Playwright?   *David Frost*   140

New Tennessee Williams Rises from "Stoned Age"
   Don Lee Keith   147

Tennessee Williams Survives   *Tom Buckley*   161

Tennessee Williams Turns Sixty   *Rex Reed*   184

Meeting with Tennessee Williams   *Jeanne Fayard*   208

A Talk about Life and Style with Tennessee Williams
   Jim Gaines   213

Playboy Interview: Tennessee Williams   *C. Robert Jennings*   224

Interview with Tennessee Williams   *Cecil Brown*   251

Tennessee Williams   *Charles Ruas*   284

"Life Is a Black Joke"   *Lothar Schmidt-Mühlisch*   296

Orpheus Holds His Own: William Burroughs Talks with
   Tennessee Williams   *James Grauerholz*   299

Roundtable: Tennessee Williams, Craig Anderson, and T. E. Kalem Talk
   about *Creve Coeur*   *Ira J. Bilowit*   308

Bard of Duncan Street: Scene Four   *John Hicks*   318

The Art of Theatre V: Tennessee Williams   *Dotson Rader*   325

Index   361

Introduction

The "conversations" of Tennessee Williams have been chosen from the hundreds and hundreds of interviews that he granted during his distinguished literary life. That it was a literary life seems sure. Tennessee Williams could seldom think of himself apart from writing, even when the financial rewards were slight or when the criticism, or so he felt, had turned to "absolutely merciless ridicule." For Williams, writing was not a formal process, nor did it adhere to any "conscious, intellectual framework." Instead, the writing of plays, stories, and poems for fifty-odd years was inevitable. "I *couldn't* stop writing," Williams explained in 1979. Of his apprentice days, extended and bitter in physical want, he testified eloquently to their aesthetic motive—"I kept writing, not with any hope of making a living at it, but because I found no other means of expressing myself" (Don Lee Keith, "New Tennessee Williams," 1970). This is a knowing self-portrait and not one that sets aside or expunges from the record Williams' acute ambition to succeed. The "whomped-up myth" of Tennessee Williams is a miracle of self-promotion—of self-defense, as well—whose amplitude and cunning construction will impress even the most intrepid booster. But this myth or legend was not born of itself. Formed out of the intensity with which Tennessee Williams lived the life of the American theatre, the myth expresses in more knowable terms and in a personal drama that often partakes of caricature an artistic integrity whose sources lie beyond compulsion.

As literary forms go, the interview is among the more troubling. It must steer in a narrow channel that runs between vanity and lucre and compete with more substantial craft—the achieved work of art. Rarely does it completely relieve the strangeness of the interviewer and his subject who speak at cross-purposes. Mark Twain understood these problems of genre, and in a brittle aside entitled "An Encounter with an Interviewer" he satirized the apparent futility of this relatively modern invention. The " 'peart' " reporter from the "*Daily Thunderstorm*" has arrived and Twain feels some call to speak to him. " 'How do you spell it?' " Twain asks, as he looks in "the Unabridged." " 'Spell what?' " " 'Interview.' " " 'Oh, my goodness! What do you want to spell it for?' " replies the " 'peart' " young man. " 'I don't want to spell it; I want to see what it means.' "

Tennessee Williams was skeptical as well. On more than one occasion, he either stated or implied his impatience with the interview; his eloquence, he seemed to say, could be found elsewhere and in purer form—in *The Glass Menagerie* or *Streetcar* or *The Two-Character Play*, in stories that he treasured, such as "Two on a Party" or "Rubio y Morena." Still, Tennessee Williams granted an astonishing number of interviews. Many, if not the majority, are perfunctory and occasional, undertaken to promote a new play or to satisfy reporters who must intercept a celebrity whenever he comes to town. These interviews are usually quite placid notwithstanding the nimbus of notoriety and decadence that traveled with Williams. Occasionally, however, an otherwise formulaic exchange will flare into life and reveal the strength of the interview, which is finally its spontaneity. The more serious interviews are also purposive, but their calculation is more far-reaching and touches the quick of Tennessee Williams' literary life—the fear, tension, and ambiguity that attend the practice of modern American letters and that indenture the artist to a search for his identity and function. As a man upon whom no dramatic occasion was ever lost, Williams frequently molded the interview to this search and implicitly at least answered Mark Twain's mock-innocent question.

The interviews selected for *Conversations with Tennessee Williams* encompass five decades of an intense literary life and range from the standard and well-known to the more obscure and specialized. They are conducted with varying degrees of acumen, information, and goodwill toward the subject, who only rarely shows his irritation with the few inevitable questions. The interviews are filled not only with revealing insights into Williams' works and career but also with contradictions, self-promotion, and more than a little misleading information. A fairly large number of interviews employ the essay-interview format. This kind of report can provide an otherwise stark occasion with a warmer and more familiar "world" of discourse. Its drawback, of course, is that we may hear the subject's voice less frequently and that his words may be subordinated to the interviewer's "fiction."

In part at least, the three-dozen or so interviews in this volume have been chosen to retrace the progress of Williams' long career by marking important dramatic productions and documenting telling moments in his personal and artistic life. Representativeness was not, however, an absolute editorial value. Tennessee Williams' best advice to a young playwright was "Don't bore the audience!" (Dotson Rader, "Tennessee Williams," 1981). Accordingly, the interesting, revealing, or provocative interview has been included whether or not it advances any temporal scheme. "Orpheus Holds His Own: William Burroughs Talks with Tennessee Williams" (James Grauerholz, 1977), for example, does not support such development, but this meeting of mutually admiring writers—not the usual configuration of an interview—subtly evokes a fellowship of artists who in discussing their work protect it like magicians from undue disclosure. "We're having a very literary discussion, aren't we?" preens Tennessee Williams before erupting into a hearty laugh.

Still, the Williams interviews are literary—his "talk" with Burroughs especially so—and they disclose basic truths about the practice of modern American letters. The critical elements of the Williams myth or legend were present in 1940 in his first major interview, suitably an AP wire release. The distinctive name and "warm drawl" of this outsider from Mississippi, his flight from mundane occupation and "footloose" wandering of the "48 states," the dynamic of attraction to and retreat from the "high powered" landscape of Broadway—these elements, which comprise for Williams "that most common American phenomenon, the rootless, wandering writer," would be considerably embellished in his later travels; but they were first hardened into myth in Boston when *Battle of Angels* failed only a month after this hopeful interview. The failure of Williams' first major production was nasty and notorious and taught him no doubt that success and failure in the commercial theatre resemble twins who answer to the same name. In *Conversations with Tennessee Williams* the elaboration of a distinctive persona may be traced through three phases: the years 1944-1955, when Williams is very much the toast of Broadway; a second period that begins to emerge with the failure of *Orpheus*

Descending (21 March-18 May 1957/68 performances), reveals thereafter deepening nuances of emotional disturbance, and culminates in 1969 with Williams' commitment to Barnes Hospital in St. Louis; and a concluding phase, a curious amalgam of strength and debility when Williams has almost constant recourse to the interview. Perhaps Rex Reed has put best the perplexity of any sensitive Williams-watcher during these years: "What to make of this Halloween goblin?" ("Tennessee Williams Turns Sixty," 1971).

Tennessee Williams did not exaggerate when he described some of his later critical notices as "absolutely merciless ridicule." In his preface to the *Collected Stories* (1985), Gore Vidal has speculated that such meanness was punishment for Williams' homosexuality, which was never much of a secret in the theatre world and became widely known after 1970. In part at least, Williams' homosexuality was the signature of an outsider and thus reinforced his legendary status. But the virulent and gratuitous criticism of Williams that Gore Vidal notes was more broadly based than sexual orientation could alone account for.

In late September 1940, Williams wrote to his friend, Joe Hazan, from the Hotel Costa Verde in Acapulco. He confessed feeling drawn like a fragile moth to the excitement of Broadway, but he realized as well that its intensity would soon pall and he would flee to some such remote place as Acapulco. This is an early and accurate description of the dynamic of attraction and resistance to the theatre world that formed the core of the Williams myth—that "artifice of mirrors," as he described it to Rex Reed in 1971. The selected interviews make clear the degree of Williams' absorption in the excitement of Broadway. He helped to oversee innumerable major productions, each with its own myriad intersections of highly charged personalities. Williams pursued a mass audience and savored its applause. He competed with other playwrights for attention and finally was thrust into competition with himself. He yearned for one last popular success while his better artistic instincts pointed to a more experimental kind of drama.

The Williams myth projected a self that had entered with uncommon energy into a compact with the commercial theatre. Williams' chronic debilities, addictions, and breakdowns charted the perils and panics occasioned by this compact and, more generally,

indicated the equivocal nature of an art that best exemplifies the
dilemma of all imaginative writing in a consumer age. But the myth
projected resistance as well. The success of *The Glass Menagerie* was
coincident with Williams' recognition that fame was a betrayer. For all
his address to a mass audience and his entanglement in literary
politics, Williams periodically asserted aloneness by travel, the
breaking of long associations, and the violation of expected patterns
of behavior. In writing to Joe Hazan from New York City, Williams
prayed in August 1940 for the courage to remain alone and
uncompromised in his artistic values.*

To recall Williams' simile, a moth is vulnerable and elusive, and
resembles rather precisely the complex self that Tennessee Williams
compounded in interviews and on other public occasions. The harsh
criticism of the 1960s and '70s—only an undertone in the brighter
years—evolved, I would think, from misapprehension or
simplification—and perhaps resentment, too—of Tennessee Williams'
larger-than-life persona. Critics failed to see that it was not merely a
charlatan's self-promotion, nor could it be dismissed more charitably
as embroidery of language fit for a self-confessed effusive poet. The
legend of the writer that Williams created allowed him to restage the
inner drama of modern American letters and to adjust himself subtly
to its inherent strains and tensions. By dramatizing the artistic self in
search of balance and coherence, the interview played a heuristic role
that should not be underestimated in studying Tennessee Williams'
life records.

Seeing the Williams persona as a way of moderating the pratfalls of
the literary life may be a distinct critical advancement, but it contains
its own special distortion as well. Tennessee Williams emerges as the
modernist poet that he surely was—a type that Donald Davidson, a
fellow southerner, had likened to "a noble exile" whose specialized
art was threatened by separation from ordinary life. But Williams was
not this exotic "Bird" or "Halloween goblin" in all or even in his most
important manifestations. An engaging strain of the ordinary
persisted—in Williams' familial relations that were always held taut
but never broken, in his social conscience and the close attention he

---

*The Williams-Hazan correspondence is of considerable importance and may be examined
at the Humanities Research Center, University of Texas at Austin.

paid to the politics of the republic, and especially in the act of writing itself. Here the writer's motives might lie beyond compulsion, but his daily practice betokened the faithfulness of an old-fashioned artisan.

Williams' habitual writing contributed at least five major plays to the repertory of modern drama. Among other things, his interviews ask that we give more serious regard to the writing that followed *The Night of Iguana* (1961), the last play widely deemed "successful." References to a looser, less talky, more presentational kind of drama are frequent in Williams' post-*Iguana* interviews. Characteristically, they are not attended with academic pomp or even with Williams' own peculiar brand of precision. But these references are persistent, and they do have at least the hypothetical virtue of challenging the "decline and fall" thesis that governs many popular and academic evaluations of the Williams *oeuvre*. He would, I think, have approved this term because it conveys as no English substitute can the sense of a life's work.

The University of Missouri-Columbia Research Council and the English Department have generously funded research travel and editorial assistance. Professor Timothy Materer, chair of English, has been supportive throughout the preparation of *Conversations with Tennessee Williams*. I wish to thank also those who helped materially in gathering sources and preparing the typescript—Jeanice Brewer, Marilynn Keil, Barbara McCandless (Humanities Research Center, Austin, Texas), and Mary Weaks, a most valued co-worker and editorial assistant; those who undertook the several translations and their refinement—Kathryn Wright Brady, Marlene J. Devlin, Martin Camargo, Betty Littleton, and Luverne Walton; and those who provided good advice and friendly support for the project—Jackson Bryer (University of Maryland), Virginia Spencer Carr (Georgia State University, Atlanta), Larry Clark, Ken Craven (Humanities Research Center), Allean Hale, and Thomas Quirk. A special gratitude remains for the interviewers who graciously answered correspondence and granted permission to reprint. Two instructive interviews were not available for reprinting and should be consulted by the reader: George Whitmore, "Interview: Tennessee Williams," *Gay Sunshine*, 33/34 (1977), 1-4—the best of Williams' interviews in the gay press—and Charlotte Chandler, *The Ultimate Seduction* (New York:

Doubleday, 1984), 317-355. In editing the text, no material has been omitted from the question-answer format of interviews that use this method. In several cases, routine biographical-bibliographical passages and plot summary have been deleted from essay-interviews to facilitate their reading. Annotations—bracketed and identified as the editor's—have been provided for the reader who may require more precise identification of productions, reviews, texts. I am much indebted to Drewey Wayne Gunn and John S. McCann whose bibliographical studies of Tennessee Williams greatly eased the preparation of this volume. Throughout, Lyle Leverich has been a model of patience in answering questions and sharing with the editor his extensive knowledge of Williams.

AJD
May 1986

Chronology

1911   Thomas Lanier Williams: born 26 March; Columbus,
            Mississippi; to Cornelius Coffin and Edwina Dakin
            Williams. Rose Isabel and Walter Dakin, sister and brother
            of TW, born in 1909 and 1919.

1918   Family moves to St. Louis, Missouri.

1929-31   Attends University of Missouri; member, Alpha Tau
            Omega fraternity.

1931-34   Works as clerk for the International Shoe Company, St.
            Louis.

1936-37   Attends Washington University, St. Louis.

1937   Rose Williams institutionalized at Farmington State
            Hospital (Missouri) for schizophrenia which led to a
            prefrontal lobotomy.

1938   Graduates with B.A. degree in English from the University
            of Iowa.

1939   Receives Group Theatre Award for *American Blues*
            (collection of short plays). TW represented by Audrey
            Wood of Liebling Wood, Inc. Receives Rockefeller
            Foundation Grant.

1939-44   Period of itinerancy in New York, Massachusetts, Georgia,
            Florida, Louisiana, New Mexico, California, and Mexico.
            May-October 1943, MGM scriptwriter in Hollywood.

1940   *Battle of Angels.* Boston: Wilbur Theatre, 30
        December-11 January 1941. Revised as *Orpheus*
        Descending, New York, Martin Beck Theatre, 21
        March-18 May 1957.

1944   Death of "Grand," Rosina Otte Dakin, maternal
        grandmother of TW, 6 January.
        The Summer Belvedere. Five Young American Poets.
        Third Series. Norfolk, CT, New Directions.

1945   *The Glass Menagerie.* New York: Playhouse Theatre, 31
        March-3 August 1946. Wins New York Drama Critics
        Circle, Sidney Howard Memorial, and Donaldson awards.
        Important European productions include Luchino
        Visconti's direction, Rome, Theatro Eliseo, 12 December
        1946, and John Gielgud's direction, London, Theatre
        Royal, 28 July 1948.
        You Touched Me! (with Donald Windham). New York:
        Booth Theatre, 25 September-5 January 1946.
        27 Wagons Full of Cotton and Other One-Act Plays.
        Norfolk, CT, New Directions.

1947   Association with Frank Merlo begins.
        A Streetcar Named Desire. New York: Ethel Barrymore
        Theatre, 3 December-17 December 1949. Wins Pulitzer
        Prize and Drama Circle Critics and Donaldson awards.
        Important European productions include Luchino
        Visconti's direction, Rome, Theatro Eliseo, 21 January
        1949, and Jean Cocteau's adaptation, Paris, Théâtre
        Edouard VII, 15 October 1949.

1948   *Summer and Smoke.* New York: Music Box Theatre, 6
        October-1 January 1949. Revised as *The Eccentricities of*
        a Nightingale, New York, Morosco Theatre, 23
        November-12 December 1976.
        American Blues: Five Short Plays. New York, Dramatists
        Play Service.
        One Arm and Other Stories. New York, New Directions.

1950   *The Roman Spring of Mrs. Stone* (novel). New York, New
        Directions.

1951   *The Rose Tattoo.* New York: Martin Beck Theatre, 3
        February-27 October. Wins "Tony" award for best play.
        *I Rise in Flame, Cried the Phoenix: A Play about D. H.
        Lawrence.* Norfolk, CT, James Laughlin.

1952   Election to National Institute of Arts and Letters.

1953   *Camino Real.* New York: National Theatre, 19 March-9
        May.

1954   *Hard Candy: A Book of Stories.* New York, New
        Directions.

1955   Death of the Rev. Walter Edwin Dakin, maternal
        grandfather of TW, 14 February.
        Cat on a Hot Tin Roof. New York: Morosco Theatre, 24
        March-17 November 1956. Wins Pulitzer Prize and
        Drama Circle Critics and Donaldson awards. Important
        French production under Peter Brook's direction, Paris,
        Théâtre Antoine, 18 December 1956. Revised version,
        New York, ANTA Theatre, 24 September 1974-8
        February 1975.

1956   *Baby Doll.* Filmed for Warner Brothers by Elia Kazan,
        director. Stage version, *Tiger Tail,* Atlanta, Alliance
        Theatre, Winter 1978.
        In the Winter of Cities: Poems. Norfolk, CT, New
        Directions.

1957   Death of Cornelius Coffin Williams, 27 March.

1958   *Garden District* ("Something Unspoken" and *Suddenly
        Last Summer*). New York: York Playhouse, 7 January.

1959   *Sweet Bird of Youth.* New York: Martin Beck Theatre, 10

March-30 January 1960. Adapted by Françoise Sagan, Paris, Théâtre de l'Atelier, 1 October 1971.

1960   *Period of Adjustment.* New York: Helen Hayes Theatre, 10 November-4 March 1961.

1961   *The Night of the Iguana.* New York: Royale Theatre, 28 December-29 September 1962. Wins New York Drama Circle Critics Award. Important British production, London, Savoy Theatre, Spring 1965. Wins London Critics' Poll for Best Foreign Play.

1963   Death of Frank Merlo.
            The Milk Train Doesn't Stop Here Anymore. New York: Morosco Theatre, 16 January-16 March.

1965   Receives Brandeis University Creative Arts Award.

1966   *Slapstick Tragedy* ("The Gnädiges Fräulein" and "The Mutilated"). New York: Longacre Theater, 22-26 February.
            The Knightly Quest: A Novella and Four Short Stories. New York, New Directions.

1967   *The Two-Character Play.* London: Hampstead Theatre Club, 12 December. Revised versions produced (as *Out Cry*) in Chicago, Ivanhoe Theatre, 8 July 1971; in New York, Lyceum Theatre, 1-10 March 1973; and in San Francisco (as *The Two-Character Play*), Showcase Theatre, 20 October 1976.

1968   *The Seven Descents of Myrtle.* New York: Ethel Barrymore Theatre, 27 March-20 April. Revised as *Kingdom of Earth,* Princeton, NJ, McCarter Theatre, 6 March 1975.

1969   Receives honorary degree of Doctor of Humane Letters, University of Missouri-Columbia; awarded National

Institute of Arts and Letters Gold Medal for Drama. Committed for psychiatric care, Barnes Hospital, St. Louis (September-December).
In the Bar of a Tokyo Hotel. New York: Eastside Playhouse, 11 May-1 June.
Dragon Country: A Book of Plays. New York, New Directions.

1971   Dismisses Audrey Wood, literary agent of thirty-two years.
The Theatre of Tennessee Williams. 7 vols. New York: New Directions, 1971-81.

1972   *Small Craft Warnings.* New York: Truck and Warehouse Theatre, 2 April; New Theatre, 6 June-17 September.

1974   *Eight Mortal Ladies Possessed: A Book of Stories.* New York, New Directions.

1975   Receives Medal of Honor for Literature, National Arts Club.
The Red Devil Battery Sign. Boston: Shubert Theater, 18-28 June. Revised version produced in Vienna, English Theatre, 17 January 1976.
Moise and the World of Reason (novel). New York, Simon.
Memoirs. Garden City, NY, Doubleday.

1976   *This is (An Entertainment).* San Francisco: American Conservatory Theater, 20 January 1976.
Tennessee Williams' Letters to Donald Windham, 1940-1965. Ed. Donald Windham. Verona, Italy, Sandy M. Campbell; New York: Holt, 1977.

1977   *Vieux Carré.* New York: St. James Theatre, 11-15 May.
Androgyne, Mon Amour: Poems. New York, New Directions.

1978   *Creve Coeur.* Charleston, SC: Spoleto Festival USA, 5

June. Revised version produced (as *A Lovely Sunday for Creve Coeur*) in New York, Hudson Guild Theater, 21 January 1979.
Where I Live: Selected Essays. Ed. Christine R. Day and Bob Woods. New York, New Directions.

1979   *Kirche, Kutchen, und Kinder.* New York: Jean Cocteau Repertory Theatre, September.

1980   Death of Edwina Dakin Williams, 1 June.
Will Mr. Merriwether Return from Memphis? Key West, Fla.: Tennessee Williams Performing Arts Center, 24-28 January.
Clothes for a Summer Hotel. New York: Cort Theatre, 26 March-April 16.

1981   *A House Not Meant to Stand.* Chicago: Goodman Theatre, Spring 1981/Spring 1982.
Something Cloudy, Something Clear. New York: Jean Cocteau Repertory Theatre, 24 August-13 March 1982.

1982   Receives honorary doctorate, Harvard University.

1983   Dies during the night of 24-25 February, Hotel Elysée, New York City.

1984   *Stopped Rocking and Other Screenplays.* Intro. Richard Gilman. New York: New Directions.

1985   *Tennessee Williams: Collected Stories.* Introd. Gore Vidal. New York, New Directions.

Conversations with Tennessee Williams

Newest Find on Broadway Is a Mississippi Playwright Named Tennessee Williams
Mark Barron/1940

From *The Commercial Appeal* [Memphis, TN], 24 November 1940, sec. 1, 14. ©1940 by the Associated Press. Reprinted by permission.

New York, Nov. 23—Tennessee Williams is a young playwright with the soft, warm drawl of Mississippi in his voice and the footloose urge of 48 states in his feet. About six months ago he drifted in from his many wanderings to Broadway, lugging a roll of manuscripts under his arm. After politely dropping his plays on a literary agent's desk, he disappeared again without leaving a forwarding address.

That night the agent read a couple of the plays, excitedly hurried over to the Theatre Guild and got an enthusiastic acceptance for immediate production. But young Williams was the little man who wasn't there and the few meager clues his agent could track down didn't locate him.

There was nothing to do but wait. And wait the Guild did to start rehearsals of his drama, *Battle of Angels,* which is to be his first play on Broadway. Then, a couple of months ago, Tennessee's curly-head popped into his agent's office again.

The Guild sent for Miriam Hopkins to desert her film chores in Hollywood and hurry East to play the leading role. The famed woman director, Margaret Webster, who has staged such lauded productions as Maurice Evans' Shakespearean appearances, gave up several other assignments to direct this performance.

So *Battle of Angels* is swinging into rehearsals with as high powered a lineup of talent as even Bernard Shaw or Eugene O'Neill could command. But Williams already is yearning to move on from the bright lights and has no intention of staying in their glow a minute after his play opens.

"I was born in Mississippi," he said as he began telling of

3

wanderings that have taken him from Coast to Coast and in and out of scores of varied jobs. He is still in his twenties.

"But I got the name of Tennessee when I was going to the University of Iowa because the fellows in my class could only remember that I was from a Southern State with a long name. And when they couldn't think of Mississippi, they settled on Tennessee. That was all right with me, so when it stuck I changed to it permanently.

"Before I went to Iowa I went to Washington University in St. Louis first because my family lives there. My father is in the shoe business and he wanted me to be a shoe salesman. I hated the job, but I stuck with it until I had saved enough money to move on to the University of Iowa, where I worked as a waiter in the school cafeteria.

"By the time I got there I had trained myself to be a pretty good waiter. But earlier, when I waited on tables in a hospital, the doctors all moved away from my section of the dining room because they said I was the world's worst hash slinger."

Williams soon took to the open road again, roamed down the shores of the Pacific states until he came to the little town of Hawthorne, Calif. There he got a job on a pigeon ranch which, he explained, isn't as big or romantically Western as it may sound. On a pigeon ranch you operate on a range about as big as a big backyard.

"But I was always up to my neck in squabs," he says.

As Williams moved on, he began to be influenced by the psychoanalytical writings of D. H. Lawrence, the late British novelist who did much of his work in New Mexico.

"When I reached New Mexico, I stopped there awhile to meet his family and friends because I had become convinced that his life would be an extraordinary and dramatic subject for a play," he states.

"Then after I had gathered the material I discovered that someone else had already written a play about him. But I still plan to do either a play or book about him. And I've dedicated *Battle of Angels* to him."

On his way from New Mexico Williams stopped over in New Orleans, where he had more trouble trying to convince restaurant owners that he really wasn't such a bad waiter. He finally was put to work in a cafe in the French Quarter because he wrote a slogan for the proprietor which read: "Meals for a Quarter in the Quarter."

In his wanderings Williams has been writing continuously and arrived on Broadway not only with his *Battle of Angels,* but also with an armful of other plays, of which two more are to go into rehearsal soon.

"The one I'd like most to get on is my *Stairs to the Roof,* which is a social comedy about a lowly paid clerk trying to escape his economic cage. My interest in social problems is as great as my interest in the theater and traveling. I try to write all my plays so that they carry some social message along with the story.

"I've changed to the full length play form of three acts now," Williams said, "but when I first started I did only one-act plays because I was even more social minded then and found it easier to get across a message and with more impact if I made it brief. All of my one-act plays are about such social groups I ran across in my wanderings."

Now that Broadway producers are holding open the door to him, Williams definitely has no plans to settle down in one of the luxurious penthouses most Broadway playwrights bask in once they write a hit.

"No, siree. I'm getting out of town the minute my play opens and maybe sooner. Where I'll go I don't know. Just wherever my feet take me. I'll probably go back somewhere and take a postgraduate course on how to sling hash without getting it on the customer's vest."

Williams, who was born in Columbus, Miss., is the son of Cornelius Williams, now of St. Louis. The elder Williams was originally from Knoxville, Tenn., and is a descendant of John Sevier, a Tennessee pioneer. Young Williams is also a grandson of the Rev. Walter E. Dakin, an Episcopal minister in Memphis who retired recently.

Williams' mother was born in Ohio. He doesn't remember which town because when she was a baby she was taken South, the South to which he says he is returning the moment he can finish with this strange business of producing a play on Broadway.

"Tennessee" Williams, Playwright, Author
William Inge/1944

From the *St. Louis Star-Times*, 11 November 1944, 11. Reprinted by permission of International Creative Management, Inc., on behalf of the William Inge Estate.

Another name to add to the already elongated list of St. Louis' literary sons and daughters is that of "Tennessee" Williams. Now at the age of 30, he has published poetry and stories in America's most discriminating periodicals and is about to have his second play produced on Broadway.

He feels very hopeful about his new play which, incidentally, has a St. Louis setting. It is being prepared to open in Chicago Christmas and there is some chance it will play in St. Louis before settling down for what he hopes will be a long run in New York.

His real name, of course, is not Tennessee. That is a tag that was given him by his brothers in Alpha Tau Omega at the University of Iowa and the way he came by it deserves telling. He was born in Mississippi and still speaks with a southern accent, which was rare in Iowa. The first time his fraternity brothers heard him speak, they started calling him by the name of the first southern state they could think of. Williams accepted the nickname and later decided that it would make an excellent pen name.

His real name is Thomas Lanier Williams and he is the son of Mr. and Mrs. Cornelius Williams, 53 Arundel pl., Clayton. He comes by his talent honestly for Lanier is a family name, and the family is the same that produced, much earlier, the famous American poet, Sidney Lanier, who wrote "Song of the Chattahoochee."

Tennessee has been in St. Louis this week paying an annual visit to his parents. Next week he will go back to New York to attend the opening rehearsals of his new play, *The Glass Menagerie,* which is being produced by Eddie Dowling, who also will star in the production with Julie Haydon and Laurette Taylor.

6

He was only 25 when the Theatre Guild produced his first play, *Battle of Angels*, which starred Miriam Hopkins. The play had been submitted to John Gassner, drama critic and historian, with whom Williams was studying at the New School of Social Research in New York.

Tennessee feels that he was a little gullible at the time for he let the Guild talk him into a lot of changes of which he did not approve. And by the time the play opened in Boston, it was pretty badly torn apart. The play was a serious treatment of sex and love which Boston, typically, found "highly objectionable." New York, typically, had no moral objections, but just regretted that it didn't get across.

"I'm glad now that the play was not a success," Williams says. "If it had been, it would have gone to my head and I would have thought I knew all there was to know about playwriting. As it was, I was forced to realize I had much to learn so I set out to learn it."

When *Battle of Angels* closed after two weeks in New York, Tennessee felt a little ridiculous, he says, because obviously he had been oversold. He felt he didn't dare to show his face in a producer's office so he started publishing some of his poetry and short stories. His work has appeared in *Story* and *Poetry: A Magazine of Verse* and just recently he was selected by publisher James Laughlin to appear in an anthology of *Five Young Poets,* published annually by New Directions.

In the first of these volumes, published about five years ago, another Clayton resident, Clark Mills, one of Williams' boyhood friends, was represented.

His professional career started in 1939 when the Group Theatre in New York gave him a $100 prize for a group of one-act plays called *American Blues*. Previous to that, the St. Louis Mummers produced two of his full length plays, *Candles to the Sun* and *Fugitive Kind,* which met with enthusiastic audiences here. This was when he was still a student at Iowa from which he got his A.B. degree in 1938. He also attended Washington University and the University of Missouri.

Tennessee has written for as long as he can remember and always has been content with the meager subsistence his writing at times has provided him. "My salaries have ranged from $50 a month to $250 a week, but I preferred the $50 job because it enabled me to live in New Orleans. My largest salary was earned in Hollywood where I worked on the writing staff at M-G-M. I didn't like it, but it enabled me to save something for a change."

Playwright with "A Good Conceit"

Robert Van Gelder/1945

From the *New York Times*, 22 April 1945, sec. 2,1. ©1945 by
The New York Times Company. Reprinted by permission.

Tennessee Williams, the 31-year-old author of *The Glass Menagerie*, has what someone called the greatest gift—"a good conceit of himself." His mannerisms are those of one who is extremely absent-minded. "I'll have milk," he said one day recently in a cafeteria, and at that reached for a bottle of beer and refused milk.

When shaking hands both hands come forward as though the choice of whether to shake with the right or left hand had to be made each time. But when his attention is caught he talks with that quick candor that marks a writer as distinctively as might a jewel set in the middle of the forehead, with the openness and frankness that only those adults who are habitually and strictly honest with themselves ever achieve. He is a composed, confident dreamer who is both observant and self-centered, sympathetic and remote.

One of his relatives, the late John Sharp Williams, former Senator from Mississippi, once remarked: "I'd rather be a hound dog and bay at the moon from my Mississippi plantation than remain in the United States Senate." Tennessee Williams feels similarly about New York. "I have no interest in the intellectuals or pseudo-intellectuals that I find here," he casually comments. He adds, "They mean nothing to me creatively."

The applause that he is hearing these days isn't important to him, he says, and there is no good reason why he should not be believed. His interest is in writing and in the "creative theatre" and though he believes that his *The Glass Menagerie* is good as plays go, he is the author of two plays that he prefers to it, and hasn't the slightest doubt that he can write more plays that will be far better.

He is convinced that the Theatre Guild "messed up" his earlier *Battle of Angels*—"which is the best play I've written yet; it may not

9

be quite so polished as the one that is now on but it has an epic quality, it has sweep, and I think that is more desirable than finish." But when *Battle of Angels* was tried out in Boston it "fairly set the teeth of the audience right on edge, it just wouldn't do for Boston," and the production was scrapped. His second-best play, he thinks, is *Stairs to the Roof,* which also failed to reach Broadway.

The Glass Menagerie is "semi-autobiographical—that is, it is based on the conditions of my life in St. Louis. The apartment where we lived wasn't as dingy and poverty-stricken as that in the play, but I can't say much for it, even so. It was a rented, furnished apartment, all over-stuffed furniture, and the only nice room in it was my sister's room. That room was painted white and she had put up a lot of shelves and filled them with little glass animals. When I'd come home from the shoe place where I worked—my father owned it, I hated it—I would go in and sit in her room. She was the member of the family with whom I was most in sympathy and, looking back, her glass menagerie had a meaning for me. Nostalgia helped—it makes the little flat in the play more attractive really than our apartment was—and as I thought about it the glass animals came to represent the fragile, delicate ties that must be broken, that you inevitably break, when you try to fulfill yourself."

The success of the play, he said, has brought at least as many complications as pleasures for it means that more people want to see him, to take part of his time, and some old friends have already accused him of going high-hat because he can't see as much of them as he formerly did. "There is a kind of problem in personal integrity," he said. "The real fact is that no one means a great deal to me, anyway. I'm gregarious and like to be around people, but almost anybody will do. I'm rather selfish in picking my friends, anyway; that is, I prefer people who can help me in some way or another, and most of my friendships are accidental."

"Don't you think that goes for most people?"

"Well, maybe it does, but I don't want to be like most people. And I do think there is a problem of personal integrity involved."

Williams worked in Hollywood for six months. "They gave me $250 a week, which was just peanuts compared to what the names are getting, but it was riches to me because I had come to it from $18 a week I was getting at the Strand Theatre out there in Los Angeles.

William Fadiman out at Metro had hired me on the strength of two of my printed plays. They put me to work to turn out a picture for Lana Turner and then they didn't like what I did, so after one and a half months working on the Turner picture I spent the other four and a half months out on the beach at Santa Monica doing my own work."

"Didn't you have to go into the office?"

"No, they didn't even want me in the office. One time my agent called Mr. Fadiman to tell him that one of my plays was going on in Cleveland and to ask if I could go on for the opening. Mr. Fadiman said I could go all right, on one condition, and that was that I never came back."

"Well, don't you feel kind of an exultation in the way this play has gone over, because so many people who kicked you around can't kick you any more?"

"No, I don't feel that very much, because I don't think that bothered me particularly. All that they did was sort of on the periphery of my existence."

He said that he really enjoys writing. There is no pleasure in the world like writing well and going fast. It's like nothing else. It's like a love affair. It goes on and on and doesn't end in marriage. It's all courtship.

Williams will soon go down south to Texas. He says that for creative work the best conditions are those where you have some simple routine of life, a routine that is fairly good for you and doesn't take any thought or any doing. That way you are not interrupted with too much stimulation from outside. His creative materials come from the South, and he said he is at home there. There are too many cross-currents here in New York. "Margo Jones had a grant of Rockefeller money and some more money coming from rich people in Dallas. With that she's going to try to start a real creative theatre down there and she wants me to come and work with her. I want to do it. That is my real interest. I find very little that interests me here."

The Life and Ideas of Tennessee Williams
Jean Evans/1945

From *New York PM Magazine,* 6 May 1945, M6-M7.

Within a week or two after *The Glass Menagerie* had won the Critics Award as the outstanding Broadway play of the year, almost every newspaper in town had carried stories about its author, Tennessee Williams.

The stories presented a good many essential details. They said, for instance, that Mr. Williams was 31, that he had been born in Mississippi, and that his parents had named him Thomas Lanier. They said also that Williams had written eight or 10 other full-length plays, only one of which had been produced, a dozen or more one-act plays, a book of poems and many short stories.

One of the most interesting accounts, a short piece in the *Herald Tribune,* had been written by Mr. Williams himself to explain why he had called his play *The Glass Menagerie.* [*New York Herald Tribune,* 15 April 1945, sec. 4, 1—Editor] When his family had moved to St. Louis from the South, he said, they had been forced to live in a congested apartment neighborhood. His sister had helped to brighten her room by collecting a large assortment of little glass figures, mostly animals. When he left home, Mr. Williams said, these articles "came to represent in my memory all the softest emotions that belong to recollection of things past."

In spite of all these stories, some of our questions about Tennessee Williams were still unanswered, so we asked Jean Evans to have a talk with him. She made an appointment to see him at the Hotel Shelton one Tuesday morning at 10:30.

When I arrived at the Shelton, she says, I called Mr. Williams' room on a house phone. I heard the bell ring four times. In the middle of the fifth ring, a sleepy voice interrupted with, "Yes?"

I identified myself, but the silence on the other end of the wire told me I hadn't registered. I started all over again.

12

"Oh yes—yes—sorry—I was asleep. Won't you come up?"

Up on the 12th floor, I rapped on his door. Mr. Williams opened it. He looked very young as, bare-legged, bare-footed, and wearing an ample robe, he stood for a moment against the dim background of his room. He rubbed his eyes and short-cropped hair with the palms of his hands.

"Come in," he said finally. "I'll just wash my face and brush my teeth," and he retreated into the bathroom.

His windowshades were still drawn. There were two islands of order in the room, the scarcely rumpled bed in which he'd slept—it was like an envelope he had slipped neatly out of—and a small desk holding a shiny portable typewriter and several tidy stacks of paper.

The rest of the room was all disorder. A tall dresser was cluttered with scraps of paper, a couple of ties, some coins and other odds and ends. On a bed that was the twin of the one he'd slept in were a brief case, a manila envelope, more scraps of paper with jottings on them, a half-full pack of camels, a topcoat, and a black-and-white-checked vest. The rest of the suit had been dropped across the arm of a chair. I raised a shade to let in some light, shoved aside some of the stuff on the bed and sat down.

Mr. Williams, still bare-footed and in his bathrobe, looked wide awake when he came back a few minutes later. He was tanned, bristly-haired, blue eyed. He asked if I'd had breakfast. I had. He picked up the phone, ordered orange juice, boiled eggs, and cinnamon buns, and coffee for two, then hung up. The phone rang, and he picked it up again.

"Hello—Oh', hello Mr. C———. Won't you tell me what you want to see me about?—I'm sorry, but I'm busy just now—yes—that would be better."

There was curiosity in his face as he hung up. "He's a tall man with an umbrella," Mr. Williams explained. "He stopped me in the lobby the other day. I was in a hurry and he said he'd phone later. He won't tell me why he wants to see me."

I said maybe he'd written a play, and Williams nodded dubiously. Then we settled down to the business of the interview, though Mr. Williams seemed still to be wondering about Mr. C———.

I'd seen *The Glass Menagerie* the night before. The play is set in the slums of St. Louis during the depression years and tells about a

faded Southern belle and her crippled daughter Laura, whose chief
interest is a display of charming little glass animals. Laura's brother,
Tom, adventurous and full of high dreams, works in a warehouse and
tries to escape the monotony of his life by going to movies. The
action revolves around the desperate desire of the mother to get
security through marriage for her gentle, moon-struck daughter;
finally, one evening, a gentleman caller arrives.

I'd read four of Mr. Williams's one-act plays. All but one had been
about poverty-stricken people whose situations seemed hopeless. I
asked Mr. Williams if he always wrote about unhappy, trapped,
hopeless people. He'd been half-reclining against a pillow on his bed,
but he sat up now.

"I hadn't thought of them as being hopeless," he said. "That's not
really what I was writing about. It's human valor that moves me. The
one dominant theme in most of my writings, the most magnificent
thing in all human nature, is valor—and endurance.

"The mother's valor is the *core* of *The Glass Menagerie*," he went
on. "She's confused, pathetic, even stupid, but everything has *got* to
be all right. She fights to make it that way in the only way she knows
how."

We talked a little about his other plays and then, a trifle anxiously,
he asked if I had found them without humor. I said no. There was a
great deal of humor in them if he meant the wry kind that sprang out
of incredibly miserable situations, the kind that made an audience
want to cry while it was laughing. He nodded.

"George Jean Nathan, in his review of *Menagerie,* said I was
deficient in humor," Williams remarked. [*New York Journal
American,* 9 April 1945, 11—Editor] His manner was casual, but
there was an edge of annoyance in his voice. "He said that all the
humor had been embroidered into the play by Mr. Dowling."
(Dowling is co-producer of the play, plays the narrator, and the son,
Tom) "I'd love for somebody who knows my other work to refute
him."

He paused, and then went on defensively, "Not one line of *Glass
Menagerie* was changed after the final draft came back from the
typist. A scene was inserted, the drunk scene. That was Mr. Dowling's
idea, but entirely of my authorship. And one line by Mr. Dowling, was
added. The last line, where he says to the audience, 'Here's where

memory stops and your imagination begins.'" He paused. "Mr.
Dowling did a great job. A magnificent job. But there was humor
contained in the play. I had that in mind, along with the rest, when I
was writing it."

Mr. Nathan had also written that the play, as originally written, was
freakish. I wanted to know if Mr. Williams liked writing plays
unconventional in form.

"If you mean unconventional in that my plays are light on plot and
heavy on characterization, yes. But not in structure. *Glass Menagerie*
is not at all freakish in structure.

"Have you read Saroyan's *Get Away, Old Man?*" Williams gave a
peal of gay, sudden laughter that rang through the room. "There's a
play that would give Mr. Nathan pause. The curtain goes up and
down, up and down, all through the play."

He said he liked Saroyan very much, "his short stories perhaps,
more than his plays."

I said I'd like Saroyan better if he were able to admit there was evil
under the sun. Mr. Williams smiled. "His point of view—his attitude—
I suppose you could say, is childish," he said. "Saroyan's characters
are all little Saroyans. He multiplies himself like rabbits. But he is
himself so interesting, that he usually gets away with writing only
about himself."

How did he think the human situation could be improved? I asked.
He looked as though the question had startled him.

"It's a social and economic problem, of course," he said, "not
something mystical. I don't think there will be any equity in American
life until at least 90 percent of our population are living under
different circumstances. The white collar worker, for instance. Most
people consider him pretty well off. I think his situation is horrible.

"I'd like to see people getting a lot more for what they invest in the
way of effort and time. It's insane for human beings to work their
whole lives away at dull, stupid, routine, anesthetizing jobs for just a
little more than the necessities of life. There should be time—and
money—for development. For living."

About this time Mr. Williams's breakfast and my coffee were
brought up. Half way through the meal, the phone rang. It was Mr.
C———. Mr. Williams explained politely that he was still busy.

"You say your business will take only five minutes. Why not come up now?" Mr. C—— didn't want to disturb him. Mr. Williams said very well, hung up, and eyebrows slightly knit, returned to our conversation.

He was born in Columbus, Miss., he said. He has a sister, two years older than himself, and a brother, six years younger. When he was young his father had been a traveling salesman, so the family lived with his mother's parents.

"My grandfather was an Episcopalian minister. We were brought up in an atmosphere of Southern Puritanism," he said. "It's like Northern Puritanism, except that it's more fractious. Also more old-fashioned.

"Life was pleasant—gracious, full of imaginings," he went on with nostalgia in his voice. "Perhaps that's why, when writing, I nearly always return to the South. We lived in small Mississippi towns. We always had a large back yard. My brother didn't figure in my childhood because he was a baby so long. But my sister and I played together. We invented games. The poor children used to run all over town, but my sister and I played in our own back yard. We were seclusive."

Had he envied the other children their freedom? "Oh, no," he protested. "My sister was an ideal playmate." He paused. "My sister was very charming—very beautiful. She had an incredible imagination. We were so close to each other, we had no need of others."

I asked him about the games they'd invented. He thought for a moment, then laughing, said, "I'll tell you about a secret game of mine. I used to have cards flying through the air, and nobody knew what I was doing. It must have looked very stupid to others, but I would never explain. I was very secretive."

He went on to tell me about the cards.

"I'd take a deck of cards. The Kings, Queens and Jacks were royalty. The rest were the soldiers and ordinary people. Each denomination, the diamonds, clubs, hearts, spades, were different kingdoms. You'd be amazed at the number of stories you can act out with that beginning.

"More than any other game, I used to act out the Siege of Troy," he went on, enjoying the remembrance. "I'd divide the cards into Red and Black. The Greeks were the Reds, the Trojans, the Blacks.

Then I'd take the Greeks in one hand"—he held one arm straight out at his side—"and the Trojans in the other"—he held out the other arm—"slap them together"—he did it—"and then throw them into the air. The ones that fell face down were dead.

"Besides the games, I used to have the quality of seeing things with my eyes shut, wonderful things." He squinted for a moment. "I get only dim images now, but when I was little, I'd see whole scenes, like the *Arabian Nights*."

About the time he was ready for high school, his father got a desk job with the National Shoe Company [sic], and the family moved to St. Louis. All through his high school and part of his college days, they lived in crowded, unattractive apartments which, he said, were horrifying after the life he had had in Mississippi. In one of the apartments, his sister's sunless little room overlooked an alley and Williams helped her paint the walls and furniture white, and install her collection of glass animals, making a place of white and crystal in the midst of squalor.

His first year at college—the University of Missouri—he devoted to "writing and an infatuation with an Irish girl."

His grades had been so bad at the end of that year, that his father made him go to work for the shoe company.

"I stuck to that damned shoe office nearly two years," he went on. "They tried me at everything. I was a miracle of incompetence."

Part of his incompetence, he said, probably had been due to the fact that he was in a state of perpetual exhaustion. He worked long days, and stayed up nights trying to write.

"My father thought writing a lot of foolishness, especially poetry writing," Williams said. "At the end of two years—I guess I willed myself into a state of sickness—I collapsed." Two weeks later he was told he would not have to return to the shoe company, and he got well right away.

Freed from the shoe company, Williams worked his way through the University of Iowa by waiting table at Iowa State Hospital, then he put in a period at the University of Washington [sic]. "After that I traveled almost continuously, writing, and doing odd jobs to keep alive."

"I lived carefully and whenever I'd saved enough to go some place else, I'd get a bus ticket and go."

He went to New Orleans, Florida, California, New York, New England, and stops en route.

In 1940, he went on, the Theatre Guild had bought his *Battle of Angels* and had given it a "superb" production with Miriam Hopkins playing the lead, and Margaret Webster directing. But the show, which dealt with sex and religion, opened in Boston, and died there.

"After that I was in the peculiar position of being fairly well known in the theater, but having no productions."

I asked if the Critics Award had made up for all that. He replied dispassionately, "Of course, I'm very happy about it, but the climax came a long time ago.

"In Chicago, the play looked like a sure failure. Miss Taylor [Laurette Taylor, who plays the part of the mother] gave no indication during rehearsals of how she would play the part. We were depressed. All the time we were rehearsing," he went on, "she was working, but it was an inward process. Then, on opening night, the thrill of seeing Miss Taylor come out with the greatest performance I'd ever seen—well, everything afterwards has been eclipsed by that."

The phone rang again. Mr. C———, of course. Williams had a 1 o'clock appointment, it was 12 then, and he hadn't dressed. But he urged Mr. C——— to come right up.

He had scarcely hung up the receiver when a tall, immaculately dressed, cadaverous looking man stood in the doorway. Mr. Williams introduced us. "I really wanted to talk to you in private," Mr. C——— said. "I'll come back another time." I said I'd step out into the hall, and did.

A minute later the door was opened, and Mr. Williams, with a dead-pan face, beckoned me in. "Mr. C——— is a violinist," he said, his grave manner warning me not to laugh. "He wants to play in the salons of artists and writers. I don't know how to help him. Do you?"

I said perhaps he should join the musicians' union, and get an agent. Mr. C——— didn't like that. Mr. Williams explained gently that he didn't give parties, but that he'd be glad to take Mr. C———'s name and address and let him know if he heard anything.

Mr. C——— gave his name and address. Mr. Williams said, "Thank you very much." But Mr. C——— didn't leave.

There was a long, embarrassing silence. I rigged my camera and in an attempt to bring the situation to a normal level, I handed a flashlight to Mr. C——— and asked him to hold it. Mr. Williams shot me an annoyed look. I took a picture. Mr. Williams remarked that the violin was a beautiful instrument. Mr. C———'s large dark eyes glowed in agreement.

Mr. Williams repeated that though he never gave parties, he'd certainly let Mr. C——— know if he heard of one. Mr. C——— thanked him, and left.

We didn't say anthing at all about Mr. C——— when he'd gone. I took another picture, and then dismantled the camera. Just as I left, Mr. Williams asked worriedly: "Do you think he looked destitute?"

The Role of Poetry in the Modern Theatre
George Freedley/1945

Transcription of "Theatre Time," WNYC-Radio, 3 October 1945. Printed by permission of the New York Public Library, Performing Arts Research Center, Rodgers and Hammerstein Archives.

GF: We've got Tennessee here tonight to talk with us and answer a few questions. How do you feel about being quizzed, Tennessee?

TW: Well, I'm always a little intimidated by a mike, just as I am by a footlight.

GF: Well, that really ought not to bother you, after all. Just treat the mike as your friend. But I'll tell you, first of all, what we want to know is, what do you think is the role of poetry in the modern theatre?

TW: I think that's going to depend pretty largely on two factors. As everyone knows poetry has a limited audience. It cannot compete on Broadway with comedy hits like *Harvey* or *Dear Ruth,* or even with a play like *Glass Menagerie* which is poetic, but not a verse play. I wonder how many people listening to us tonight know or like or possibly have even heard of Hart Crane, and yet he's conceded generally to be the greatest America poet since Whitman. Therefore, if we're going to have poetry of this stature in the theatre, we'll have to have theatres that can afford to run without reaching a very large audience. The answer to that is decentralized theatre, I think, national theatres like that outlined by Robert Breen and Bob Porterfield. ["Toward a National Theatre," *Theatre Arts,* October 1945, 599-602—Editor]

GF: Oh yes, that was what we were talking about last week. We had Newbold Morris and Bob Breen on here discussing that plan. Don't you want to say something more about that, Tennessee?

TW: Well, I've read the plan and I think it's a tremendously sensible, workable plan, and I think it is the salvation for the poetic theatre. I don't think poetry can play an important role in the theatre as long as it has to be on Broadway because there it can't survive, it can't compete there. And I think Margo Jones' plan that she's working out in the Dallas theatre is another hope.

GF: Well, she's a grand gal, Margo. I know her well and I saw, as a matter of fact, you've gone on the Board of Directors down there. Tell me, what are you going to do in connection with that Dallas theatre?

TW: Well, I hope to go down there and learn how to direct plays while I'm writing them. I haven't heard from Margo yet, she hasn't completed her financing campaign.

GF: Well, of course, that takes an awful lot of digging—I mean even in a rich city like Dallas—but I understood from Lynn Riggs the other night at the opening of your play [*You Touched Me!* New York: Booth Theatre, 25 September 1945—Editor] that things are moving along very satisfactorily, and I think that undoubtedly she's going to take poetic plays into consideration when she is choosing her repertory. Is that right?

TW: That will be her first consideration, I'm sure. She's already gotten a number of scripts that are poetic in quality, though not in verse form.

GF: Those are new plays, I take it?

TW: Yes, I read one particularly fine one that was written by the drama editor for the *St. Louis Star-Times,* William Inge, and we've taken an option on that already. [Inge's *Farther off from Heaven* was the first production of Theatre '47, Dallas, 3 June 1947—Editor]

GF: Well, is she going to take any of the great plays of the past?

TW: Yes, she's going to include Shakespeare in her repertory and Chekhov, of course, and, I hope, Marlowe and Webster—

GF: And Webster and Jonson perhaps?

TW: Yes.

GF: But we ought to get back to the point that we were making about the role of poetry in the theatre. Do you feel that the theatre in modern times has sufficiently employed poetic resources?

TW: I could answer that better in two words that would be very emphatic but get us thrown off the air.

GF: Well, don't do that please, after all this is the Municipal Broadcasting System.

TW: No, definitely not. The poetic resources are there, but they won't be fully employed until we have a theatre that can afford to give fine productions without running at a profit. And go on giving them and giving them finely. I seem to be leading back to a national, decentralized theatre again, but all roads leading to poetry in the theatre seem to lead there.

GF: Well, that of course is a perfectly sound idea and we're all working towards it. I mean Cheryl Crawford and Margaret Webster and Eva Le Gallienne with their American Repertory Theatre. After all, Horace Schmidlapp has offered a prize for a plan as to how to raise money for a national theatre. Blanche Yurka, the chairman of the committee, a lot of awfully good people are connected with it.

TW: Yes, I know, Miss Yurka called me and asked me to submit a plan. I told her I couldn't think of any better one than Mr. Breen and Mr. Porterfield and Margo Jones were already working on. They're the real active authorities in that field right now, it seem to me. All I can do is sit and hope and pray.

GF: Yes, that's true, but to get back to that question of your concept of what poetry means in the theatre. Do you think of poetry as merely being a question of lines in the play, lines that you might write, or Archibald MacLeish might write, or some other person? Is it auditory or visual? Do you think that ballet and dance are the logical development of poetry?

TW: Well, I'm glad you brought that up because it seems to me that the visual and the plastic elements in theatre are the things that have been neglected too much by poets who are trying to write for the theatre. Now there have been a good many wonderful library poetry plays. They've been turned out by first-rate poets like W.H. Auden, T.S. Eliot, Delmore Schwartz, and Louis Untermeyer, and even Edna St. Vincent Millay has written one.

GF: You mean *Aria da Capo*?

TW: Yes, that's the one I was thinking of. But unfortunately most of them haven't acquainted themselves with the theatre. They worked as poets and their poetry is verbal. They haven't exploited all the wonderful plastic and visual things that the theatre offers. They haven't learned how to use movements and gestures in place of long speeches. Now the trouble is that when a lot of critics and audiences meet poetic speeches in the theatre, [they expect] . . . highfalutin, long-winded speeches.

GF: Yes, I'm afraid we do sometimes. Sort of a temptation.

TW: And the trouble is as much in the poets themselves as it is in the people who view their works, because they haven't learned how to dramatize instead of simply write.

GF: You think that acting plays a great part in that, don't you? I mean, after all, the movement of an actor can be extremely poetic. Have you in mind any scene in any play that you've seen or any play of your own for that matter?

TW: Whenever you speak of acting, my mind immediately goes to Laurette Taylor.

GF: I don't blame you.

TW: I don't think Laurette reads poetry. I don't think she ever curls up in bed with Hart Crane or even William Shakespeare, but I've never known a person who could put more poetry, more of the quality of poetry, into a reading. What the poetic theatre needs is more fine, intuitive actors of her caliber. We've gotten in the habit, actors in the Broadway theatre, of talking like parrots. And poetry dies through that form of delivery.

GF: You think that's the effect of long runs, Tennessee?

TW: It can be the effect of long runs but it needn't be. I think it's the effect of appearing in too many hit-and-run comedies. [laughter]

GF: Well, tell me, do you think films have the same influence? Do you think that they have a damaging effect on the reading of poetry among actors? When I say reading of poetry I don't mean their sitting by the fireside, I mean their reading poetic lines on the stage, or over the air for that matter.

TW: Well, there should be theatres that can put on repertories of poetic plays where actors can be trained to read poetry. That's the only answer I can think of, and that gets it around again to a decentralized theatre, a theater that does not have to live on profit. That does not have to compete with Broadway successes in the comedy and musical field.

GF: Well, then, you think that this old idea that was worked out long ago by the Federal Theatre, by the National Theatre Conference, a decentralized theatre, a decentralized professional theatre, is the important thing?

TW: The trouble with the old Federal Theatre Project was that it was government controlled in its policy. Now this Breen-Porterfield plan would not have government control, it would just have government funds.

GF: Yes, of course, that is based on using money that is raised from all kinds of sources—I mean from private and public sources—and using them to make the best possible adaptation of our modern theatre. I mean our theatre in all its aspects. In other words, it would never in any way be a relief program. It would be a realistic treatment of the modern theatre in the best possible terms that we know. And that, of course, is the plan that the U.S. Public Theatre Foundation is putting forward and the plan, which we understand, that the American National Theatre has under consideration.

Well, I think we've had a very interesting discussion. I think, Tennessee, that you've brought us something that is quite unusual. It isn't often that we have the opportunity of having a poet on the air, a poet who is successful. There are lots of unsuccessful poets, we believe, living according to tradition in Greenwich Village. But I think you live in a high hotel towering above Lexington Avenue in what is known as the Grand Central Zone. Well, at any rate, I want to thank you for being here tonight, Tennessee, and I want to say that this has been, to my mind, the most interesting of the programs so far with no detriment to anyone else.

TW: Well, thank you, George. It's been fun for me too. More fun than I thought it would be.

A Playwright Named Tennessee
R.C. Lewis/1947

From the *New York Times Magazine,* 7 December 1947, 19, 67, 69-70. ©1947 by the New York Times Company. Reprinted by permission.

In 1940 in Boston a new play, *Battle of Angels,* a production wearing the colors of the Theatre Guild and directed by Margaret Webster, opened for a two-week tryout. At the tryout's end, it closed—with an apology from the Guild to its subscribers. . . .

However, the Guild's apology was hopeful. It expressed regret at the play's failure to please and wound up: "*Battle of Angels* turned out badly, but who knows whether the next one by the same author may not prove a success?"

The author in question was Tennessee Williams, and his "next one" was indeed a success; it was *The Glass Menagerie,* which ran for 563 performances on Broadway, won the Critics Circle Award in 1945, and made Tennessee Williams the theatre's best-known young playwright. Now he has a new play in New York, *A Streetcar Named Desire.*

A few days ago I talked with Williams in an East Thirty-sixth Street apartment he had borrowed while *Streetcar* was in rehearsal. In the old-fashioned, high-ceilinged bed-living room there were, among other things, a copy of André Gide's Journal, a fifth of Scotch and the compounded untidiness of one who is both bachelor and writing man. Williams, in his shirtsleeves, sprawled on a couch.

He in no way resembles what seems to be the popular fancy about him. Perhaps because of his name, perhaps because of the plays he writes, people usually expect him to be a romantic type, either built along the monumental lines of the late Thomas Wolfe or lean and hungry-looking like Gary Cooper. Actually, the name Tennessee is his own idea; he adopted it, in place of the Thomas originally given him, in honor of his Tennessee forebears. And, at 33, Williams is short and

stocky, with dark hair, a small mustache, blue eyes and an antebellum accent. When he is being serious, which is much of the time,
his manner is intense, methodical and ingrown, rather like that of a
youngster who has just graduated summa cum laude from Harvard.

Though he is heavier and much more at ease than when I last saw
him—when *The Glass Menagerie* was ending a three-month run in
Chicago and was about to strike out for New York—he is still far from
the silk-dressing-gown school of playwrights. His only sartorial
characteristic seems to be an affection for bow ties. He is habitually
amiable to callers and he answers questions with disarming honesty.

Nevertheless, he is uncomfortable when he attempts to talk about
himself or even his work. Asked to explain the origin of one of his
plays he struggles with the question for several moments, then gives
up: "Perhaps my unconscious could tell. I can't."

Whether he is essentially humble or essentially self-centered is a
moot point among those who have worked with him. There is no
doubt that he has humility, stemming from the knowledge he has
acquired at first hand that writing is hard work. During a rehearsal of
Streetcar Williams had an idea for the production that he wanted to
offer to the director, Elia Kazan. He turned to a colleague beside him,
explained what his idea was and asked whether it would be all right
to speak to Kazan about it. His companion, who had never
encountered such diffidence in a successful playwright, said "Of
course." Williams nevertheless waited for a break before approaching
Kazan.

Most of the allegations of conceit with which Williams is sometimes
charged arise from his absorption in his work, as well as his
consciousness of his own undeniable worth. Speaking recently of the
future of the theatre, he paused to list the more promising of the
younger American playwrights, and named: "Arthur Miller, Saroyan,
Williams. . . ." He meant Tennessee Williams, but the intonation of
his name was exactly the same as that of the others.

His modesty and his interest in perfection make him listen readily
to suggestions about his plays while he is working on them. At the
same time he takes umbrage quickly at stories that a produced play
has been substantially altered on the advice of a director or someone
else.

After the opening of *The Glass Menagerie* a Broadway rumor had

it that much of its success was due to textual emendations by Eddie
Dowling, who, besides acting with the late Laurette Taylor in the play,
co-directed and co-produced it. Williams declared at the time that the
only changes from his final draft had been the insertion of one
episode, the drunk scene, at Dowling's suggestion, and the omission
of a screen on which magic-latern slides bearing images and titles
were to have been projected. Later in his "Production Notes" for the
published play, he felt moved to write: "There is only one important
difference between the original and acting version of the play"—the
deleted screen. So that no one would miss the point, he put it in
italics.

Unlike a small army of writers, Williams is reluctant to discuss the
theatre in terms of trends or theories, but he has set down on paper
what might be called his credo: "The straight realistic play with its
genuine Frigidaire and authentic ice cubes, its characters that speak
exactly as its audience speaks, corresponds to the academic
landscape and has the same virtue of a photographic likeness.
Everyone should know nowadays the unimportance of the
photographic in art." In the two years since these words were
published, Williams' views haven't changed appreciably, and neither
has Broadway.

Current conditions, Williams says, make the prospect for a young
unknown playwright pretty dim.

"The obvious and biggest millstone is expense. That's why fresh
plays don't get put on. The cost of producing a play is up three or
four times even since 1940. It took only about $20,000, if I
remember, to stage *Battle of Angels*. *Streetcar* cost at least three times
that. The solution to this problem, like a lot of others in the theatre, is
theatres off Broadway. In London I hear you can still put on plays for
a few thousand dollars. I think we should study England's methods.
They certainly produce just as artistic results.

"If a new playwright writes a really good play, nothing can stop
him. But a beginner can always use experience. And there are hardly
any theatres off Broadway to give him that."

Williams' work to date includes ten full-length plays—not counting
Camino Real, a Mexican fantasy that he wrote this year and has not
yet shown to anyone—as well as a score of one-acters, some short
stories and a number of poems. Unlike Saroyan, who is noted for the

celerity of his muse and to whom Williams is sometimes compared, he is a relatively slow worker. He devotes a year and a half to his major plays and each exists in three or four drafts. Among his favorite writers are Chekhov and the Spanish poet and dramatist Garcia Lorca, and it is probable that they, more than any others, have contributed to his own particular style.

Williams' plays share at least two distinctive characteristics. One is a feeling for evanescent moods and conditions. Another is an emphasis on psychological peculiarities, which brings up the characters as if one were to substitute binoculars for spectacles in looking at them. The effect of these qualities is a static, dreamlike atmosphere, in which action is sometimes limited to the agitation of the dialogue.

Plot as such has always had a secondary interest for Williams. "My chief aim in playwriting," he says, "is the creation of character. I have always had a deep feeling for the mystery in life, and essentially my plays have been an effort to explore the beauty and meaning in the confusion of living." In writing *The Glass Menagerie,* he says, his ideal was a static drama—"a play whose interest does not depend on incident or situation but holds its audience through the revelation of quiet and ordinary truths."

Williams' views on social progress, the place of man in the cosmic scheme and other serious questions are implicit in all of his plays, especially his earlier ones. On some points they approach an attitude that has come to be identified with Saroyan. Exclamations like the following are not infrequent with his philosophical characters, most of whom have been pushed to life's extremities: "Is there no mercy left in the world anymore?" cries one. "What has become of compassion and understanding? Where have they all gone to? Where's God? Where's Christ?" . . .

The failure of *Battle* was the supreme test of Williams' courage and devotion to the theatre. His difficulty was that he was the author not merely of a first failure—an obstacle that a number of young dramatists have surmounted with distinction—but of a spectacular flop.

"I thought for a while I was washed up even before I'd got started," he subsequently related. But he didn't know his own strength. For more than two years before 1940 he had been "that most common American phenomenon, the rootless, wandering writer"—living in various parts of the country and working at a dozen menial jobs to keep alive.

He became a wanderer again. "I had already discovered," he says, "that the life of a young writer was going to be something similar to the defense of a stockade against a band of savages." He did not stop writing. . . .

Williams' preoccupation with his work limits his natural gregariousness. He has relatively few close friends and they usually have some connection with his career—such persons as Audrey Wood [literary agent of TW—Editor]; Margo Jones, co-director of *The Glass Menagerie* and director of Theatre '47, which presented *Summer and Smoke* in Dallas last summer; and James Laughlin IV, proprietor of New Directions press, which has published many of his poems and plays. Williams has explained his social habits this way: "I am gregarious and like to be around people, but almost anybody will do. There is a problem of personal integrity involved."

Another reason for Williams' few close attachments is his enthusiasm for travel, something of a habit acquired in the days of penury and peregrination before he came into his own. Although he keeps an apartment in New Orleans, in the French Quarter, he may not see it more than three months in twelve. The other nine he will probably be in Florida, New Mexico, Texas, California or Mexico. New York he visits only on business. . . .

As for future writing, he has two projects, neither of them definite. One is on a Southern theme. "I'd really like to do something different," he says. "I don't think that after *Streetcar* and *Summer and Smoke* I should write another Southern play, yet at the moment I don't feel close enough to anything else."

No one, including Tennessee Williams, however, can be sure of what he will do next. He does not feel bound to one style of writing for the theatre and he is interested in a great number of subjects. "People who live in glass menageries," a friend has said of Williams' literary talents, "will leave no stones unturned."

Tennessee Williams—Last of Our Solid Gold Bohemians
Henry Hewes/1953

From *Saturday Review*, 28 March 1953, 25-27. © 1953 by
Saturday Review Magazine Co. Reprinted by permission.

Early in Tennessee Williams's new play *Camino Real* (here
pronounced CAMino REEL and not camEEno rayAl) one of the
characters asks, "What'd he say?" While Mr. Williams did not write
the line with this in mind, he has discovered, since he opened in
Philadelphia, that it sums up perfectly the reaction of a large segment
of the audience. Theatregoers who spot the short, lightly moustached
playwright in the rear of the orchestra bear down on him with
questions about the play's meaning that he accepts with a mixture of
amusement and amazement. "You give me another $4.80 and I'll
give you a lecture," he jokes to earnest-minded patrons.

The most frequent question concerns the play's locale, which
though not specified in the program seems to be a Spanish-speaking
tropical resort. The majority of inquirers figure it out as some kind of
limbo or purgatory where the soul discovers its final disposition,
much like the ship in *Outward Bound*. However, Mr. Williams feels
only that his locale represents the general atmosphere of life. On the
other hand, he does admit that the characters imprisoned in his locale
have been offered certain terminal points. They are the Siete Mares, a
swank tourist hotel where the nonconformist guest is in constant
danger of eviction when hoped-for remittances fail to arrive; the
Ritz—Men Only, a delapidated "pad" across the street where the
evicted guest may go; the Fugitivo, a nonscheduled airline which
caters to those who believe they can escape by flight; the Laboratory,
where people who die without five dollars in their pocket are taken
by the street cleaners in order that their bodies may be dissected; and
some stone steps leading through an arch and out over uncharted

deserts and snowy mountains, which is the terminal Mr. Williams would choose for himself.

"I haven't worked these things all out consciously and I never realized they might be confusing until I started reading the play to prospective backers," says Tennessee, whose formula for writing is to drink a cup of coffee and then let the words flow without advance blueprints, even though the procedure usually requires him to do several drafts. "I thought of *Camino Real* as sort of a fairy tale or masque. When I originally wrote it as a one-act six years ago, the character of the locale was Mexican. But since that time I have been back and forth to Europe and Africa a few times and I've added touches from Fez, Tangiers, and Casablanca. Also each time I return here I sense a further reduction in human liberties, which I guess is reflected in the revisions of the play. In making the play longer I have added the character of Lord Byron, and have expanded the roles of Jacques Casanova and Marguerite Gautier."

That these characters, along with such fictional gentlemen as Baron De Charlus (the homosexual masochist from Proust) and Don Quixote, can coexist in a contemporary setting comes from the playwright's notion that ordinary time can be suspended onstage. Instead of diurnal chronology, he has substituted a feeling of time by dividing the play into sixteen blocks on the royal or real highway (the ambiguity is intentional). Each block corresponds with a French scene (a character enters or exits) and is announced to the audience by the hotel proprietor, a man who seems to take delight in toying with the romantics who wander about in degradation and in low spirits.

"I wanted the regular announcement of the blocks as they come along to have the whiplike quality of time," says the poetic dramatist, who as an author having his most complex play tried out for only three weeks prior to its Broadway opening is supremely conscious of the flagellative relentlessness of clock and calendar.

Equally conscious of the approaching deadline is the play's director, Elia ("Gadge") Kazan, who has been working with Tennessee Williams on the *Camino Real* project over a period of two and one half years. Mr. Kazan thinks that the reason for any confusion comes from the fact that *Camino Real* instead of having the usual unity of story that limits expression has a unity of theme expressed far more completely than it could have been in a tight story. For that theme he will refer you back to Tennessee with the warning that you have the right to question him about it, but that he, in turn, has the right not to answer.

"The theme," says the playwright affably, "is pretty much the same as that of a play I wrote in 1941 called *Stairs to the Roof*, which was produced at the Pasadena Playhouse. [26 February 1947—Editor] It is, I guess you could say, a prayer for the wild of heart kept in cages. *Camino Real* doesn't say anything that hasn't been said before, but is merely a picture of the state of the romantic nonconformist in modern society. It stresses honor and man's own sense of inner dignity which the Bohemian must reachieve after each period of degradation he is bound to run into. The romantic should have the spirit of anarchy and not let the world drag him down to its level. Don Quixote, who appears at the end of the play, is the supreme example of the obstinate knight, gallant in meeting ultimate degradation, and unashamed at being the victim of his own romantic follies." . . .

When the playwright was asked to lift the veil on some of the symbols used within the play, he had this to say: "To me, using a symbol is just a way of saying a thing more vividly and dramatically than I could otherwise. For instance, the hotel proprietor's dropping Casanova's shabby portmanteau of fragile memories out the window is a clearer expression of an idea than you might be able to do with a thousand words. However, I don't believe in using symbols *unless* they clarify."

By clarifying Mr. Williams doesn't mean that he feels a compunction to iron out the complications or contradictions within his play, because he intends it to be infinitely suggestive and filled with half-truths and intimations. "Now if *Camino Real* purported to deliver a message, I would have had to be clearer, but it doesn't, and I don't think the people who find it confusing in its present form would like it any better if it were clarified."

The problem that does concern him as he moves into his final tryout week is Kilroy. Kilroy, an ex-boxer, is the play's most important character, but in the expansion from the shorter original, Mr. Williams has had to stop Kilroy's story and make him a minor character for almost the entire second act. "Right now I can see no way of extending the Kilroy story, so the only thing I can do is to try to make Act II so vivid that the audience won't mind Kilroy being in abeyance.

If I had written this script in one setting, I wouldn't be having this problem. On the other hand, if the play concerned only Kilroy, it would have been much less of a play."

Aside from this, the only other major effort that will be made will be directed towards making the whole production move as swiftly as possible. "We're trying," says Mr. Williams, "to find the points where it is impeded, and fix them so that the play will have a smooth dreamlike quality."

Kazan, who faced somewhat similar problems when he directed Thornton Wilder's bewildering *The Skin of Our Teeth* ten years ago, recalls that prize-winning play as being cooler, more objective, and less complicated.

"*Camino Real* is the most direct subjective play of our time," says Mr. Kazan.

"It's Tennessee speaking personally and lyrically right to you. That's one reason we've pulled the audience inside the fourth wall by having the actors frequently speak directly to the spectator and by having some of the exits and entrances made through the aisles of the theatre. This device also gives a feeling of freedom."

Both Kazan and producer Cheryl Crawford are highly pleased to be doing a work that moves so far away from the strict naturalistic drama that prevails on Broadway. "No one," says Mr. Kazan, "appreciates how much *A Streetcar Named Desire* did to open the avenue to a less literal approach toward the theatre. Because of *Streetcar* we had *Death of a Salesman*. Now we all hope people are ready for this."

While both Kazan and Williams are grimly concerned with the success of *Camino Real*, they are at the same time infected with the wild spirit of anarchy within the play, and when last seen were walking relaxedly down Walnut Street on their way to "dig" a night club appearance by one of their favorite performers, the equally wild-spirited Johnny Ray.

Tennessee Williams: Ten Years Later

Arthur B. Waters/1955

From *Theatre Arts*, July 1955, 72-73, 96.

When *Cat on a Hot Tin Roof*, which recently won for Tennessee Williams the Pulitzer Prize and New York Drama Critics Circle Award, had its Broadway première at the Morosco Theatre on March 24, it was exactly ten years—give or take a few days—since *The Glass Menagerie* catapulted this same playwright into the ranks of the very top brass of the theatre. Has the intervening decade made any conspicuous change in him? Has it altered very radically his views on playwriting, the theatre? A double negative seems to be in order. There is now an easy and quite obviously sincere tolerance of varying aspects of the theatre.

During the years between *The Glass Menagerie* and *Cat on a Hot Tin Roof*, Williams believes the legitimate theatre in this country has most certainly held its own. "I'm sorry," he says, "that I haven't been able to follow personally the results achieved by some of the young playwrights, but I know there are a lot of promising ones, and more and more, their work is reaching the stage. Talent—real talent— doesn't go unrewarded these days." Two young writers who elicited his special admiration are Robert Anderson, who handled delicately and sensitively the difficult theme of homosexuality in *Tea and Sympathy*, and William Inge, who won the playwright's admiration in *Bus Stop* for a mastery of warm, sympathetic characterizations and easy, fluent dialogue.

On the subject of *Cat on a Hot Tin Roof*, Williams remarked gravely, "I would regret it very much if this new play had to rely, even in a minor degree, on the public's appetite for salaciousness. In fact I feel so strongly on the subject that I suggested we take out most of the four-letter words that were in the original script. I conscientiously believed they helped establish some of the characters, most of all the crude and uncouth Big Daddy. I still feel that a number of these were quite in character and, to my mind, unobjectionable. But when I heard that word was getting around that we had a dirty show filled with dirty dialogue, I strongly advised their removal."

The playwright is very emphatic in coming to the defense of his central character Brick, the play's lonesome and sympathetic near-alcoholic against whom charges of homosexuality are made. "Brick is definitely not a homosexual," he declares, and points out that in one key speech he has Brick's wife attest to her husband's innocence. "Brick's self-pity and recourse to the bottle are not the result of a guilty conscience in that regard. When he speaks of 'self-disgust,' he is talking in the same vein as that which finds him complaining bitterly about having had to live so long with 'mendacity.' He feels that the collapse and premature death of his great friend Skipper, who never appears in the play, have been caused by unjust attacks on his moral character made by outsiders, including Margaret (Maggie), the wife. It is his bitterness at Skipper's tragedy that has caused Brick to turn against his wife and find solace in drink, rather than any personal involvement, although I do suggest that, at least at some time in his life, there have been unrealized abnormal tendencies."

When I sought a parallel between the new play and A Streetcar Named Desire, Williams only partly agreed. "Aside from the locales which are somewhat similar, there is a surface likeness between the leading feminine characters, but only a surface one. Blanche DuBois and Margaret share certain attributes, notably strongly passionate natures, but they are really as unlike as a moth and an eagle. Both find themselves brought into turbulent, head-long collision with the rock of life, but whereas Blanche is weak and pitiful—almost a mental case—Margaret is sturdy, strong and resilient. Because she is violently, almost possessively in love with Brick, doesn't mean she is oversexed or abnormal."

The knowledge that in recent years Williams has been dividing his time between Florida and Rome, with occasional prolonged stopovers in New York, caused me to ask him why he continues to deal in most of his plays with the people and settings of the Deep South of his struggling boyhood.

"Because I know and understand their moods and personalities better and because I am both familiar and in complete sympathy with the flavor and mode of their speech," was his unhesitating reply. "But I don't feel that the characters in *Cat on a Hot Tin Roof* are bound by the setting of the play. Their problems and feelings and the inner tragedy of their whole tortured lives would be very much the same if the story were laid elsewhere."

Williams himself does not feel restricted to locale. After the play's opening he was off to Florida again; then he planned to fly to Rome for a writing assignment with Anna Magnani in mind.

There also is a new tolerance in his attitude toward Hollywood. "Film standards have improved a great deal in recent years," he points out. "They've done a very good job by my *Rose Tattoo* (which stars Miss Magnani), and this summer I expect to work with Elia Kazan (director of *Cat on a Hot Tin Roof*) on a film to be called *Hide and Seek*, which will be based on a short play of mine, *27 Wagons Full of Cotton*." The latter came to Broadway in April as part of a triple bill called *All in One*.

Williams is a tremendous admirer of Kazan, who previously directed his *A Streetcar Named Desire* and *Camino Real*, and feels that if Kazan had staged *The Rose Tattoo*, it would have been the smash hit it just missed being. Before *Cat on a Hot Tin Roof* arrived, the playwright felt he hadn't had a real success since *Streetcar*, for he classes *The Rose Tattoo*, as well as *Summer and Smoke* and *Camino Real*, as failures. "If this new one doesn't make the grade, I'll have to go back to writing plays for art and little theatre groups," he remarked with a wry and not altogether humorous movement of his lips.

His favorites among his plays are *The Glass Menagerie, Streetcar,* and *Cat on a Hot Tin Roof*. What about *Camino Real*? "Well," he said, "I think I was entitled to that one. Every author has to do something like that sometime in his writing career. It was a kind of literary catharsis. As a matter of fact, while I was writing them, I suppose I've liked all the plays I've tackled, with the possible exception of *You Touched Me!*" (an adaptation of a D. H. Lawrence story, written with Donald Windham). In the fall Wlliams will complete the revision of his first full-length produced play, *Battle of Angels*, under the new title of *Orpheus Descending*.

Compared with the Tennessee Williams of 1945 who was on the threshold of his first major success—after a period of anxious years, straitened circumstances, a deadly grind and a variety of jobs that ranged from waiter to teletype operator to usher at a movie theatre on Broadway—the Williams of today has comparative security, and his new tranquility of mind is mirrored in his manner. Perhaps it will be mirrored in his writings too: *Cat on a Hot Tin Roof* has a relatively cheerful conclusion.

A close perusal of the script called my attention to a facet of Williams' talent as a writer that I had previously overlooked. Not only is his dialogue both trenchant and moving, but his stage directions are embellished with the author's personal feelings about the characters and their problems. Somewhere about the middle of Act II, I found what I thought to be a graphic description of just what Williams was aiming at in his latest play. I was pleased to find him not only willing but enthusaistic for me to quote it, because to him it is the real nub of his play.

So here it is—Tennessee Williams' own vivid analysis of his aims:

". . . The bird that I hope to catch in the net of this play is not the solution of one man's psychological problem. I'm trying to catch the true quality of experience in a group of people, that cloudly, flickering, evanescent—fiercely charged!—interplay of live human beings in the thundercloud of a common crisis. Some mystery should be left in the revelation of character in a play, just as a great deal of mystery is always left in the revelation of character in life, even in one's own character to himself. This does not absolve the playwright of his duty to observe and probe as clearly and as deeply as he legitimately can; but it should steer him away from 'pat' conclusions, facile definitions which make a play just a play, not a snare for the truth of human experience."

Williams in Art and Morals:
An Anxious Foe of Untruth
Don Ross/1957

From the *New York Herald Tribune*, 3 March 1957, sec. 4, 1-2. ©
I.H.T. Corporation. Reprinted by permission.

The other night we climbed up to Tennessee Williams' second-floor
two-room apartment in E. 58th St. and had a little talk about several
subjects such as why he writes plays, what kind of people he writes
about, does he try to shock his audience, is he an optimist or a
pessimist, and does he consider himself a moralist.

He has a home in Key West where he spends much of his time and
does his best work. He was at his New York apartment because his
new play, *Orpheus Descending*, opens at the Martin Beck March 21,
and he had to be close by during rehearsals.

A pleasant-faced short man a little on the plump side, Mr. Williams
fixed vodka on the rocks for his guest and himself, and settled himself
comfortably on the sofa and waited for the first question.

Some people accuse you of filling your plays with sordid
characters. Are they right?

Mr. Williams took a long pull on the vodka and answered the
question with a somewhat indignant inflection to his voice, which is
an unusual blend of Dixie-British. He was born in Mississippi but has
spent much time abroad.

"I don't think Blanche DuBois was sordid," he said, hissing the
word sordid in a way that indicated he didn't think much of it. "I
think she was rather noble. I don't think deeply troubled people are
sordid. She was troubled. Miss Alma in *Summer and Smoke* was
almost a puritan. Is that sordid? Tell me who was sordid in *The Glass
Menagerie*? In *The Rose Tattoo* Serafina was earthy and sensual.
These things can be very beautiful, I have always thought."

It was clear that the more Mr. Williams thought of the word sordid
as applied to his people, the more preposterous it became.

"Coming to *Cat on a Hot Tin Roof*, I don't think either Maggie or Brick was sordid. Brick was troubled. Maggie was desperate. I thought both were admirable people in different ways. I thought Big Daddy had a certain stature and bigness, almost a nobility, in his crude ways.

"I can't think of any of my main characters who have been sordid. I think pettiness and meanness is sordid. I would never choose a person of that sort for a main protagonist because they don't interest me."

What kind of people do you like to write about?

"Deeply troubled people. I think most of us have deep troubles. I've yet to find people I didn't think were deeply troubled. This is the age of anxiety. I think that if most people look at others they'll see deep trouble under the skin. There is an increasing tension and anxiety in people I know."

Mr. Williams knows a lot of different kinds of people he's met in different places. He's been an elevator operator in New York. He's waited on tables and recited verse in Greenwich Village. He's worked as a teletype operator for the Army Engineers in Jacksonville, Fla. He's been a waiter and cashier in a restaurant in New Orleans. He's ushered at the Strand Theater in New York.

Another drink of vodka and he resumed in his warm, fluent voice.

"So often the theater doesn't try to get under the skin. That's all right for comedies and musicals, but I can't write this sort of thing. I have to write of people as I know them.

"A writer's view of the world is always affected by his own state of being. I am an anxious, troubled person. I can't write about anything I don't feel. Maybe some day I will suddenly become hilarious and write something very bright." He laughed at himself as he said this.

"I once wrote a romantic comedy, *You Touched Me*. It was about troubled people but in a funny way. I wrote it with Donald Windham. It ran for three and a half months at the Booth Theater in, I think, 1945. Well, really, I don't think my works are terribly solemn. There's a good deal of humor in most of them. People howled at *Glass Menagerie*, you know."

Are you a moralist? Mr. Williams comes from a line of moralists. His grandfather was an Episcopal minister in Columbus, Miss., where Tennessee was born.

"I would say so. I have a distinct moral attitude. I wouldn't say message. I'm not polemical, but I have a distinct attitude toward good and evil in life and people. I think any of my plays examined closely will indicate what I regard as evil. I think I regard hypocrisy and mendacity as almost the cardinal sins. It seems they are the ones to which I am most hostile. I think that deliberate, conscienceless mendacity, the acceptance of falsehood and hypocrisy, is the most dangerous of all sins.

"The moral contribution of my plays is that they expose what I consider to be untrue. But I don't want to pretend that I'm a great moral evangelist. I'm an entertainer and a playwright—a profession that is at least partly entertainer.

"I don't write for frivolous reasons. I always write to express myself. But I want to succeed also as an entertainer. I want to be a playwright that holds an audience, amuses them. I'm not a preacher, at least not consciously."

Are your plays optimistic or pessimistic?

"I think it's very necessary to discover those things in life one can believe in. I think life is meaningless unless we find something to which we can be faithful, believe in, consider valuable, hold to in ourselves. In that sense, I think I am mostly optimistic. I believe very strongly in the existence of good. I believe that honesty, understanding, sympathy and even sexual passion are good.

"So I don't think I'm a pessimist altogether. I find life a mysterious and terrifying experience. I don't think I'm as gloomy as a lot of people who write. I'm sure I've never written anything as gloomy as *Long Day's Journey Into Night.*" This is the Eugene O'Neill play now at the Helen Hayes.

What are the moral values of *Cat on a Hot Tin Roof*, for example?

"I meant for the audience to discover how people erect false values by not facing what is true in their natures, by having to live a lie, and I hoped the audience would admire the heroic persistence of life and vitality; and I hoped they would feel the thwarted desire of people to reach each other through this fog, this screen of incomprehension. What I want most of all is to catch the quality of existence and experience. I want people to think 'This is life.' I want to offer them my own individual attitude toward it."

Mr. Williams himself brought up the fact that some critics have accused him of writing sensational plays to make money.

"I've never written for money. I'm always happy to get it. But I've never written for it. When critics say that of me I think they're avaricious themselves. My kind of work can be bad, primitive, childish, but it should be apparent to any one with a critical faculty that it isn't the kind of thing you do for money. With what I know about the theater, I could really write for money if I wanted to.

"Nor do I ever try to shock people. Well, yes, I do. I want to shock people but not to have a *succes de scandale*, not to shock per se, but because I want to give people a jolt, get them fully alive. I like strong effects and boldness, and perhaps sometimes I go overboard, but I never do it for commercial reasons.

"I do it only to make a point more strongly. I don't like vulgarity in any medium. I've been offended by certain works of mine, by things over which I had no control."

As an example of offensive things, Mr. Williams brought up the famous elephant story, a ribald tale told by Big Daddy in *Cat on a Hot Tin Roof*. It was removed shortly after the opening.

"I wasn't crazy about the elephant story. I was glad to have it taken out. Kazan (the director of the play) told me that the third act had to be rewritten to get Big Daddy back on the stage. I felt Kazan was imperative for the play. In my great longing to hold his interest, I rewrote the third act to bring Big Daddy back on. I thought I could do it without violating the essential meaning of the play.

"Then when I got Big Daddy back on I couldn't think of anything for the old man to say. So I had him tell the elephant story. I sent the story up to Kazan's room and he immediately said: "This is marvelous." If Kazan says something is it, you think it's it. So it went in. I'm very susceptible to people's opinions, especially those I respect very highly."

The word sordid came up again. Mr. Williams had been thinking about it in the intervals of talk, with increasing dislike, and this time he decided to demolish it.

"Sordid? I prefer not to classify people according to that yardstick. I don't think in those terms. Sordid is just a term used by a second-rate reviewer. It has no critical validity."

Orpheus Descending, which is directed by Harold Clurman and presented by the Producers Theater, is an 85 per cent rewrite of a play called *Battle of Angels* which closed in 1940 after its tryout in Boston and never got to Broadway.

It has been rewritten numerous times. In the latest rewrites Mr. Williams had Anna Magnani, considered by him the greatest living actress, in mind as Lady Torrance, the wife of Jabe Torrance, proprietor of a general store in the Mississippi delta country.

Magnani agreed to do the play but only for two months because she felt that with her limited and painful English, a longer run would be too great a strain. Mr. Williams asked Magnani to agree to a longer run. She said no.

So Maureen Stapleton, who created the role of the widow in *Rose Tattoo*, will be Lady Torrance. "I think Maureen is very likely the greatest actress in America," said Mr. Williams. "There was nobody else here I thought could do it." The movie role has been promised to Magnani.

"I tried very hard to get Brando for Val," Mr. Williams said. Val Xavier is "a sort of honky tonk guitar player and singer" who works at the Torrance store. The role will be taken by Robert Loggia.

"Brando said he thought it was my best play. He was going to do it. But then he became evasive. I could never pin him down. I don't know whether he's scared to go back to the stage. I think he was afraid at first of playing opposite Magnani, afraid of being overshadowed. Well, maybe it's not fair to say that.

"The play deals mostly with what I believe is corrupt in life," said Mr. Williams. "One of the characters is very definitely a representative of evil. The evil takes the shape of brutality and viciousness. There are quite a few gossipy, bitchy characters in the play, but I don't think that any of them could be described as sordid." The word no longer angered him and he chuckled at it.

That Baby Doll Man: Part I

Louise Davis/1957

From *The Tennessean Magazine* [Nashville, TN], 3 March 1957, 12-13, 30-31. © 1957 by *The Tennessean*. Reprinted by permission.

Tennessee Williams, controversial playwright whose scenes of degradation have infuriated Southerners and brought down bans on his *Baby Doll* from New York to Nashville, has a surprising explanation of his work:

"I write out of love for the South," he said during an exclusive interview at a rehearsal hall in New York where his new play was being whipped into shape.

"But I can't expect Southerners to realize that my writing about them is an expression of love.

"It is out of a regret for a South that no longer exists that I write of the forces that have destroyed it."

A hard man for the press to catch any season, Williams has been their special target since *Baby Doll* was banned by Cardinal Spellman when it opened in New York last December. During the three weeks that Williams was in New York recently for rehearsal of his newest stage play, he granted one of his rare interviews, and gave *The Nashville Tennessean Magazine* what is probably the first full-length discussion of his work ever to appear in any newspaper.

"I don't write about the North, because I feel nothing for it but eagerness to get out of it," he said. "I don't write about the North because—so far as I know—they never had anything to lose, culturally.

"But the South once had a way of life that I am just old enough to remember—a culture that had grace, elegance . . . an inbred culture . . . not a society based on money, as in the North. I write out of regret for that."

A quiet man, with almost Oriental serenity, Williams had a special

43

gentleness in his voice when he spoke of his kindergarten days in
Nashville—in 1916, when his grandfather, the Rev. Walter E. Dakin,
was rector of the Church of the Advent, on Seventeenth Ave., S.

And he wondered if the Nashville he remembers with such
affection would see through the harshness of his plays for the truth
underlying them.

"I hope people don't associate me with *Baby Doll* alone," he said.
"I am not ashamed of it, but a movie is the creation of the director. It
is a very different medium from the stage.

"Elia Kazan, who directed the movie, is a fine director. I think he
did a fine job. But the movie has many things in it that I did not write.
It has at least one scene that I objected to when it was being filmed. It
was symbolic in a way that I considered it bad taste."

What scene?

Williams declined to identify it—surprisingly enough, in the interest
of good taste.

"Too evil," he said, but would add no more.

Middle Tennesseans who have seen *Baby Doll* in Lebanon,
Franklin and other communities will have to do their own speculating
on the one offending scene.

Is it where the "other man" pretends to make love to Baby Doll in
the swing? Or where he traps Baby Doll in the old parked car? Or is it
something insignificant but symbolic in the background? Williams
wouldn't say.

The rotting Mississippi mansion itself tells the story. Williams said
the house where *Baby Doll* was filmed was shown just as Kazan
found it when he drove up with camera crew and cast.

"We didn't move a stick," Williams said. "All of the Negroes and
most of the white people in the movie lived in communities near the
old house."

In its ruins—symbolic of a vanished way of life in the South—new
and crude inhabitants rattle around as ludicrous misfits throughout
the play.

"I am not a sociologist," Williams insisted. But *Baby Doll*, like so
many of his plays, shows the hideous disintegration of character in
men trapped by poverty, by their own ignorance, by greed. . . .

But Williams said that even *Baby Doll* has one character who,
however tenuously, represents the grace that once warmed the

South. The frail spinster aunt who is dependent on Baby Doll and her husband shoos chickens out of her kitchen, but she never loses a touch of elegance.

"Aunt Rose Comfort had a grace and a poetry about her . . . and a dignity," Williams said. "I have never written about the South any other way."

He had pulled up chairs against the wall of the warehouse-like rehearsal hall on New York's West 65th Street, and relaxed in easy conversation while he kept an eye on the cast going through the lines of his new play, *Orpheus Descending*.

"What I am writing about is human nature," he said. "I write about the South because I think the war between romanticism and the hostility to it is very sharp there."

"Romanticism," for him, stands in direct contrast to materialism. It is a reverence for all that is idealistic and beautiful.

"I wish that the people of the South could realize that I am writing about its romanticism," Williams said, almost wistfully.

"And the charm of its speech appeals to me, even in *Baby Doll*. I love the accent, the beautiful speech. Southerners express things in a way that is humorous, colorful, graphic."

A mild-mannered man with a fierce contempt for sham, Williams did not dodge my questions about the plays that have brought down the wrath of the South.

From the time his *Streetcar Named Desire* became one of the all-time shockers of Broadway in 1947, he has had a hard time convincing some playgoers of his loftier motives. *Streetcar*, which won the Pulitzer prize and was made into a movie, shocked all the South by its picture of depravity and squalor in New Orleans. . . .

"Blanche DuBois had a natural elegance, a love of the beautiful, a romantic attitude toward life," Williams said. "My main theme is a defense of that attitude, a violent protest against those things that defeat it."

Williams says he bears no resentment against those who misinterpret his plays. He surveys the scene thoughtfully without surprise or bitterness or regret.

His blue eyes narrowed into thoughtfulness when I mentioned the vile vocabulary of *Cat on a Hot Tin Roof*.

Was it necessary to the story?

"It had to be," Williams said. "'Big Daddy' was a rough man, a self-made man, not the typical Mississippi plantation owner, but the ignorant man who has bullied his way into power. I had to make him violent to make the character clear." . . .

"Maggie was the only aristocrat in *Cat on a Hot Tin Roof*," Williams said. "She was the only one free of greed."

Her handsome husband, who could never quite face life after the realization that his golden days in the stadium were over, was the most tragic figure in the play. Whether his alcoholism covered his guilt—or his anger at being suspected—is debatable at the end of the play.

But Williams left nothing unsaid about Brick's ambitious brother, Gooper, and his wife, Mae, who had been "queen of the cotton carnival" in Memphis. They were social climbers, fawning over "Big Daddy" for the fortune that they expected to inherit from him.

"Gooper and Mae correspond to the New South," Williams said. "They are the country club type."

Williams admitted that his plays show a dark picture.

"But these are dark times," he said.

"It doesn't help to sentimentalize. An artist has to express the things he regards as true . . . You analyze your observations, and you have to write what you see."

The shocking quality of his work reflects the shocking state of the world today, he said.

"There is a lot of violence in my work, but there is a lot of violence in life," he said. "I don't think it is false."

He looked out the windows of the hall where Director Harold Clurman, seated at a table in center of the room, had the *Orpheus* cast gathered about him in a semi-circle—schoolroom style. Outside, the rain was turning to snow; inside, actresses in galoshes were working doggedly to catch the proper Delta accent.

Williams listened to their speech, occasionally took up the script—at the director's suggestion—and showed the cast what an authentic Mississippi accent sounded like.

For Tennessee Williams (christened Thomas Lanier Williams) was born in Columbus, Miss., in his grandfather's rectory, on March 26, 1914. And—except for one year in Nashville—he spent his first seven years in Mississippi and visited there often during his boyhood.

"And I can still talk Southern," he said with some pride.

His ear is so attuned to accents that he picks them up before he realizes it, and the mixture is difficult to place.

"Some people call it British, but it changes frequently—depending on where I have been," Williams said.

His legal residence is at Key West, Fla., and he has a cottage there where he keeps up a furious pace of writing. In the 12 years since his first hit, *The Glass Menagerie*, opened on Broadway, Williams has had 11 plays, two short stories, one novel and a volume of poems published. Five of the plays have become sensational successes and *Streetcar* won for him both the Pulitzer prize and the Drama Critics Circle award.

But Williams, looking back over the work, found it difficult to estimate how long it takes to turn out a play.

"In Florida, I begin work around daybreak and work until I get tired," Williams said. "In New York, I get up much later. I work very rapidly, type very rapidly, but I go over things time and again."

He glanced toward the cast of his *Orpheus Descending*, to open on Broadway March 21.

"I've been working on this one off and on for 17 years," he said. "I have rewritten it many times—once especially for Anna Magnani, who was to have had the leading role. But that didn't work out. (Miss Magnani played the lead in the movie version of his *The Rose Tattoo*.)

"I write on a play a while, get discouraged, put it aside, pick it up again. Ordinarily the work on one play is spread out over two years, but I suppose it would amount to about eight months of solid time if I could write that way."

For relaxation from the tension of writing, he tries to get in some swimming every day.

"A playwright is especially tense," he said. "He has to work up the same tenseness as the character in the play. I find swimming the best relaxation from that tension."

Williams comes to New York infrequently—only when a new play is in rehearsal or when he is on the way to Europe, ordinarily.

The bachelor playwright allows himself about four months in Europe every year. He used to rent an apartment in Rome and travel from there in whatever direction he liked, but he doesn't bother with the Rome headquarters now. He travels without any fixed center.

"I am increasingly restless as I grow older," he said, looking slightly worried about that. "That's just the opposite of what it should be, isn't it?"

But he does plan to settle down—and *not* in the remote future, he said.

New Orleans will be his home then.

"My happiest years were there," he said. "I was desperately poor . . . hocked everything but my typewriter to get by, and that was when you could get a good room for $5 a week. New Orleans is my favorite city of America . . . of all the world, actually."

Williams, not quite 43, says that he feels the strain of writing more as time goes by.

"I don't feel any lack of material to write about," he said. "The material is not depleted, but the energy is. After 40, you have to content yourself with working longer and harder."

Five feet, six inches tall, Williams says he is fighting a tendency to gain weight. He moves about quickly, talks rapidly, and yet manages an unhurried air. He cocked an ear to the actors going through his lines and hesitated about correcting them on their interpretation.

"Do you think I should interrupt them?" he asked.

The director had two actors sounding angry because one of them had lost "100 nickels" in a slot machine.

"No Southerner should be angry in that situation," Williams said. "He would think it was funny. But that's something the North doesn't understand."

Critics have blamed Williams for giving in too easily to directors, but he has a tremendous respect for their particular skill. And he has a gallantry, a courtesy that would be perfectly at home in his grandfather's rectory.

He walked across the bleak rehearsal hall to get a better look at the snowy rain, decided against having sandwiches sent in for our lunch, and offered to help with my galoshes.

"This place is too ugly," he said. "Not very pleasant for a meal."

And a few minutes later, when the shaky self-service elevator had delivered us to the building entrance three floors below, he surveyed the winter scene happily: the snow on huge round storage tanks down the block, the contrast of their curves against the solid cubes of warehouses surrounding them.

"I don't even mind this weather, for a change," he said. "I've always liked this view."

The man who has been called the "most poetic of American playwrights today" struck a brisk pace in search of a cheerful restaurant—not minding in the least the snow that settled on his brown hair and highlighted every rooftop against the graying sky.

Williams On a Hot Tin Roof
Don Ross/1958

From the *New York Herald Tribune*, 5 January 1958, sec. 4, 1, 7.
© I.H.T. Corporation. Reprinted by permission.

Tennessee Williams disclosed the other night that he is in psychoanalysis. This is of interest to theatergoers because it could mean that a different Williams, a playwright less concerned with distraught people and violence, will eventually emerge. This is what he hopes.

Tuesday two of Mr. Williams' short plays under the title *Garden District* open at the York Playhouse, First Ave. and 64th St. The longer of the plays—it is almost a full-length play—is called *Suddenly Last Summer*. It was written during the period, beginning last summer, that Mr. Williams went into analysis. It is violent and shocking, he feels, but it is in a sense a catharsis, a final fling of violence.

"I think if this analysis works, it will open some doors for me," said Mr. Williams the other night before a log fire in his New York apartment. He spoke freely, almost eagerly, of his problems, as though there were some therapeutic value in unfolding them.

"If I am no longer disturbed myself, I will deal less with disturbed people and with violent material. I don't regret having concerned myself with such people, because I think that most of us are disturbed. But I think I have pretty well explored that aspect of life and that I may be repeating myself as a writer. It would be good if I could write with serenity."

Mr. Williams, a short man with a soft, almost prim mode of speech ("I talk a little pretentiously, don't you think?"), got up to attend to the fire. Smoke was billowing out into the room, and a fine rain of wood ash was settling on him.

"I don't think I'll ever be a bland, comfortable sort of writer," he said. "I think I'll always be a protestant, an outraged romantic, or a

Puritan, shocked by things that are reflected in my own character. I don't think I'm more virtuous than the people in my plays that shock me. I'm just as bad or worse."

From his early childhood, Mr. Williams said, he has been neurotic. He is now in his middle forties. He was bothered increasingly by periods of sheer panic in which he feared he would die of a heart attack. He was afflicted by claustrophobia. He could no longer sit in the middle of a theater with people crowded around him.

He was afraid to walk down a street unless there was a bar in sight—not that he took a drink in each block but simply because he needed the assurance, in case he panicked, of knowing he could get a drink. A drink was the only thing that could calm him at such times.

Now, after six months in analysis, the fearful spells are much less frequent. He has had only two since the analysis began. (Formerly, he might have as many as twenty in this period of time.) The claustrophobia has subsided. He is more serene. In his apartment house in the East Sixties, there is what may be the world's smallest elevator. It holds only one passenger and it gives a rider—or did this rider—the frightening feeling of being in an upended coffin. Mr. Williams is able to step into this conveyance without a twinge of his old claustrophobia.

He spends fifty minutes a day, five days a week, at the office of his analyst. He doesn't intend to become a permanent analysand; he figures that he will give it a year or so.

For years, Mr. Williams tried to muddle through without help. Then, a year ago, the last of his plays to appear on Broadway, *Orpheus Descending*, got bad notices and closed after a short run. In it the Williams violence reached a peak: at the close a man was torn to pieces by a pack of dogs.

"I was terribly shocked by its reception," said Mr. Williams. "I had invested so much of myself in it. I had worked longer at it than any other play. I thought it had lyricism, the feeling of tenderness, the striving to understand, the longing, but I did feel that the ending didn't come off quite right."

"I didn't blame the critics or the public. I felt I had failed. I associated this with the extreme difficulty I had in writing it. *Orpheus* brought all my problems to a head. I knew I must find help or crack up, so I went to an analyst and poured out all my troubles. I felt the most enormous relief." Incidentally, many of Mr. Williams' friends, like Marlon Brando, Elia Kazan and Irene Selznick, had been urging him for a long time to consult a psychoanalyst.

Some people believe that analysis has a bad effect on a writer. "I do not believe this," Mr. Williams said. "If I did I would never have gone into it. I would not hazard or risk my ability to work. I would have preferred to remain confused and troubled. I'm very happy that I had writing as an outlet to my reaction to experience. Otherwise, I would have gone really off my trolley. That's the only thing that saved me."

Like any other writer, Mr. Williams is troubled by a fear that he may have said all he has to say. "I believe I wrote my best play early," he said. "It was *A Streetcar Named Desire*. My writing has, I think, followed a declining line since then. My plays have obviously not been as good. I did feel, though, that *Cat on a Hot Tin Roof* brought the line up suddenly. I thought that this was in many ways as good as *Streetcar*. It didn't have its lyric qualities, but the second act was as good as anything I've ever done. With *Orpheus* I felt I was no longer acceptable to the theater public. Maybe, I thought, they'd had too much of a certain dish, and maybe they don't want to eat any more."

Understandably, Mr. Williams does not like to reveal the plot of his plays. But he did say enough about *Suddenly Last Summer* to indicate that it is about a young woman who witnesses the shockingly violent murder of a man. In order to clear herself of suspicion, she tells a story of the death which damages the man's reputation. The man's wealthy and powerful mother has the girl locked up in an insane asylum and, somehow, a psychoanalyst is called in to straighten out the tangle. Mr. Williams believes it is one of his best plays. The other play on the York Theater bill, called *Something Unspoken*, was written five years ago when Mr. Williams was in London.

"It's not a realistic play," said Mr. Williams of *Suddenly Last Summer*. "The set lighting establishes a nonrealistic mood. I hope people will realize it's a moral fable of our times."

The off-Broadway theater is fine for experimental and controversial works, Mr. Williams thinks. He intends to write other plays for it, but the next thing he has in mind is for Broadway. It's a revision of his *Sweet Bird of Youth*, a full-length play which was produced in Florida a couple of years ago but has not been seen in New York. [Coral Gables: Studio M Playhouse, 16 April 1956—Editor] He hopes to have it ready by August or September.

He has concluded that *Bird's* ending is too violent and theatrical, and he will tone it down. As it stands now, the hero is emasculated off stage at the end. Mr. Williams will substitute for this physical violence the psychological equivalent of emasculation.

Tennessee Williams
Mike Wallace/1958

From *Mike Wallace Asks: Highlights from 46 Controversial Interviews*, ed. Charles Preston and Edward A. Hamilton (New York: Simon & Schuster, 1958), 20-23. © 1958 by Newsmaker Production, Inc. Reprinted by permission of Simon & Schuster, Inc.

It's said that a nation's art reflects a nation's soul. In Tennessee Williams, America has elevated to the top rank of playwrights a poet preoccupied with tragedy, avarice and spiritual cannibalism. This says much about our times and much about Mr. Williams, who has written such disturbing plays as *A Streetcar Named Desire*, *The Rose Tattoo*, *Cat on a Hot Tin Roof*, and the film *Baby Doll*.

MW: Richard Watts, whom I know you admire, has described your characteristic mood as "steeped in passion, hatred, frustration, bitterness and violence."

TW: I don't contest that at all, Mike. It's quite true.

MW: What I am after is, if you want to tell me: Do you really feel that way about the world?

TW: I'm having a big argument on this subject with my analyst, Mike. I tell him that I don't feel that way and he—he wants to find out if I do or I don't, and we're still exploring it. I think I feel more affection and love. He thinks that certain early conditions and experiences in my life made—created a lot of anger and resentment in me, which I am taking out now through my writing. He may be right, I can't say.

MW: What kind of conditions?

TW: Have you ever heard of the term—he didn't want me to use these analytical terms, he doesn't approve of them, but I do a lot of reading and I use them to him, he doesn't use them to me—a term that I've come across lately is "infantile omnipotence."

MW: "Infantile omnipotence"?

TW: That is what we all have as babies. We scream in the cradle, the mother picks us up, she comforts us, she suckles us, she changes the diaper, whatever is giving us discomfort is tended to, and through this she rocks us to sleep and all that. And whatever gives us discomfort, we find, is—is relieved in response to an outraged cry.

MW: Well, this is an experience that is common to all of us, yet we don't all see the world the way you seem to in your writing.

TW: This is the infant feeling omnipotent. All it has to do is cry out and it will be comforted, it will be attended to. All right. We grow up a little and we discover that the outcry doesn't meet this tender response always. After a while the mother realizes that it's no longer an infant, she gets impatient with its outcry or maybe the father gets impatient with it. Anyway, it meets a world which is less permissive, less tender and comforting, and it misses the maternal arms—the maternal comfort—and therefore, then, it becomes outraged, it becomes angry. And that's where most of our neuroses spring from, from the time when we—when the maternal world which has made us feel omnipotent because every time we cry out, we're given attention, and love, and care—that ceases to work any more. We meet a more indifferent world, and then we become angry. That is the root of most anger. That is the root of it in the world.

MW: Should your analysis be successful, can we then expect happy comedies from Tennessee Williams?

TW: Never. Never. Never. I can't hope to please every critic.

MW: In *Orpheus Descending*, Tennessee, one of the main characters says this, "Nobody ever gets to know nobody, with all of us sentenced to solitary confinement inside our own skins for life. We're under a lifelong sentence to solitary confinement inside our own lonely skins for as long as we live." How much of Tennessee Williams is talking there?

TW: I think about ninety per cent.

MW: Truly?

TW: At least a lot of that. I think there are moments when we can get out of it, and those are the great moments in life. The moments we must wait for are the moments when we escape from our—the prison of our skin.

MW: Would you help me to understand a little bit more what you mean when you say escape from the loneliness, the solitary confinement of our skins?

TW: Where we can feel truly and deeply and passionately for another person—that's what I mean.

MW: Communication with another person?

TW: Yes, when it really happens—and it does happen. Even for a person as introverted as I am, it can happen occasionally.

MW: You've also told me, and I think that you have demonstrated it here, that for a long time, you were a lonely man and rather afraid of friendship.

TW: Not afraid of it, but suspicious of it. I'm never certain whether they're liking Tom Williams or Tennessee Williams, you know. And I didn't use to be like that and I deeply resent the fact that becoming a prominent playwright has made me like that.

MW: Tennessee, you've admitted that one of the reasons that you gave this latest play of yours, *Garden District*, to an off-Broadway theater is that you didn't want to stand the strain of a big on-Broadway opening.

TW: Yes.

MW: Now, to me it was very difficult to understand that one of America's major playwrights would be that insecure about his talents.

TW: Well, it's not strange, Mike, if you think about it. All reputations in the theater are inflated reputations.

MW: How do you mean?

TW: I mean nobody is as good as publicity makes them appear, and if he's reasonably objective with himself he knows that that's true and it gives him an awfully shaky feeling. And this increases with each production—the reputation grows as he becomes more conscious of the discrepancy between the reputation and the actual self.

MW: In other words you, Tennessee Williams, do not feel as important a writer as the rest of the world seems to regard you?

TW: Certainly not.

MW: You certainly don't feel that you're a fraud?

TW: No, I'm not a fraud, but I'm not—I'm not the kind of a writer that I want to be and that a lot of the world seems to—

MW: What kind of a writer do you want to be? What does the world want of you that you feel that you cannot live up to, Tennessee?

TW: In every one of my plays I fall short of my objective.

MW: Do you consider the body of your writing an important body of writing?

TW: I'm not the person to answer that. Important to me, yes, because—in all of it—it contains things that I felt passionately.

MW: Now then, Tennessee, an attack came on your writing from Cardinal Spellman in reference to your recent film, *Baby Doll*. How do you feel about that criticism?

TW: Well, I don't wish to reply aggressively to a beloved dignitary of a great church. I would like to say this, that as I wrote it I was not conscious of writing anything that corresponded to these terms that he's used against it. I don't think that it had any corrupting influence on audiences. I think it should have been forbidden to adolescents— to anyone under the age of sixteen. I think I might ask Cardinal Spellman how he feels about the opposition of the Church to birth control, because I think our primary human problem now is overpopulation and the production of children by families in economic condition not—who bring them up under circumstances that don't give them a fair chance in the world.

MW: Tennessee, may I ask you this: What do you think personally about religion, formal religion?

TW: I regard myself as being a very religious man. Every time I have a play opening, I close a door on a certain room and kneel down and pray to God. And I very often receive an answer—in fact, I've always received an answer. The may sound very corny . . .

MW: No, not at all.

TW: . . . But, even before plays that I suspected were going to be failures, for instance *Garden District*, I did that, and I suddenly had a feeling—you know, as if in response to the prayer—that was affirmative.

MW: Well, this is the prayer of the supplicant. Do you feel any identification with a specific faith, or is God a part of your everyday life?

TW: Well, the two most wonderful people in my life were my grandfather, who was an Episcopal clergyman, and his wife, my grandmother. I was born in the Episcopal rectory and I grew up in the shadow of the Episcopal church. I can't say that I've continued to go to it, but my grandfather was devoted to the church and certainly his sincerity and depth as a person made it impossible for me to ever be against formal religion per se.

Lonely in Uptown New York

W. J. Weatherby/1959

From the *Manchester Guardian Weekly*, 23 July 1959, 14. ©
1959 by W. J. Weatherby. Reprinted by permission.

Tennessee Williams's home in uptown New York was a slightly
dishevelled fifth-floor apartment in which one sensed an impatience
with housework. A large Spanish parrot perched on my shoulder and
inspected one of my ears while Mr. Williams showed me the paintings
he bought in Italy that adorned the walls of his sitting-room and
bedroom. A typewriter was balanced on the pillows of his bed and
papers were scattered over the bedclothes: such signs of early
morning industry recalled the remark of Elia Kazan, the director, that
Tennessee Williams was the hardest working man he had ever
known. The guided tour of his apartment completed, Mr. Williams
curled up on a couch and talked through veils of cigarette smoke in
that intriguing voice of his, a slight Mississippi drawl with an
undertone of sharp irony: a wicked combination, ideal for deflating
other people if he were not such a gentle man. His complete
frankness in fact gave him an unguarded quality; one remembered
the warning of a producer years ago that he should not wear his heart
on his sleeve "for daws to peck at." Much of his work deals with the
problem of self-expression, of communication between people, and
his deliberate honesty in his own personal life is a moving example of
a writer practising what he preaches.

He thinks he has had only "one or two major themes" as a writer,
and it is easy to see what they are: an obsession with the passage of
time, with lost youth and the corruption of innocence, is to be found
in all his writings, poetry and prose and plays. His latest play in New
York, *Sweet Bird of Youth*, has two main characters, a middle-aged
film star and a fading young gigolo, who first appeared in an
unproduced one-act play entitled *The Enemy: Time* several years
ago. Almost all his major plays have begun as poems or short stories

59

or one-act plays, and have grown gradually into full-length works, but even then he is never satisfied with them and has rewritten plays after they have opened in New York. *Sweet Bird* opened there in March and is one of the big successes of the season, but the author is still unhappy about it. He simplified the character of the gigolo by cutting the second act extensively during rehearsals, but the bridge passages he substituted and some of the minor characters were still worrying him when I talked with him in New York. As soon as possible he was setting off for about six months to the Far East—Japan, Hongkong, and perhaps China "if they will let me in." A view of the Far East through Tennessee Williams's eyes seemed to promise a new harvest for a Broadway still going through an Oriental phase. But . . .

TW: I'm not going there for that. I have never before been so depressed or found it so hard to work. I reckon I have been going through a nervous breakdown by slow stages, a sort of controlled nervous breakdown. I have been living with it, working along with it, instead of giving in to it. It might have been better to have had it quickly. I have never been to the Far East and I'm hoping the new places might be diverting enough for me to lay off the work for five or six months. The trouble with me is that I can't think of anything to do but work.

Q.: You described *Sweet Bird* as "the toughest one I've ever done."

TW: *Sweet Bird* was in the works too long. The whole second act was particularly hard for me. I was deeply interested in the two main characters, but the other characters did not have the same interest for me, and it was awfully hard for me to write the second act, which was largely about the social background of the story. Sometimes I wish I had made it a shorter play and not tried to deal with so much. I was already tired when I came to the rehearsals and I was in no condition to do all the rewriting I had to do, and I was inundated with notes suggesting changes—from somebody other than the director. I felt castrated. Any other point of view except the director's and author's together should be left alone. Otherwise it creates chaos. They demoralise the writer, sap what is left of his confidence.

Q.: Hasn't your great success made your own self-confidence impregnable?

TW: I have no self-confidence at all. I don't have any opinion about anything I have done for years after it is finished. I read that Eugene O'Neill always said anything he was working on was the finest thing he had ever written. I always feel it is the worst. I find it is a terrible disadvantage because you need confidence to create energy, the necessary vitality to push the thing through.

Q.: Is it easier for a playwright to win recognition now than when you first started?

TW: I think it is much easier, particularly because of the off-Broadway movement. And the fact that producers are more adventurous in the type of material that they accept. The concept of theatre has become broader, much more plastic in the last twenty years.

Q.: Your own work has obviously had a strong influence. But is the theatre adventurous enough for you yet?

TW: I always write about what I want to write about and let the fur fly where it will. The great danger for me is repeating things. I have always felt that an artist has only one or two major themes anyway on which he writes variations. I think I have worked only one or two. I can't write about anything that does not seem to involve me, that I'm not emotionally involved in. I'm limited to the sort of material that is personal. You could say I write about two extremes, the great tenderness between individuals and the terrible circumstances which surround them. As a boy I discovered writing as an escape from a world of reality in which I felt acutely uncomfortable. I used to be morbidly shy. Another thing I have always been haunted by—a fear, an obsession, that to love a thing intensely is to be in a vulnerable position where you may well lose what you most want. Perhaps such a fear, a terror, tended me towards an atmosphere of hysteria and violence that is expressed in much of my writings . . . (musing, behind a cloud of smoke). Writing is always such a lonely thing—or it should be.

Q.: Do you plan to write any more novels?

TW: I don't think so. The one time I wrote a novel (*The Roman Spring of Mrs. Stone*) was just to organise material for a film for Greta Garbo. It started out with that intention but she obviously wasn't interested in making it. I like writing short stories, but I enjoy writing plays so much more. I have a much lighter play, a serious

comedy (*Period of Adjustment*), that will be my next major theatre
production. I have tried it out in Florida but I don't know when I'm
going to do it here. [Miami: Coconut Grove Playhouse, 29 December
1958—Editor] My energy is really very, very low. Ever since *Sweet
Bird* it has been awfully hard for me to work.

Q.: What do you think of the American critics?

TW: They are tolerant on the whole. They simply demand you do
it well. They do demand that you write with taste. That I always like
to do if I can. When I was in London recently I was asked how I felt
about the censorship of my language. A lady reporter gave me an
example of some words that had been cut out. I said, "Oh, my God,
did I write that?" (He threw back his head with a shy, boyish laugh.)
A lady reporter, I tell you, repeated some of the words.

Q.: Lady reporters can be downright?

TW: I guess so. I sometimes put it in the manuscript the way a
character would talk in life, expecting that in production something
else may have to be substituted.

Q.: What was your impression of the London theatre?

TW: I thought *The Long and the Short and the Tall* [by Willis
Hall—Editor] was a very good play and I liked John Osborne's
musical *Paul Slickey*. It was entertaining. I didn't understand why
they treated him so badly.

Q.: How important do you think an author is at rehearsals?

TW: Virtually indispensable, especially in a foreign production.
When my plays are put on I should be there. I don't think any
director can tell from the script exactly what I had in mind. I have
seen a lot of foreign productions of my plays, but I have seen damn
few that were what I meant. (Suddenly a pigeon flies past the
balcony window of the room.) I like pigeons, don't you?

Q.: Don't they give you a sense of open space, of freedom, in New
York?

TW: Yes, that is right.

Q.: But they're flat-footed—

TW (a little indignant): But they always are—

Voice (from next room): Ten, Anna (Magnani) is on the phone.
When will you be ready for dinner?

"Soon, soon," he said, and we talked a little longer but with no
notes taken. He said he was reading *Part of a Long Story*, a book of

reminiscences about Eugene O'Neill by his second wife, and as he picked up the book it made a memorable picture of Tennessee Williams: America's greatest dramatist of the present reading about her greatest dramatist of the past.

Williams and Kazan and the Big Walk-Out
Arthur Gelb/1960

From the *New York Times,* 1 May 1960, sec. 2, 1, 3. © 1960 by
the New York Times Company. Reprinted by permission.

Tennessee Williams emerged from the workroom of his apartment in
an East Side brownstone at noon the other day, poured himself an
outsized martini and talked about a few things that were uppermost
in his mind.

His chief preoccupation, at the moment, is Elia Kazan's withdrawal
last week as the dirrector of the new Williams play, *Period of
Adjustment.* Mr. Williams professes to regard the withdrawal as the
termination of what had been a fabulously successful dramatist-
director alliance, which began in 1947 with the production of *A
Streetcar Named Desire.*

Mr. Kazan has said, officially, that he had to give up *Period of
Adjustment* because it conflicted with work on a movie that would
keep him busy well beyond September, when he was to have staged
the play.

Mr. Williams does not credit Mr. Kazan's official excuse, nor does
Mr. Kazan sympathize with Mr. Williams' emotional interpretation of
the situation.

"Kazan," said Mr. Williams, "has suddenly gotten the crazy idea
that he is not good for my work. We met Monday night for drinks. He
showed up looking rather shaky and gray in the face, and told me
definitely he couldn't do my new play. I tried my best to make him
change his mind, but he was adamant."

(Apprised of Mr. Williams' comment, Mr. Kazan insisted: "I offered
to do the play when I was through with my movie, but Tennessee
was not willing to wait till then. I consider him the greatest living
playwright and would certainly like to work with him again, if he will
ask me.")

Mr. Williams is the second Pulitzer Prize-winning playwright whose alliance with Mr. Kazan has become a subject for public speculation. In 1952, Arthur Miller and Mr. Kazan parted company, after Mr. Kazan had directed *All My Sons* and *Death of a Salesman*; in that instance, however, it was the playwright who, for personal reasons, ended the association.

In the present case, Mr. Williams feels, a "misunderstanding" is responsible for Mr. Kazan's walk-out, and it is a misunderstanding that apparently goes deeper than the technical problem of juggling a time schedule. Evidently Mr. Williams believes that a public airing of his interpretation of the facts is in order.

"I think," Mr. Williams said, "that Kazan has been upset by people who accuse him of looking for popular success—people who snipe at his so-called melodramatic interpretation of my plays." ("I'll admit that the sniping has annoyed me," said Mr. Kazan. "But I'm used to being sniped at, and would never give up a play for a reason like that.")

"I've been so preoccupied with my own work," Mr. Williams went on, "that I wasn't aware of how much sniping was going on. The fact is, Kazan has been falsely blamed for my own desire for success." ("He should have said that earlier," declared Mr. Kazan, who recently wrote Mr. Williams, accusing him of being "terrified of failure.")

"It's quite true," Mr. Williams said, "that I want to reach a mass audience. I feel it can dig what I have to say, perhaps better than a lot of intellectuals can. I'm not an intellectual. And perhaps, at times, I've exceeded the dignified limits in trying to hold an audience, but it's wrong to blame Kazan for this. My cornpone melodrama is all my own. I want excitement in the theatre. Wherever I've been excessive, it's due to a certain hysteria on my part that takes over. By accident of nature, I have a tendency toward romanticism and a taste for the theatrical.

"The charge that Kazan has forced me to rewrite my plays is ridiculous. Nobody can budge me an inch. Kazan simply tried to interpret, honestly, what I have to say. He has helped me reach my audience, which is my aim in life—the bigger the audience, the better. His withdrawing has been shattering for me. I felt at home with him."

Looking something less than shattered, Mr. Williams, who is sun-

tanned and trim from a recent stay in Key West, continued to defend
his defecting director at his own expense.

"There are people," he said, "who have put the blame on Kazan
for the ending, which they didn't like, of *Cat on a Hot Tin Roof*."
("Read the preface Tennessee wrote to *Cat*," suggested Mr. Kazan,
somewhat ominously. "The sniping all started then.")

"Kazan has also been blamed for the poor second act of *Sweet
Bird of Youth*. The truth is, the second act of that play is just not well
written. I was in a terrible state of depression at the time, and couldn't
function, except on just a craftsmanship level. Kazan wanted a great
second act, and I couldn't give it to him. I'm re-writing the act now,
for the published version; I'm going to stick with my two main
characters, whom I should never have left in the first place. The act is
weak because I couldn't really identify with Boss Finley."

As for *Cat on a Hot Tin Roof*, said Mr. Williams, it was true that he
wrote two different endings, one at Mr. Kazan's suggestion. "But both
those acts are mine. I wrote them, not Kazan."

Mr. Kazan, Mr. Williams went on, was the most courageous
director he knew.

"He had the courage to do *Camino Real* seven years ago and to
believe in what it said, even though his own wife didn't like it, and I
had to read it aloud twice to backers who stalked out without
comment. Kazan certainly wouldn't have done *Camino Real* to
achieve commercial success. I don't think a director ever showed
such courage."

The play was a controversial failure, but Mr. Williams regards it as
Mr. Kazan's greatest production, "with the possible exception of
Death of a Salesman and *A Streetcar Named Desire*."

Having gotten that off his chest, Mr. Williams thought it expedient
to point out that there were other directors who could mount his
future plays on Broadway. He said that José Quintero, who directed
Summer and Smoke off Broadway after it had failed uptown, and
who is preparing an off-Broadway revival of *Camino Real* for a May
16 opening, was "just as brilliant as Kazan."

Mr. Williams also thinks a great deal of George Roy Hill, who has
replaced Mr. Kazan as director of *Period of Adjustment*. Actually, Mr.
Quintero was thought of also as Mr. Kazan's replacement, but he was
already committed to direct *Laurette* early next season.

"There will be another new play for Quintero, and I'm glad he's doing *Camino Real*. He's a great artist. He may bring out new facets in the play. There is as much of a contrast between two directors as between two writers."

Mr. Williams is exorbitantly fond of *Camino Real,* calling it the closest he has come to making a philosophical statement about life— "that despite all contrary conditions, it is necessary to cling to romanticism, not in the sense of a weak sentimentality, but in the sense of adhering as far as you can to a gallantry, like Don Quixote's; the play is a plea for a romantic attitude toward life, which can also be interpreted as a religious attitude—religious in an august, mysterious sense."

The opening of *Camino Real* on March 19, 1953, was, Mr. Williams recalled, the worst night he had ever spent in his life.

"We had a good audience, with great applause," he said. "One can be taken in by this, you know. I went home and as the hours wore on and I got no congratulatory calls, I became panicky. Then Kazan arrived with his wife and the John Steinbecks. He had brought them to present their condolences. I guess I flipped my lid. I shouted to Kazan: 'How dare you bring these people!'

"Then I slammed into my bedroom. A friend of mine explained to the Kazans and the Steinbecks that I was hysterical and served them a round of drinks; then they left. It was terrible. I did love that play so much."

Mr. Williams' new play is, he said, as much of a departure as *Camino Real* was. "The two plays are poles apart, though; *Camino* is a fantasy, and this is perhaps my most realistic play. Actually, it is a comedy, set in Memphis of today, but we are not calling it that because there is a danger of the actors gagging it up. It's written as a play with humor and has an ending that's non-tragic. The people at the end still have problems, but they have found each other, and maybe they can now solve their problems together. It's an unambitious play. I only wanted to tell the truth about a little occurrence in life, without blowing it up beyond its natural limits."

As far as Mr. Williams' immediate future is concerned, he claims it will be movieless, as well as Kazan-less. He will never, he said, do another movie adaptation. (Someone else is currently adapting his novella, *The Roman Spring of Mrs. Stone,* which Mr. Quintero will direct.) *The Fugitive Kind,* which Mr. Williams adapted from his own *Orpheus Descending,* is, he said, his last movie.

"There comes a time in life when you have got to conserve your energy for what's most important to you. And the theatre is what's most important to me."

Interview with Tennessee Williams, Yukio Mishima, and Dilys Powell

Edward R. Murrow/1960

Transcription of "Small World," CBS-TV, New York, 8 May 1960. © 1960 by CBS Inc. All rights reserved. Printed by permission.

EM: Good evening. Tonight on "Small World" three writers: prolific, provocative, and exercising an influence far beyond their own countries. From London Miss Dilys Powell. Dean of film critics, author of five books, three of them on Greece. Incapable of writing pedestrian prose. Miss Powell, if we could travel the Atlantic on A Streetcar Named Desire, we would pass a Sweet Bird of Youth flying over a Cat on a Hot Tin Roof near The Glass Menagerie. And then Suddenly Last Summer or tonight, there in Key West, Florida, would be Tennessee Williams, where he is right now. Have you two met?

TW: Yes, we met just now, not face to face, not vis-à-vis, but over this strange hookup.

EM: And here in Tokyo a young thirty-five-year-old triple threat man, Yukio Mishima. A novelist—twelve of them—playwright, director and actor. One of the most talented writers in Japan whose works have been widely translated into English. Tennessee, you and Mishima are old friends, aren't you?

TW: We met in New York, in a rather unfashionable district and in a rather bohemian quarter, but we had a marvelous time. [laughter] He entertained us lavishly at the typical Japanese restaurants when I was in Tokyo last September for about a month I guess it was. And as a parting gift he gave me a most beautiful ivory apple with a little Japanese fishing village carved out inside the apple, which I treasure most highly.

YM: In Tokyo your movie, *Suddenly Last Summer,* is going on at movie theaters.

69

TW: Oh, my gosh. You know I can't take full responsibility for it, Yukio.

YM: Why?

T: You know the screenplay was mostly written by our wonderful new playwright, Gore Vidal, who's just had a huge smash hit in New York. [*The Best Man,* Morosco Theatre, 31 March 1960—Editor] I think he did a good job of it. Of course I prefer the play, naturally. You know, one always does.

DP: I really must break in. May I break in on this lovely, friendly conversation?

TW: Yes, yes, please, Miss Powell.

DP: I'm very much interested in what you say about not writing your own screenplay. Now Mr. Williams, or shall I call you Tennessee? May I call you Tennessee?

TW: Please call me Tennessee, Miss Powell. Can I call you Dilys?

DP: Yes, please, otherwise I shall feel out of it.

TW: It's a beautiful name.

DP: Thank you. Well now, Tennessee, do you choose your own screenwriter?

TW: Yes, I chose Gore because we were old friends and I have a great admiration for his work.

DP: Have you had experiences of not choosing your own screenwriter and wishing to complain of it?

TW: Yes, only with my first play, Miss Powell.

DP: Which one?

TW: *The Glass Menagerie.* After that I either wrote them myself or I had the choice.

DP: Yes, now I was thinking about *The Glass Menagerie* because the film, as I recall it, was not enormously changed from your play.

TW: Oh, it was enormously changed, and somehow they managed to botch it all up, you know. It was a mess, to tell you the truth. [laughter]

DP: But now, you don't like it because it's changed from your play?

TW: Well, I almost never like my plays on the screen, Dilys. [laughter]

DP: Do you think that, necessarily, a film should follow very closely the play or the book on which it's based? Well, then I'm bound to say I don't.

TW: No, I do not. I think they should create something entirely new in a cinematic form, you see.

DP: Yes.

TW: But they don't somehow get organized that way. They're afraid to. I don't know why they are. But they stick too close to the stage play and a stage play is not always effective on the screen, you know.

DP: No, I quite agree. But is it perhaps because you are the author and you feel very close to the play yourself that you dislike a different rendering of it on the screen?

TW: I think that's quite probable because I'm very jealous about my work, you know. And it's very hard for me to like anybody else's treatment of it, you see. [laughter]

DP: Of course it is. But I'm bound to say that I thought, for instance, *Streetcar* came off extremely well on the screen.

TW: Yes, well you know we had a screenwriter down here working on it, and he started off like it was *The Cherry Orchard*. You know, he said that outside the mansion, outside Belle Reve, you could hear them chopping down trees. And I said, "Oh no, this isn't *The Cherry Orchard* quite." And so this poor gentleman from Hollywood was taken off the script and I had to write it myself, which I probably subconsciously wanted to do all along, so I gave him the ax. [laughter]

DP: But tell me now, the ending of the film, this is the thing which interests me very much. I have a feeling that perhaps the screen cannot accept quite such stark discouragement as the stage can.

TW: Dilys, I thought the ending of *Streetcar* was profoundly uplifting.

DP: On the film it had a note of hope.

TW: I thought it ended on a note of great gallantry, which is the word I most prefer as a descriptive adjective about human people. I thought Blanche—when she rose from the floor because she saw kindness in the eyes of the stranger and walked off with him, taking his arm, to a madhouse, saying "I have always depended on the kindness of strangers"—shows that quality of gallantry which I think is the great flag, the great banner, of the human race.

EM: Mr. Mishima, what did you think of that final scene?

YM: I saw the movie about four or five years ago and I was moved

very much. Tennessee once mentioned to me that it is the most
faithful movie to his plays.

TW: I think it is the most faithful one. I was terribly distressed by
Cat on a Hot Tin Roof, although I'm living on it and it's made me
more money than anything else. People tell me it came off, but for
me it didn't. It seemed almost like a prostitution or a corruption. I
don't know.

EM: Mr. Mishima.

YM: Yes.

EM: Why aren't more Japanese plays and novels translated into
English?

YM: The translation of plays is a very difficult thing, particularly
from Japanese into English or into any foreign language, because
Japanese talking has its own characteristics and is quite different from
English or French talking. We have a different type of culture, you
know. And I think it's always such a problem. How do you translate
"love," the English word love, into Japanese?

TW: How do you translate "love" into Japanese?

YM: Yes, we have no Christian tradition, you know, and the word
love can suggest a Christian meaning, I suppose. Sometimes we use
the word love just as sex, but I think love has a very religious
meaning in your country sometimes.

TW: Well, I think love is one of those great international
commodities which we'll probably transfer to the other planets
someday and it will still not change very much, Yukio.

YM: Yes.

TW: Of course, there are two kinds of love. There is benign love
and there is malignant love. Strindberg once put it very nicely on the
subject of malignant love. He said, they call it love-hatred, and it hails
from the pit. Well there's that kind of love, but there's also a benign
love and a love that involves tenderness. Now you know in America,
and in sophisticated circles, love is beginning to be a somewhat
disreputable subject at least in the theatre, because it's been exploited
to excess. There was a recent article in *Partisan Review,* our big,
intellectual, boring weekly, but which is really intellectual and
important, but boring, I think. There was an article called "Love,
Love, Love," saying that we in the theatre are talking too much about

love and using it as an expedient to end our plays upon a note of uplift and as a very expedient solution to problems which are far from expediently solved. [Gore Vidal, "Love, Love, Love," *Partisan Review*, 26 (1959), 613-620—Editor] This I buy, but I think we could go too far in disavowing love as the thing that the human race must depend upon finally.

DP: But isn't the present unfashionableness of love as a subject due to the fact that it has been terribly overdone?

TW: Terribly, terribly, in our films, in our TV soap operas, and in our plays, the subject of love has been used for expedience.

DP: And so one welcomes current films and current plays which are not about love. For instance, in this country we have just produced a film called *The Angry Silence*.

TW: Beautiful title, I haven't heard about it.

DP: It's a beautiful title about a savage subject. It's a social, an industrial, politic subject. It's a subject of a strike and a man who refuses to strike and is therefore sent to Coventry. Well, one welcomes that. One is so thankful to see a film which does not end with the couple falling into one another's arms, walking away into the sunset, riding away across the prairie.

TW: I think Mishima-san, and you and I, we all agree about that. [laughter]

DP: Yes, but I have to admit being occasionally, not puzzled, but extremely interested by the handling of love in the Japanese cinema. And I'm thinking in particular of the film of Mr. Mishima's own novel, *Conflagration*, in which love is the cause of destruction. It's because the boy loves the temple that he destroys it, is that not so?

YM: Yes.

TW: I saw it in Tokyo. It's a screenplay of such philosophical subtlety that I think it needs seeing a couple of times.

DP: But the point I should like to make is, how difficult it is for the ordinary European audience to accept the difference in approach and, as it seems to us, the very complicated mode of expression and of thought. They seem to the ordinary western European, I think, very complex, the modes of thought of the Japanese cinema.

TW: Miss Powell, you have to be a decadent Southerner to understand the Japanese cinema. [general laughter]

DP: Well, it is difficult for the ordinary person.

YM: Miss Powell, I think a characteristic of Japanese character is just this mixture of very brutal things and elegance. It's a very strange mixture, and may I say your country's culture lacks similar characteristics of culture, doesn't it?

DP: What, of extremes of brutality and elegance?

YM: Shakespeare's plays have beautiful delicacy and elegance.

DP: Yes, that is so, but let's accept it that even in England, you know, the ordinary member of the public would not be able to accept the works of Shakespeare unless he had been brought up with them. If Shakespeare were to write today, I think he would have a terrible flop in England. I think, you see, that there is a great barrier between countries because of the difficulty of understanding their art. You see, art should help us to understand one another, but very often I think it makes it more difficult. Shouldn't it?

[Commercial Pause]

EM: Tennessee, as you were saying when I was forced to interrupt you . . .

TW: Yukio, you were talking about brutality and elegance. I think I understand what you mean. I'm not being snobbish when I say that, but I think you in Japan are close to us in the southern states of the United States.

YM: I think so.

TW: And I think I am able to understand how you could put those two terms together, brutality and elegance. I could not define why.

YM: And I couldn't say why, either, but it is why I feel sympathy toward your work. I find our same characteristic mixture in your works, in your plays. For instance, *Suddenly Last Summer,* I think, is the most representative mixture of brutality and elegance.

TW: It isn't very elegant except in the performance of a couple of actresses.

YM: Yes.

TW: But certainly there have been films in America that have had brutality and a kind of elegance. I can't name them, but you in Japan have certainly achieved that thing. I think what you meant was that we must depict the awfulness of the world we live in, but we must do it with a kind of aesthetic, you know, a kind of grace and aesthetic, so that although it is a horror, it is not just sheer horror. It has also the mystery of life which is an elegant thing.

YM: Yes, it's a mystery, but even in contemporary Asia we are always looking for such a pure genuine elegance that when—

DP: This is too much for me. May I break in, please.

EM: Yes, Miss Powell.

DP: I'm suffering here, I'm suffering terribly. Brutality and elegance. All right, I accept it in your plays Tennessee, I accept it in the Japanese cinema, but you say that the southern states of America have perhaps a kind of fellow feeling with Japan because of this incongruity of brutality and elegance.

TW: I think we're a little less abhorrent of it, of the combination of it, than you in England are at the present time. I think you're still a little frightened of treating brutality in a fashion which is almost elegant or graceful.

DP: We are frightened. I do think, you know, that violence is getting an appalling hold on art, particularly in America. I think that is one of the things which is, at the moment, dividing Britain and America. That you, in America, have gone much farther in violence than we have. We feel really that the new world is moving into violence, while we are—well, I'm afraid, I hope—standing still. I really do shrink from this savagery and brutality and violence. I understand about the aesthetic of violence, I accept it, but I feel that the movement is getting out of hand, you know.

TW: Dilys, when we depict violence, do you think that we are praising it or denigrating it?

DP: Sometimes you are accepting. Sometimes under cover of denigrating, I think you are exalting it. I really do.

TW: You have a possible point, darling, provided we're all masochists. [general laughter]

DP: Well, I suppose most people are masochists and most artists as well. There you have brutality and elegance.

TW: Let us not deny all the dark things of the human heart, but let us try to cast a clear light on them in our work.

DP: A great friend of mine once said to me the human heart is desperately wicked. And it is you know—

TW: Oh, it is, but it's also desperately [DP: desperately good?] desperately tender, dear, and hungry for tenderness.

YM: Miss Powell, I heard that you are deeply interested in ancient Greek plays. How about the theme of ancient Greek theatre, it is destiny or something else?

DP: Ah, that's very nice of you to ask that because I think it puts much better than I could have myself something which I am trying to get at. You see the ancient Greek theatre, although it expresses the violence and the brutality which is in life, doesn't put the violence coldly before one. And that is what I really do deplore very much in a great deal of modern writing, modern films, modern art. That by presenting violence as it does, it appears to condone it. The ancient Greeks, as I see it, translated violence, savagery and the terror of life into an overruling serenity. And I think, you know, that Shakespeare does that too, in spite of the savagery, in spite of the brutality.

TW: Dilys, Dilys, please. Shakespeare translated it into vast poetry, great poetry.

DP: Into great poetry which is ultimately serene.

TW: That is what gave the catharsis to Shakespeare. What gave the catharsis to Greek tragedy was the stateliness of its performance.

DP: The stateliness and a religious serenity.

TW: The serenity was simply a product of a style of production. You know they wore masks and everything was very formalized, but, darling, did it add up in idea, in essence, to anything less violent than what we sometimes are doing now? Now I know you're going to say that we seem devoted to violence, infatuated with it, but I think you're also going to say that our violence is more clinical. Well, you see, we need the eloquence of a Shakespeare which none of us has. Or we need the elegance of production, the august and stately production of the Greeks perhaps, to give us what you call this serenity.

DP: You've said a lot of things so I'm going to say, well now let me—

YM: Today is a very suitable and fitting age to write plays because plays need such a violence of life, such a terror of life. But even though we have the Atomic bomb in the contemporary age, I think the ancient Greek people had the same amount of terror of life, the same amount of violence of life, in their small society, in their small world. Don't you think so?

DP: Surely, everybody, I mean people living quiet lives in quiet streets in London, Paris, Tokyo when there's no war on, is a victim of appalling violence. Every death is a violence, every birth is a violence, every illness is a violence. But to insist that violence is the overruling element in life seems to me to be wrong. Let me remind all of us, including me, of a Franco-Japanese film called *Hiroshima, Mon Amour*. It doesn't depict violence, it suggests it, it implies violence, it tells us of the savagery which underlies all our lives, and which lies in wait in every heart, but it doesn't insist that violence is the major part of life. And that is, at the risk of repeating myself, that is what I deplore so very much in a great deal of modern writing, both for the screen and for the printed page.

TW: We show both the light and the shadow, and the shadow is the violence which we live threatened by. I mean we're threatened with world extinction through violence. In our lives violence, not physical violence but emotional violence, is so much a part of us. I have seen so much depicted of people's longing to meet each other tenderly with love, and violence is represented because it's the obstacle, it's the other side of the coin, it's the dark side of the moon, however you want to put it, but the dark side of the moon is in the sky and we want to show both sides of the moon you know.

YM: Yes, and now our civilization seems to be coming to its climax. But I don't think a culture comes to its climax. Sometimes culture seems to descend into hell. But I think a culture has its own way, compared with civilization, and I think culture is a phoenix. Sometimes civilization is destroyed but culture is a phoenix. Even when it goes down to hell, I'm sure it will come up from hell sometime.

EM: And so we must quietly terminate this conversation that had so much to do with violence. Would you care to say goodnight to each other?

YM: Good night, Miss Powell, Tennessee.

TW: Good day it is here. [laughter]

DP: Well, it's good afternoon here. And it's been lovely talking to you both.

EM: Thank you all very much.

Studs Terkel Talks with Tennessee Williams
Studs Terkel/1961

Transcription of "Studs Terkel," WFMT-FM, Chicago, December 1961. © 1961 by Studs Terkel. Printed by permission.

ST: Any discussion of Tennessee Williams, I think, must keep one factor in mind: that any discussion of Tennessee Williams *evokes* discussion, even, I found out, at bars, thank God. And if ever a time when discussion involving the human spirit or the disspirited human is needed, it is now. We're delighted to be guests of Mr. Williams in his suite at the Blackstone Hotel. We know that in Chicago *The Night of the Inguana* is playing until December 21st before it opens in New York at the Royale Theatre.

TW: Twenty-third.

ST: Twenty-third, correction. Mr. Williams, I remember something you wrote on the back of a Caedmon record on which you were reading "The Yellow Bird." You spoke of your childhood, of your Episcopalian, clergyman grandfather and your father who was a deft poker player, and you spoke of the puritan and cavalier strains in you. It occurs to me this is America, isn't it? The puritan and the pagan, always embattled.

TW: [light laughter] Yes, I think it's most of the world, actually. But I don't think there's anything like that on the Caedmon record, at least I didn't say it. Was it written on the—

ST: Well, it was written on the back.

TW: Oh, written, oh yes, yes.

ST: Now, I am trying to explain the fact of conflicting impulses in all of your heroes and heroines. I thought perhaps this might reflect our country. You know, we speak of the pagan and the puritan always in battle here.

TW: I think puritanism is an element more of the Protestant countries, you know, predominantly Protestant, than it is of the Mediterranean nations that are predominantly Catholic. I'm not trying

78

to make a pitch for one religion against another, but I have noticed in the Mediterranean nations like Italy and Spain and France that the puritan complexes are not so evident. But out of these puritan complexes seems to come a great deal of that friction that makes interesting art.

ST: We'll come to the Mediterranean in a moment. Was it Kenneth Tynan who spoke of you and hot climates? That is, your figures in *hot* climates in the Mediterranean were so much more free.

TW: Yes, well you see I spent most of my life in a very puritanical background. My homelife was dominated by a very wonderful but rather puritanical mother, who was in conflict with a very wonderful but rather profligate father. [laughter] First I sided with the mother's side and then after my father's death, for some strange reason, I began to see his point of view better. [laughter] After they put him away in Old Gray, that's the name of the cemetery in Knoxville.

ST: In Knoxville this was. Moving to St. Louis from Mississippi was a big factor, was it not, in your experience?

TW: Oh, yes. There have been these two biographies about me that came out this season. I find it very disturbing to have these two things come out. They examine my background and they dissect my plays as if I were no longer living, it seems to me.

ST: As though they were museum pieces.

TW: Yes, as if I were totally out of the picture now and were just a retrospective item. Well, when my agent informed me last spring that she had first drafts of these two biographies on her desk, I said, "My God, they must think I'm going to kick off!" I was really frightened by it. [laughter] Well, now I've got to live with it and they've got to live with me, 'cause I'm still living and I'm not about to kick off.

ST: You said that you found the rich and the poor, this big split, when you were young.

TW: Oh, yes, yes. Well, that was only apparent in St. Louis; it wasn't apparent in Mississippi.

ST: Why was this, why was it apparent in St. Louis and not in Mississippi?

TW: Because, you see, in Mississippi we lived in small communities, small towns as a rule, and being grandchildren of the Episcopal minister we always had our social acceptance, you know. It was taken for granted. But in St. Louis there was this money aristocracy—plutocracy, I think, is the precise word for it. And if you lived in the wrong neighborhood, you just weren't the right people. And we *had* to live most of the time in the wrong neighborhood because there wasn't the money to live in the right one, you see. And we had to go to public school, we couldn't go to Country Day School. The equivalent for girls, what was it called now? Well, you know what I mean.

ST: I suppose this is often asked you, I'll ask it though it be a cliche. In *Glass Menagerie,* if we may start at the beginning, Jim, the son, pretty much reflected your feelings, didn't he, to a great extent?

TW: Tom.

ST: Tom, I mean. Jim was the Gentleman Caller. Tom, rather.

TW: At that time nobody knew my real name was Tom, they all thought my real name was Tennessee, I suppose. I let the character be named Tom. Yes, he did pretty much. I tried to keep him in the background of the play except as a narrator. The leading characters were the mother and the girl.

ST: We think of Amanda and her sham gentility. We think of Blanche, too, to some extent. But in thinking of T. Lawrence Shannon, your defrocked clergyman in *Night of the Iguana,* it occurred to me that he and Blanche were two figures in the same boat. He's at the end of his tether. Blanche coming to visit her sister was at the end of hers.

TW: I've said this very same thing, and I'm glad you make that point. In the portrait of Shannon I think I was drawing a male equivalent almost of a Blanche DuBois.

ST: I hadn't heard you say this. It occurred to me that he was a male—

TW: But I knew I was doing it. I don't know if that's good in the play or bad? But that's what it is, undoubtedly. Of course, there are many important differences, such as the fact that Shannon is a man who is very much concerned with what is going on in society. If you listen carefully to certain parts of the play, you realize this is a person whose great redeeming virtue is that he has a true and deep social conscience.

ST: Shannon does?

TW: Yes, even though at this point at which we see him exposed, he is in a state of extremely personal disturbance. But still, through that personal disturbance you see the presence of a deep awareness of social inequities, the starvation and the misery. You know of the places he's conducted tours through. He says there's a great deal that "lies under the public surface of cities."

ST: He is aware of this, whereas Blanche was—

TW: Blanche's personal situation seemed to eclipse everything for her. You will notice that she didn't—well, there is a speech in which she said we must not "hang back with the apes!"

ST: Yes, we must not hang back with "the brutes" or with the apes. She says that to Stella.

TW: That speech shows a sort of general philosophical feeling of hers. But in Shannon's case it seems to be more particularized and on a more impersonal level somehow.

ST: And yet, though Blanche at the very end says I will depend upon "the kindness of strangers" and finds no kindness really, Shannon does—

TW: I think people always find kindness.

ST: Well, did Blanche find it as that man took her away?

TW: I think even in asylums one can find kindness if one is willing to give it.

ST: You're asking Blanche to give after the play ends in a sense, aren't you? Blanche is taken—

TW: I have no idea what happens to Blanche after the play ends. I know she was shattered. And the meaning of the play is that this woman who was potentially a superior person was broken by—

ST: Brutality?

TW: Was broken by society.

ST: Society?

TW: The falsities in it.

ST: Isn't it funny, I said brutality and you said society.

TW: Well, we were thinking along slightly different lines.

ST: And yet perhaps not too different.

TW: And yet they converged a bit, didn't they? I think in our time the condition of society is pretty terrifying.

ST: Because all of your heroes and heroines are, I suppose in their own way, not only rebels—I was about to say lost—but they seek to find themselves. Shannon, for example, in *The Night of the Iguana* does meet the kind stranger, doesn't he, in Hannah, the role played by Margaret Leighton?

TW: He does indeed, yes.

ST: How would you describe Hannah, since we have perhaps a new figure in American theatre in the role played by Margaret Leighton? Was it Kenneth Tynan who spoke of your love for what we call the "incomplete" people? That is, he was not denigrating them, he merely meant our society makes them incomplete, I believe.

TW: I've always regarded myself as an incomplete person, and consequently I've always been more interested in my own kind of people, you know, people that have problems, people that have to fight for their reason, people for whom the impact of life and experience from day to day, night to night, is difficult, people who come close to cracking. That's my world, those are my people. And I must write about the people I know. Perhaps that limits me, I'm sure it must limit me as an artist, but nevertheless I couldn't create believable characters if I moved outside of that world. That doesn't mean that I'm altogether a crackpot, because I'm not.

ST: *Does* this limit you? I mean aren't these people a basically sensitive people up against a brutal framework?

TW: I think, of course, they are. There's never been any question about that, I don't think. And I don't think you will find many artists who aren't more or less in the same situation. Give a person an acute sensibility and you're bound to find a person who is under a good deal of torment, especially in this particular time.

ST: Think of Blanche for a minute. I'm asking you, the creator, to think of Blanche. I'm thinking of her for the moment. She represented so many good things too, despite the sham that she seemed to evoke.

TW: Well, as she said, "I don't tell truth, I tell what *ought* to be truth." She had the courage to admit that she occasionally embellished upon the real facts and when her back was to the wall, she had courage and truth and eloquence, I thought.

ST: Think of another figure, someone else who was hurt very easily. Earlier I asked you about the conflict of the pagan vs. the puritan, the battle. In *Summer and Smoke,* that will soon be coming to Chicago with the magnificent Geraldine Page in it—

TW: Yes, Gerry Page.

ST: —as Alma Winemiller, you have someone who is outwardly so caged by her inhibitions that when she breaks through, there is a wildness within her.

TW: There always was, yes, that's what gave her the palpitations. She was caging in something that was really quite different from her spinsterish, puritanical exterior.

ST: Isn't this figure almost an archetype—not that all your characters aren't different—but isn't this figure, the one who is caged—

TW: It seems to be an obsessive figure with me as a writer. I'm gradually beginning to find other types to deal with in my work. But it is gradual and the question is, will one man's life be long enough to complete the discovery of these other types?

ST: Well, I'm sure you will indeed. Your creative—

TW: Well, I'm fifty now.

ST: That's a beginning.

TW: Life doesn't begin at fifty, my friend, don't kid me.

ST: Tennessee Williams, I'm thinking of this new figure in *Night of the Iguana,* Hannah, who's a little different from the others. A spinster perhaps, she *is* a spinster. Not too acquainted with the flesh of life, yet very much with the spirit of it. Yet there seems less conflict within her than, say, in Alma.

TW: She has come to terms, of a kind, with life, yes. She's a very, very modest person, Hannah, and in that sense, to me, a very beautiful person. I meant Hannah, the part of Hannah Jelkes in *The Night of the Iguana,* almost as a definition of what I think is most beautiful spiritually in a person and still believable. I'm still exploring the character of Hannah and thank heavens I have a great artist like Margaret Leighton to help me. Because Maggie and I are exploring this woman. And Maggie is portraying each night with the most consummate artistry—the woman, as far as I've created her. And then after the show and between shows, we talk over this woman, and we explore between us still further. You know, Maggie seems to dig this woman, that's why she took the part.

ST: Even now, while you're here in Chicago—*Iguana* is now in its third week or so—even now, you are honing and polishing more.

TW: What astonished me about some of the reviews—I won't

mention names but at least one or two reviews—is that they didn't
see what I was trying to find through the creation of Hannah. I don't
see how a woman as unique and as lovely as Hannah Jelkes could
be ignored, you know, in a play. Especially when she was portrayed
as beautifully as she was—

ST: It's interesting that it's Hannah you see—offhand, we think of
the defrocked clergyman, Shannon, as the focal figure, yet, as you
say, he's had a prototype in a way in Blanche DuBois at the end of
her tether. But the new figure in your world, then, is Hannah, is it not?

TW: She's the new one, yes. And as I say, she's still in a process of
creation. The first production of a play isn't for me the final one.
Even if this one should close, you know, after a short run, I would go
on working on this play until I had created Hannah completely.

ST: This is a fascinating avenue, if we may explore it a bit. Even
though *The Night of the Iguana,* you say, might close after a short
run—

TW: Well, we've had—

ST: *Battle of Angels*—

TW: Yes, *Battle of Angels* eventually became *Orpheus
Descending,* not that it was ever successful in either form, but I
certainly continued my exploration of the characters in the play over
a long period, and I think I will with this one too. I don't think
whatever happens to the Broadway reception of *Night of the Iguana*
will finish my work on *The Night of the Iguana.*

ST: Where the characters will outlive whatever the framework at
the moment may be?

TW: Oh, yes, for me the production of a play is only an incident in
the life of a play. I mean there's not only the continued work on the
play but there are other productions of the play. Sometimes it's a
failure on Broadway and it's a success off-Broadway, as happened in
Summer and Smoke. Sometimes it's a failure in one country and in
another country it's a great success. And consequently I feel that a
play is dynamic and living far beyond the time of its Broadway
opening and the press the following morning. And I don't think I'm
going to be too much concerned this time with the critical reception
of this play because I know this play, as long as I am living, will live in
me and I will keep it alive within myself and do all I can do to
complete it.

ST: In that sense it is dynamic, this very play. You will not be bothered by its present framework or how that framework is received?

TW: No, I won't be limited by its reception, no.

ST: Somewhere you mentioned your leaning more and more toward off-Broadway when it comes to future projects?

TW: That's only because I feel that too much of my nervous energy is expended on needless tensions, things that are quite extraneous to the creation of a work. I would rather concentrate on writing the work and then having it done by unestablished but excellent players off-Broadway than go through this so exhausting hassle, you know, of putting on a $100,000 or a $125,000 production with all the responsibilities outside the one that you have to your work.

ST: Another reflection of what you were saying a moment ago—that it's the play itself or perhaps even more the characters within this play who are most important to you.

TW: Yes, they come alive, they are like living beings to me, they're more alive to me than I am to myself. They are my life and I don't feel that their life terminates with a Broadway opening, a Chicago opening, a Detroit opening, or any opening. Until I have created them as fully as I can create them, they're still going with me. Once I'm totally satisfied that they're completed as fully as I can create them, then they will have their own lives to lead without me.

ST: Right now you are living with Hannah and with Larry Shannon—

TW: Hannah and Larry Shannon and even with old Maxine Faulk. [laughter]

ST: We haven't spoken of this figure filled with animal spirits, Maxine, who is a third figure of this group in Mexico. Again the hot climate. Was D. H. Lawrence a big factor in your life?

TW: Not as much as people imagine. Chekhov more, I would say.

ST: Chekhov more?

TW: Yes, especially where this play is concerned, the influence of Chekhov is much stronger. I call this a dramatic poem, this play, more a dramatic poem than a play.

ST: In that the hurts, the hidden hurts, of people one way or another bounce against each other?

TW: No, in the sense that it's composed rather like a poem. It's not constructed very well as a play, but it has more the atmosphere of a poem, I think.

ST: Well, don't all of your plays have a poetic flavor to them?

TW: I hope so. Some of them more than others. *Cat on a Hot Tin Roof* is the most realistic play I've done. *Suddenly Last Summer* is perhaps the most poetic.

ST: I remember at the end of *Suddenly Last Summer* on opening night here in Chicago with Diana Barrymore, who was excellent, as I recall, in the role of the girl—

TW: It wasn't her best role, her best role was as Maggie in *Cat on a Hot Tin Roof.*

ST: She didn't do that in Chicago.

TW: She was excellent as Blanche in *Streetcar,* but when I saw her in Chicago in *Suddenly Last Summer,* I realized that she was doing a brilliant virtuoso performance of a part in which she was basically miscast, just as Liz Taylor was miscast in it on the screen.

ST: I remember outside on the sidewalk—whether people are pro or con Williams, what is most important is that you create a great deal of animated discussion at a time when there is so little of it and that this discussion involves man one way or another in stress.

TW: I'm glad to hear that.

ST: What, don't you believe that?

TW: Yes, I do. I gather that.

ST: One of your favorite quotations is that we are all in "solitary confinement" in our skins. You know that phrase—

TW: Oh yes, that's from *Orpheus, Orpheus Descending.* "We're all of us sentenced to solitary confinement inside our own skins."

ST: Well, does this find its way into all of your characters, whether it be Blanche or Alma Winemiller or Shannon?

TW: Well, the drama in my plays, I think, is nearly always people trying to reach each other. In *Night of the Iguana* each one has his separate cubicle but they meet on the veranda outside the cubicles, at least Hannah and Larry Shannon meet on the veranda outside their cubicles, which is of course an allegorical touch of what people must try to do. It's true they're confined inside their own skins, or their own cubicles, but they must try to get out as much as—they must try to find a common ground on which they can meet because the only truly satisfying moments in life are those in which you are in contact, and I don't mean just physical contact, I mean in deep, a deeper contact than physical, with some other human being.

ST: A matter of communication, then, that is so lacking today perhaps.

TW: I think it's the only comfort that we have, of a lasting kind.

ST: To communicate.

TW: And I have seen it happen between two people. I can't think of any better example than my grandparents who were so close together they were like one person.

ST: This was in Columbus?

TW: No, in Mississippi, various places in Mississippi. Finally in Memphis where they retired to after my grandfather completed his service to the Church. They remained so close they were like that old Greek legend, Baucis and what?

ST: Philemon.

TW: Baucis and Philemon, yes, that's what they were like. And it's been a great inspiration to me. On the other hand there was my mother and father who were quite the opposite. They were in constant conflict. But I thank God that I have seen exemplified in my grandmother and grandfather the possibility of two people being so lovingly close as they were that they were almost like a tree. Two people who had grown into a single tree. That was the story wasn't it, the Greek legend?

ST: That's right, after they were so good to the two strangers, Mercury and his friend. This is interesting. There were two kinds of lives you saw from the very beginning, and this reflects itself in—

TW: Two different couples, my grandparents who grew together in wholeness and in love, and my parents who split violently apart and tore the children apart through division and conflict. Those are the two backgrounds that I had as a forming person.

ST: I think of the gentle Laura of *The Glass Menagerie,* in a way a victim, Laura.

TW: Oh, yes, she was. Laura was sort of an abstraction of my sister, Rose.

ST: There are so many questions I want to ask you, Mr. Williams. Everything you're saying connects with what I am asking. We think of the two playwrights of the American theatre. And again I quote

Kenneth Tynan who speaks of the two best writers of American dramatic prose: Miller, the social playwright who seeks the "attainable" summit, the other, Williams, the poetic playwright who speaks of the "unattainable" summit "because his aspirations are imaginative." [*Curtains* (New York: Atheneum, 1961), 257-266— Editor] Do you follow that?

TW: Yes, I do. I never read that bit but Mr. Tynan is a very good critic. Even when he lambasts you he does it with such eloquence and wit that you enjoy it.

ST: But he paid tribute to you very much indeed, I remember, in this particular essay that—

TW: We're good friends. Ken and I have always been friends in spite of the occasional times when he's felt it necessary to take a negative point of view.

ST: He speaks of *Cat on a Hot Tin Roof* as his favorite.

TW: Yes, I like his choice.

ST: Do you think he was justified, you may recall, in critizing Kazan, whom he felt had tampered with a superior product—the original script—in his production?

TW: Well, when you're dealing with an artist as creative and as great as Kazan, you can't use the word "tamper." Kazan brings to bear an intensely creative imagination. He cannot help but leave his own stamp upon what he does, and who would want him not to. I don't want him not to. I just want the meaning of my play to come through, and essentially whenever Kazan has worked on a play of mine, he has magnified that play in a good way. He hasn't diminished it ever. Sometimes we've had a little variance. My viewpoint about how a certain act might go may be divergent from his viewpoint, but after all a play is published, you know. People can take their choice. I can't say that my viewpoint is right, perhaps it isn't, and perhaps I need someone like Kazan to modify my viewpoint.

ST: I imagine this is par for the course, is it not, the conflict between playwright and director?

TW: What isn't par for the course is to have such a great director do your work. That's what isn't par for the course, that's very exceptional.

ST: One thing that's significant about your plays is the feeling of actors toward them. We think of the number of actresses in the American theatre today and just about the top five you can name have found their way as a result of your plays. There's Maureen Stapleton, *Rose Tatoo;* there's Geraldine Page, who was in *Summer and Smoke* and *Sweet Bird of Youth*—

TW: I've been very fortunate in having great actors and actresses—

ST: Uta Hagen, Jessica Tandy—

TW: I think I've had the advantage of having nearly all the very distinguished stage actors in America in my work.

ST: But isn't there something else here, the theatricality, the theatricality of your writing, that it plays no matter what the circumstances.

TW: Even if the plays themselves don't come off, there's always a part in them that is very good for an actor.

ST: Excitement that is there continuously—

TW: There's always a part that attracts a fine actor.

ST: Because you are continuously defended by actors, almost invariably it's the actor who comes to your defense.

TW: I hope that will always be so.

ST: Lonnie Chapman, a young actor I know, was making this point. Every actor that he knows who has played Williams may agree or disagree with you on one point or another, but the excitement of the role is something that is a part of his good memory. I have a question that I want to ask you, Mr. Williams. Your admiration for Carson McCullers—

TW: Yes, I suppose next to my sister, Rose, Carson is, of all the women that I know, now living, the one closest to me. With the possible exception of my mother, but of course my mother is of another generation and Carson and I are of approximately the same generation. I feel very close to her even though often I may not see her for months at a time. That's because we seem to have similar attitudes toward life.

ST: Toward "incomplete" people?

TW: That's true, yes. I'm afraid that's true.

ST: I'm not afraid. Again, if I may, the references made to you and your feeling for incomplete people—they could be complete under other circumstances, couldn't they?

TW: They could, I think, under ideal circumstances, but to tell you the truth, I'm not sure I've ever met a complete person. I've met many people that seemed well-adjusted, but I'm not sure that to be well-adjusted to things as they are is a desideratum—is that the word? that which is to be desired. I'm not sure I would want to be well-adjusted to things as they are. I would prefer to be racked by desire for things better than what they are, even for things which are unattainable, than to be satisfied with things as they are. I don't think the human race should settle for what it has now achieved at all, any more than I think America must settle for its present state. My people fought for the beginning of this country. I am totally an American, and I'm an intensely patriotic American in the sense that I feel a longing for this country to go forward and be unafraid. I feel intensely American, but I am not satisfied with the present state of things in this country and I'm afraid of complacency about it. I'm afraid of our thinking that all the rest of the world is in error and we're totally right. Nobody is right. And the whole meaning of all my work is that there is no such thing as complete right and complete wrong, complete black, complete white. That we're all in the same boat and really the boat is the world, you might even say it's the universe. All creation is the boat, not just one nation, not just one ideology, not just one system. That everything is in flux, everything is in a process of creation. The world is incomplete, it's like an unfinished poem. Maybe the poem will suddenly turn to a limerick or maybe it will turn to an epic poem. But it's for all of us to try to complete this poem, and the way to complete it is through understanding and patience and tolerance among ourselves. That's my idea of patriotism. It's patriotism to the world and to humanity. I'm afraid of Birch societies, I'm afraid of that sort of thing. That's the most fearful and dreadful thing that we have to face now in this world.

ST: In your way, as a playwright, you are saying this when you speak of your incomplete people. You will not adjust to that which is evil, that you feel is evil.

TW: Oh, I have plenty of evil in me, I'm not a nice person.

ST: All of us have the same sins in us.

TW: Yes, but I think I know what evil is, I think I can recognize evil. I think most people can if they will try to. My business, my vocation, whatever you want to call it, compels me to weigh evil and good, and consequently when I'm working I'm always in a state of examining. I think I am.

ST: You're a highly moral man is what it amounts to. You are.

TW: Are you talking about my behavior?

ST: No, no, I'm talking about your outlook on the world.

TW: [hearty laughter] I'm glad you're talking about my outlook because I couldn't make such a claim for myself as a person in his behavior.

ST: Who can?

TW: Who can? Well, I don't know about other people, I only know about myself.

ST: You are a very moral person.

TW: I'm a moralist, yes.

ST: And thus you're a surgeon who would perhaps probe the canker and the sore, and being a good surgeon, you dig pretty deep.

TW: Yes, I want to discover all that is evil and all that is good. I hope that I have a chance to, I hope the public will bear with me while I continue the exploration. I'm not a very good writer, but I seem to be a man who has this obsession to explore good and evil.

ST: If we may continue with this exploration. In *Camino Real,* doesn't your Byron speak of taking chances and risks?

TW: Yes, he says, *"Make voyages!—Attempt them!—there's nothing else . . ."*

ST: Is this pretty much your credo?

TW: That's my philosophy, my credo, yes. I don't know where they'll lead, the voyages, and neither did Byron actually, in the *Camino Real.* But certainly this just sitting still is of no constructive purpose.

ST: So what's this itch in you, this creative spirit, this restlessness, then, that in a way—

TW: I think one must try to go forward in this world without stepping on other people. The way to progress is by daring to go forward but not trampling on other beings as we go, if we can help it. God knows, I can't say that I have made whatever progress I may have made in life without stepping on people. I suppose I've stepped on many toes.

ST: Perhaps one more thing. In *Camino Real,* doesn't your Don Quixote speak of the violets cracking through rocks?

TW: Yes, at the end of the play, *"The violets in the mountains have broken the rocks!"* That's the final line of the play.

ST: Do you believe that can be done? Well, that's done, isn't it?

TW: That's done occasionally. As I say, I think the world is an unfinished poem; it could turn to a limerick or it could turn to an epic. I don't know which it will turn to, or it could just sputter out. Still, at moments, certainly the violets do break the rocks. There are moments when they do. I'm not sure one should cling to that image too much because after all it's rather a pretty image; it's an effective image but it isn't a very comprehensive one perhaps.

ST: Isn't the non-violent movement of all these students in a sense a parable of violets breaking through rocks?

TW: What movements?

ST: The sit-ins of the students of Nashville, the theory of non-violence they're practicing, you see. The Ghandiesque approach in a way is that too, strangely enough.

TW: I think the Negro race has conducted itself with the most extraordinary nobility—

ST: And patience.

TW: —and patience. We should be very proud of them as Americans, that they are our people and they have conducted themselves with such nobility and patience in these disgraceful circumstances.

ST: Perhaps one last question. There are many last questions I want to ask you, but are you pressed for time?

TW: No.

ST: Oh, good. Because I remember, since you're speaking of the Negro and the Blues, that you like the Blues very much. I think of when Brownie McGhee and Sonny Terry were here in *Cat on a Hot Tin Roof* and a broadcast was done and you included, didn't you, a Blues backing?

TW: Oh, yes. We had a wonderful Negro band playing backstage. Fabulous.

ST: You chose the best harmonica Blues player in the world.

TW: Great, great, great. Kazan chose them, not me, he found them.

ST: Music. I know you're interested now and then in certain aspects of jazz. You've written some songs too, haven't you?

TW: I have written a few Blues lyrics, yes, which have been set to music by Paul Bowles, who's a very dear friend of mine. *Blue Mountain Ballads.* [New York: G. Schirmer, 1946—Editor]

ST: Is there something on your mind now that you feel like talking about? There are other things coming to me as we're sitting here talking. About the figures in your play—as you say they're with you all the time, you're living with them all the time.

TW: Well, they're most of my life, I have a little life outside of them, but comparably very little. I hope that now after *The Night of the Iguana* opens I will have a little more. I will take a rest and try to find, try to live a little more as a person outside the theatre.

ST: You've done a good deal of writing outside the theatre too, short stories and some poetry.

TW: I rarely write poetry or short stories anymore. I find that I put my stories into my plays and my poetry into my plays now.

ST: So you're wholly, then, a man of the theatre?

TW: Almost completely, I rarely ever write a short story or a poem anymore. I find I must conserve my energies for what I'm best at, and I think I'm best at plays.

ST: How do you feel when someone like *Time,* for example, speaks of your nonheroes? I know this is a difficult point—

TW: Well, the show business department of *Time* magazine is my bête noire.

ST: I was afraid of that—

TW: They rag me incessantly, and if it gives them great satisfaction, let them *have* it, but I don't know why they are so unremitting in this. Just recently they compared *Iguana* to a turkey. They said that my incoming play to Broadway appeared, from all indications, to be a massive turkey. And then they proceeded to quote *carefully* selected bits from the reviews in Chicago, selected only for whatever damage they could do. They ignored whatever was said that offered promise and expressed admiration. Then they lifted out of context something that I'd said on a interview with Mr. Kupcinet. They pretended that a remark that I'd made about my desire to work off-Broadway was made in reference to this play, *Night of the Iguana.* It was not made in reference to this play at all. It was only made in reference to my desire to rest for a while and to work off-Broadway until I have recovered my energies after this present work.

ST: Has it ever occurred to you Tennessee Williams—
remembering your talking earlier about adjustment—that *Time* is a
magazine of adjusted people? You are a non-adjusted man—

TW: I should not care to be as adjusted as the gentlemen from the
show business department of *Time* magazine whom I encountered
on a parlor car on a train between Philadelphia and New York when
they insisted that I come and join them, and they showed themselves
to be merciless sadists.

ST: That's the point I was coming to, forgetting about *Time* for the
moment. Dr. Hutchins, Robert Maynard Hutchins, recently said
something very beautiful about adjustment courses at universities. He
blasted them, and this matter of adjusting he equated with
complacency.

TW: I don't care to adjust on the level of certain types that appear
to be adjusted. No, I don't, I'd rather stay an outsider, even if it
means an outcast.

ST: Coming back again to your plays in every respect, this then is
it, basically, is it not? I mean you in a sense *are* the outcast from that
which you consider evil of another kind, evil—

TW: I think adjustment and conformity to that which is basically
wrong and unjust is not the kind of adjustment we should want. Even
though it is acceptable in society, I don't find it acceptable. And I'd
rather accept exile from that kind of society.

ST: Tennessee Williams, another question. I wander a bit and yet
all these questions are part of a design, I think, I hope. Southern
writers in recent years—the resurgence of creativity on the part of so
many, whether it's Carson McCullers or Eudora Welty or Flannery
O'Connor. Do you consider yourself a southern writer?

TW: Well, my roots are in the south, at least my creative roots are.

ST: Is there a way of explaining this, the past, say, twenty years or
so?

TW: I think the group of writers you're referring to, Eudora Welty
and Carson McCullers and myself—we're far from being the new
wave, you know. [laughter]

ST: Nonetheless, prior to that time, there wasn't too much coming
from the South, was there, creatively?

TW: Oh, yes!

ST: Wasn't there a desert period?

TW: Well, there probably was aside from the poems of Sidney Lanier. There wasn't much writing—

ST: Your middle name incidentally.

TW: Yes, we're related collaterally. Aside from that, there wasn't much except a polite sort of writing going on. There was a sudden efflorescence of writing that began with Faulkner, don't you think? I think he began the Southern Gothic movement, as it's called. And Robert Penn Warren. I think a great many wonderful writers have come out of the South, say in the last thirty years. But in the last five or six or maybe ten years, I don't know if there've been any new ones. I think the shift may be in the other direction now.

ST: Do you see any trends, by the way?

TW: I think there's a great deal of creativity going on in England now, in the English theatre particularly with a man like Harold Pinter, author of *The Caretaker,* and a man like Samuel Beckett, he's an Irishman though, isn't he? But still, I think of them as all belonging to the British Isles. And John Osborne, fabulous. I like all these new writers from England.

ST: Since you've mentioned Pinter and *Caretaker* and Beckett. The new wave—

TW: The New Wave writers, yes. And in America there's Edward Albee, of course, brilliant artist, and a very brave man, I think. Well, there've been several others. Gelber—

ST: Richardson.

TW: I'm not so crazy about Richardson, but I can see that he can be amusing.

ST: Albee, Pinter, the young writers. You said something very moving that I remember hearing on the program. You, an established playwright—our most celebrated—find yourself inspired by the younger playwrights.

TW: Yes, I do. I like their attitude toward the commercialism of the theatre. They say go take a flying jump at the moon, that's what they say to the commercial theatre, it seems to me. And I admire them for it.

ST: And apparently that's what you're saying too, you're about to say.

TW: I've been saying it all along, but still I've been having plays produced on Broadway. [laughter] I know that I've made some compromises, naturally I have, but I hope that when I have rested a while and go back to work that it will be off-Broadway and that I will not be so divided a person, that I will not have as much difficulty in resisting the myth of success as the thing that one must have. The big success, the rave notices, the pleasing of the big mass of people. It hasn't affected my work while I'm working, but I think it has proved to be an infection that you can't resist if you're continually surrounded by it. Certainly it doesn't help you as an artist to be surrounded by it. It filters in somehow.

ST: You want to be more free?

TW: Yes, I want to be more free, I want to work for myself really, without thinking anymore about whether it will get rave notices or be a smash and all that. Have a big line at the box office the morning after it opens.

ST: This is a tough one, I suppose. Being human, how immune can one be from it or how free can one be from it, from that to which we're accustomed?

TW: That's the big question.

ST: That's the question, isn't it?

TW: That's the big question. I'll find out. [laughter]

ST: Anything else you'd care to say, Tennessee Williams?

TW: No, I think we've covered a lot of ground, maybe too much.

ST: No, I don't think so. I think in a way this is a portrait and I should volunteer at this moment, a very endearing portrait of a thoughtful man and playwright, Tennessee Williams. Thank you very much.

TW: Thank you, I enjoyed it very much.

Williams on Williams

Lewis Funke and John E. Booth/1962

From *Theatre Arts*, January 1962, 16-19, 72-73. Reprinted by permission of John E. Booth.

We interviewed Mr. Williams at his New York apartment, the top floor of a one-time private house in New York's East Sixties. It is a modest apartment, the living room, in comfortable disarray, furnished with random taste, with an eye-catching bronze here, a stained glass window decoration there. Lots of books around—but none in evidence by Mr. Williams. It was noon, but for Mr. Williams this was still quite early, for the night before had been a late one—and a tense one—working on his new play *The Night of the Iguana* which had just started rehearsals with Bette Davis, Margaret Leighton, Alan Webb and Patrick O'Neal under the direction of Frank Corsaro.

Interviewer: Did you find there were many changes to make?

Williams: I came in kind of resentful. Not resentful, that's not the word. I mean, I came in with great trepidation because when you come into rehearsal with a script that says all you want to say—and it has already been pruned down quite a bit—and, you know, I think the cutting should come mostly when you reach the point of the run-throughs—well, I thought this was all a little premature for cutting. I had just come from the dentist's office and I still had a lot of novocaine and I wasn't . . . you know, it was very difficult for me. I knew the third act needed pruning, but it is always a traumatic experience to do that. But toward the end of the evening I suddenly saw the light—that there were enough long speeches, which is my specialty, unfortunately, and that at least five or six pages earlier in the act could be reduced to sort of a dynamic, you know—rather than talk—it would be more effective that way. I realized there was too much talk. I mean there were speeches of five lines where half a

line could have done it. Right now I'm engaged in trying to say—
trying to express a play more in terms of action. Not in terms of
physical action; I mean, in sort of a gun-fire dialogue instead of the
long speeches that I've always relied on before. Let me say that I
depended too much on language—on words.

Interviewer: Does this portend some new direction for your
work? Do you want to reach audiences in a new way, somehow
touching them in other ways, less directly?

Williams: You mean more allusive rather than on the nose?

Interviewer: Yes, that's right . . .

Williams: Yes. That I'm conscious of more than ever. I've been
writing too much on the nose, you know, and I've always sensed the
fact that life was too ambiguous to be . . . to be presented in a cut
and dried fashion. I've always been conscious of that, but I think I'm
getting surer now. I think the one beautiful and great thing about the
new wave of playwrights is that they approach their subject matter
with this kind of allusiveness. The whole attitude of this new wave of
playwrights is not to preach, you know. Not to be dogmatic, to be
provocatively allusive. And I think that's much truer . . .

Interviewer: You mean the playwrights like Beckett, Gelber,
Albee . . . or maybe Harold Pinter and his new play, *The Caretaker?*

Williams: Christ, that's a fabulous work. To me the play was
about the thing that I've always pushed in my writing—that I've
always felt was needed to be said over and over—that human
relations are terrifyingly ambiguous. If you write a character that isn't
ambiguous you are writing a false character, not a true one.

Interviewer: The new playwrights, then . . .

Williams: You see, they're exploring subtleties of human relations
that haven't been explored.

Interviewer: And their writing, the spareness, the style, is
something you admire?

Williams: It's something that drives me crazy with jealousy. I love
it. While I'm in the theatre, I'm enthralled by it and I say, Oh, God, if
I could write like that. If only I were twenty-five and just starting out,
what these boys could have given me.

Interviewer: But ninety per cent of the present playwrights would
probably be just as blind with jealousy to write the way you do.

Williams: I think my kind of literary or pseudo-literary style of writing for the theatre is on its way out.

Interviewer: Wouldn't you always want to write plays that are, well, poetic?

Williams: But poetry doesn't have to be words, you see. In the theatre it can be situations, it can be silences. Colloquial, completely unheightened language can be more poetic, I think. My great bête noire as a writer has been a tendency to what people call . . . to poeticize, you know, and that's why I suppose I've written so many Southern heroines. They have the tendency to gild the lily, and they speak in a rather florid style which seems to suit me because I write out of emotion, and I get carried away by the emotion. Sometimes what Kazan refers to as the arias, sometimes they come off very well, and other times they stop the play.

Interviewer: Who are some of the other modern playwrights you like?

Williams: I'm not crazy about Ionesco. I'm crazy about Anouilh at his best, I'm always enchanted by Giraudoux and I love Albee, best of our American playwrights. Of the English playwrights I love Harold Pinter and I like Osborne. I like the bite in his writing, the fearlessness that he shows.

Interviewer: You feel that really if these young playwrights had been writing twenty-five years ago they would have had an influence on you . . .

Williams: Not influence so much as an enlightenment on how to say what you have to say in short forms, and without reliance so much on speech; and in their psychological subtleties which I have only arrived at. Now I think I know more about people . . . and they seem to know about it long before I did. Yes, the theatre as it exists Off Broadway, in the new wave of playwrights—let's exclude Mr. Kopit, who I wish would stop it—I feel that here is my country, you know, and why wasn't I in it before, you know, why have I been writing these long, long plays?

Interviewer: You mentioned Kazan a moment ago. Do you feel any freedom being away from Kazan?

Williams: No, no, no. I don't. One of the most regrettable things in my life is that I don't think that Kazan and I will ever work again together, and it wasn't my choice. It was his. I think that he is the most brilliant director we have.

Interviewer: Then there is a complete break between you and Kazan?

Williams: Well, there was certainly—on my part at least—there was certainly no change in my friendship for him, and I think probably he still likes me, but our liking is ambivalent, you know.

Interviewer: This is curious, because now Kazan is separated from both you and Arthur Miller.

Williams: Yes, well Arthur Miller hasn't been writing plays since *A View From The Bridge* and I think that Kazan would be perfectly willing to do another Arthur Miller play, if Arthur came up with one that was ready. There would be a reconciliation between them; I heard there had been.

Interviewer: To get back to *The Night of the Iguana* . . .

Williams: You know, there's nothing I dread more than trying to tell about a play. A play only exists on the stage. It really does. And when you try to tell about it . . . well, I can say this about it, it has no relation to the short story that bears the same title except for the Iguana itself, and for the Mexican background.

Interviewer: Well, what is the significance of the Iguana itself?

Williams: The Iguana? If I start talking about the significance of it, people will say I'm talking in symbols again and people don't like the symbolic quality of my work, I don't think. They think I overdepend on symbols.

Interviewer: Some time ago you said you were hoping someday to write one play that would encompass everything that you've been trying to say. Is *Iguana* the play?

Williams: I was trying to work on it in *Iguana*, yes, at least a kind of summation of what I've derived finally from these mixed feelings and attitudes.

Interviewer: You might say, then, that from your point of view *Iguana* is the most important of your plays.

Williams: For my own personal selfish satisfaction at least. I hope it will reach other people too, but, God knows, not everybody has the same life, or problems that I have and maybe it won't communicate to them. I can only hope that it does.

Interviewer: After *Iguana* have you anything in mind?

Williams: I intend to work Off Broadway from now on.

Interviewer: Entirely Off Broadway from now on?

Williams: Yes, from now on. I've gone through too many of these Broadway stage plays and I've suffered certain attritions of time and energies. I've been writing for thirty-five years—since I was fifteen years old—I'm a man of fifty now—and now I want to write . . . I've always loved writing, but now I want to write with love as the main objective because I just can't go through any more of these big productions. They kill me, you know, the tensions. I'm a very tense person. If you put a very tense person . . . a person who is naturally very tense . . . into terrifying tensions of putting on a Broadway play—he's pushing his luck you know, he's gonna crack.

Interviewer: This decision doesn't reflect any feeling that you haven't been well represented artistically on Broadway?

Williams: Oh, no, no. I've always been represented artistically very well indeed. I can't think of a single instance when I wasn't.

Interviewer: And you think you'll fare as well Off Broadway?

Williams: That troubles me because it's much easier to get the best director and the finest stars, the finest actors—stars, that's a terrible slip of the tongue, isn't it?—it's much easier to get them in a Broadway production. Now, I couldn't assemble a cast like I have for *Iguana* in an Off-Broadway production. Bette Davis, Margaret Leighton can't afford to go Off Broadway. Kazan couldn't afford to go Off Broadway. But the marvelous thing is that so many of these new playwrights and these directors, and even these new actors, seem to be less concerned with commercial aspects. And they do beautiful things and the audiences seem to enjoy it just as much. Now I would never get the kind of performance Off Broadway that Miss Leighton is going to give, for instance, and Miss Davis, in their respective roles, or Mr. Patrick O'Neal, whose name isn't known but will be known.

Interviewer: You were pleased with the Off-Broadway production of your *Suddenly Last Summer,* weren't you?

Williams: Yes, indeed. Herbert Machiz gave it a very beautiful directorial job and we had some fine actors in it, but unfortunately we kept losing them. We'd have them for a month and then they would be offered another part on Broadway. And you have that continual replacement problem.

Interviewer: But on the other hand it will be worth it for your peace of mind.

Williams: Yes, I've got to. I want to survive. I love life even though people think I'm very indifferent to it, but . . .

Interviewer: Yes, people have remarked on a negative quality in your works. But you do, then, highly value life—and the relationships with people in life?

Williams: The only satisfactory thing we are left with in life is the relations—if they're sincere—between people.

Interviewer: There is an impression that some people get from your plays that love as a personal relationship cannot be a satisfactory one.

Williams: Not totally, no. But I mean it's better than most business relationships turn out to be. (*Laughing*)

Interviewer: But I mean, isn't love the finest personal relationship in the end, the most complete?

Williams: I think it's the closest we've come to, you know, a deeply satisfying relationship between people . . .

Interviewer: But haven't you indicated that when one loves there is also something of defeat?

Williams: I don't think I ever could have said quite that . . . but I think that's part of this ambiguity that is, I suppose, in my characterizations. It's the thing I'm most concerned with, the fact that there isn't any absolute in people's feelings for each other.

Interviewer: But beyond that don't you feel that human relationships are rarely as rewarding as you would wish them to be?

Williams: Oh, of course not, no they never are.

Interviewer: And in marriage . . .

Williams: People marry usually when they are very young, and sexual attraction between them is what really brings about the marriage, but then after awhile they discover they not only have to sleep together, they have to live together. And just sleeping together ceases to be the be all and end all of the relationship, and they begin to discover things in each other that irritate them now because they didn't really know each other. That's why, especially under the pressures that exist in a place like Hollywood and New York, every few years, you know, married people . . . I guess the average longevity would be around five years, wouldn't it?

Interviewer: To go back to something you said before—what did you mean when you said from now on you wanted to write "with love?"

Williams: I want to—now I don't mean loving everybody, no, no. I hate about eighty per cent more people than I love, believe me. (*Laughing*) But I have to understand a person. I have to understand the characters in my play in order to write about them because if I just hate them I can't write about them. That's why Boss Finley wasn't right in *Sweet Bird of Youth,* because I just didn't like the guy, and I just had to make a *tour de force* of his part in the play.

Interviewer: Do you want to like all your characters, then?

Williams: Understand them. If I understand them I like them. (*Laughing*) The one thing I cannot—I can understand maybe—but, no I don't even understand it, is that kind of self-infatuated, self-blindness and cruelty, you know, such as he . . . Finley . . . personified.

Interviewer: I wanted to get back to something you have been talking about—saying, in a sense, good-bye to violence in your plays. You have made a point of this in talking recently.

Williams: I didn't mean to, and I think I protested too much.

Interviewer: You don't have a particular feeling about eliminating violence from your plays?

Williams: It if occurs naturally, of course, it will be there. Right now I don't feel inclined to use violence, and I don't know why. Just maybe, it has to do with personal fatigue. I just don't feel inclined to. I sort of said to myself, "All right, stop fighting them," you know, "don't join them, but stop fighting them . . . stop fighting so violently the people that you hate."

Interviewer: Were you aware of a tendency in some quarters to be discouraged with the extremes of violence in your plays? Does that disturb you?

Williams: I have always tried to find the dénouement that seemed predicated by the earlier . . . by the play as a whole.

Interviewer: Why do you say stop fighting the people you hate? Is that cynicism, do you think that there's no more point in it or do you just not wish to be violent for other reasons?

Williams: I'm not quite sure. Could it be despair? It might be, you know. Actually *The Night of the Iguana* is a play whose theme, as closely as I can put it, is how to live beyond despair and still live.

Interviewer: For someone who loves life, why should despair be so strong in you?

Williams: Because I'm a romantic . . . an old-fashioned romanticist.

Interviewer: What is it actually that you despair of?

Williams: I despair sometimes of love being lasting, and of people getting along together . . . as nations and as individuals . . . of their realizing how important, how necessary it is to do that. I've just despaired of it . . . I hope I'm wrong . . . It may be just the product of a temporary exhaustion.

Interviewer: You mean a spiritual exhaustion?

Williams: Yes. A spiritual exhaustion—well, I'm pretty tired physically too. Anyway, I know I still love my work best. It's the best part of my life. But I know that the work is harder for me. It takes me, say, two years to do what I would do in one year before.

Interviewer: That's part of growing older, isn't it? And you are not as "hungry" as you once were.

Williams: Yes. But there are certain artists who seem to preserve a happy, non-despairing attitude toward life. Now certainly Mr. Kazan's new film is affirmative, you know. And I had the impression that *Period Of Adjustment* was a happy play, but when I saw it this summer in the stock production with Dane Clark, I realized that it was about as black as *Orpheus Descending,* except that there was more tenderness, perhaps, less physical violence.

Interviewer: What accounts for your restlessness?

Williams: It's physiological, I would guess. I never can remember the time when I wasn't restless. Even when I was a child, I never wanted to finish a game. I wanted to try and play something else, you know . . .

Interviewer: Well, doesn't your daily swimming release this?

Williams: That's the only thing—liquor and swimming— Milltowns, liquor, swimming. Last night after the cutting session, I took two Milltowns.

Interviewer: What discipline do you observe while you are working?

Williams: What discipline do I observe? The only discipline that I observe is when I get up in the morning. It wouldn't be possible for me to do anything but work. I've been doing it every—for thirty-five years, you know. I have been writing every morning except for very brief periods—when I had an eye operation, and once right after the *Menagerie* opened—no, just before it opened, when it was in rehearsal. I stopped writing for about two months, or a month and a half because I thought I'd had a terrible heart attack and that I couldn't stand the tension of writing—if I wanted to live, you know.

Interviewer: Did you have a heart attack?

Williams: I just drank one cup too many of too strong a coffee. I was trying to make the coffee so strong that, you know, it wouldn't pour—and I just didn't get my breath—and instead of doing the sensible thing and going to bed, I rushed out in the street . . .

Interviewer: Well, you got scared. I mean you had a legitimate right to get scared. Then when you say you write every morning—what time do you start working?

Williams: I will wake up at around seven—around daybreak—and I'll make my coffee and I'll go into what I call the "madhouse"—in Key West, it's a studio, here it's this little room in there.

Interviewer: And how many hours do you put in at the typewriter?

Williams: Three and a half as a rule . . .

Interviewer: And that's all for the day? You don't do any work in the afternoons?

Williams: Well, I shouldn't. But then if the afternoon is very boring, I'll come home and start again. But I've discovered that in the afternoons I'm only good for about half an hour. I can't, you know, by that time, I've had it.

Interviewer: Well, now, when you say you write every day, you're writing short stories, you're writing plays. I mean, do you ever just sit and write without any purpose?

Williams: Write without any purpose?

Interviewer: I mean, for instance, you get up in the morning and you're not—you're in between plays and you're in between short stories—but you must write. What do you write during that period?

Williams: Oh there's always unfinished scripts lying around. I just reach in, you know . . .

Interviewer: How can you do that? Don't you need time to get into the mood?

Williams: Well, I'm a compulsive writer—because what I am doing is creating imaginary worlds into which I can retreat from the real world because I'm . . . I've never made any kind of adjustment to the real world."

Williams: Twenty Years after *Glass Menagerie*
Joanne Stang/1965

From the *New York Times,* 28 March 1965, sec. 2, 1, 3. ©1965
by the New York Times Company. Reprinted by permission.

Tennessee Williams once wrote, at the beginning of the self-typed
script of his first success: *"The Glass Menagerie,* a rather dull little
play by Tennessee Williams."* Incredibly, it will be twenty years this
Wednesday since actor Eddie Dowling stepped forward in the
Playhouse Theater, and quietly began, "Yes, I have tricks in my
pocket, I have things up my sleeve . . . "

Since that moment, the American theater, indeed theater
everywhere, has never been the same. Year after year, the
"menagerie" has grown into a steamy zoo of Williams characters—
riddled by violence and aberration, steeped in despair—but
illuminated by the poetry and compassion that comprise his great gift.
As a body of work, the plays pronounce to many that Tennessee
Williams is one of the outstanding living playwrights, but he is still
using "dull little," "meager little" and "trivial little" as descriptions of
his dramas. When he finishes a new play, its imagery must march
through the abbatoir of self-abasement permanently fixed inside his
head.

One recent early evening Williams sat in a rented penthouse on
West 55th Street, and gamely tried to talk about himself. Interviews
seem painful for him. He stares straight ahead, wetting his lips from
time to time, his speech punctuated by sharp, loud laughter. One is
used to seeing him—in photographs—in a gaudy T-shirt, lounging in
some warmer climate. In the chill of a Manhattan March he was
subdued in a gray flannel suit, the moustache not so rakish. He said:
"I've never felt at all secure—and I'm leveling with you now—about
anything I've ever written, not anything at all. Each year I think I
become more devastatingly critical of my work. I hate everything I do.
I was talking this matter over with Carson McCullers once, in the

summer of 1946. I had just finished writing a play called *Summer and Smoke,* and I said, 'I think I will never again be able to write another play,' and she said to me very wisely and kindly, 'an artist always has that feeling, that dread, when he finishes a new work. The feeling that he'll never be able to do another.'

"Finishing a play, you know, is like completing a marriage or a love affair. You're totally absorbed in the play or the novel or the piece of writing, and when you can't do any more with it, it ceases to be the center of your life. You feel very forsaken by that, that's why I love revising and revising, because it delays the moment when there is this separation between you and the work."

Two occurrences make this an auspicious week for Williams. Tonight, Brandeis University will honor him with a Creative Arts Award commemorating his "distinguished contribution to the American Theater," and on Tuesday a revival of *Glass Menagerie* opens at the Paper Mill Playhouse, starring Maureen Stapleton, Piper Laurie, Pat Hingle and George Grizzard. Williams admits he pretends not to care about awards and prizes, "but when the Drama Critics Award is about to come out and I have a play on Broadway, I sweat blood hoping I will get it. When a Pulitzer Prize is about to come out, it's *enormously* important to me, I need all the kind of assurance that prizes give me.

"It's amazing to me that the 20th anniversary of *Menagerie* is here already. I remember those days when it was first produced. Of course everything is much more fun and much more exciting when you're young. Now, of course, it isn't so exciting, but still there's the compulsion to go on working as best I can. I think time is the enemy of the writer more than it is of the athlete, for instance. A writer has to compensate for what time takes away from him by working harder and trying to think things out more carefully if he can."

Williams feels the agony is sometimes worth it if the play succeeds. "If a play is received well opening night I have a feeling of great, great joy. If it's badly received on opening night I am plunged into an almost psychotic state of gloom. I remember when *Orpheus Descending* opened on Broadway, I went to a party afterwards, and the reviews were rather bad. I had worked very long and hard on the play—actually I had been working on it longer than any of my other plays, and I flew into a kind of mad frenzy." He laughed. "I got on

the phone and called an airline and had myself booked straight from
New York to Hong Kong, leaving about seven the next morning.
Well, it was already around 2 A.M., and I then fell into a deep,
exhausted sleep—oversleeping the hour at which I was supposed to
depart. Then very happily the afternoon reviews were better, and I
decided to stick it out. I would say that the effect of a play's reception
lasts about a week with me. After that, its effect is dissipated, at least
on a conscious level, and I'm once more involved in some new
work."

Williams's latest effort is a pair of plays jointly entitled *Slapstick
Tragedies*. They were scheduled to be done this season, but then ran
into what Williams refers to as "an unhappy situation. We had
everything lined up for the production. We had Alan Schneider to
direct, and Kate Reid and Leueen McGrath for the two female roles,
then comes the deadline, and the money wasn't there. It was
financed at $150,000 which is a little high, you know, for two rather
crazy plays.

"They're not Theater of the Absurd but they *are* very offbeat plays.
My commitment to the producer, Charles Bowden—he was also the
producer of *Night of the Iguana*—expires the end of April, but I've
extended it to the end of June. Mr. Bowden, being an Irish optimist,
thinks by then he will have raised the money. Well, I can only pray
that he will. Mr. Bowden and I were both very religious when *The
Night of the Iguana* was to leave Chicago and come into New York.
We went to a church, had a mass said for it. I'm not a Catholic
myself, but I love the Catholic mass, and by golly it opened well, and
got the Critics Award that year."

Williams says he derives very little comfort from the fact that his
plays may make him immortal. "It's strange, I guess, but I don't seem
to have any concern with that. I think when I'm dead, it won't matter
a damn to me whether people remember me well or not. The
hereafter is for the living, not for the dead. If I were coming back at
all, I wish I were coming back as a frog (he pronounced it frawg) or
an alley cat, or even a cockroach. If I were a little more Buddhist,
perhaps I would be comforted that I would come back as one of the
lower beasts, but unfortunately I haven't turned Buddhist—or
anything much."

He misses his home in Key West. "I'm in a terrible dilemma. I

know I can't stand living in Manhattan, but at the same time I know I
need the psychiatric treatment, and the medical treatment I receive
here. So I can't go away, and I can't stay. But somehow it will solve
itself, things do. I'm taking a little trip to London, to see if I can go
away for awhile. I sound as if I'm some terrible invalid. Well, I'm not,
really. I have a great deal of stamina. My family, all of them, have a
great deal of physical vitality, and thank God I have a share of it, too.
I suppose I will go on much longer than I really want to. But I hope
that I can make up my mind soon where to go.

"One of the few times I ever cried in my life—I had had a quarrel
with someone—I burst out crying and said, 'I have nowhere to go'—
and I really didn't. I didn't have anywhere to go then—that I really
wanted to go. But maybe soon I'll be able to go to Rome. If I could
get a little villa near the Via Appia, I could happily spend the rest of
my life there. I've always loved living in Rome. I have very dear
friends in Rome. No, I don't have very dear friends, I have a dear
friend, Anna Magnani."

Williams says his only goal "is the one I set for myself every
morning—that I will be able to go on working, because that is my
great joy. It's odd, I was talking this over with a psychiatrist not long
ago, and he said, 'How could you have so little confidence in
yourself, with this body of work behind you,' and I said I only think of
what I'm doing now, and what I may be able to do later. That's all
that matters to me, because writing or creating plays, or sometimes a
story or a poem, is my way of life."

Williams has an obvious affection for all the flawed people
populating his plays. "I have always been more interested in creating
a character that contains something crippled. I think nearly all of us
have some kind of defect, anyway, and I suppose I have found it
easier to identify with the characters who verge upon hysteria, who
were frightened of life, who were desperate to reach out to another
person.

"But these seemingly fragile people are the strong people really.
They have a certain appearance of fragility, these neurotic people that
I write about, but they are really strong. Blanche was much stronger
than Kowalski. When he started to assault her, he said, 'Tiger—
Tiger!' She was a tiger, she had much more strength than he, and she
surrendered it to him out of desire. These fragile people—they're

always spiritually stronger, sometimes physically stronger, too. They hold up better, though it costs them an awful lot."

From time to time Williams finds himself confronted with someone who tells him how much they enjoy his work. "I'm afraid I often think they are trying to make a fool of me. I have an unfortunate inability to believe in people's admiration, or even their acceptance. But I am so tortured each day by my failure to quite do at the typewriter what I intended to do at the typewriter, that it casts a shadow over the rest of the day, and it's during the rest of the day, naturally, that people might come up to me and tell me that they loved this or that. Under that shadow of the disappointment of the morning, I can't say that I believe them."

He looked disturbed. "But that's awful. I know it is."

Finally, Williams was asked about the influences on his life and work. He spoke without a second's hesitation, loudly and clearly, as though the answer were a bit of catechism he had learned by heart. "The strongest influences in my life and my work are always whomever I love. Whomever I love and am with most of the time, or whomever I *remember* most vividly. I think that's true of everyone, don't you?"

Tennessee Williams

John Gruen/1965

From *Close-Up* (New York: Viking, 1968), 86-95. ©1965 by
John Gruen. Reprinted by permission of Viking Penguin Inc.
"The Inward Journey of Tennessee Williams," a much briefer
version of the following interview, was published in the *New York
Herald Tribune Magazine*, 2 May 1965, 29.

Interviewer: The first question, Mr. Williams: Why do you write?

Williams: I know that there's nothing else I could do but write. I
don't believe there's such a thing as a born writer, but I—I couldn't
face a day without writing. The day would seem so completely empty
to me that by the time the evening came I would feel like shooting
myself.

Interviewer: When did you realize that writing was your particular
calling? What prompted you, as a child, or as a young man, to put
pen to paper?

Williams: Well, I didn't start writing until I was ten years old; I
startled the high-school English teacher by writing what she thought
was a very good theme. You remember they called them "themes" in
those days. I suppose they still do. A written assignment of more or
less creative kind. My subject was the Lady of Shalott. The teacher
told us to look around the room—there were many framed
pictures—and pick out a picture to write about. In one of the pictures,
the Lady of Shalott was drifting down the river on a boat of some
kind—and having even then a somewhat romantic attitude toward
things, I picked her out for my theme. I read it in front of the class,
and it met with a very good reception. From that time on, I knew that
I was going to be a writer. I thought I would be a writer—you know—
without a success; I never was optimistic at all.

Interviewer: What was the climate of your childhood?

Williams: My childhood was happy until the age of seven, when I
took very ill. We had a family doctor who was rather puzzled by

112

diseases, I think mine at least: he diagnosed my disease as diphtheria; say after four or five months of it, I developed a disease which he diagnosed just as inaccurately as Bright's disease. By that time, I was so weak that I had to push myself along the floor. I couldn't walk. Naturally, I became, and from that time on remained, a neurotic and introverted child. I remember developing my first true neurosis at the age of ten. I was terrified to go to sleep at night, because sleep seemed to me so similar to death. I had my first nervous breakdown—this sounds awfully maudlin—when I was in the shoe business in Saint Louis. I had stuck at it for three years. Working all day at the shoe company as a clerk typist and staying up all night writing—drinking black coffee, as black and strong as I could make it—and banging away on a typewriter.

I was a pretty good quick typist, and I could bang the hell out of the machine. But I was banging the hell out of myself at the same time, and all of a sudden one night something funny happened in my chest. My heart, which I had never been conscious of before in my life, began to beat like something syncopated, you know, one, two, pause, three. It was simply all that black coffee and the strain of my unhappiness in the shoe company. I did what I suppose is the most inadvisable thing that a person *could* do under those circumstances: I rushed out of the house. Pell-mell. And I walked for hours with my heart going like that, and I thought—let's see, I must have been twenty-three at the time—I thought I was about to drop dead any minute. I never even thought about *having* a heart—you know, having an organ in my body—and here I was suddenly confronted with the frantic heart. And in my chest.

I walked at a very fast pace for about three hours. And I remember I passed—it was very early in the spring when this happened—I remember I passed under some trees that were just beginning to bloom. Now this sounds very corny and romantic, I know, but I looked up at them, and somehow they gave me a feeling of comfort. I knew I was going to survive.

Interviewer: What was the first play you saw?

Williams: In Saint Louis, where I lived as a schoolboy and as a young adult, there was only one theater, called the American, downtown toward the river. Road shows came in there. I only made sixty-five dollars a month, and so I couldn't afford an orchestra seat or even the first balcony. I had to sit up in what we called the peanut gallery. I saw *The Barretts of Wimpole Street* with Katharine Cornell, which I liked. I wasn't terribly thrilled by it, but I liked it. And then I saw one I can't remember. But the third I will never forget . . . that was Ibsen's *Ghosts* with Nazimova. And it was so fabulous, so terrifyingly exciting, that I couldn't stay in my seat! I suddenly jumped up and rushed out and began pacing the corridor of the peanut gallery, trying to hear what was being said on the stage, but at the same time I couldn't stand to watch it anymore. It was the scene in which Mrs. Alving realizes that her son, Oswald, you know, is afflicted with syphilis and that it has gone to his brain.

Interviewer: Had you been reading plays before that?

Williams: I'd been reading the plays of O'Neill and Shakespeare. I began reading Shakespeare when I was still in grade school. My grandfather had a complete set of Shakespeare. I was particularly enchanted by all the very violent plays.

Interviewer: If you would call any of the material you read "influences," which would they be?

Williams: I believe that the chief influence on me, as a playwright, was Chekhov.

Interviewer: What are your writing habits—that is to say, your *modus operandi* or ritual?

Williams: I'm glad you said "ritual," because it *is* a ritual. I write as soon as I get up in the morning—facing that terrible question as soon as possible: Will I be able to write today? And *how* will I write? I begin with two cups of coffee, rather strong coffee. And then I go to my bedroom and I give myself an injection to pick me up. At first, I was terrified of taking the injections—giving them to myself. But I've gradually learned to do it. And I give myself one c.c. of whatever the thing is, the formula—I don't know what it is. I just know that immediately after it I feel like a living being! Then I can go to my table and work. Some days, of course, the work doesn't go at all well. Other days it does go well. I type very fast. And if a page is marred at all, I tear it out of the typewriter and start another one. It's a terrible habit, because I should be able to scratch things out. But I hate a page covered with scratchings.

Interviewer: Do you write primarily in the morning, and how many hours?

Williams: Almost exclusively in the mornings. I write for two and a half hours, and sometimes on my good days, I will write for as many as five hours.

Interviewer: Can you write anywhere?

Williams: I have to write anywhere I am. Because, as I said, unless I begin a day with writing, the day is utterly vacuous for me. I feel it a lost day. That obviously indicates that my life is insufficient, you know, that my daily life is insufficient matter.

Interviewer: Do you work on more than one thing at a time? That is, are you able to skip from a play that you may be writing to a novel or some poetry?

Williams: Some mornings I get up and what I've been working on is repugnant to me. It doesn't seem to attract me at all. And I feel as if I'll never get anywhere with it. So then I shift to some other thing that I've been working on. So I find it absolutely necessary to have two things going at once, then I can shift back and forth.

Interviewer: What do you think it is in your plays that has ignited the imagination of the public?

Williams: I have a great desire to *excite* people! I find it easier to do in plays than in stories or poems. I've never felt that I was a good poet.

Interviewer: Your agent, Audrey Wood, once said that you liberated subject matter for a whole new generation of young playwrights. Do you feel that is true?

Williams: I don't think so, no. Though she's more inclined to put me down then to pay me compliments! I think she was paying too high a compliment there. On that occasion, I remember that I replied, "I'm very happy if I have opened doors for playwrights, but you know, Audrey, I don't want to be just a doorjamb."

Interviewer: Was it difficult for you to get your plays put on?

Williams: Yes, there was a tremendous trouble about that! And maybe a lot of it is understandable. I've always had a tendency to go overboard, I think—to write too violently. This morning—no, it was early this afternoon—I told my doctor about a dream I'd had. He said that, yes, well, we *know* you have a lot of violence in you. But we can't take that out right now.

Interviewer: You wrote an article in the *New York Times* in which you described the sudden success that came to you when *The Glass*

Menagerie opened . . . a moving account of suddenly finding
yourself famous and of having rented an extraordinary suite in a very
expensive hotel . . . beautiful damask covers on the sofa, and so
forth. But you suddenly realized that all this wasn't what you wanted
from fame at all. [30 November 1947, sec. 2, 1, 3—Editor]

Williams: I don't think the furnishings of that little suite would
bother me anymore. Because it was just an ordinary hotel suite. But
I'd been living in the YMCA, you know, and the Men's Residence
Club, and places like that, where you can get a room for seven-fifty
or ten dollars a week. So naturally, it seemed very posh to me to be
in that suite. And I was on a high floor and had a wonderful view
over the East River. But the most important thing always was simply
to sit down and write. Nothing else was terribly important.

Interviewer: You also found a very peculiar change in the
attitudes of your friends.

Williams: Yes, I suddenly realized that I was in the position of
being a professional writer. Always, before, I had been an amateur
writer in the sense of one who loves to write. Now I was a
professional writer, and that disturbed me terribly.

Interviewer: To what extent are your plays autobiographical?

Williams: All creative work is autobiographical.

Interviewer: You have created a most provocative gallery of
female characters—like Blanche DuBois to the Gnädiges Fraülein.
Have you an *idée fixe* regarding women, and Southern women in
particular?

Williams: I don't know why I find it much easier, much more
interesting to write about women. My sister and my mother were
both very articulate women. They talked with great charm. In most of
my writings I try to recapture the charm of the way they talked.

Interviewer: Many of your women have a streak in them either of
violence or of great vulnerability—such as Blanche DuBois—often a
layer of refinement underneath, which, in many cases, is a broken
spirit.

Williams: I never find broken spirits in women I admire. My sister,
as everyone knows by this time, is a mental invalid, afflicted with
schizophrenia. I can say this because she would never hear it. But her
spirit is much stronger than my spirit. Nobody who tried to put her
down could possibly put her down.

Interviewer: Your male characters, on the other hand, seem marked with characteristics that suggest either a kind of ruggedness, à la Stan Kowalski, or weakness, like Brick?

Williams: I'm afraid I don't identify very easily with these Stanley Kowalskis and so forth. Maybe I should. They are a sort of mystery to me.

Interviewer: Among your plays, which is your favorite?

Williams: That's a question that would naturally come up. It's a question that I never know how to answer. Naturally, one is always hopeful that the play he's working on at the present time is the play that means most. There are certain plays where I've felt that. Others I realized were not important plays—I don't think that *Period of Adjustment* was important. I'm not sure I thought *Rose Tattoo* was an important play, although I worked on it very intensely. I wrote it during a period in which I was very happy in my life. The plays of mine which I think had more importance were *Streetcar, The Glass Menagerie*—the two most people think are my best—and *Cat on a Hot Tin Roof.*

Now, the longest play—that is to say, the play that I worked on longest—was *The Milk Train Doesn't Stop Here Anymore.* It has had several productions. First with Hermione Baddeley, who was incredibly good in it, though the play failed despite her brilliance. And then the following year, I managed to have it done again, and this time Tallulah Bankhead played in it with Tab Hunter. Tab Hunter was not my choice, although he proved to be a better actor than I would have expected of a Hollywood juvenile. But Tallulah Bankhead, she was just right for it. Why did it fail? It did fail. [New York: Brooks Atkinson Theatre, 1 January 1964—Editor]

Interviewer: I recently read that there was still a third version of *Milk Train.*

Williams: I went to San Francisco to work with the Actor's Workshop there. A very brilliant young director named John Hancock dug it as a Gothic play. And he did the most extraordinary things—I have a whole set of colored pictures of it. While I don't think it received good notices, it still is playing to full houses there. [Encore Theatre, 23 July 1965—Editor]

Interviewer: You believe, obviously, in revision?

Williams: Yes, I revise continually, because I'm never quite satisfied. I set for myself a certain thing to say. And I never am sure that I've said it exactly. *Camino Real* was a mutilated play. It had my best writing in it. But there were things in it that didn't quite seem rational, even in the terms of the wildness of the play. There were puzzling dichotomies. After his death, Kilroy snatches the gold heart from his own body and he rushes to a pawnbroker with it. The pawnbroker can *see* him. Which is odd. Since he is dead. The pawnbroker can *see* him and accepts the gold heart and gives him all kinds of . . . all kinds of things that would appeal to a gypsy's daughter. And he rushes to the gypsy's daughter with them, and he cries up to her. And the gypsy's daughter thinks it is just a cat!

Interviewer: You recently told an interviewer that your particular contribution to the poetic or lyric drama may no longer be wanted by today's theater public.

Williams: At present, the theater is reduced to so many musicals, you know. And the theater of the absurd, which can't appeal to me. I can't really work in the theater of the absurd. I can work in fantasy— in romantic fantasy—and I can work in very far-out plays. But I could never just make a joke out of human existence.

Interviewer: What do you suppose has happened to the theatrical climate—I mean even in serious plays?

Williams: The obvious answer is that people have lost their sense of decency.

Interviewer: A number of your plays, such as *Camino Real* and *Night of the Iguana* and *Suddenly Last Summer*, have exotic backgrounds which provide wonderful atmosphere. When such milieus are used, do you mean them to be adjuncts to the texture of your plays, or are they locales that all have a personal and special meaning for you? *The Night of the Iguana,* for example, was set in Mexico.

Williams: I was in Acapulco when it was still a primitive and charming Mexican village. With a great deal of poetry about it, I thought. Now it is more like Las Vegas, I'm afraid.

Interviewer: In reading each of your plays, one detects that the strong are ultimately the most vulnerable, and the weak turn out to have the greater strength and endurance. Is this your observation of life in general?

Williams: I think the weak—if they are not just pusillanimous—

are compelled to have more strength than those who are overtly strong. They wouldn't survive at all unless they had this inner strength. They may suffer a great deal for it—and I suppose they do. But I've always felt that Blanche was stronger than Stanley Kowalski.

Interviewer: What is your reaction to theater criticism? Do you consider it valuable, or do you consider it destructive?

Williams: I'm always profoundly impressed by how critics turn out the reviews in such a short time. But I always think that they try to be as fair as possible. They have certain prejudices, like all of us. There are one or two plays of mine that I felt they could have been kinder to. Notably *Orpheus Descending,* and perhaps my last play, *Milk Train.*

Interviewer: You're noted to be shy and a lonely person. How have these qualities colored your work?

Williams: Sometimes I think I'm shy as a rhinoceros.

Interviewer: But there is some truth about it?

Williams: Why do you think I go to doctors?

Interviewer: What about that school of thought that says, If you are an artist, avoid psychoanalysts?

Williams: Well, I discussed that with the doctor today, and he said, "Tom"—which is my name, not Tennessee. He said, "Tom, don't you know you're doing most of the work?" He said, "I'm learning from *you—you're* telling me, I'm not telling you." I don't know if I'm crazy about Freud or Karen Horney, or any of them—I just know that if I like the analyst (and I like the one I'm going to now), something does happen to help me get through the day.

Interviewer: What about those plays of yours that have been made into films? Which film versions, for example, have pleased you and which have not?

Williams: Every film which Kazan made of my work—he made two. *Baby Doll* pleased me very much—that was an original film script. What Kazan did with *Streetcar,* of course, pleased me enormously. I also loved what was done with *Orpheus Descending* on the screen—Magnani and Brando, although they didn't get along very well, you know.

Interviewer: What happened?

Williams: Sid Lumet directed it brilliantly. Against great obstacles.

Interviewer: What about *Cat on a Hot Tin Roof?*

Williams: I was not happy about the film of *Cat on a Hot Tin Roof.*

Interviewer: Did you think Liz Taylor was miscast?

Williams: No, I think she was brilliantly cast. I thought that the screenplay itself, which I did *not* write, was somehow, not quite what I meant to say.

Interviewer: Would you comment on your latest plays at all?

Williams: *Slapstick Tragedy.* I don't think they'll work. These plays are in the same vein as *Camino Real, and Camino Real* didn't go over well. Besides, I'm considerably older than I was . . . and it's harder as you get older. You have to work much harder and much longer on everything you do. The human animal is subject to attrition, he gets tired. And he has to go to wonderful doctors like Doctor Max.

Interviewer: Which of the younger playwrights do you admire?

Williams: It's so very easy to answer that. I'm sorry you said "younger," because I am going to say Beckett, who isn't younger. I have a great feeling for Edward Albee. I've never seen any play of his that I didn't think was absolutely thrilling. He is truly a major playwright, America's major playwright.

Interviewer: What about such contemporaries as Arthur Miller?

Williams: Arthur has a great deal of dynamic quality. He's a fine writer. When I went through Greece a year ago last spring, some reporters told me that he had been through a little before me and that he said that I didn't write from my head or from my heart but from my abdomen! It did put me off a bit (I don't know how you hit a typewriter with your abdomen), but I still haven't changed my opinion of Arthur Miller.

I met Faulkner three times. He seemed as shy as imaginable. He was with a very beautiful girl, and he could only talk in whispers to her. I didn't try to draw him into a conversation. The second meeting was in Paris and a very beautiful girl was with him again. Again, there was the situation of his looking down, not up, and not talking. I had that situation too: it's very hard for me to talk sometimes, and one of my phobias is that I will not be *able* to talk. But Faulkner actually didn't talk *at all*. And finally I felt, you know, that I had to talk directly to him. So I did. I talked to Faulkner directly. Suddenly he lifted his eyes, and I saw such suffering in them that I felt tears coming into my eyes.

Interviewer: How does a playwright observe life?

Williams: It's a gradual process. It's very gradual. My day-to-day life has a great deal to do with it, I suppose. I don't think I know how to answer that.

Interviewer: If I may intrude on a kind of personal situation of yours. Do you have a very active inner life?

Williams: Oh, terrifyingly active, yes.

Interviewer: What are the sorts of things that occupy your thoughts?

Williams: Life and death. In the past two years, I have had two dear friends who died—and it shocked me unbearably. And I thought they shouldn't have been allowed to suffer as they did. I don't know why. One of them was on the bed that has to tilt back and forth like a seesaw to keep circulation going. And the movement of the contraption caused agony. So I don't think death is a thing that one should go through except of his own volition in his own way. I don't believe in hospitals. I hope I will never be confined to one. I hope that when I have to die I will arrange it myself.

Hemingway had the great feeling for man's ability to choose. He was an existentialist—he understood it long before Sartre did, you know. Perhaps we all understood existentialism before Sartre did. Hemingway did the brave and the right thing, the dignified thing, I believe. Because what could the end of his life have been, you know, but a thing that might have reduced him to crying—people become almost deprived of their will at the end of their lives. They mustn't allow themselves to reach that point. Maybe their doctors must not allow them to reach it.

Interviewer: Do you find it difficult to live? Is it a struggle for an artist?

Williams: It all depends on how well you've worked that day. If you've worked, if you think that you've accomplished *something* that day, the day is brighter for you, and you get through the day reasonably well.

Interviewer: Do you feel that there is an end of the road for a writer, as far as his creative energies are concerned?

Williams: Why yes, everyone knows that.

Interviewer: I have read many biographies of writers, and autobiographies. Every writer finds it increasingly difficult to write after his youth has been gone through, though in some ways, he is able to compensate by the accumulation of experience.

Williams: You should remember that you're always competing with your earlier work. You have to. In my particular case, they all say, Oh, that *Glass Menagerie!* until you almost begin to hate it! Because you know you have been working fiercely all the time since. And it's not quite possible to believe that you haven't created something since then.

Interviewer: What about acting? And directors, and the whole milieu of the theater? Do you enjoy the by-products of being a playwright?

Williams: I've always been very shy around actors, because I don't believe they can help resenting the playwright. The playwright has written the play, and they're playing it. They conceal it very nicely, but still the playwright feels that they must resent him.

Interviewer: Some actors have nothing but the greatest admiration for you.

Williams: There are certain ones, yes. Those that see that you're as tortured as they are.

Interviewer: How do you feel about Tallulah Bankhead playing Blanche DuBois? [Miami: Coconut Grove Playhouse, 16 January-4 February 1956; New York: City Center Theatre, 15 February 1956— Editor]

Williams: I thought she finally delivered a very powerful performance. She was like a tiger—a tigress, I mean!

Interviewer: There were so many snickers at the performance. Why was that?

Williams: That is because poor Tallulah attracts a certain public which is inclined to laugh—not at her, but at her public image.

Interviewer: Why did Elia Kazan succeed in giving such aura to the plays of yours he directed?

Williams: The relationship between the director and the playwright is a very delicate, dangerous relationship. Kazan and I worked it out extremely well. We enjoyed working together, and

Kazan seemed to dig my work, and I certainly was crazy about his direction.

Interviewer: Is there any area of the theater that you have not yet explored that you would like to try?

Williams: I can't think of any area of the theater that I *haven't* tried to explore. I've written realistic plays, I have written fantasies, I've written allegories. This year I've worked on a novella. But a terrible accident occurred. Yesterday morning. I took the novella out of its envelope and all the pages spilled on the floor. Two-thirds of the pages are not numbered, and it's going to be a terrible task to reassemble the pages.

Interviewer: Can you tell us what it's about?

Williams: It's called *The Knightly Quest.*

Interviewer: What is it about?

Williams: I would never dream of telling you.

September 1965

PS   The above interview, done in September 1965, did not pass muster with George Plimpton, who had asked me to do it for his "Art of the Theater" series in the *Paris Review*. In all fairness, it should also be stated that Williams himself was not particularly pleased with the above. I, on the other hand, found it enlightening, often poignant, and certainly interesting, but the reader must arrive at his own conclusions about that. . . .

Tennessee Williams
Walter Wager/1966

From *The Playwrights Speak* (New York: Delacorte Press, 1967), 213, 224-237. © 1967 by Walter Wager. Reprinted by permission of Curtis Brown, Ltd.

Tennessee Williams flew up to New York in January 1966 from his home in Key West, Florida, for the production of *Slapstick Tragedy*, and it was during the first week of rehearsals that this interview was recorded in the playwright's pleasant apartment on one of the upper floors of an ultra-modern "co-op" monolith on West 72nd Street. The questions were put by the editor of this book; a very brief edition of the interview was published in the March 1966 number of *Playbill*.

Q.: How do you literally write a play; where do you begin? Does an idea nurture within you for a long time? Do the characters come first and then the story?

Williams: It is almost impossible to pinpoint the start of the play, at least for me. I think that all plays come out of some inner tension in the playwright himself. He is concerned about something, and that concern begins to work itself out in the form of a creative activity. Sometimes I will get up in the morning and feel a little more energetic than usual and I will just start writing.

Q.: With a pen or with a typewriter—how do you work?

Williams: Typewriter—I typewrite very rapidly.

Q.: You were saying that sometimes you get up in the morning and start to write dialogue.

Williams: Yes, something on a page or two pages of dialogue will spark in the way of characters or situation and I just go along from there. I am a very wasteful writer. I go through several drafts, as many as four or five before I finish a work. I am sure that any playwright would give you practically the same description.

Q.: Albee said to me that he writes a play when it becomes more painful not to write it than to write it.

Williams: That's a very good way of putting it, you know.

Q.: Then the subject literally forces itself out?

Williams: Yes, some people accuse you of being too personal, you know, in your writing. The truth of the matter is—I don't think you can escape being personal in your writing.

Q.: Impossible.

Williams: That doesn't mean that you are one of the characters in the play. What it means simply is that the dynamics of the characters in the play, the tensions correspond to something that you are personally going through—the concerns of the play and the tensions of the play and your own concerns and tensions at the time you wrote it. I have always found that to be true.

Q.: I have noticed that in many of your plays there is poetry or one of your characters is a poet, and I have heard from someone you know, the former drama critic of the St. Louis *Post-Dispatch*, that you began or have done a great deal of poetry writing, and yet you don't write much poetry now. Why have you given up poetry? I have read your poetry and it's excellent.

Williams: I found that I had written enough poetry—I mean in the form of poems; I think plays can be just as lyrical as a poem can be; you can use just as much personal lyricism in a play as you can in a poem; and also I have noticed as writers get older—that is, poets—they tend to write less poetry. I think actual poetry is a medium more for the young than for the middle-aged.

Q.: I think the question of age is an interesting one because in the introduction to one of your plays, I think *The Rose Tattoo*, you mention "the continual rush of time that deprives life of dignity and meaning." Does this question of aging trouble you now that you have turned fifty? Is it something that you are going to be writing about?

Williams: I think I have always written quite a bit about it. We were having a poker game up here last night and at one point the game got too mixed up and somebody knocked a glass off the table accidently; there was no violence involved; and suddenly all at once I began to talk about age. I said, "I can't believe it, I am fifty-four years old now, and I think the reason it is so incredible to me that I have suddenly reached this age is that each year is not another year to me—it's a play." And sometimes three years are a play and my life seems to be chalked off not in years but in plays and pieces of work, and so I am taken by surprise by how much time has passed and my being as old as I am.

Q.: I am stunned, myself, when I read your biography this afternoon—to see the numbers—your age; but I have no sense of the writing of this being the work of a man of forty or fifty or any age. I have read them as plays; none of that has come through, although some of your recent plays have been concerned with older people, such as the *Slapstick Tragedy*, which is about to open now.

Williams: There is no particular age in that.

Q.: There are elderly women in it.

Williams: It seems to exist outside of any specific time and, no, they are not elderly women. We are not going to age the women in the plays; they are going to appear the same ages as the actresses actually are playing. Well, the play is so "way out" that it will not have to be pinpointed in time.

Q.: The question of pinpointing them in plays is also an interesting one. Most of your plays, I believe, are set in the South, where you grew up, yet, do you consider yourself a Southern writer, because the questions you raise seem to be universally applicable to me?

Williams: I think I am becoming less associated with the South than I was originally. I was a Southern writer because my parents were Southern and I was born in the South. Now, my father was from Tennessee and my mother from Ohio, so it was a sort of split between. Would you say Ohio is the North?

Q.: Well, I guess you would say that it is on the verge of the South.

Williams: She was from Southern Ohio but she went to East Tennessee when she was a very young girl, so she grew up to be a Southerner.

Q.: Why did you take the name of "Tennessee"?

Williams: Because my father's family were Tennesseans. They were very active in the making of the State of Tennessee.

Question: And everyone calls you "Tennessee" now?

Williams: No, I prefer people to call me "Tom," my real name. Of course, you know in professional meetings people call me "Tennessee."

Q.: Your good friends call you "Tom."

Williams: People with whom I am close to, I always ask them to call me "Tom"; it's easier and I like the name "Tom."

Q.: You are the grandchild of an Episcopal minister?

Williams: Oh yes, he was almost my closest relation.

Q.: Are you still actively involved in any discernible religion?

Williams: Well, I keep a Russian icon by my bed. It was given to me by a dear friend in London for my birthday. It is a very beautiful Russian icon and I don't suppose I would keep it there if I didn't have some religious feeling; it is obvious that I do have religious feeling. It may seem ingenuous to have religious feeling to a lot of people but to me it seems necessary.

Q.: Could you define this religious feeling?

Williams: Well, it isn't associated with any particular church. It's just a general feeling of one's dependence upon some superior being of mystic nature.

Q.: Does God or religion come up much in your plays? I haven't seen it specifically.

Williams: Oh, yes, I notice the word "God" occurring several times in the recent disaster.

Q.: In one of your interviews you said that in only a few moments of life is there really human contact. Does that mean you feel it is basically a rather lonely existence?

Williams: Now, that is probably some quotation that is not an exact quotation, because I certainly don't feel that. I feel that in many, many moments in life there is almost continual contact; under what circumstances I said that I can't imagine, because it isn't what I feel—at least not what I feel *now*.

Q.: When you were a child, I heard an anecdote told that you once were out in the back yard digging.

Williams: Oh yes, that was one of my mother's favorite stories.

Q.: What were you digging for—devils?

Williams: Yes, she said—I am sure she was telling the truth—it was quite a funny story. She found me digging in the back yard. She said, What are you digging for? I said I was digging for the devil.

Q.: In a sense, do you still think you're digging for the devil in these plays?

Williams: In a sense, yes; but I am also digging for the opposite of the devil.

Q.: For the angels?

Williams: For God.

Q.: In one of your comments you state the plays represent a struggle between good and evil—of man's struggle between good and evil. How would you define good and evil in our contemporary society?

Williams: I don't think it needs definition. It is so obvious. We all know—when I look at the papers that arrive every morning, it is just incredible what is going on; you know that so much is fantastically abominable going on. This whole Vietnam bit is so incomprehensibly evil to me.

Q.: You mean the killing that is going on there?

Williams: Yes, the naphtha—what is that?

Q.: Napalm.

Williams: The way they burn people alive and the way they spray chemicals over the rice fields so they will starve; I don't need to list the instruments . . .

Q.: You are talking about the cruelty of modern weapons rather than the political connotation.

Williams: Yes, they are incredibly cruel and, believe me, nothing that will be won out of this war will be worth the life of a single man who died in it, in my opinion.

Q.: Do you have equally strong feelings about the civil-rights movement in the South?

Williams: Yes, equally strong.

Q.: Because you haven't touched that much in your writing, or do I do you an injustice?

Williams: I always try to write obliquely. I think the closest I came to writing directly was in *Orpheus Descending* about my feelings about what goes on in certain parts of the country.

Q.: I have found it interesting that a number of the Southern writers, such as yourself and the late Mr. Faulkner, didn't really comment too directly on this question. They were primarily concerned with human struggles of a more general nature.

Williams: I don't see the difference between them. I think they were so closely interrelated that I don't see how you can divide the two things.

Q.: Do you think that you would ever write directly on this question?

Williams: I am not a direct writer; I am always an oblique writer, if I can be; I want to be allusive; I don't want to be one of these people who hit the nail on the head all the time.

Q.: Have you always been this sort of writer—I mean as a child? By the way, did you write as a child?

Williams: I started to write around twelve.

Q.: And did you start writing in this allusive manner then, or probably less so?

Williams: Less so, of course, because children are more simple.

Q.: I hate to keep bringing up your past remarks as if to belabor you with them, but in one of the interviews you gave you spoke of the depravity and bestiality in life and went on along those lines—is this a current concern of yours?

Williams: I think it is of anyone who pauses to think and who has some perception.

Q.: Now, on the question of perception, I recently read a critical study of your plays that made reference to the obvious influence of Freud on your work. Is that a fair statement? Have you read a lot of Freud?

Williams: I looked into maybe a book or two of Freud but I never read any of it.

Q.: You observed it in life?

Williams: To the extent that I have any connection with Freud—I think Freud did illuminate many dark areas in the human unconscious, and I think I write mainly from my unconscious mind.

Q.: And do you write day or night? Is there any special time you write?

Williams: I find it almost impossible to write any time but the morning, when I have more energy to write.

Q.: Is it early morning, or after breakfast?

Williams: Immediately after breakfast.

Q.: And do you require any special conditions?

Williams: Oh, yes, I require many special conditions. I have quite a ritual.

Q.: Tell us about it.

Williams: Do you want to know about the whole ritual? I think that should be a secret of my own. I think that should be my secret . . . whatever makes it possible for me to work, I should do, because I must work. Up to 1955 I found it much easier to work, and after 1955 I was conscious of a certain fatigue, and now, well, when I get up in the morning . . . let me give you a few little clues—I have anemia, which is rather a problem. I don't know how severe it is, or if anemia is the right word for it, but it is the word that is used; and I have to get up in the morning and give myself an injection, which peps me up sufficiently to get to the goddam desk. And combined with the shot, there's also the two strong cups of coffee; and then I always have one of these martinis on my writing table; I don't take more than one. But I found after 1955, specifically after *Cat on a Hot Tin Roof*—that I needed these things to give me the physical energy to work; and the intelligent thing might have been to stop working, to rest. But I am a compulsive writer. I have tried to stop working and I am bored to death. . . . I don't know what I am here for . . . what is the purpose of my being here.

Q.: I am pleased that you are so compulsive . . . and we all benefit from it every year or two.

Williams: Well, occasionally I hope that somebody gets something out of it.

Q.: Do you have any sense of being isolated now or lonely? I have heard somebody say that, that because one or two of your plays haven't been received as some of the earlier plays, that this has troubled you.

Williams: I have never been without terrific anxiety about all of my work. You know, it's constitutional with me to be anxious as all hell about all of my work. I'll never get over that and I never hope to; I just have to live with it.

Q.: I guess that's the nature of being a writer—you put your head on the block every time you put a piece of paper into the machine.

Williams: Yes, of course you do, and it takes a physical toll of your nervous energies. You've got to do all kinds of things to try to make yourself stand up under it. Now, I am not a self-destructive person; I try to keep myself going. Every afternoon I go to the YMCA and I will swim sixteen or twenty lengths of the pool; that is when I am in New York. When I am in Key West I will swim, I would say, about half a mile in the sea.

Q.: Do you do most of your writing in Key West or here?

Williams: I enjoy writing in Key West more than I do here; but I have to be here right now.

Q.: Now, about the other playwrights—first of all, which playwrights do you think have interested you or influenced your work in the past?

Williams: Strindberg and Chekhov—if you are talking about master playwrights of the past.

Q.: And which of the current playwrights interest you, American or foreign?

Williams: American or foreign—nobody now, because I have my own way which has crystallized for me and nobody influences me anymore.

Q.: Which playwrights interest you rather than influence you?

Williams: Interest me? They all interest me if they're good. I think in America Edward Albee is by a good margin the most interesting of the new American playwrights.

Q.: Do you read much in the way of novels?

Williams: I don't have much taste for fiction recently—that is, in the last ten years or so, I prefer to read journals and books, collected letters of writers and of the people's biographies. Right now I am reading *The Diary of Anäis Nin,* who is one of our very fine writers.

Q.: You don't travel as much as you used to; does this mean you are settling down more in America, you are more at ease in America?

Williams: It means, I think, mainly that I don't have the energy to bat around the world like I used to. I went around the world once and lived a good deal of my time during the last fifteen years or more in Rome, Italy, and I saw most of the interesting cities in Europe, cities interesting to me, but now I don't know whether I can resume that sort of traveling or not; I am rather dubious that I can.

Q.: There are two more questions that I would like to ask you. One, you have stated in an earlier interview that you found the state of contemporary society terrifying.

Williams: That I am sure I have said because I really do find it so.

Q.: What sort of things do you particularly find terrifying to you?

Williams: All the things you see on the front page of the morning paper.

Q.: Violence, cruelty, dishonor?

Williams: All those things—the senseless wars going on; you know, so many things—the struggle for civil rights. . . . I'm not a person dedicated primarily to bettering social conditions, because I am not able to, except through my writing, and I doubt whether people will pay enough attention to writing for writing to have any effect.

Q.: You said one more thing. You said, "I don't think America must settle for its present state; you must go forward and be unafraid." In what areas must we go forward, do you think; in what areas must we move?

Williams: I think we are moving in some good areas now. We were just talking about the civil rights.

Q.: That's important?

Williams: That's very important and we are making progress— not as fast as we might hope for—and there is some very ugly opposition to it; but it seems to me we are making some remarkable progress in that direction. I feel that finally American people have a sense of justice. It may take them a while to formulate it because there are so many false leaders—you know, politicians like Senator Dirksen and Mr. Nixon; and there was the late Senator McCarthy; there are so many people like that who are impeding the spirit of American people—their understanding, I mean.

Q.: On the question of the spirit of American people, do you have any particular feeling about the young people today?

Williams: I love what the young people of today are doing. They don't seem to be scared of anything, except their own shadows, maybe, and that's wonderful. It's wonderful how they can go out and face police bullies in the South, Ku Klux Klan, the whole bit, and they do have that courage, and it's marvelous. I think this is one of the great generations of young people that we now have.

Q.: Finally, you said: "I'd rather stay an outsider than adjust to injustice." Do you still think of yourself as an outsider?

Williams: Outside of what?

Q.: Outside of the main social stream, in America.

Williams: I am very much a part of it, I hope; I hope to be always.

Q.: So you don't feel outside anymore?

Williams: No, I never did really; if I said that I was kidding somebody, not myself.

Q.: I thank you very much, Mr. Williams. You were very kind and generous with your time. You make a wicked martini, too.

Williams: I hope it made some sense.

Talking with Tennessee Williams
Dan Isaac/1969

From *After Dark,* October 1969, 46-50. ©1969 by *After Dark.*
Reprinted by permission.

"I hate living in hotels. I don't know why I picked this one."
Tennessee Williams laughed as he said this. We were sitting in his
suite at the Plaza, and I had just commented on how antique the
grand old place was getting to look. There was too much white in the
room—white tables, white chairs, white walls—making it look
somehow like a badly fashioned set for a play he never wrote but
might have. *Color isn't passive. It has a fierce life to it.* It was
Saturday night, and Mr. Williams had just postponed by a week the
opening of his new play, *In the Bar of a Tokyo Hotel.* Having decided
to do some rewriting, he had taken over the direction of the play as
well.

The first thing I had noticed when I walked into his hotel room was
a copy of Merton's translation of *The Way of Chuang Tzu.* (Because
of his involvement with Eastern thought, Williams' plays have become
increasingly recondite—but for those who understand them,
increasingly beautiful.) Williams told me later that his publisher had
sent this book to him, along with a couple of others: collections of
poems by Lawrence Ferlinghetti and Gary Snyder. But it was the
Chuang Tzu that he apparently was reading. *Inner Sources of
Serenity.* When he sat down, Mr. Williams cleared the little table in
front of the couch so that he might serve me a drink. And as he
carried off some scraps of paper with fragments of dialogue written in
longhand—most probably lines that would soon be inserted into
Tokyo Hotel—he said: "File this crap under crap." He was, of course,
quoting a line from his own play, *Camino Real.*

Maybe Tennessee Williams was quoting himself to me as a way of
getting through an interview at an hour that was difficult for him.
There were moments when nothing was said and a thick silence hung

between us. Curiously, though, during those moments I heard his voice in my head answering me from the silence with fragments of dialogue from *Tokyo Hotel: Crossing the frontier of a country I have no permission to enter.* I had been to the first preview and thought it to be a great play. But it was also a difficult and unyielding one. In some ways, it didn't give much to the audience. *In the beginning, a new style of work can be stronger than you.*

Tennessee Williams looked tired and moved slowly. He apologized for having just woken up a few minutes before, commenting that the strain of rehearsals and rewriting was beginning to get to him. He said that he missed his two or three hours of swimming a day, admitting that he was obsessive about it, that it was his therapy. Then he added that not getting this exercise was causing him to deteriorate physically. This too was spoken with a wry smile, a smile that was more in the weary tone of voice than in anything visual, causing whatever he uttered to come out whimsically hyperbolic. "I'm too old a man to be going to the Y."

Having heard that he had been seriously ill during the winter, I asked him about the current state of his health. "Deplorable," was the answer that came with a kind of comic majesty. It was the same grandiose tone that he had used with a sophomoric middle-aged lady who approached him deferentially during the intermission of the first preview of *Tokyo Hotel* to ask if he was the author of *The Rose Tattoo.* His mock majestic reply on that occasion was: "Indisputably."

We had been waiting some time for room service to send up some coffee, when the bellboy finally knocked and entered with a single long stemmed yellow flower in a huge white vase. There was no note, but Williams was certain it was from his leading lady, Anne Meacham. "She sends me flowers every night," he said gesturing toward several arboreal collections in different corners of the room, one of them the young sprouts of a dogwood tree. *The disguised rapacity of a flower means nothing to me.* The yellow flower that neither of us could identify was placed next to a vase already choked with petals, left to languish leaning against a lamp. For a while Mr. Williams talked about how wonderful both Anne Meacham and Donald Madden were in the leading roles of *Tokyo Hotel,* particularly the marvelous way they had of learning the new lines he would give them at rehearsals, integrating them immediately into the flow of their performance. "Madden is amazing. I hardly have to write the lines for him, he memorizes them right after my reading them aloud."

Still waiting for the coffee, we discussed the critics. Williams was very concerned with what Clive Barnes would say about the play. "He's a tough critic and I don't think he likes me very much." He had great praise for Walter Kerr who he thought was the best around. Williams went on to say that he probably wouldn't even read the reviews, for the day after the opening he was flying to Italy for a vacation that would include much swimming in the sea. I wondered if he was bluffing, or was he really that cool that he could take off without even bothering to read the notices after having worked so long and hard on the play. I told him that I thought *Tokyo Hotel* would get the good reviews it deserved, but not entirely for the right reasons. I gave him my theory of how I thought the critics every once in awhile got the guilties, and after having been extraordinarily cruel to one play were extraordinarily kind to the next one the playwright produces, and even the next one after that. With some hesitation I pointed to the laudatory reviews given *Sweet Bird of Youth*. I argued that it wasn't that good a play. "The critics," I continued, "were still overcompensating for what they had done to *Orpheus Descending.*" To my surprise Williams agreed with me on *Sweet Bird.* In fact, he had made his own critical assessment of this play some time ago. Two years *after* its successful Broadway run, he had done considerable rewriting of the play for a production in Los Angeles. [Civic Playhouse, 1 November 1961—Editor]

The coffee finally came and we began to talk a little about *Tokyo Hotel.* It reminded me so much in style of the one act work, *I Can't Imagine Tomorrow,* (published only in the March, 1966 issue of Esquire)—a two character play where the man is so inarticulate that the woman has to complete all of his sentences for him—that I wondered aloud if *Tokyo Hotel* grew out of this play. Mr. Williams gave a negative to this suggestion, and after a silence replied somberly: "I don't complete many sentences these days." *I have no plans. I have nowhere to go.* I asked Mr. Williams if *I Can't Imagine Tomorrow*—which I have always regarded as a neglected masterpiece—had received a performance anywhere. Again there was a silence and a sense of sadness in his voice. "No attention, no production." Going back to my question about the inspiration for

Tokyo Hotel, Williams mentioned that down in Key West he went through a period where he was always falling down. *An artist has to lay his life on the line.*

In The Bar of A Tokyo Hotel is about a great artist whose most recent experimental work is beginning to exhaust, overpower, and finally destroy him. There is a great ambiguity about the nature of his illness. Subject to falling fits, the artist collapses and dies. In many ways it is a play about the most intimate and mystical of subjects: The relationship of an artist to the act of artistic creation.

There were questions about *Tokyo Hotel* that I wanted to ask—but something held me back, and now the silence was coming from me. Maybe it was the realization that everything I wanted to know had been said in the play itself. At one point in the second act the artist steps forward to the edge of the stage, looks out at the audience, and announces: "You thought I was talking to you. I was really talking to myself." What is the worth and sense of an interviewer's questions when a writer has already spoken so clearly—and despairingly—of his own work within the protective context of a fictive form. *You've always had your own style, but it's not what you're doing now.*

I turned the conversation to other things and asked the kinds of questions expected of an interviewer. Who were his favorite playwrights? "Beckett and Albee," he replied as though the answer were so obvious he couldn't quite understand why the question had been asked. Had he seen anything since coming back to New York? He had not had time for much, but had seen the last twenty minutes of *I Am Curious*—but was not curious enough to stick around for the rest of the picture after the intermission. What did he think of the newest movements in the theatre? "I don't want naked bodies in my plays. I want naked minds and naked hearts."

We talked a bit about some of the things that had brought the name of Tennessee Williams into the news over the course of the last year. During the winter, while he was sick with the Hong Kong flu, he had converted to Catholicism. Since then he had been to Rome, met and talked with the head of the Jesuits. And when the conversation turned to Williams' interest in Zen Buddhism, he said: "I don't think any church has fastened on to any great mystery." I waited for something to follow this remark, mysterious in itself, but it was left unilluminated. *If I should say the circle of light is the approving look of God it would sound romantic.* I asked him what had happened last summer when he was sending out reports that he was in the hands of unscrupulous people, saying that if he should die suddenly it would not be a suicide even though it might look that way. [*New York Times,* 29 June 1968, 19—Editor] *I was . . . always willing . . . to die.* To my surprise he readily volunteered an answer. "Last summer I got panicky, hysterical—put everything I owned in storage and went from hotel to hotel in New York." *A restless creature that lives in a private jungle.*

Knowing that Tennessee Williams is an obsessive writer as much as he is an obsessive swimmer, I asked what else he had in the works. *I've always approached my work with a frightened timidity.* He went to his bedroom and returned with four manuscripts that he placed on the table before me with a certain shy pride. One was a scenario based on his short story, "Three Players of a Summer Game." The other three were typewritten first drafts of one act plays. I was intrigued by the titles: *Now and at the Hour of Our Death; A Rectangle with Hooks; A Recluse and His Guest.* Sitting there on the table they seemed to radiate with a kind of restless energy, and for a moment I wanted to forget about talking to Tennessee Williams and read the plays. I looked at the first page of one of them and had to stop myself from going further. I also asked about the play he had referred to in his Sunday New York *Times* article last year, when he quoted a good hunk of dialogue from an unnamed work in progress. [24 March 1968, sec. 2, 1,3—Editor] A broad smile flashed across his face as he informed me that I must be thinking of *Will Mr. Merriwether Return from Memphis?* "It's about two women, neighbors," he told me, "both of whom receive apparitions." Bill Glavin, secretary and loyal friend to Tennessee Williams who had joined us at some point after the arrival of the coffee, also lit up at the mention of this work. "It's a very funny play," he warmly volunteered. Suddenly Williams was busy looking for the play and concerned that he couldn't find it. "That's what I ought to work on next, and I think I may have left it in my house down in Key West." Right then and there phone calls were placed down to Key West, but connections could not be made. Worried that the woman who minds the house for him might have fallen ill, even the local hospital was given a try—but all to no avail.

It was nine o'clock now, and time only for a fast dinner if Williams and Glavin were to get to the 79th Street Playhouse in time for the late performance that the theater ran at ten on Saturday nights. I thanked Tennessee Williams for letting me talk to him and apologized too much for taking his time. His response was kind, and he apologized in turn for being depressed and uncommunicative as he plainly was. He invited me to come back later in the week.

When I walked alone into the warm and summery night, I realized I was very high—inordinately so for having had but two drinks, scotch to Williams' coffees. I knew that part of this high was from at last having sat down and talked with the man whose work I so greatly loved—whose later plays, the mysteries, remain lamentably unknown and unappreciated. *He thought he could create his own circle of light.*

Then I remembered the story Bill Glavin had told me, the story about what happened at the first preview of *Tokyo Hotel* just after the play ended. A young man very much in the style of a hippie had come up to Tennessee Williams and said: "Man, that was a very deep trip." Talking with Tennessee Williams—the unfinished sentences and the silence—had been a very deep trip for me. *You thought I was talking to you.* Suddenly I looked up and saw a girl waiting for a bus whose young face was marred by a mask of makeup. *I was really talking to myself.* Thinking about how theatrical she was trying to look in a brave but pathetic way, I came back down into a world outside the circle of light where things were dark but more familiar. I was standing on the edge of Central Park and there were green leaves on the trees.

No division between us any more. Suddenly last spring.

Will God Talk Back to a Playwright? Tennessee Williams
David Frost/1970

From *The Americans* (New York: Stein and Day Publishers, 1970), 33-40. © 1970 by David Frost. Reprinted by permission of Stein and Day Publishers. The following interview is a briefer, edited version of Frost's conversation with Tennessee Williams on "The David Frost Show," WNEW-TV, New York, 21 January 1970.

Frost: A lot of your life has changed since you converted to Roman Catholicism, hasn't it?

Williams: Oh, yes. That was while I was around the bend. Not that I don't love the Church, I do. I love the Church very much, but I don't go to it. I work, instead.

Frost: But you did convert to Roman Catholicism?

Williams: Yes, I did.

Frost: Have you stopped that now?

Williams: It's hard to say. The Church can be so beautiful to look at, you know. I like to go in at odd hours, so none of the congregation is there. I like to go in when it's empty and just kneel down and sort of communicate with whatever there is to communicate with. I hope there is something.

Frost: Do you think there is something?

Williams: Yes, I do, strangely enough.

Frost: Do you call him God?

Williams: What other word is there? Godot, I suppose.

Frost: Not that a human being can define God if he is God, but what do you understand by God?

Williams: Whoever is responsible for the universe. Including us, you know.

Frost: Do you know anything about him? I mean, what is whoever is responsible for the universe like?

Williams: I think he has odd moments of compassion. I know that every time I have a play opening I will go into a room alone and kneel down and pray, and sometimes it's just a bathroom and I'll kneel down by the bathtub and I'll pray, and I always get a sort of affirmative or negative answer, meaning the show will go or it won't go, you know?

Frost: So you know before it goes on.

Williams: Not until after I've prayed.

Frost: But after you've prayed, and before it's opened, you know how it's going to do?

Williams: I get a sort of response, yes.

Frost: And when you say he is responsible for us and for the world, where does his responsibility leave off?

Williams: Oh, I don't think he's up in the sky or anything like that, you know. Where does our responsibility begin?

Frost: Yes.

Williams: With ourselves. We have to take that responsibility, it's a terrible one, but we have to assume it.

Frost: And what is the responsibility we have, each of us to ourselves, do you think?

Williams: We have to see that we are behaving in some sort of a decent fashion toward our fellow creatures, animal and human, don't you think?

Frost: I think particularly human, yes.

Williams: Particularly human, but animals, too.

Frost: Your plays are full of people with terrible problems and afflictions and so on; do you see life basically as a joyous thing or as a painful thing?

Williams: I find life quite pleasurable, even though I am insomniac. For instance, I don't sleep until about six in the morning, generally. But I enjoy those hours. I love reading and I even love just lying there and thinking.

Frost: Do you think your plays are basically gloomy?

Williams: People tell me they are, but I've never thought so.

Frost: Which would you say was the most hopeful play you've written?

Williams: Certainly *Period of Adjustment.* It is the only comedy I ever wrote, but then I saw it again and I suddenly realized it was not funny. There were laughs in it, but it was really more serious than I had thought. It had another title, which was a better title, actually, *Hi-Point Over a Cavern*. It was laid in the suburbs of a city and the suburb was named Hi-Point. My mother's house is built over an underground cavern. She discovered that after she'd bought it and moved in it began to sink little by little, and cracks appeared in the wall and the ceilings.

Frost: Has your own life influenced all that you've written a great deal? People say that they can see you in your plays.

Williams: I'm very personal as a writer, yes. I don't mean to be, I just am. Unavoidably.

Frost: Which is the most personal of your plays?

Williams: Perhaps *Camino Real*.

Frost: Why do you pick that?

Williams: It was sort of a statement of my own philosophy, a credo.

Frost: What is your credo?

Williams: That romanticism is absolutely essential. That we can't really live bearably without a good deal of it. It's very painful, but we need it.

Frost: By romanticism do you mean fantasy?

Williams: A certain amount of that and the ability to feel tenderness toward another human being. The ability to love.

Frost: And what gives people that ability?

Williams: Not allowing themselves to become brutalized by the brutalizing experiences that we do encounter on the Camino Real.

Frost: How would you define the word "love"?

Williams: Love is a feeling, isn't it?

Frost: What sort?

Williams: Oh, well, there's sexual love. The first time I felt that, I was really just a child of eleven. I had a childhood sweetheart. I was sitting next to her in a moving picture theater called the Lyric—the West End Lyric in St. Louis, and she was a redheaded girl with brown eyes and she had no sleeves on her dress and I wanted to put my arm around her and feel her bare arm, and that was my first awakening of sexual love. Later I began to feel great tenderness toward her of a nonsexual nature.

Frost: What sort of love would you call that, as opposed to sexual love?

Williams: We'd call that the purification. Wouldn't you? I think that sexual love is usually the best introduction to love, but I do think there is something beyond it, just as I know that people at very advanced ages still feel great love for each other.

Frost: It doesn't necessarily replace sexual love, but goes beyond it?

Williams: Sometimes it even replaces it. In cases of couples who are married for fifty or sixty years, I don't suppose they still want to have sexual relations. I shouldn't imagine so, although it's possible, they tell me.

Frost: I heard they go on forever.

Williams: Oh, really? That's encouraging.

Frost: But you mentioned experiencing the first sexual love feelings at the age of eleven. How often have you felt that purification of love, how often have you gone beyond that?

Williams: I've never enumerated the times. I've never lived without feeling love, though.

Frost: Really?

Williams: Yes. I'm talking too intimately to you. Let's get on to something more general.

Frost: All right. What was the spur that initially started you writing, do you think?

Williams: My mother bought me a typewriter when I was thirteen and I think I'd already shown some interest in writing. Probably around eleven, you know, but at thirteen she bought me a typewriter and then I went to business school and became more or less a pro.

Frost: Did the school know you were training to do something artistic like plays?

Williams: No, they thought I was training to become a clerk-typist, which I did later on.

Frost: For how long?

Williams: For three years, in the International Shoe Company in St. Louis, and I had to have a nervous breakdown to get out of it.

(*Laughter*)

Frost: How did you manage that?

Williams: I just had it. You would have, too, if you'd been in that. But I wouldn't take anything for those three years. I got to know those people so well. Otherwise I might have grown up knowing only long-haired artists, writers, and poets. I love them, but that's not the world.

Frost: What was it you learned in those three years that you couldn't learn from artists?

Williams: These people's lives were rather barren, and their great joy was in communicating with each other and telling every little detail of their daily lives to each other, and bonds were formed. I've never had any similar relationship since, because I've been sort of isolated with the typewriter most of the time.

Frost: Would you say your life has been lonely?

Williams: No, no. No, I've always found it necessary to have one person, at least one, very close to me. It's awful when the person dies. I've had that experience. At the age of fifty-eight, which is my age, it's natural to have had that experience. And then you have to start building a new world.

Frost: Is that difficult?

Williams: Or else you drink yourself blind or something like that. Or retreat into some false world of liquor, pills, or drugs, or what have you.

Frost: You were, thank God, cured recently.

Williams: Yes, they gave me the cold-turkey treatment and I had three convulsions in one morning. I don't know how I survived it, but I did.

Frost: You survived it and you look incredibly well now. You really were quite close to death. Does death frighten you?

Williams: Not nearly as much, not nearly. There was one moment in this psychiatric hospital when I had a heart attack and I felt the stabbing pains. What I felt wasn't fear, but a sort of a cold concentration on the moment. There happened to be a sadistic nurse in the room. She had followed me in because I had gone out of the room very angry and said that there was too much disturbance and I couldn't sleep and all that. She had followed me into my little cubicle. It wasn't a plush hospital at all, it was sort of a snake pit with almost no refinements. And she had followed me into this cell and she said, "Well, what's next on the agenda?" And I turned to her and

I said, "You're a mean little bitch." And then, all of a sudden I began having these stabbing pains and I said, "Go get me a nitroglycerin tablet."

Frost: And did she go and get it?

Williams: She did. So it shows that they're never really that mean.

Frost: You say that you're not lonely. Would you say that you're a happy person.

Williams: I think so. Relatively. I try not to feel sorry for myself.

Frost: What is being happy, really?

Williams: I don't know. Does anyone? I think that the greatest happiness is felt in moments of great tenderness between two people. Isn't that about as much as we know?

Frost: Is it that any one person yearns to communicate with another and it's only in those moments of love that they can most deeply communicate? Why are those the peaks of happiness?

Williams: Because we all have a great desire to escape from ourselves and to feel joined to another human being.

Frost: Why do we like to escape from ourselves?

Williams: Because to be alone is to be lonely. Unless you're a writer and you have your typewriter.

Frost: Do you like yourself or not? Or do you adore yourself?

Williams: I don't adore myself, no.

Frost: Do you find yourself good company?

Williams: I never stopped to think about that very much. I'm more or less saddled with myself. I can't do much about it. Do I like myself? No, I don't like myself very much. I often wonder, how can anybody like me, and yet occasionally I discover that somebody does.

Frost: Given that you're not lonely and that basically you try to be happy, why is it that your plays are so full of the less cheerful topics, like cancer and lobotomies and rape and adultery and incest and nymphomania and homosexuality and—

Williams: You're merely picking things out of the plays.

Frost: Nevertheless, the abiding impression that people get from reading your plays is of those spectacularly cheerless subjects.

Williams: Don't you know that those are the things that we are all obliged to live with? You may not die of cancer, and yet eventually

you might. So it's a part of human existence, isn't it? I've only dealt
with cerebral lobotomy once. In a play called *Suddenly Last
Summer.* It was a dramatic necessity.

Frost: What put that subject into your mind?

Williams: I happened to know about it, not to experience it on
my own, but—

Frost: Or through the family?

Williams: Some person that I had known well that had a cerebral
lobotomy.

Frost: It just comes back again and again to the fact that all your
plays do come out of your personal life, don't they?

Williams: Out of everybody's personal life. I think we all live with
rape. My God, we're all victims of rape, symbolically.

Frost: How?

Williams: Society rapes the individual.

Frost: Do we all live with cannibalism in this same symbolic way?

Williams: Yes, we all devour each other, in our fashion.

Frost: What about things like the homosexuality and so on, does
everybody live with that, too?

Williams: I think that everybody has some elements of
homosexuality in him, even the most heterosexual of us.

Frost: That no one is all man or all woman, you mean?

Williams: Oh, in my experience, no. I don't want to be involved
in some sort of a scandal, but I've covered the waterfront.

(*Laughter and applause*)

New Tennessee Williams Rises from "Stoned Age"

Don Lee Keith/1970

Adaptations of the following interview were printed in *The Times-Picayune* [New Orleans, LA], 18 October 1970, sec. 3, 6, and in *After Dark,* August 1971, 28-35. Printed below is an edited version of the original copy text. Printed by permission of Don Lee Keith.

If Williams is anything but a novice at an interview, at least he is somewhat out of practice, and that, perhaps, accounted for his nervousness. "I haven't granted a real interview in years. Eight years, I suppose, or more. Oh, occasionally, I may speak to a newspaper reporter, very briefly, when I have a new play opening, just for promotion. But that's only for a few minutes, and I certainly don't think that's an interview. Do you?" . . .

After arranging a stray carnation in the bowl on the coffee table, he did the same for his thoughts on interviews, emerging with, "I've learned to avoid such things, because no matter what you say, it seems to come out in print twisted and not what you actually said at all. A year ago, one of those big fancy magazines couldn't get an interview; so finally they wrote their own. [Donald Newlove, "A Dream of Tennessee Williams," *Esquire*, November 1969, 172-178, 64-80—Editor] I was terribly ill at the time and wasn't physically able to sue them for the libelous story, much less grant an interview. For instance, they said that I'd been beaten up by some sailors in a Key West bar, and they built up some idiot story around this. Listen, I've never been beaten up by sailors in a Key West bar. Then, there was that story by that thing, whatever he is, who calls himself a writer. It was in the *Atlantic* and you'd think they'd have better sense, at least the editors. Oh God! What errors and misquotes and, well, you wouldn't believe it. [Tom Buckley, "Tennessee Williams Survives," *Atlantic Monthly,* November 1970, 98, 100-106, 108—Editor]

"People, even my neighbors at my house in Key West, are all too willing to believe such things. Jesus, I've grown so tired of being a target. Yet, what can you do? It never stops."

For the record, *Esquire* located the attack incident in Miami, and it was a pair of hitchhiking sailors, no one in a bar. Nevertheless, the conversation was no time to cavil, for Williams was beginning to discuss his current physical condition.

"Now, I limit myself to one sleeping pill before bedtime. And I've cut down on booze. My thinking is clearer than it has been in years. Physically, I feel better than I can remember. And I can reflect and realize how adversely my work was affected by the pills and liquor, which had both become an uncontrolled urge.

"I'm glad we're finally in a new decade. I have an entirely different outlook. The sixties were dreadful for me. Baby, that decade was a catastrophy. It almost killed me. I wish I'd slept through the whole thing. Maybe I did and didn't know it. I told Gore that, and he assured me I hadn't missed anything.

"Until September of 1969, you see, for several years, I'd been taking very strong sleeping pills. I'd take them in the morning, all day long. And, of course, I was mixing them with liquor, too. The pills, while they were for sleeping, produced a sort of euphoric effect. I somehow needed that. I also had a witch doctor—I used to call Max that, but actually, he's a very respected physician in New York—who would provide me with these vials of, well, a vile concoction. I don't know what was in them. I'd give myself injections periodically, sometimes twice a day. All this kept me going. Of course, I would go to sleep, or, rather, pass out, and then later, I'd wake up and start all over. And I was trying to write, all at the same time.

"This went on for years, I tell you, and it might be going on now, and if so, I wouldn't be here talking to you, if something hadn't happened early one morning.

"I came to about two o'clock, and before I started to write, I went out on my patio to make a cup of coffee. At that time, they had moved my kitchen stove out there because a new one was being installed, but it had been delayed in delivery. The coffee got to boiling, and I lifted the pot off the stove, and I must have had some kind of blackout spell or something, because I fell, and the coffee spilled on me and blistered my right shoulder. Severely. Second-degree burns."

He rubs his right shoulder and chest, then turns to pour another drink.

"My younger brother Dakin came down from Collinsville, Illinois, where he lives. He's a despicable person. My agent, Audrey Wood, had called him and said, 'I think you ought to have Tom committed.' And he did. Dakin is notorious for his political maneuvers."

Williams slips again into his chair, rests the drink on one knee, covers his eyes with a hand, and leans his head far back. "The family has never been involved in such things, politics. We've all been above board. But anyway, I accompanied him back to St. Louis. I was still very hazy in the head, but I understood that he and Mother and I were going to the hospital. I thought it was for physical treatment, but they put me in the psychiatric ward. Not the real bad one, but when they came back the next day, I told Dakin and Mother that I demanded to be released.

"I put on my clothes and was leaving. When I got to the elevator, a big brute of an orderly refused to let me get in the elevator. So, I went back to my room and again demanded that my brother tell them to let me out. That's when they put me in solitary confinement.

"It wasn't a hospital, that psychiatric place at Barnes Hospital. It was a snake pit, a looney bin. In the first place, I was sick. It all stemmed from the death of my very best friend a few years back. And I was exhausted from work. They couldn't understand something like that, the people at that place, the doctors. They gave me the cold turkey treatment.

"The first thing they did was take away my pills, which I had to have. And alcohol. The last thing I remember is struggling to get my pills back. After that, I must have become unconscious.

"They tell me I had three convulsions in one day. And within four days, two heart attacks. I stayed there three months, and I tell you, I almost died.

"Until recently, I swore I'd never speak to Dakin again; I didn't even want to see him. But he came down to Key West a couple of months ago, and we had, I guess, a kind of reconciliation."

It was his brother, Williams admits, who figured prominently in the playwright's conversion to Catholicism in early 1969. "It wasn't my idea," Williams insists. "I don't really think I wanted to do it, but that happened during my Stoned Age. As far as I was concerned, I would have been happy just staying an Episcopalian. My real religion is my writing. I didn't go to church before my conversion, and I don't go now that I'm officially Catholic. When I'm scared, I do pray a lot, though, and I do believe there is a God. I don't believe He's dead, like some people say. But I don't know where He is, or what He's doing.

"Now, I'm not sure whether this attitude of mine is necessarily reflected in my work; I'm just not sure. Certainly, some of my plays may deal with a meaninglessness of existence, or the need for a meaningful philosophy. I suppose that if you live your life with a definite concept of the hereafter, heaven and all that, then life has more meaning. But suppose heaven is a fantasy that has been needed all along! Then we're down here with our wits, and our wits only, to get us through. Do you know what I mean? As I've said, the only victory is how we take it. And besides, many times, hell is yourself, if you allow it to be. I know, Baby. Believe me, I know."

A half block away, the bell of St. Louis Cathedral struck three dull thuds, resounding in every French Quarter direction, and Williams pulled on the jacket of his white linen suit. In the hotel lobby, he thumped the bloom of a yellow chrysanthemum—"Hmmm, real"— and loped out into the tourist crowds, slithering through them with the agility of a minnow through seaweed. . . .

At the corner of Royal and Toulouse Streets, Williams paused and looked around with a glance of recognition: "Ah, Toulouse Street. See that cottage down there, the one with the arched doorway? Yes. I lived there in 1939, trying to write. It was a little rooming house then. The woman who owned it needed money and decided to serve lunches. I devised an advertising slogan, 'Meals for a Quarter, In the Quarter.' I would pass out handbills on the streets and then I'd rush back and get on my white coat and be the waiter. That's how I paid my rent.

"It was also about this time when I started to use the name Tennessee. I had already tried Valentine Xavier (revived for the male lead of *Orpheus Descending*) but that seemed a bit pompous. Like Thomas Lanier Williams. Besides, Tennessee was justified somewhat in that the Williamses had fought the Indians for the State of Tennessee, and I had already discovered that the life of a young writer was going to be somewhat similar to the defense of a stockade against a band of savages.

"In New Orleans, I found the kind of freedom I had always needed. And the shock of it against the puritanism of my nature has given me a subject, a theme, which I've probably never ceased exploiting." . . .

A lengthy conversation with Williams is almost certain to be sprinkled liberally with mentions of Miss Wood, his longtime agent. His references to her are not always gracious, however, and depending on his strength of the dramatic, there seem to be varying degrees of his recurring paranoia, a trademark that has always hung over him like a swamg fog.

"Audrey Wood is a tough lady. Did you read that book last year? The one about the theatre and all. Now I can't remember its title. Oh, *The Playmakers.* [Stuart W. Little and Arthur Cantor, Norton 1970, 185-186—Editor] There's a picture of Audrey in it, and this bit about how she and her late husband, Bill Liebling, kept me alive back in the forties. It said they gave me $25 a week to keep me going, which is the most ridiculous thing I ever heard of, and I can't understand why Audrey or Bill would have said a thing like that. My God! They wouldn't even pay to have my plays typewritten for years. The only time Audrey helped me financially was in the winter of 1941. I'd just been thrown out on the street by an abstract painter with whom I was sharing an apartment. I had no money. I had an awful cold. Practically no clothes. I'd even hocked my typewriter. So, I went to the Lieblings' apartment, and Audrey said she'd call the Dramatists Guild. The Guild said they'd give me $10 to get me through the weekend. Later, I did get a $1,000 grant from the Rockefeller Foundation, which was renewed for $500, but in the meantime, while I was trying so desperately to be a playwright, I worked at everything from running an all-night elevator in a big apartment hotel to reciting verse in the Village to operating a teletype for the U.S. Engineers in Jacksonville, Florida. I even plucked birds on a squab farm. All the while, I kept writing, not with any hope of making a living at it, but because I found no other means of expressing myself.

And I am, quite frankly, offended at the implication that I was subsidized." . . .

When Williams rounded the corner in New Orleans' French Market and came in view of one of the city's newest tourist attractions, he stopped for a moment. He looked head-on at a refurbished leftover from the now retired Desire streetcar line, spitpolished for the occasion because it was his first visit there since the car had been put on display. He giggled.

A tourist bureau official asked for an autograph on a poster from a production of the play which June Havoc had directed at Repertory Theatre, New Orleans. Inside the car, Williams stationed himself at the controls. "What do you say to a streetcar? It's not gitty-up."

The pace of his steps began to slow, somewhat, on the more leisurely walk back to the hotel. Standing beneath iron lace galleries and peering occasionally into antique shop windows, he would sometimes seem to be transfixed, ephemerally, into another time, taken there through the magic of memory. His head would be at a delicate tilt, his mouth would form just a trace of a smile, and if he happened to be in the right light, there would be a peculiar peace about him.

But peace and Tennessee Williams have not walked together often. Throughout his life, and particularly for the past 15 years, Williams has been plagued with gnawing emotional difficulties. During one of his early adventures in psychoanalysis, the psychiatrist figured the playwright's distresses—claustrophobia, fear of heart attacks, drinking—were the result of too much intense work. The doctor would shift appointment hours to try to make it impossible for Williams to write. "But if he said I had to come in at eight in the morning, I'd get up at four and do my writing," he said, waving away the offer of a cigarette. "I couldn't face a day without it. It was compulsive." . . .

Back in his hotel suite, he poured another Campari and soda. A mild one. "Let them call me crazy if they want to, but almost all of my best plays have been written in spite of, and sometimes because of, emotional stress. Very few have been written when I was in a comparatively tranquil mood. In fact, I just came across a play which I'd forgotten I'd written. It was done during my Stoned Age. It's called *Will Mr. Merriwether Return from Memphis?* I discovered it in a pile of old manuscripts. But anyway, back to the subject. I think that some kinds of emotional stress can suffocate creativity, while others may give you a drive to create.

"My own creativity, I believe, has tended to mirror reality. Certainly, the language used has always been realistic. For some people, back with the earlier productions, the lines were quite shocking. But compared to today, those lines were mild. Now, you see a play on Broadway and they're saying things like motherfucker and cocksucker, and nobody arches an eyebrow.

"And as far as my motivation is concerned, well, I suppose it has, of course, been a form of compensating for something else. When I was a very small child, my mother managed to alienate me from my father, who wanted me to play baseball. I loved him only after he was dead. A sad thing to say, maybe, but by that time I could at least try to understand him.

"My mother never wanted me to go out with the boys, so to speak; she wanted me only to have friends who were girls. Consequently, I grew up being a sissy. But I was devoted to my grandfather. When I was a little boy, he'd be making parish calls and I'd always beg to go with him, so I could hear what everybody said. After I grew up and had a place of my own, I kept him with me at least half the time. He loved Key West. We even went to Europe together. Such a joy to be with, he was, not the rough sort of man, but gentle and sensitive, like Nonno in *Night of the Iguana*, who he was, of course. He liked things like silk handkerchiefs and nice tea cups, but he was totally masculine, never effeminate.

"I had a very special feeling for my sister, too, but Rose, bless her, has been a total schizophrenic since she was 27 years old. She became that way after a dreadfully tragic love affair. She was a beautiful, warm person, but eventually she became convinced that everyone was trying to poison her. It was necessary for her to have a lobotomy, a frontal lobotomy. Of course, that destroyed all possibility of recovery, but she's peaceful now. It was one of the first such operations in this country. I feel I must provide for Rose, and I do."

Some writers have insisted that Williams patterned Blanche DuBois (*A Streetcar Named Desire*) after his sister, but he says if that's true, he did so subconsciously, that Blanche was more like his "Aunt Belle in Knoxville."

"But I'll be the first to recognize the similarities between my sister and Blanche. In her transition to St. Louis, removed from security and thrown into a world of alarm and despair, Rose had hideous inner turmoil in trying to cope with life. She was fragile and sensitive, and she couldn't cope. Blanche, also fragile and sensitive, couldn't cope either. But Blanche was certainly not a virgin, and I'm confident that my sister, to this day, is.

"It's funny, how Blanche has been depicted, how differently, both on stage and screen, and well depicted, I think. Jessica Tandy, I liked. Julie Harris played Blanche in one production. I told her she was good, and she was. But in the last act, she failed to capture that certain desperation. She needed a Kazan as director. She had the ability, and a good director would have brought it out. . . . Tallulah Bankhead told the world, practically, that I wrote every good role for her. Poor Tallulah, dead now, was dreadful as Blanche in Coconut Grove. There, she played to the faggots. In New York, she was fabulous, because she played against the faggots."

If Williams' opinions of the stage treatment of his plays are favorable, this approval does not necessarily extend to adaptations for the movies.

"Generally, I don't like them. I liked *A Streetcar Named Desire.* And I liked *Sweet Bird of Youth,* except for the ending, which was nothing more than a cop-out. I hated, absolutely hated, *The Glass Menagerie,* and also *Cat on a Hot Tin Roof,* although I made a lot of money from that one.

"When Sam Spiegel bought *Suddenly Last Summer,* we agreed on the casting. At first, I wasn't sure about Katharine Hepburn as Violet Venable. I thought she was quite too young to play such an older woman, as I visualized the part. In the stage production, Hortense Alden played the part in a wheelchair. But I admitted that casting Miss Hepburn might be daring, and it took me a while to get accustomed to the idea. Now, of course, I know she was brilliant. So was dear Monty Clift as Dr. Cukrowicz. But while Elizabeth Taylor was very good as Maggie in *Cat on a Hot Tin Roof,* she simply wasn't right as Catherine Holly in *Suddenly Last Summer.*" . . .

Williams is not one to revise in bits and pieces. When he does revise, it is almost always in a play's entirety. He prefers, however, to leave his plays as much like they are originally written as possible.

"First, I do a full draft, which is just exploring and getting the characters into focus. Then I do a second draft to perfect the material. The third draft is about as good as I can do, and if I do a fourth, then that's the one that's published.

"When I'm working, which is almost every day, it helps to work on more than one play at a time. I'm afraid I'm a pitifully sloppy writer. I make incredible mistakes.

"And when I've finished an intensely dramatic scene, I'm just exhausted. I mean it. Limp. Sometimes I can't catch my breath. Until recently, I would have to rush to the medicine chest and wash down a pill, usually with straight vodka. And yet, I still can't think of writing as working."

While Williams has generally enjoyed an amicable relationship with most other writers, he has never been an integral part of any particular clique. "Carson McCullers was one of the most wonderful and remarkable persons I've ever known. But other than Carson, and a very few others, I haven't been involved with the literary scene. I've found that writers don't often get along together very well.

"William Faulkner practically never spoke to me, although I was around him a good deal at a particular point in my life. Maybe it was because he was in love with a girl, a dear friend of mine, who was involved with the production of *Cat on a Hot Tin Roof*. He was in Philadelphia fairly often at the time, while the play was trying out there.

"Hemingway and I never established a rapport either. One night Frank Merlo and I were at a dinner party with him. Kenneth Tynan had arranged it. Hemingway seemed shy to me; we didn't have much to talk about. In a way, it was embarrassing. Tynan later wrote something rather unkind, something about the gay company, but I don't think Frank and I came off very gay in the situation.

"Then, there was a time back in the late forties when I was quite close to Gore Vidal and Truman Capote. That was when we were all traveling, mostly in Italy. We'd run into each other at various places and have dinner or whatnot. I rarely see them anymore, and Carson was the only writer I remained close friends with.

"The last time I saw Gore was in Rome. I was giving a party for Maria Britneva, a dear friend of mine from London. It was in Gore's apartment, and he had invited all these, oh, I don't know, these

effete snobs, or whatever. They kept coming and coming—the son of
J. Paul Getty, the richest man in the world, the daughter of so-and-so.
And finally, maybe I'd had just enough liquor to make me
courageous, so I announced: 'There is just too much piss elegance
here.' Which put Gore into a fit."

Williams lets out with a high-pitched giggle.

"Well, Maria quickly ushered me out on the balcony. The next
morning, Gore told Oliver Evans, the professor, that The Bird—that's
what he calls me, The Bird—had just gotten to be too, too much, and
that you couldn't very well introduce The Bird to anybody in polite
society anymore. I love it. I just love it.

"Truman, on the other hand, has a real sense of humor. He can be
genuinely funny. Years ago, he and I were on the same boat going to
Europe, and there was this Catholic bishop who had a crush on
Truman. Truman was rather attractive in those days, with his bangs
and all. So, this bishop would come over to our table sometimes
when we were having dinner. One night, Truman looked over and
began admiring the bishop's ring. Truman said, in that quaint little
squeak of his . . . "

Then, Williams widens his eyes and goes into a near-perfect
imitation of the "little squeak," complete with nasal tones and vocal
inflections.

" 'This sure is a nice ring. I've always wanted a ring like this,'
Truman said. The bishop replied, 'But this is a bishop's ring. However
did you expect to get one?' And Truman answered, 'Oh, I thought I
might find one that some defrocked bishop had hocked in some
pawn shop along the way.'

"Those were very funny years. Some of the people were very
funny. But, as I've said, it was Carson who was the important one."

His friendship with Carson McCullers began in 1946 after he read
her novel, *The Member of the Wedding.* His play, *The Glass
Menagerie,* had been the hit of the past Broadway season, but he
had convinced himself that he wouldn't live much longer. He wrote
Mrs. McCullers a letter, telling her that he wanted to meet her before
he met death. That summer, she spent several weeks at his rented
cottage in Nantucket. They sat at opposite ends of a long wooden
table while she adapted her novel for the stage and he completed
Summer and Smoke. In late afternoons, they would take bicycle

rides, and at regular intervals, would lie on the grass, reading aloud their own accomplishments of the day.

Such soothing souvenirs must be gem precious to the present-day Tennessee Williams, considering that since *Night of the Iguana* opened in 1961, he has known nothing but dismal failure from his creative efforts. For the most part, the critics have drawn and quartered the man, and magazine articles have consistently tried to bury whatever was left.

And peculiarly enough, he does not seem to have developed any tougher skin. "I don't know whether I'm overly pessimistic, or incurably paranoiac, or if it's just an attempt to prepare myself for what might be coming. But I always expect complete failure. I've never thought of myself as a really good writer, and I find it amazing that I have been able to write as long as I've written, and as much.

"Do you want to know something? I really find it hard to believe people when they say that they like, or sometimes they say love, what I've done. I mean it, and I'm not trying to be modest. God knows I could hardly be modest when there are such incriminating reviews that have been written.

"There have been times when I have been truly crushed, humiliated, over the unkind remarks of critics. Some playwrights say they pay no attention to reviews, but I guess I'm not that strong, because the bad ones hurt me. Really hurt. Yet, I don't feel confident enough, actually, to answer a critic, even if I were invited to, which, of course, I never have been and never will be.

"The problem is that when you write something that people love, they love you for doing it. But this love fades, only to be replaced by something else, sometimes hate. You're always expected to outdo yourself, to be better than you ever were, and if you're not, then they say you're bad. Inevitably, you are put in competition with your own self, your own talent. It's sad.

"Right after *In the Bar of a Tokyo Hotel* opened, *Time* or *Life*—I believe it was one of them—ran a story saying that Tennessee Williams was finished. [*Life*, 13 June 1969, 10—Editor] I decided they were right. Anne Meacham called and said let's get out of here, and we flew off to Tokyo. But, of course, I came back.

"Every time—almost every time, at least in ten years—I had a play on Broadway, I swore I'd never write a Broadway play again. There, you can be so damned vulnerable. But as you start to write again, and when you've written something that has potential, there are pressures. There are producers and there are agents. And you find yourself giving under those pressures and going back to Broadway, where you said you'd never go again.

"Yet, regardless of what they say, what anybody says, I don't think I could ever stop writing. I've just finished the revised version of a new play called *The Two-Character Play,* which I wrote for Margaret Leighton. I've done the screenplay for *One Arm,* which will be the only short story to date to be made into a movie. Other than *Night of the Iguana,* which I don't count because it has no resemblance to the story, except the title."

In the other room, a phone rang. "The professor will get it," Williams predicted, and within moments, "the professor" stuck his head in and said, "It's the doctor."

"The professor" is Williams' term for Oliver Evans, poet and biographer and one of the playwright's oldest friends. He is also a traveling companion of Williams' with whom he would be leaving the next day for an extended trip to the Orient.

The call was a short one, and as he returned, Williams told Evans, "Sam doesn't think there's much reason for concern. He says it's a matter that can easily be seen about over there."

Back in his chair, he fingered lightly one side of his chest. "It's my tit," he remarked. "I'm the victim of a fatty tumor, but if anybody asks, I'm claiming it's breast cancer. Now, where was I? Yes, *The Two-Character Play.* Well, I'm not coming back until it's ready for production."

Then he stood again and began to move about. He seemed a bit uneasy. "It will be the last of my long plays, full-length ones. From now on I'm going to concentrate on shorter pieces. And maybe another short novel."

As he spoke, he suddenly seemed to be staring at an undetermined point somewhere in mid-air. His eyes were sadder now, and the lines around them were more obvious. . . .

"I travel more now, I've found. Somehow, I almost dread the idea of Key West again. After that last article came out, it hasn't been the same there. They come by and throw rocks at my house and yell, 'Faggot.' Sometimes they throw eggs.

"I've never hidden my homosexuality, I don't think. I haven't meant to. But then, I haven't tried to flaunt it, as some have said. In many ways it has been such an integral part of my creativity, however. When Luchino Visconti was directing a production of *A Streetcar Named Desire,* he turned to me once and said, 'Tennessee, you *are* Blanche.' He was wrong, because I wasn't. She was mostly my Aunt Belle. Aunt Belle in Knoxville. But his production, done with Communistic focus to make Stanley the hero, was actually more effective than the one by Kazan.

"Yet, I'll admit to being other heroines. I was Alexandra del Lago from start to finish. I've probably made every speech she made. And I meant them twice as much. Anyone who knows my plays well knows that."

He moved toward the windows. "Oh, but I love Key West. I really do. I settled there many years ago because it's the only place in this country where it's warm enough for me to swim every day of the year. The sky is always clear, and the water's so blue. I simply cannot endure cold weather. I'd die if I had to live where it's cold.

"In Key West I have my pet bulldog bitch, Gigi, who's getting so old she's having geriatric problems. And I have a rose garden with a special Gypsy Rose Lee Memorial Rose Bush—I planted it the day Gypsy died—and my gazebo I call the Jane Bowles Summerhouse.

"But lately, I've been thinking of taking a place in New Orleans for a while. Some place quiet and pleasant. I own property here, have for years, but I can't move into it quite yet. Right now, I think the place is full of dykes."

There was a pause, and he began a slow pacing of the floor, his gaze scrutinizing the room as a prize leopard assesses an elegant cage. But with each thought, each phrase that stretched into a sentence, his steps seemed heavier, more burdensome.

"Some folks have said that the plays of Tennessee Williams are *passé,* that their time has come and gone. Perhaps they're right, certainly if they're talking about plays that have to do with verbal values.

"But the use of the word *passé* doesn't bother me so much anymore, because after all this time, I've finally reached a point where I'm more concerned about survival as a person than I am about survival as a playwright."

He stood, now, at the wide fan window in the livingroom of his hotel suite. He looked out across the French Quarter skyline. It was dusk; the street lights flickered on, sending shadows of beat-up garbage cans skittering along the cracked and uneven sidewalks.

"That's Chartres Street down there, isn't it? My, but it looks so different from up here. I walked down it this morning, and I thought, 'This is the same street I walked down thirty years ago. Most of the same buildings.'

"Somehow it seemed to have changed so much."

And then I thought, "So have you, Tom. So have you."

Tennessee Williams Survives
Tom Buckley/1970

From the *Atlantic Monthly*, November 1970, 98, 100-106, 108.
© 1970 by Tom Buckley. Reprinted by permission.

In "An Open Response to Tom Buckley," *Atlantic Monthly*, January 1971, 34-35, Tennessee Williams castigated the interviewer for "the most dangerous misquotations, distortions, and libel by venomous implication." In replying, Buckley defended the accuracy and sympathy of his essay/interview. See *Atlantic*, January 1971, 35—Editor.

Tennessee Williams picked up a postcard from the coffee table in the living room of his house in Key West, Florida. "My mother's crazy again," he announced. Then he tilted his head to one side and laughed. The laughter was mellow and bubbling. The tip of his tongue darted between his even white teeth as though to savor it before it escaped.

He handed the card to his old friend Andrew Lyndon. "Miss Edwina's saner than I am," Lyndon said doubtfully.

"Hell," said Tennessee, "she's saner than *I* am." He laughed again, and the other people in the room—John Young, his secretary-companion; David Loovis, a novelist who has known Tennessee for twenty years; and my wife and I—laughed, too.

When the card came around to me, I saw that it was an antique, something that Tennessee's mother must have found in the back of a seldom-opened desk drawer. The front showed a tinted photograph of a mountain scene, the colors thin and faded now. The caption read, "Where Three States Meet—Harpers Ferry, W. Va., on the Baltimore & Ohio Railroad."

It was addressed to "Mr. Thomas L. (Tennessee) Williams" at Key West, and had been postmarked only a week or so earlier. The

message, written in the spidery hand of the aged, said, "Dearest Son,
This is the view from the Knoxville 'Country Club.' I'm sure Rose
must have seen it when she made her debut. Love, Your Mother."

"I just can't understand it," said Tennessee, rubbing the back of his
neck. "Mother is eighty-eight years old, but she isn't senile at all. Her
mind is just as quick . . . "

"Rose is Tennessee's sister," Loovis told me in a quiet aside. "She's
been a patient in a sanitarium in Ossining, New York, for years."

Tennessee heard him. "Rose," he said, "had the first prefrontal
lobotomy ever performed in the United States. That was in . . . " He
paused, thinking. "She was twenty-six then and she's sixty now, so I
guess it was 1936. It was a terrible operation. My mother gave
permission to have it done while I was away. I think she was
frightened by Rose's sexual fantasies. But, y'know, that's all they
were—fantasies. I'm sure she's still a *virgin.*"

Tennessee asked John Young to bring him a martini, the one drink
of hard liquor that he allows himself each day, and the conversation
drifted on to other topics.

I had gone to Key West in mid-May to complete a convalescence
from a difficult illness. It was Loovis, an old friend of mine, who
suggested that I meet Tennessee and write an article about him.
"He's a new man," Loovis said. "It's the most wonderful thing I've
ever seen."

In October, 1969, Loovis told me, Williams had entered the
Renard psychiatric division of Barnes Hospital in St. Louis. During a
two-month stay there he seemed to have broken a dependence on
pills—stimulants, tranquilizers, sleeping potions—and alcohol that
had imprisoned him for years in a deepening emotional fog.

"He never knew where he was most of the time," Loovis said. "He
staggered. His hands shook. He was incoherent. He'd get paranoiac,
and scream and shout and cry."

In 1968 the *Times* carried a story about Williams. It said that he
had disappeared from his apartment on West Seventy-second Street,
leaving behind a note that said, "If anything of a violent nature
happens to me, ending my life abruptly, it will not be a case of
suicide, as it would be made to appear. I am not happy, it is true, in a
net of con men, but I am hard at work, which is my love, you know."

During the few hours a day of comparative lucidity that he

experienced, Williams tried to keep writing. His plays were produced, but the critics received them with growing disappointment. They ranged downward from the respectable failure of *The Milk Train Doesn't Stop Here Anymore* in 1963, to *Slapstick Tragedy* and *Kingdom of Earth,* to the final fiasco of *In the Bar of a Tokyo Hotel* in 1969, of which *Time* said, "It seems more deserving of a coroner's report than a review." [23 May 1969, 75—Editor]

But the man I met in Key West gave reason to hope that the verdict that Williams, who is generally regarded as the country's foremost living playwright, was finished as a creative force was premature. I had seen him in a New York café three or four years before, and he had been puffy-faced and pasty white. Now he was tanned, and his gray-blue eyes were clear behind his heavy-framed spectacles. His chestnut-colored hair had begun to thin at the top but was still full at the back and sides. The British officer's mustache that he has worn for years was frosted with gray, but it seemed to fit his face better than when he was younger. He had lost twenty pounds, I was told, and looked trim and well muscled, wearing a high-fashion shirt of a crepe-like material, with long collar points and puffed sleeves, tan shorts, and heavy leather sandals. He seemed calm, indubitably lucid, and mildly amused at himself and the world.

"Y'know, baby," said Tennessee, pulling out the word "baby" like a string of taffy. "I spent seven years behind a veil of pills and whiskey, and I've never enjoyed life as much as I'm enjoyin' it now. If I can just get my ticker regulated, I'll probably live to be as old as my grandfather—he was ninety-eight when *he* died—and I'd adore it. . . . I've *almost* died so many times, but I *don't* die just because I don't want to."

"You're goin' to live to be *one hundred and thirty-nine,* Tom," said Lyndon, arching back his head and letting his glance dart around the room. Tennessee's oldest friends call him Tom. Lyndon, who is also a Southerner, in his middle forties, from Macon, Georgia, has been a peripheral figure in the literary world for twenty-five years or so, including a considerable period as the companion of Christopher Isherwood. Now, seemingly down on his luck, he was staying with Tennessee as a houseguest.

"I survived," Williams said, raising his head. "The soles of my feet

were cut open and pebbles sewn inside so I could not run away—I
survived."

Andrew chimed in. "I survived it all."

This speech, which I found was from a melodrama of the 1920s,
The Shanghai Gesture by John Colton, was a sort of recognition
signal in Williams' circle. It was often quoted from, and is spoken by
Mother Goddam, the owner of the largest brothel in the world, in
febrile Shanghai. In it she describes how she was sold to the sinister
"junk men," operators of floating houses of prostitution, as a gently
reared young girl:

> Yes—yes—yes—all—all I survived—whippings with hippo hide
> when I was stubborn—hot dung thrust into my nostrils and stinging
> leeches in my ears—so I could not sleep—I survived!—sulphur burned
> on my naked back to make my tired body gay . . . soles of my feet cut
> open and pebbles sewn inside so I could not run away—I survived! I
> survived it all! Hate helped me—black gods helped me—hell and the
> devil helped me—I lived! I lived!

Since getting out of the hospital Williams has been spending most
of his working hours revising *Two-Character Play*. Produced in
England in 1967, it received generally unenthusiastic reviews,
although the critic of the *Times* of London wrote, "Mr. Williams
succeeds quite brilliantly in sustaining the idea that nothing whatever
is to be relied upon and that if we get through one veil there is
another just beyond."

"Two Character Play," in Tennessee's words, "is a play within a
play within a play." Its two characters are a brother and sister, Felice
and Claire, and the setting is an empty theater in a cold, distant place
"that could be the North Pole."

"It's my best play since *Cat*," Tennessee said. "Maybe better. But
it's got to be more than that. It's got to be totally *invulnerable*. The
critics don't like to find out that they've been *wrong*."

A lifetime around the theater has given Williams many stagy
mannerisms. His conversation often sounds like dialogue in an as yet
unwritten play. He changes pitch, intonation, and timing, and
thickens his Southern accent, or makes it disappear, to suit what he's
saying.

"I think that Audrey Wood thinks I'm dead," he said quietly,
looking at his hands. "She thinks that *Two-Character* should be

produced off-Broadway. I think she wants *all* my work produced off-Broadway." (Miss Wood has been Tennessee's agent since his first commercial production in 1940. "A thirty-year love-hate relationship," she calls it. She had spent the preceding week with him. When I relayed his comments to her in her New York office, she said, "Of course I want to see him produced on Broadway. That's just Tennessee's 'normal' paranoia.")

Tennessee's voice got darker. "Well, she's *wrong!* Work is what I've given my life to and what I'll dedicate my death to, and if she . . . gets . . . in . . . the . . . way . . . *Out!*"

His mood lightened. He mentioned that he had asked Miss Wood to talk to Margaret Leighton about appearing in a fall production of *Two-Character Play*. To him, she is "the best actress in the world." His all-time favorite is long-dead now—Laurette Taylor, who played the mother in his first great success, *The Glass Menagerie*.

"In the dressing room, Maggie is the most nervous person in the world," Tennessee said, miming the shaking hands, clattering elbows, and collapsing knees of the tall, cadaverously thin actress. "She shakes so . . . she just rattles. Why, she can't even make herself up." He aimed a make-believe powder puff at his cheek, missed, and sent it out past his ear. "But something happens in the wings." His gestures flowed into calm beauty, and he paused at the wonder of the transformation. "Oh, I love her!" he said. "She makes a play come together. I thought she was marvelous in *Gnädiges Fräulein*. She couldn't help *The Mutilated*, though." He paused again. "Nobody could."

"Maggie turned down *Sweet Bird of Youth,* y'know," Tennessee said. "She didn't think it was for her. [Geraldine Page scored an enormous success in the role of the aging actress, Alexandra del Lago.] But *Bird* has never been done in England. Maggie could do it there. I told her I'd rewrite the second act for her so that the action remained at the hotel. That way she'd dominate the play even more completely."

Almost all of the great roles in Williams' plays have been written for actresses—Vivien Leigh, Jessica Tandy, Barbara Bel Geddes, Anna Magnani, Maureen Stapleton, Julie Harris, Bette Davis, Anne Meacham, Helen Hayes. The only one he criticized was Miss Hayes, who appeared in the Laurette Taylor role in a revival of *The Glass*

Menagerie. [Washington: National Theatre, March 1961. Hayes also appeared in *The Glass Menagerie* in 1948 (London, Theatre Royal) and 1956 (New York, City Center Theatre)—Editor.] Tennessee said, "She can't act! She acts in rehearsal, but as soon as she gets in front of an audience she becomes a monkey. All those ridiculous grimaces."

He went on to say that he regretted that Greta Garbo had never appeared in one of his plays. "A wonderful woman," he said. "I read a screenplay for her one night years ago in her apartment in New York—at the Ritz Tower, I think. One of the big Hollywood directors—I can't think of his name—said to me. 'Garbo *must* go on acting.' [As he said it, Tennessee sounded like Cecil B. De Mille.] I said, 'I couldn't agree with you more, and I think I have a script that might interest her.' 'Well, for God's sake, go up and see her,' the director said. Well, I did. And all the time I was readin' we were drinkin' schnapps and she was saying, 'Wonderful . . . wonderful . . . how beautiful.' I thought I had her. When I finished, she said, 'Wonderful . . . marvelous . . . but I'm afraid it isn't for me.'" He laughed his big booming laugh, and we joined in.

Tennessee visited Key West in 1941. He was bruised in spirit. His first commercially produced play, *Battle of Angels,* had been booed off the stage during its Boston tryout. "The Theatre Guild [which had produced it] gave me $100 and told me to go away and rewrite and I came here," he said. "I stayed in a little cottage behind the old Southern Winds. Cora was very kind to me." Tennessee nodded to Loovis, who had worked at the hotel, now demolished, and used it for the setting of a novel, *The Last of the Southern Winds.*

Williams earlier received a Rockefeller fellowship of $1000 that Audrey Wood doled out to him at the rate of $25 a week. During the war years he worked at a variety of menial jobs, including a brief stint as a screenwriter at MGM, but he kept working on his plays. He returned to Key West, he said, in 1946, after the triumphant opening of *The Glass Menagerie,* with his beloved grandfather, the Reverend Walter Dakin, an Episcopal priest who was by then retired from the pulpit.

"We drove down from New Orleans—Grandpa was staying with me there—in a secondhand Pontiac," Williams said. "We stayed at

the La Concha Hotel. Key West was still very, very lovely, primitive
and completely unspoiled. I loved it . . . I still do!"

In those days Key West was much more a part of the Caribbean
world than of the mainland United States—closer to Havana and
easier to get to than it was to Miami—a town of weathered white
houses with wide verandas, the brawling fishermen, smugglers, and
sailors of *To Have and Have Not.* Hemingway lived there before he
crossed the straits to Cuba. The present reality is not so pleasant or
picturesque, but Williams stays faithful to the memory and, indeed,
re-creates it around himself.

In 1949 he bought, for a few thousand dollars, the house we were
sitting in. It's a tiny place, really, white clapboard with bright red
shutters, a dollhouse that suggests Nantucket rather than the tropics.
Over the years Tennessee has made additions—a pool, a covered
patio, and most recently an elaborate kitchen at the rear. Behind the
pool is a garage that he uses as a workroom. His next construction
project will be a gazebo that he will call the Jane Bowles Summer
House. Mrs. Bowles is the author of a play called *In the Summer
House;* she and her husband, Paul Bowles, the writer and composer,
are old friends of Williams', and he often stays with them at their
home in Tangier.

The entrance to Williams' house, on the corner of Leon and Duval
Streets, the edge of the old section of Key West, is shaded by a bushy
traveler palm. It is one of more than 300 varieties of tropical plants
that he had planted on the grounds. There are screw pine, coconut,
Washingtonian fan, and areca cluster palms, pandanus, crotons with
shiny crinkly mottled leaves, begonia, bougainvillaea, hibiscus, many
varieties of hybrid orchids, pink allamanda, split-leaf philodendron,
and cocos plimosa, to name a few. By night their leaves stir softly,
illuminated by lights on the patio and around the pool.

The living room of Tennessee's house is only about 10 feet wide
and perhaps 20 feet long. Most of the furniture is made of wicker; the
cushions are covered with faded chintz. Two of the occasional chairs
have elaborately woven backs that form a kind of peacock's eye
pattern. Tennessee said they came from Havana. A copper and brass
chandelier dangling crystal and blue glass hangs over the glass-and-
wrought-iron dining table at the far end of the room. Built into the

wall behind the table are shelves on which are oddments of china
and glassware. There is an Irish Belleek cream pitcher and cup, all
that remains of a set that was too fragile to last, given to him by his
friend Carson McCullers.

His paintings are pleasant and unobtrusive, the sort that are picked
up here and there at moderate prices as keepsakes rather than
investments. There are faintly impressionistic oils by Henry Faulkner,
a Key West artist who is an old friend; an ant's-eye view of grasses,
silvery greens and browns, that he bought in Tangier from a
Moroccan artist; a thoughtful sketch of himself, done perhaps twenty
years ago; a Toulouse-Lautrec poster of La Goulue. A model of a
square-rigger stands on a bookshelf. Replying to my question,
Tennessee said it was the ship on which his ancestors had arrived in
America. "In 1491," he said. "They were . . . uh . . . bond servants
of the first settlers, and they came over to get things ready for them."
He assumed a Deep South darky dialect. "They was a-polishin' up
the silver and cleanin' the lamp chimneys fo' dere mastuhs . . . "

The household has three pets—a Boston bull terrier bitch called
Gigi, who wears a rhinestone collar and is beginning to suffer from
obesity; a skinny tan tomcat named Gentleman Caller after one of
the characters in *The Glass Menagerie;* and an iguana of uncertain
sex that bears the compromise name of Mr. Ava Gardner. (The Ava
Gardner of no uncertain sex appeared in the film version of *The
Night of the Iguana.)* The iguana lives in a glass cage on the patio,
subsisting on a diet of lettuce leaves and hibiscus blossoms and
whatever insects come within reach of his, or her, long pink tongue.

Gigi may be in better spiritual shape than her master. In the winter
of 1968-1969, at the nadir of Williams' depression, he twice became
seriously ill with pneumonia. At the urging of his brother, who
became a convert to Roman Catholicism while serving in India in the
Army during the Second World War, he permitted himself to be
baptized as a Catholic. ("He was stoned out of his mind," a friend
told me.) Lately he has been embarrassed by this defection from the
faith of his fathers, but the priest who guided his conversion
continues to call on him every week or two.

"There's nothing Tennessee can do about it," a friend said. "He
likes the priest and doesn't want to offend him. But the whole thing
makes him uncomfortable. The last time the priest was here

Tennessee asked him to bless Gigi. He told the priest"—and here the friend assumed Williams' mellowest, stagiest voice—"'Her only sin, Father, is *gluttony.*'"

For several days I saw a good deal of Williams—at dinner, afternoons at his pool, playing bridge, and chatting over cocktails. Nothing broke the flow of conversation quicker, I found, than a direct question; but left to himself he got around to most of the things that seemed to be on his mind. From time to time he talked about his early life.

Williams' vanished Eden is Columbus, Mississippi. He lived there for the first twelve years of his life with his mother, sister, and brother in the rectory of Grace Episcopal Church, where Mrs. Williams' father was the rector. Her husband, Tennessee's father, a shoe salesman, spent most of his time on the road. In the second decade of this century, rural Mississippi still dozed and dreamed of its magical antebellum past, and Tennessee's grandfather, a member of an old family, a graduate of Sewanee, a minister of the church at which Columbus' best people worshipped, provided a local definition of gentility and high status.

It was Tennessee's aggressive, hard-drinking, poker-playing, womanizing father who destroyed it all when he became a sales manager for his company and moved his family to St. Louis, where the home office was situated. Good-bye magnolias, good-bye status. Under the influence of his mother, that slightly cracked Southern belle, Tennessee grew up hating his father. That has changed now, he said. After the failure of *Orpheus Descending* in 1957, Tennessee's depression became so profound that he spent a year in psychoanalysis with Dr. Lawrence Kubie in New York. Although Dr. Kubie tried unsuccessfully to change his sexual orientation, which was bound to fail, Tennessee said, "because I was in love at the time," he regarded this period of therapy as successful.

"I stopped hating my father, and when I did I felt like a great load was lifted from my mind," he said. "I was able to understand him better—his drinking, for one thing. My mother would scream, 'I know where his liquor is. He's hidden it behind the bathtub.' If only she'd've sat down and had a sherry with him. . . ."

As it happened, the sum total of influence on him led Tennessee to become homosexual, a circumstance that I think no longer particularly disturbs him. He nevertheless is his father's son in many ways—boastful of his masculinity, not inclined to run from a fight, and, at least until a few months ago, a notable drinker and poker player. I would hazard a guess that he prefers to see himself as an old-school Southern gentleman-playwright-man-of-the-world, with a sexual preference that he shares with kings, rather than as an aesthete in the traditional lavender-scent mold.

At Loovis' house one afternoon Tennessee got to talking about fraternity life at the University of Missouri. Because of the influence of his father, who had been a member, he became a pledge of Alpha Tau Omega. The brothers did not approve of him, he said. The solitary, poetry-writing youth was not regarded, correctly enough, as fraternity material.

"They thought I was a sissy boy," said Tennessee, making the sibilance of "sissy" sparkle in his mouth. "They were right!" He laughed. "And I thought *they* were a bunch of drunken bums, but there were a couple of good guys, too."

He closed his eyes for a moment. "I used to go to their parties," he said. "I used to take an Alpha Delta Pi. She was a *nymphomaniac,* y'know. They just *loved* her. When I picked her up at the sorority house I'd give her a slap right here [he cupped an imaginary breast] and she'd giggle and shake so."

The pledges were paddled, of course, the sort of thing that in English public schools has for centuries planted the seeds of sadomasochism; and once, Tennessee said, he was required to drink a glass of grain alcohol. "It almost killed me," he said. "I passed out, and when I came to I went into the bathroom and vomited green, and I mean *green.*"

In time, he went on, he became good friends with another of the pledges, a companion in misery, with whom he shared a bedroom in the fraternity house. Friendship ripened into intimacy, and the two youths began sharing each other's beds.

"The first time," Tennessee said, "he just scratched my arm, and I *came.*" A few nights later the other youth, whom he referred to only as "Green Eyes"—"Oh, those green eyes," Tennessee interjected lasciviously—sought to display his affection again. "He slid into my bed," said Tennessee, letting his voice go falsetto in what I presumed was a vocal parody of a frightened virgin, "and I said, 'Wh-a-a-t do you want?' "

Tennessee said he returned to the fraternity house several years ago at the time he received an honorary degree from the university. He found no obvious changes in fraternity spirit; the brothers seemed as crass and dull to him as they had during his days there. They returned the compliment by largely ignoring their distinguished visitor, fearful perhaps that he might help them carry out their fantasies.

Since the first years of his fame, Tennessee has had a companion-secretary to shield him from the irritations of daily life and comfort him during the savage hours of loneliness and anxiety. The first of these was Frank Merlo. He was a young merchant seaman when Williams befriended him about 1950. They remained together until Merlo's death from lung cancer about five years ago.

Some of Williams' friends think that Merlo's death was the most important of the events that led to his dependence on drugs. "Tom was closer to Frank than he has ever been to anyone else," I was told. "He was in terrible shape after Frank died. Yet Tom ran away from him during his final illness. He paid all the hospital bills, of course, but he didn't go to see him. The only thing was that Tom got so frightened, he quit smoking for good."

Merlo's replacement was a tall, slender, extremely handsome would-be actor named Bill Glavin. It was his misfortune to have to put up with Williams during a period of fairly steady emotional deterioration. He also functioned as a grand vizier or presidential appointments secretary, denying access to many persons who considered themselves friends of Williams, leading them to say that Glavin was responsible for "isolating" him and enslaving him to drugs. In the months before his hospitalization, Tennessee, in his paranoia, also became convinced that Glavin was plotting against him. Soon after he was released, he dismissed him, reportedly continuing to pay him $300 a week "to stay out of Key West."

A calm, pleasant man in his late thirties named John Young, a onetime YMCA secretary and assistant film director, had the job while I was there. He cooked for Tennessee, drove him in Tennessee's maroon convertible, answered the phone, arranged assignations, and kept the household running smoothly. He was paid $200 a week, I was told, and from what I saw, he more than earned it.

The advent of Young had almost completely changed the membership in Tennessee's inner circle. Most of Glavin's friends, including the woman editor of the *Key West Citizen*, were no longer welcome, while several persons who had been *persona non grata* during the Glavin regime, including my friend Loovis, were again made welcome.

In the hermetic atmosphere of Key West, these intrigues were analyzed in endless detail. Why, for example, had the *Citizen* failed to list Loovis as among those present at a certain party? Was Leoncia McGee, Williams' longtime black housekeeper, engaging in espionage for the Glavin faction? Was she supporting an army of relatives on food abstracted from Tennessee's elegant kitchen and attempting to undermine John Young by placing the blame for the missing chickens and smoked hams on him? Someone else would whisper in my ear as softly as rustling silk, that Andrew Lyndon was trying to displace John, and tempting Tennessee back down the primrose path, by his own excessive drinking.

As befits a monarch, Tennessee appeared to take no notice of the Byzantine complexities that flourished in his little court, but I'm sure he was aware of them and, indeed, did what he could to help them along, delighting in the consternation that was caused, for example, when he invited the local horticulturalist, a man closely allied with the Glavin faction, to visit him, ostensibly to discuss additional plantings.

For a couple of years Tennessee had been taking Doriden. It was fairly dependable in getting him to sleep, but it made him feel good, he said, even when he was just lying in bed. He wouldn't mention the name of the drug, which is a synthetic described as a "potent nonbarbiturate sedative," as though it was a cabalistic password. His brother, Dakin, told me what he had got himself strung out on, and about the fact that he had another substance that he administered himself by hypodermic syringe to bring himself back to alertness. "I don't know what it was," Dakin Williams said, "but I think it was speed."

In May, 1969, *In the Bar of a Tokyo Hotel* was produced in New York. It was Tennessee's worst disaster in a lengthening chain of disasters. He then decided to accept an invitation to go to Tokyo to

see a Japanese production of *A Streetcar Named Desire.* He took
Anne Meacham, who had starred in *In the Bar of a Tokyo Hotel* with
him.

After his return, he divided his time between his apartment on
West Seventy-second Street in New York and San Francisco. He
stayed at both the Mark Hopkins and the Fairmont Hotels. Dakin,
who visited him, said, "His temper was so horrible that neither could
satisfy him." Bill Glavin was ill in New Orleans during this period, and
except for Dakin's visits, Tennessee was by himself.

He returned to Key West. Early in October, Dakin recalled.
Tennessee called him at his home in Collinsville. " 'Dakin,' he said,
'an attempt will be made on my life tonight.' Well, I knew what the
score was," Dakin said, laughing. "So I said, 'Tennessee, I can't do
anything about it tonight. Will it be all right if I fly down tomorrow?'
So I arrived the next morning. In the back of my mind I wanted to
get him to the Barnes Hospital in St. Louis, but I couldn't do
anything without his permission. When I got there he was in dreadful
shape. His arm had been badly burned by scalding water in an
accident with a coffee pot a few days before, and he was badly panic-
stricken. So I asked, 'Don't you think we better get you to a
hospital?' I'd hoped to spend a couple of days in Key West myself,
but he said, 'Yes, tonight.' Well, that's the way he is. So I immediately
made reservations and we flew back to St. Louis.

"He was very bad on the plane going out because they'd only
serve two drinks to a customer," Dakin went on. "It was a Sunday
and we couldn't get anything in St. Louis either. He was furious, but
fortunately I had a bottle of liquor at my mother's place in Clayton.
We spent the night there. He was pacified by the bottle of liquor, and
he promised me he'd go to Barnes the next day. I made a reservation
at the hospital's Queeney Tower, which is very exclusive. But the next
morning Tennessee was very belligerent. He said he wouldn't go.
Then he got sick from the liquor. He told Mother he wanted to go to
the hospital in an ambulance. I ordered the ambulance. Then he
changed his mind—he said he'd go by cab—so then Mother took
him in a taxi.

"I went by that evening and he was sitting up in the Queeney
Tower. He had his bottle of booze and his bag of pills, and he looked
like he had the world by the tail. Everything was fine. But the

hospital was just making routine tests. The next day they came to
some conclusions about him. They took away the booze and the
pills. Tennessee did what he always does—he started to walk out. I'd
sent him a big bouquet of flowers in hopes of getting a nice welcome,
but he was furious with me. The doctor was there—a neurologist—
and he was going to just let him walk out. So I said to myself, 'Good
God, I've got him this far, I'm not going to let him leave if I can help
it.' I got hold of another doctor I knew—he had treated Mother—and
he said, 'If Dakin will take the responsibility, he can sign him in for
ten days, even against his will.' So he thought when he went to the
elevator that he was going to New York, but the intern got up behind
him and inoculated him with something in his arm that put him to
sleep, and he woke up in the only place in the hospital where they
can force people to stay—Renard, the psychiatric division. I
understand that when he woke up he looked around and said,
'Where am I, the Plaza?'

"I didn't see him for three days because he was so infuriated. He
also had three convulsions coming off the Doriden. He nearly died.
The doctors said so. I was there every day except when he would get
angry at me. Then I'd stay away for two or three days to pacify him.
After a while he became very friendly and very much himself. I
hadn't seen him that way in several years; I'd almost forgotten what it
was like. Y'know what one of the doctors told him? 'Tennessee, if
you play ball with us, you'll write better than you ever wrote before in
your life.' That was very clever, I thought, motivating him like that.
After that first month he stayed in voluntarily the second month. He
could've gotten out in ten days if he had known his legal rights, but I
didn't tell him.

"He also was having some problem with his heart," Dakin went
on. "The electrocardiogram showed some damage. I mentioned it to
him to try to motivate him some more, and he said, 'Dakin, I wish
you hadn't told me that.' " Dakin laughed again. "The doctors were
all very proud to be working with Tennessee, and he got along very
well with the other patients. He played bridge almost every night.
Several of the women proposed marriage to him. Once it happened
while I was there. Tennessee was embarrassed. 'Oh, this is just a *put-
on*,' he said, but the woman had a very intense look."

Dakin said he hadn't seen Tennessee since he left the hospital. In

January, Dakin said, he received a telegram from his brother, asking him *not* to attend the premiere of the revival of *Camino Real* in New York. "For reasons of my own I don't feel I can see you right now," the wire said.

"I've attended every opening but that one," Dakin said, "but I didn't mind. My own attitude toward Tennessee of course is unchanged. I'm delighted that he's well enough to be angry at me. He's eight years older than I am, and we were never close until a couple of years ago, when he felt he needed me. For three years, you know, I paid all of Tennessee's bills. His accountant would send me the checks and I would sign Tennessee's name. Now that he's gotten well and has developed a phobia against me, I've been relieved of that responsibility. I've also had the chance to pay some attention to my legal clients"—he laughed—"and my business has gone way up."

Tennessee's recollections of his stay in what he calls "the snake pit" or "the looney bin" are rather different. His mind dwells on the convulsions—"They took me off cold turkey," he said. "They didn't have to do that"—on the three heart attacks which he believes he suffered after the convulsions, on the cruelty of the nurses, the insensitivity of the physicians, and the monstrousness of his brother.

"The day after my second heart attack, y'know, when they made me get out of bed and go into the dayroom for breakfast, I said, 'Please get my brother here,'" Tennessee said, sounding pitiable.

"When he got there, I said to him, 'I've had a terrible heart attack, and I'm not going to live but a day or two at most, I don't think.' And he said, 'Good.' [Tennessee stretched the word into an expression of pure malevolence.] He said, 'I'll take you down to Florida,' and then he disappeared for four days. I said, 'Why didn't my brother come back?' and they said, 'Because it's unnecessary.'"

Tennessee had given Dakin some laundry to have done. Dakin told me that his wife had washed and ironed it herself. When Dakin returned it, Tennessee denied that it had been washed at all. "I said, 'Well, listen, Dakin, you put me in this snake pit, and I don't want to look like a fuckin' bum in here *all the time*, so you get me some clean shirts, heah. You take these dirty ones that Joyce forgot to wash to a Chinaman or get me some new ones.' You know what he did? He got me four shirts made in *Hong Kong*." His intonation underscored the absurdity of Tennessee Williams wearing shirts from Asian sweatshops. "And y'know, I'm very rich. I really am. I'm an extremely wealthy man—undoubtedly one of the two or three wealthiest writers in America. . . ."

Andrew Lyndon interrupted. "Oh, my God, what a *vulgar* remark," he said.

" . . . But this is the irony of it," Tennessee went on. "I had to wear shirts from Hong Kong because they were the *cheapest* in the department store. There were *threads* coming out at all the seams." Tennessee made it sound as though the threads were lice. "He didn't want to spend any of the money because he thought he was gonna git *all* of it himself."

Tennessee now sounded like the meanest banker in Columbus, Mississippi, explaining how the village idiot had tried to hornswoggle him. We laughed and he told us how he had fixed up his will to make sure that Dakin was suitably punished.

"Since I've got out of the hospital I've made three trips to Miami to make sure that Mother gets nothin' [Tennessee's logic was that his mother would leave any bequest from him to Dakin when *she* died] and to make sure that Dakin had no power of attorney. I had the power of attorney rescinded twice—I made two trips to New York to make sure of it—at the Chase Manhattan Bank."

"What will you do, Tom, apart from taking care of Rose?" Andrew Lyndon asked.

"Sweetheart," Tennessee replied, "my first obligation is to Rose . . ."

Lyndon interrupted. "Yes, I know that . . . "

" . . . and I have no legal power to keep her there [the private sanitarium in Ossining] after my death if Dakin wants to take her out. [Presumably he would transfer her to a worse snake pit than Barnes.] The only way I could get around that was by leaving him $25,000, *on condition* that he leave her there."

"When does he get the $25,000?" John Young asked. "How do you know he won't take the money and take her out anyhow?"

"He won't get the money until after my sister's death," Tennessee said patiently, obviously pleased to have anticipated this contingency. "She's not going to live much longer than me. She's not well. She's sixty years old and very unwell. After she dies, everything goes, aside

from personal bequests, y'know, everything goes to the Rose Isabelle
Williams Foundation for creative writers."

"Oh, how wonderful," said Andrew Lyndon. "Can I get a grant?"

Tennessee acted as though he hadn't heard. "This will is *airtight*,"
he went on. "It's the best goddamned will anybody ever wrote in his
life."

"Are there four hundred and twenty-seven codicils?" Lyndon
asked.

"No. No codicils *at all*," Tennessee replied. "That's what screws up
a will."

"That was the trouble with the one you had before," Lyndon said.

"Yes," Tennessee agreed. "I burned it all."

"It was six hundred pages," said Lyndon. "Like something by
Henry James."

"Don't worry about it," Tennessee said. "This will is a *masterpiece*.
It's absolutely airtight."

"I think your will is going to be like the suicide note that Nina
Capote left for Truman," Lyndon said, " 'Dearest Truman, Please take
care of yourself. I hid my jewelry under the icebox. Don't let that
woman get hold of it. Love, your mother. P.S.—On second thought,
maybe you ought to put the jewelry in my safe-deposit box, in case I
need it again.' " Lyndon threw his head back to lead the laughter.
"She did kill herself eventually, eight or ten years later," he said.

"What was the trouble?" John asked. "Truman?"

"No," Lyndon replied. "Joe Capote had lost most of his money.
There were other things. Truman was in Europe, writing 'Beat the
Devil.' "

"Nobody wrote that," Tennessee interjected. "It was all ad lib."

"They *did* have a good cast," Lyndon said.

"There was a terrific cast—Bogart, Jennifer Jones, Robert Morley,
Peter Lorre—and no script," Tennessee said, closing the
conversation.

In April Tennessee gave his first public reading in several years at
Duke University. John Young, who accompanied him, said one
evening over dinner that Tennessee had been worried about the
response of the students. He feared that he had gone out of fashion
or had been forgotten on the campuses. He needn't have. The

students, recognizing someone whose trips on the pathways of
alienation, pain, and drugs were beyond their imaginings, gave him a
standing ovation. The Durham *Morning Herald* carried the story of
his appearance on the first page.

"I read them a one-act play, *I Never Get Dressed 'Til After Dark on
Sunday*," said Tennessee, taking up the narrative. "I told them, 'It's
still sort of rough and raunchy, but you'll get the idea.' I think they
did. They seemed to like it. . . ."

Recalling something to mind, he interrupted himself. "Did I ever
get the check?" he asked Young. "They're supposed to pay me
$750."

"They wrote that they needed your social security number before
they could pay you," he replied. "It's university policy. I sent it to
them."

"Well, they damned well better send it," Tennessee said, sounding
fierce. "I want to get paid for that gig. I'm not the kind of cat who will
read for nothing."

He does though, of course. Only a week or two previously he had
given the same reading for the benefit of the Key West public library.
Generally speaking, he is a soft touch around the city, and in John
Brown's Bar, where he goes occasionally to sit at a corner table by
the window and drink a spritzer, he is frequently approached by one
of Key West's floating colony of hippies to come up with bail money
for someone who has been busted for drugs. In fact, with only mild
irony, the city manager told me that Tennessee was "our leading
citizen."

"I like young people," Tennessee said. "They're a better audience.
They listen, react, identify. Thank God I can still identify with *them*. I
thought I was old when I turned twenty-two. It was the only time I
ever worried about my age. I only love the act of creation, the giving
of the work. I like the *moment* of the applause—applause is the
wrong word—I mean the acceptance . . . the acceptance of the truth.
If I discovered that I could no longer write acceptably for the theater,
then I would go on stage in person . . ."

"And put Judith Anderson out of business," Andrew Lyndon piped
in.

". . . because I know how to communicate with an audience . . .

because I want to communicate. I've always wanted to. I see no other reason for me to live, except to communicate, to love, to fight."

After a while his thoughts returned to *Two-Character Play.* "If I live," he said, "it'll be my best play, but that doesn't mean it will run more than three weeks. In any case, it'll be my last long play."

"No, no, no," said Andrew Lyndon. "Don't make nervous statements like that."

"Yes," said Tennessee firmly. "I may write some one-act plays but that will be my last long one. The effort is too great now, baby." The thought of performing came to him again. "I feel at home on the stage," he said musingly, "facing strangers. I'm a ham at heart."

John Young took the cue. "Unless you're too tired I wonder would you read for us a little . . ."

Tennessee looked around. Everyone smiled agreement. He looked questioningly at us.

"How about 'What's Next?'" John Young asked.

"No, it would give me a bad night," Tennessee replied.

"Oh, Tom, if you don't mind, read 'The Ice-Blue Wind' to us," said Andrew Lyndon.

"Baby, I'm not a poet," he said.

"If you're not a poet, what the hell are you then?" Lyndon asked.

"Plays are my vocation," Tennessee replied. "I can write a conventional and graceful lyric, but I know I'm not a poet of any consequence whatsoever. . . . If you want to hear inconsequential verse, I'm perfectly willing to read it. D'you want 'What's Next?' I'll read that. It's full of inserts, and I'll have trouble reading it without my glasses. . . ."

Young went off to find the manuscript, and Williams turned to Lyndon, who was still, with words and gestures, disagreeing with Tennessee's low opinion of his own verse.

"Baby," he said in a kindly way, "my kind of poetry is long gone out. I can keep up with the theater but not with *it.*"

He slid his glasses onto his nose, and settled back in the wicker chair and cleared his throat. I recorded his reading, but with no way of knowing how the lines should be divided I have reproduced them in prose form.

"What's Next on the Agenda, Mr. Williams?" [*Mediterranean*

Review, Winter 1971, 15-19—Editor] Tennessee spoke the title, as
he did the rest of the poem, which he had written after leaving the
hospital, in a monotone, his voice slurred and heavy. "One.
Addressed to myself. Not every morning that you awaken could it
indisputably be proven of you that you have awakened quite well.
No, not with some mornings those tattle-tale stitches of things in the
left arm and the left side of the chest. The ones familiar at night now
persisting into the morning, reminding you not to forget the damaged
ventricle of the heart—that unnecessary memento of your three-day
stay at Brigance Division of Barnacle Hospital in the City of St.
Pollution.

"The Founding Fathers must have erred in their study of the night
sky's geography book. It must have been shrouded by mist off the
river. Otherwise, why, forefathers, did you plant the proud flag of
France there? No, I'm afraid, Mr. Williams, that there's something
under your skin that's pretty fast with the needle. They're sewing a
winding sheet for you. . . . But what is the whisper of the guru in the
moon if it isn't a tender word for me? Smile fiercely at him, you one-
quarter Hun, answer him back. Say, later I have work to do, and
maybe Maggie's still waiting.

"Two. Flashback. You say you have trouble in sleeping, inquired
the doctor, a neurologist, one of the trinity who pronounce
themselves to be the most eminent practitioners of their practice to be
encountered anywhere in the world. . . . And he looked at me as
dreamy, droop-eyed as Buddha cunningly caricatured by a devout
Seventh-Day Adventist. My reply was a sigh. I really didn't have
breath at the moment for more. Then he repeated his question. 'You
say you do not sleep well here?' he asked me. *Here* being that funny
farm, the violent ward in that city of St. Pollution to which my kid
brother had committed me—I guess no less than seven months ago
now. . . ."

There were two more long parts, and when he finished reading
them, Tennessee put the manuscript aside with a sigh. "It's a bitch of
a poem," he said. "I don't know *what* it is, y'know. It's just a venting
of venom, I suppose. Justified venom. I don't know what I'm going to
do with it. I may have it published in a little magazine in Tangier. It
won't attract any attention there, y'know, but I just want to get all of it
on the record."

The next night I completed a bridge foursome at Williams' house. He was teamed with Andrew Lyndon and I played with John Young. To my surprise, Tennessee kept his mind on the cards. He played a reasonable game, confining the repartee to the period between the deals for the most part. He had set a stake of a tenth of a cent a point, and each time that Young and I made a contract he would roar, "This house is full of degenerates—crooks, degenerates, and card sharps!"

As the evening wore on, the telephone rang. John Young, who was also in charge of refilling drinks, answered it. "It's David Massage," he said. "He wants to know if you want him to come over."

Tennessee lifted his head from his cards, which he held close to his chest and studied with the concentration of a riverboat gambler, the role he was enacting. "Tell'm to call back at eleven," he said.

Loovis and my wife moved between the living room, glancing through Williams' bookshelves, the patio, or from time to time sitting in kibbitzers' chairs, watching the game. One moment Tennessee, who was dummy, was saying something genial, and the next he had swiveled around to face Loovis.

"Y'just sittin' there smirkin'," Tennessee said, his voice dirty and mean as any Mississippi sheriff's.

"That's not true, Tennessee," Loovis said uneasily. "I'm not smirking."

"Well, I say you're smirkin', and I *know* you're smirkin', and you might as well admit it. . . ."

Loovis, a slim man in his middle forties who has known Williams for twenty years and admires him just this side of idolatry, tried to say something, but Williams, as he frequently does, just overrode him with his forceful stage delivery.

". . . I don't *recall* havin' invited you to dinner t'night," Williams said. "Y'just decided to come along."

Loovis, who had been readmitted to the Williams' circle through the intervention of John Young, seemed to go pale under his tan. He tried again to protest.

"The *truth* is all that's important," said Williams in a voice that was now a snarl. "Tell the truth! You were the first one to mark me as a homosexual in print, but you concealed your own homosexuality.

You're never gonna amount to anything as a novelist until you *learn* to tell the *truth.*"

Williams was referring to Loovis' *The Last of the Southern Winds* [New York: Scribner, 1961—Editor], which was set in Key West and had a minor character who may have been based in part on the playwright. A third novel has had Loovis hung up for the past three years or so.

"You're right, Tennessee," Loovis said weakly. "I wasn't capable of telling the whole truth at that time. That's what I'm trying to do now. That's what's making it so difficult for me."

John Young and I were making mollifying sounds in Tennessee's direction, but he seemed not to hear.

"You do anything like that *again*, baby, and you're gonna have more trouble than you *know,*" said Tenn, turning abruptly back to the card table.

Loovis, devastated, sat there silently. As soon as he could get up, John Young took him aside. "Tennessee gets this way sometimes," he said. "He doesn't mean it. Why don't you take a swim and cool off. . . ."

"He *did* invite me," said Loovis. "I'm sure of it."

"Of course you were invited," John said. "Don't worry about it. Tennessee has probably forgotten about it already. Go on, take a swim. You don't need trunks. It's dark and no one else is out there. I'll get you a towel. . . . Go ahead."

By eleven o'clock we had finished three rubbers. The telephone rang again. John Young answered it. "It's David again," he told Tennessee. "He says to please let him know if you're going to want him tonight because there's something else . . ."

This was a young man, tough-looking, his muscles rippling under a porous-weave T-shirt, whom I had met a couple of nights earlier at a bar. He was one of the drifters who gravitated to Key West during the winter, and had remained there, as though he were waiting for the next flood tide to sweep him north again.

Tennessee lifted his head. "Yeah," he said, "tell him to come on over." Turning to the table, he said, "Well, let's settle up. I've had about enough bridge for the night."

John Young figured up the score. "You and Andrew owe us $1.70 each," he said.

"Damn," said Tennessee, reaching into his pocket for the bills and the change. "The cards just wouldn't come our way tonight." He put the money on the table. "Excuse me," he said, heading for his bedroom, which is off the living room at the rear of the house.

When Tennessee returned he was carrying a lifesize doll. She had seen hard use. Her celluloid face was pushed in, and her pink stuffed body looked as though it had been run over by a car. Unseen by Andrew Lyndon, Tennessee slipped up behind him and dropped the doll in his lap.

"You've just got to take better care of your chile," Tennessee said. "God, how you're neglectin' it. Poor motherless chile."

"You mean, poor childless mothah," said Andrew, patting the doll on its bottom.

"That's right," said Tennessee, laughing. "Poor childless mothah."

Tennessee Williams Turns Sixty
Rex Reed/1971

From *Esquire*, September 1971, 105-108, 216-223. Reprinted
in *People Are Crazy Here* (New York: Delacorte Press, 1974), 12-
40. © 1974 by Stet, Inc. Reprinted by permission.

"Baby, I've been sick." Tennessee Williams sits under a chandelier
sporting a rosy suntan and a freshly thatched beard, having dinner at
Antoine's. He is eating Oysters Rockefeller and sipping cold white
wine and talking about life. If a swamp alligator could talk, he would
sound like Tennessee Williams. His tongue seems coated with rum
and molasses as it darts in and out of his mouth, licking at his
moustache like a pink lizard. His voice wavers unsteadily like old gray
cigar smoke in a room with no ventilation, rising to a mad cackle like
a wounded macaw, settling finally in a cross somewhere between
Tallulah Bankhead and Everett Dirksen. His hands flutter like dying
birds in an abandoned aviary. Tragic flamboyance masks tortured
sensitivity. At the age of sixty the world's most famous playwright
stands precariously on the ledge of vulnerability, fighting like a jaguar
and talking like a poet. "The carrion birds have tried to peck out my
eyes and my tongue and my mind, but they've never been able to
get at my heart."

He's been sick all his life. Diphtheria left him with a kidney ailment
and a childhood paralysis that took years to cure. He had his first
nervous breakdown when he was twenty-three. For the past ten
years his bouts with alcohol and drugs have made headlines. In 1969
he found himself in a psychiatric hospital. "Baby, I was out of my
skull. I could no longer remember how many pills I had taken, and
the liquor I washed them down with had a synergistic effect. I woke
up at two A.M. pouring a pot of scalding hot coffee all over my body.
When I woke up my brother Dakin had committed me to the loony
bin where I had three convulsions and two heart attacks in three
days. They were unbelievably cruel to me. Sleep is absolutely

essential to me if I'm to do my work. Four hours is adequate, but I became a pill freak because I wasn't even getting that. In the loony bin, they let me go as many as four days and nights without closing my eyes. I lost thirty pounds and nearly died. But I'm well now. I'm off the booze and I only take two Miltowns and half of a Nembutal a day. I had to give up phenobarbital. It had absolutely no effect on me whatsoever. If I still can't sleep, I take the other half of the Nembutal. I don't think I am going to die."

"Are you afraid of death?" I ask.

He stares at the swirls inside an empty oyster shell. "I think I've always been somewhat preoccupied with it. It appears in my plays as an excessively recurring theme. There have been evenings when I've been afraid to go to bed. The past few years have been suicidal. I was living a life during the Sixties that was virtually an obliteration of life, deep under the influence of pills and liquor around the clock. I don't know what I was doing if I wasn't trying to find an easy way out. Oh, I thought now and then how I would kill myself if I ever got around to it. . . ."

There is a gasp from across the table, where Tennessee's two friends sit quietly listening. They are a professor of English in a small liberal-arts college out West, who had come to see his old friend in New Orleans before he sails for Italy on another restless search for inner peace, and a young muscular beachboy named Victor Herbert Campbell, twenty-one, the latest in a line of secretaries and traveling companions. "You can call me Vic," says the young man, "it's short for Victor."

"Hah!" snorts Tennessee. "You mean, short for Victim." The beachboy blushes and returns to his steak. "I am sailing on the *Michelangelo* for Rome. George is going with us."

"How is George?" asks the professor, spilling sauce diable all over his white linen plantation suit.

"Not well," sighs Tennessee. "Last time we saw him he hadn't bathed for five weeks and cobwebs were hanging down from the garage over his car doors. The change will do him good."

"Have you see Gore?"

"Of course not. I expect I'll see him before I hear from him. I was simply furious over what he wrote about me in *Two Sisters* [Boston:

Little, Brown, 1970—Editor]. Young Victor here looks very much like
Gore when he was young."

"Who's Gore?" asks Victor, swallowing a forkful of French fries.

"He's a writer, baby. He wrote *Myra Breckinridge.*"

"Oh. I heard of that." Victor smiles triumphantly.

Tennessee turns to me: "This child doesn't know Carson McCullers
from Irving Berlin. He's a product of the television generation, aren't
you, Victor? At home in Key West, he stays up and watches the *Late
Show* and then comes up to my room and tells me the plots. We
should be home there now, except that I cannot live in Key West
anymore, because I am too ill to live anyplace where I can't get
medical treatment when I need it."

There are so many illnesses in the life of Tennessee Williams that
after a while it is not clear just when one begins and another leaves
off. I ask him about his most recent one. "I've had almost nothing *but*
illness, I, yuh, don't know which is the most recent. I did have an
operation in Bangkok for breast cancer. When I consulted my heart
surgeon, Dr. George Burch, here in New Orleans last summer, in the
course of the examination he noticed a slight swelling in the location
of the left mammary gland. . . ."

"I'm here to consult *my* neurologist *and* my cardiologist,"
interrupts the professor.

"Breast cancer is a rare thing among men, isn't it?" I can't resist the
question.

". . . yes, but baby, rare things have been happening to me all my
life. Anyway, an acquaintance of mine, who shall remain anonymous
for our purposes, was in the process of taking me to the Orient and
my doctor told me if it was malignant, I shouldn't take a chance
because the delay would be unfortunate, and he advised me to
cancel the trip. My acquaintance said that would not be necessary
because he, uh, knew the surgeon of the King of Thailand personally.
I said the hell with it, I'm going to take this trip. Well, the swelling
continued slowly but perceptibly to increase on the Pacific crossing so
that by the time I reached Hawaii [he pronounces it Hi-wah-yuh] I
was rather alarmed. I, yuh, believe I mentioned it to some members
of the press who came aboard the ship. I told them I was going to be
operated on by the King's surgeon in Bangkok. Well, when I arrived
in Bangkok, the receptionist at the Hotel Oriental called me half an

hour after I checked in and said there are a few reporters who would like to say hello to you. I went downstairs and they were passing out martinis to everyone, so I joined in . . . heheheh . . . and there was a hush and one of them spoke up and said, 'Mr. Williams, is it true you have come to Bangkok to *die?*' . . . hehhehheh . . . yah! . . . I laughed, of course, and said no, if I were going anywhere to die, I think it would be Rome. And that's how the rumor got started that I was dying of cancer last year. It's all over now, so I don't mind talking about it. It was performed with a local anesthetic and the dope wore off before the end so it was quite painful, but fortunately I had thought to bring a bottle of sherry along with me. I didn't even have a room reserved at the hospital, so I got up after the operation and returned to my hotel in time for dinner. Breast cancer develops more rapidly in a man than in a woman, so I presume it was not malignant or I would be dead by now."

"But you've had additional problems since then, haven't you?"

"Physical problems? Oh, yes. It's been a long time since I was physically well. I think my early years were very wearing on me, the years before I made any money, terrific years of physical want and punishment that left me exhausted. Along with that, I, yuh, had a good deal of hypochondria. My sister Rose has been in a sanitarium since she was twenty-seven years old. I suffer from claustrophobia. I was once put into a jail cell for driving without a headlight and the fear of dying in a damp, dark hole with prostitutes and people screaming for help completely shattered my nerves. I went to a strict Freudian analyst who attributed nearly everything to a . . . misdirected libido, shall we say? . . . hehhehhehyah wheeze . . . I thought *that* was an oversimplification . . . hahahaha . . . but ya know, I lived for years in an apartment on East Sixty-fifth Street between Park and Lexington with one of the tiniest elevators in the city. It said its capacity was five people, but it was a tight squeeze with three. . . . I always have trouble breathing in New York. The place most conducive to work for me is Key West, where I have my studio and swimming pool . . . the place is of no interest socially or intellectually, although my friend James Leo Herlihy lives there, as well as a few painters, but there is nothing to do except work. But I may not be able to live there much longer. During my stay in Bangkok, a terribly vicious and scandalous piece about me was

published in *The Atlantic,* of all places, and while I was away my
house was bombarded with rotten eggs and rocks were thrown in my
swimming pool and now that I am back I have encountered a great
deal of hostility. Three weeks ago I stepped into a fish pool while
crossing an unlighted patio toward an outside staircase. My back was
lacerated by a low wire fence and I suffered a broken rib. I called four
doctors in Key West and not one of them came or responded to my
calls. I had begun to run a high fever and I could not get medical
help, so I telephoned my doctor in New Orleans who said to take an
aspirin. 'But I'm allergic to aspirin,' I said. 'You just think you are,' he
said. So I took an aspirin and during the night my fever broke and I
was cured."

"He's a saint," says the professor. "I saw him today and he said I
could live to be a hundred. But the condition was I give up drinking. I
guess I'll stick with sherry and settle for seventy-five."

"Anyway," says Tennessee, returning to his own problems, "this
magazine also erroneously quoted me as saying I was one of the two
or three richest writers in America, which is preposterous, ya know,
absolutely pre—*pos*—terous! My total assets probably come to
$750,000 including property I own. Fortunately I make a good deal
each year from royalties. I have no particular anxieties about money.
But *The Atlantic* had me *boasting* I was a multimillionaire, which I
most certainly am not. They also said I cut my mother out of my will.
She was never *in* it! I gave my mother Edwina half of *The Glass
Menagerie,* my father gave her half of everything he owned when
they separated, she is an independently well-to-do woman of eight-
eight years who lives in a suburb of St. Louis in an exclusive
retirement home. My will provides for my sister after her death. She
is older than I am, but she had one of the first prefrontal lobotomies
performed on her brain in this country and is incurably schizophrenic
and will no doubt outlive us all. I was most upset about the vulgar
remarks about my sex life—now really, who cares about the sex life
of a sixty-year-old writer?—and the tasteless implications that I
abandoned my best friend Frank Merlo on his deathbed. My
heavens, I slept in the study and gave him the bedroom until he went
into the hospital for the last time before his death. I was with him
continually, including the day he died. So many people knew the
truth, but nobody came to my defense. My agent Audrey Wood

knew the truth. The article made me out to be a monster! Now high-school kids, delinquents I imagine, race past my house in Key West in their cars at night shouting, 'Queer! Faggot!,' and young Victor here has to go out and see if his car has been stolen. The whole attitude of the island has distinctly altered toward me. When people meet me face-to-face, they are very kind. Society is becoming very permissive to one's inalienable rights to pursue whatever personal choices make one happy in life. But among the unsophisticated, there still exists a conspiracy to destroy the sensitive people of the earth."

I ask if he feels he has been personally persecuted because of his private life-style. His mouth forms a round opal, sucking in a tiny sigh. "In the theater especially, one is exposed to a kind of criticism which will use personal lines of attack. I've seen it done time and again."

"I thought theater people were very broad-minded in protecting their own."

"The actors, yes. I'm speaking particularly of people who *write* about the theater more than those who participate *in* it. I've read things that say Blanche was a drag queen. Blanche DuBois, ya know . . . that George and Martha in *Who's Afraid of Virginia Woolf* by Albee were a pair of homosexuals . . . these charges are ridiculous!" His voice becomes high-octane, bordering on hysteria. "If I am writing a female character, goddamnit, I'm gonna write a female character, I'm not gonna write a drag queen! If I wanna write a drag queen, I'll write a drag queen, and I *have* written one, as a matter of fact, which *will* be produced someday. The setting is right here in New Awlyuns and it's called *And Tell Sad Stories of the Deaths of Queens* and it's about a drag queen and I think it's quite funny. It's a paraphrase of that line from *Richard II*—'Now let us sit upon the ground and tell sad stories of the death of *kings*,' only I changed it to *queens* . . . hehhehhehheh. . . ."

The professor has a good laugh, joining Tennessee in his private joke. Young Victor almost chokes on his cherries jubilee.

"I have not always been mistreated by the press," he continues when he has caught his breath. "I had very good relations with Stark Young and Brooks Atkinson. . . . I've had pleasant relations with Walter Kerr. I think that Mister Kerr is the most brilliant *writer* among the critics, but I'm somewhat puzzled by a man of his obvious cultivation and learning and all, that he could expose some of the predictable prejudices and biases that he does. I think it has something to do with the fact that he's a Catholic . . . hehhehheehee . . . but the viciousness of the critics will not drive Albee or me, either, from the theatah . . . it can be very wounding and demoralizing, but it can't stop me. The critical assaults on my work had something to do with my period of maladjustment during the Sixties. I think some of my work was better than it appeared to be from the notices it received, although some of it was thrown on too hastily in the Sixties under circumstances that were not auspicious. *In the Bar of a Tokyo Hotel,* for example, was not as bad as the critics said it was. *Life* magazine said I was all washed up, finished as a playwright, and they even paid for space in *The New York Times* to reproduce this obituary. [10 June 1969, 96—Editor]. I heard some people took another ad to denounce that review, but if they did, I never saw it because Anne Meacham and I ran away to Japan . . ."

"To the bar of a Tokyo hotel?"

". . . to escape the brutality of the press, and my agent Audrey Wood never sends me anything good about me. My poor little dog Gigi landed in quarantine. We left in such haste I didn't look into her vaccination papers, so I had to rent a Japanese house and hire Japanese servants at great personal expense because that was the only way they would let my dog out of quarantine. Oh, it was a dreadful mess. That was the beginning of my breakdown. I had been disintegrating for years, but that was the final culmination of events. I went out of my mind."

During the above, the professor has fallen asleep. "The professor accompanied me to the Orient and he was more ill than I was. I think he has a brain tumor." Throughout dinner, for which he arrived an hour late in a state of dazed confusion, the professor has consumed an old-fashioned, followed by a crème de menthe frappé, followed by a vodka on the rocks, followed by a stinger and polished off with a bottle of white Pouilly-Fuissé. Now he is dozing at the table, like Lionel Barrymore by the fire in *A Christmas Carol.* "Your heart, baby. You're not as young as you used to be."

Tennessee's voice, sharp as a snowflake on a sunburned nose, wakes the professor, who has turned a glass of wine upside down in his sleep. Two waiters fly over with wet cloths to wipe the grape from the carpet as the professor runs his hands through his fading hair. "I am not myself tonight," he says gently. "I think I am suffering from a terminal case of yellow fever."

"I know what you mean," laughs Tennessee in his soft, maniacal giggle. "Those Oriental boys are pure poetry."

Victor lets out a puppy yelp. Tennessee shoots him a thumbtack look. He retires to the men's room to smoke a forbidden cigarette. Cigarettes are not allowed in Tennessee's house since his closest friend for fifteen years, Frank Merlo, died of lung cancer. The subject returns to suicide. "It would probably be something dramatic," I suggest.

"No, I would never jump off of or under anything."

"You'll probably fall upon a samurai sword."

Tennessee lets out a shriek of pleasure at the thought. "Nononono, I don't think I shall ever commit suicide. As a matter of fact, I have been resurrected and come back to life. Looking back on that black nightmare, I don't understand it except that there had been disappointments in my professional career and the death of Frank, the person closest to me in my personal life, and my life was something of a shambles. When I got up in the morning after all the sedation, I gave myself speed injections administered intramuscularly. It was the only way I could write."

"Did it improve your work?"

"It gave it a momentum, ya know, during a period when I was in a clinical state of depression. It gave me a sufficient charge in the morning to get me to the type writer to feel some interest in putting words down on paper. For four years, I had no love life at all. I was only interested in sedation and the shots and writing, that was all. It was a retreat from life, a protracted death wish that lasted roughly from 1963 until my release from the psychiatric hospital where I came within a hairsbreadth of death. That's when I fell in love with life . . . hehhehhaha . . . I didn't like the feeling of death being *that* close and tangible."

"I've had brain damage," says the professor quietly, not wanting to be left out of all this.

"I don't notice, baby," says Tennessee.

"I've just had an injection of Demerol."

"I will summon young Victor to carry us home to bed," sighs

Tennessee. "Tomorrow we will both see a doctor. I have no strength.
I become exhausted [pronounced eggs-zost-id] quite easily. Right
now I am physically unprepared to continue our conversation and
young Victor will have to see me to my hotel." Victor returns from the
men's room, smelling of peppermints, and helps both Tennessee and
the professor on with their coats. At the door, there is a flourish of
starchy genuflecting as New Orleans' most famous expatriate makes
his exit. His manner is unassuming: he could be a clerk or a
wigmaker or a pornographic-movie director. I am beginning to think
he is just an ordinary man when, by some rare occult vibration, he
seems to instinctively mirror my thoughts in his glazed expression. "I
am paranoiac, baby, so I hope you do not make the mistake of
laboring under the false impression that you are talking to a sane
person!"

Outside, under the lamplights of Antoine's, the beachboy and the
staggering professor take their places silently at his side, like sentinels,
and walk into the night. "I used to depend upon the kindness of
strangers," says Tennessee, as though he were projecting across
footlights into an empty theater. "Now I depend upon the kindness of
friends."

What to make of this Halloween goblin? This gilt-edged invitation
to decadence, this life lived with constantly recurring visions in a
madhouse, laced with the beckoning insinuation of champagne and
flaming foods, of Oriental rugs and dimly lit brothels, surrounded by
exotic friends like Anaïs Nin and Anna Magnani, who has publicly
announced on several occasions she would like to marry him? He
has gathered his years slowly, savoring the lusty taste of living, taking
swooning delight in extravaganzas of brocade, crepes suzette, and a
mild scent of orrisroot. High ceilings and dust on antiques fill him
with a sense of appropriateness. He has created a myth of himself.
His temple holds much ivy. He is shy, pursued by visions of hell, and
is blind in one eye. He has done everything and seen everything. He
has won every award there is, including two Pulitzer Prizes. There is
scarcely a minute of the day when he doesn't complain about either
emotional exhaustion or being physically assaulted by any number of
undiagnosed afflictions. One senses he is his own worst enemy, that it
is miraculous that he has indeed been able to write at all. Yet, like the

old dog that has survived many seasons of distemper, he keeps
coming back, a Phoenix rising from the flames. . . .

Morning. The sky over the narrow streets that dive crazily into the
New Orleans French Quarter is bronze marble, hard and brilliant. By
the time I reach his hotel suite at the palatial Royal Orleans, he has
been up for hours, hammering away at his portable typewriter. It is a
daily after-breakfast routine. If he is excited about his theme, he may
type for eight hours straight. Other times he may brood like a
Thurber character, producing doodles. Today is a good day. He is
reworking a scene from something new called *Two-Character Play,*
which he describes as his "last long play." It will be tried out in
Chicago and the prospect worries him. "Although I feel I am only
fully alive when involved in a new production, I have great anxiety
about this one: it was conceived and written when I was almost
completely phased out, and rewritten several times after my release
from the psychiatric hospital, but it is still the work of a very disturbed
writer, and it is terribly personal and I don't know how much
audience empathy will be engaged. I do know the play will be
exposed to critics in Chicago who have been known to bring personal
bias into their criticism and at least one of them, Claudia Cassidy,
officially retired but still quite active, can be quite devastating. I
remember, when *Night of the Iguana* came dragging its ass into
Chicago, she dealt it a terrific clout, calling it a 'bankrupt play,' and
we were barely able to complete our engagement despite the box-
office appeal of Bette Davis, who had fired the director."

Victor is in the bedroom, reading a comic book. He comes in with
some Polaroid color snapshots he has taken of the house in Key
West, pert and sassy, like an art nouveau candy box, and Tennessee's
pets—a Boston terrier bitch named Gigi who looks like a canine
Colette, an orange tabby cat named Gentleman Caller, and an
iguana chained to the front porch to scare off marauders called Mister
Ava Gardner. "I feel the constant threat of hurricanes that will
someday sweep my little frame house out to sea in a tidal wave, but it
is really home to me. I went there after my first play *Battle of Angels*
with Miriam Hopkins caused a sensation of the wrong sort and was
closed down in Boston by the Theatre Guild in 1940. They gave me
$100 and told me to go somewhere and write something else. In

those days, it was possible to live on $100, ya know. So I went down
to Key West and lived in a genteel boardinghouse of solid mahogany.
That was before Howard Johnson came along and ruined it. I should
be there now. I'm too weak to travel. I don't know what I'm doing
here, payin' $80 a day in the Royal Orleans Hotel. I should have
never come here. So many painful memories. It was such a
wonderful place to be in the Thirties. Of course, I couldn't afford to
eat anything but grits then.

"I am one of the richest writers in the world now," he says,
contradicting his remarks of the night before, "but there were many
desperately poor years, even after I was well-known. I started writing
when I was twelve, but I never made any money at it until *The Glass
Menagerie*. People think Audrey Wood sent me money to keep me
alive, but that is a myth. She was once instrumental in procuring a
$1,000 Rockefeller grant which she paid to me in installments of $25
a week, so I wouldn't spend it all at once, but I lived quite frugally at
the Y. She *never* subsidized me."

I ask him about his money, since he makes continual references to
it. "But you know," he drawls, like spitting butter, "I have never
written anything for money. I have made a great deal of money and
I've tried to invest it wisely, but I have no head for financial matters. I
have a portfolio of stocks, in a custodial account. I don't fool with
them myself. I let Chase Manhattan handle them. I told them do what
you will with the stuff as long as you don't invest in anything
involving deforestation or jeopardizing the ecology. I was once
advised by a business associate to put $50,000 into a Denver
bowling alley. I sent my brother Daken out to look at it and he said it
was mahvelous, so I went ahead and invested in it. Shortly after,
another bowling alley, much bigger, was put up right beside it and it
went out of business. I lost the whole fifty thousand, and then some.
Dakin is notoriously ambitious. He'll walk up to people on the street
and say, 'Hello, my name is Dakin Williams and I'm running for the
United States Senate. Do you know Tennessee Williams? He's my
brother.' In my life, Dakin has always been the one to bring me bad
news first. When I was in the loony bin, I was just recovering from
my heart attacks when Dakin presented me with that scurrilous piece
in *The Atlantic*." [TW is probably referring to the *Esquire* article by

Donald Newlove, "A Dream of Tennessee Williams," November
1969—Editor.]

It was also Dakin who converted his brother to Catholicism in
1969. "He attributes my recovery from madness to himself and God.
I attribute it to *myself*. *And* God. Dakin did get me into the church at
a time when he thought I was about to expire. It wasn't much of a
conversion. I have never once been to confession. If I had a church
like the St. Louis Cathedral here in the French Quarter, I might get
into the habit. That is like going to the theater. I'm religious but I'm
not a churchgoer."

He prepares for his walk through the French Quarter with glee.
Victor, who has been giggling in front of a closed-circuit TV channel
that shows the hotel guests around the swimming pool on the roof,
emerges in a one-piece red jump suit. He waits silently by the door
with his camera over his arm. "I've never thrown any of my plays
away," says the writer, not yet ready to give the green light.
"Although I have burned sections of them and I've had things
disappear . . . hehhehhehheehee. . . . I started a novella on the long
voyage back from the Orient called *Hang It Loose*. It's about a, yuh,
hippie that I met on de boat. He had been thrown out of Japan. He
was not allowed to go in any of the public rooms on de boat because
he only had a pair of pants and a shirt, no socks, no jacket. . . ."

"How could he afford to be on this luxury liner. . . ."

"Well, he had to get out of the country and that was the only
passage available. He had just enough money to get him to Hi-wah-
yuh. . . ." He seems perturbed that I have interrupted his story, but
continues. "He was persecuted on the ship. One thing I detest is the
deliberate cruelty of one human being to another. He was a lovely
person. Had long, golden hair, looked like a young Greta Gah-bo,
yes that's it, a young Greta Gah-bo. . . ." He is obviously enthralled
at the vision. "He was somewhat as I'd visualize Chris Flanders, the
young man in my play *The Milk Train Doesn't Stop Here Anymore*,
who was no Richard Burton, baby. I will eventually finish the novella,
but right now I'm concentrating on my last long play. I don't think I
will ever have the energy, provided I do have the time, to write
another full-length play."

I ask if he ever feels he has dried up as a writer. "Never really," he answers quickly. "I've gone through periods when I have reached a, yuh, *impasse,* when it was impossible for me to *express* what I wanted to express, but never when I had nothing to *express*. It's very egg-*zost*-ing. I never think too much about plots, ya know. Plots just sort of happen. I create the characters first and the rest just happens. *Milk Train* was the most frustrating experience I've ever been through. It was never a successful piece of work. I keep rewriting it all the time, but I've never gotten it right. Hermione Baddeley was quite, quite brilliant in the first production, but the part of the boy was never realized. Tab Hunter was hardly what I'd call an innocent, and poor Tallulah could no longer project her voice in the second production. Her physical strength was not adequate. That play reflected a great preoccupation with death, as did most of my work in the Sixties. I'm much more stoical now, hehhehheh. I regard myself as a failed artist. I'm as happy now as I've been in many years. I've come to terms. I don't mind being sixty, I get glasses stronger each year to compensate for failing eyesight. And I've learned how to deal with success. I once wrote an article about it saying security is a kind of death, I think, and it can come to you in a storm of royalty checks beside a kidney-shaped pool in Beverly Hills or anywhere at all that is removed from the conditions that made you an artist. It happened to me after my first success, *The Glass Menagerie,* turned me into an overnight celebrity. I moved to a first-class hotel and lived off room service. Between the moment when I ordered dinner and when it was rolled in like a corpse on a rubber-wheeled table, I lost all interest in it. Once I ordered a sirloin steak and a chocolate sundae, but everything was so cunningly disguised that I mistook the chocolate sauce for gravy and poured it all over the steak. Of course this was the more trivial aspect of a spiritual dislocation that began to manifest itself in more disturbing ways. I became indifferent to people. A wall of cynicism rose in me. Conversations sounded like they had been recorded years ago and were being played back on a turntable. I suspected everyone of hypocrisy; I still do. I hated my work and was in physical agony. I decided to have another eye operation to give myself a gauze mask to hide behind. I had been afflicted for some years with a cataract on my left eye which required a series of needling operations and finally a serious one on the muscle of my left eye. I was in pain and darkness and I ran away to Mexico, an

elemental country where vagrants innocent as children curl up to
sleep on the pavements, and human voices, especially when their
language is unfamiliar, are soft as birds. My public self, that artifice of
mirrors, ceased to exist and I learned that the heart of man, his body
and his brain, are forged in a white-hot furnace for the purpose of
conflict. That struggle for me is creation. I cannot live without it.
Luxury is the wolf at the door and its fangs are the vanities and
conceits germinated by success. When an artist learns this, he knows
where the dangers lie. Without deprivation and struggle there is no
salvation and I am just a sword cutting daisies."

There isn't much to say after that. We leave the hotel suite. A maid
has left a tangle of vacuum-cleaner cords outside the door. "Snakes
in the hallway!" cries Tennessee. Outside, he leads the way to a
jewelry shop on Royal Street to buy a diamond ring. "It's only $125,
a very good bargain," says the shopkeeper.

"A genuine diamond for $125?" gasps Tennessee.

"Its not perfect. . . ."

"Who *is*?" He buys it. Guided by the sun, he continues his stroll.
"This place has so many memories. I came here in 1939 to write. I
was heartbroken over my sister Rose's confinement in a psychiatric
hospital and I suffered a breakdown myself. In New Orleans I felt a
freedom. I could catch my breath here. See that bar over there? That
used to be called Victor's. I lived just around the corner in a large
room on the top of an old house where I worked under a skylight at a
large refectory table writing *A Streetcar Named Desire*. At that time, I
was under the mistaken impression that I was dying. I didn't feel
much like eating, but in the evenings after working all day my only
close friend would bring me a bowl of oyster stew and in the
afternoons I would go around the corner to Victor's Café and have
myself two brandy alexanders. Without that sense of fatigue and that
idea of imminently approaching death I doubt I could have created
Blanche DuBois."

He talks as though Blanche is still inside him, trying to get out, a
victim in the jungle without talons. His face is sad and old as he leads
the way past antique shops, a flamenco parlor and a genuine voodoo
shop, the owner of which claims to be a warlock who, in a former
life, was a cat. The window is full of howling cats among the gris-gris,
love potions and books on Marie Laveau the Voodoo Queen. He

stops at 722 Toulouse, his first address in New Orleans, and the years
cross his face in a shadow. "In those attic windows I wrote a short
story about a tubercular poet throwing up blood—a recurring theme
in my work. I used to do it myself. I stayed alive by hocking my
typewriter and waiting on tables. It was a boardinghouse and I
thought up a slogan—'Meals for a Quarter in the Quarter.' I'd go
outside the old gray building with its green shutters and iron grillwork,
hang up my sign with my own slogan, then I'd run back inside, and
change quickly into my waiter's uniform just in time to serve the okra.
One night I came home and found an old hag who lived in the place
pouring boiling water through the cracks in the floor to scald the
tenants to death. I escaped owing $50 by sliding down from the
second story on a string of bed sheets to a trumpet player waiting
below who promised to drive me to California in his jalopy to what
he described as his uncle's magnificent ranch. It turned out to be a
run-down pigeon farm where they took me in out of pity after the
trumpet player deserted me, and I earned my keep plucking squab
feathers. I still remember how I got paid. For every squab I plucked
I'd keep tab by putting a feather in a milk bottle."

We pass stuffed mammies holding boxes of pecan pralines
wrapped for mailing. At the Cabildo, he crosses over by the Jax
brewery and walks along the New Orleans waterfront. "This reminds
me of the time I did *The David Frost Show*. He asked me if I was a
homosexual in front of millions of people. I was so mortified I didn't
know what to say, so I just blurted out, 'I cover the waterfront,' and
the audience cheered me so loud he said he guessed he better break
for a commercial and I said, 'I should think you would.'" We come to
a sign advertising bayou cruises and riverboat rides and I ask if it was
true that Truman Capote once tapdanced on a steamboat and
painted flowers on jelly glasses. "I think that was just a product of
Truman's fanciful imagination. He always lived in a fantasy, ya know.
When I first met him, he told me he had a ring given to him by André
Gide. But he was so amusing in those days, before he discovered the
Jet Set. I will never forget we were coming back from Europe
together on the *Queen Mary* once and there was a mad Episcopal
bishop on board who kept following Little Truman around. Truman
was very, very funny and kept us all in stitches by telling this poor
depraved bishop, 'You know I've always wanted to own one of those

bishop's rings for my very own,' and the poor man kept saying, 'Oh, that's very difficult . . . you have to be a *bishop,'* and Little Truman said, 'Well, I thought perhaps I could get one from some de *frocked* bishop!' . . . hehhehhee. . . . I always said Little Truman had a voice so high it could only be detected by a bat!"

He lets out a wild, weird cackle that causes people to turn around in the street. "The only *real* writer the South ever turned out was Carson." Of all the writers he's known, Carson McCullers was the only one with whom he established a lasting friendship. "She was no angel, ya know. Or if she was, she was a black angel. But she had infinite wisdom. Ours was a deep relationship that spanned many years. I first met her when I went to Nantucket to die. I had read *The Member of the Wedding* that year and I considered her the world's greatest living writer. I wanted to meet her before I died, so I wrote to her and she arrived on the boat, this tallll girl came down the gangplank wearing a baseball cap and slacks. She had a radiant, snaggletoothed grin and there was an immediate attachment. I seldom remember addresses, but this was 31 Pine Street in Nantucket, an old gray frame house with a windup Victrola and some fabulous old records, like the *Santiago Waltz* and Sousa band numbers. A big windstorm broke the downstairs windows and a pregnant cat jumped in and had kittens on Carson's bed. This was her last good year before her stroke. She did a good deal of the cooking, mostly canned green pea soup with wienies in it and an innovation called 'spuds Carson,' which was mashed potatoes with olives and onions mixed in it. She was in love that summer and mooning over somebody. Her husband Reeves had not yet committed suicide, but it was not him she was mooning over. She would go out and buy Johnnie Walker and sit in a straight-back chair at the foot of the steps and after my friend and I went to bed she'd sit up all night mooning over this romance in her head. I'd come down in the morning and the bottle would be empty. It was a crazy but creative summer. We read Hart Crane poems aloud to each other from a book I stole from the St. Louis public library, and we had a portrait of Laurette Taylor, who had just died, with a funeral wreath around it, and the fireplace was always filled with beautiful hydrangeas, and we sat at opposite ends of a long table while I wrote *Summer and Smoke* and she wrote *The Member of the Wedding* as a play. Carson is the only person I've ever been able to stand in the same room with me when I'm working. After her stroke, she was incapacitated, but my sister Rose was in a sanitarium near her house in Nyack and I would often stay with Carson when I went to see her. She kept a room upstairs called 'Tenn's Room' which was always prepared for my visits. My fondest dream was to own a ranch in Texas and have my sister Rose, my grandfather, and Carson, and we would all live together, all of us invalids."

Williams saw a lot of McCullers in her last years. He sent her money, refused to recognize her strokes ("Why honey, you jus' been havin' a li' ol' psychosomatic breakdown") and transferred to her large doses of his stifled affections for his sister Rose. He later used many of her characteristics as the basis for the female lead in *Night of the Iguana,* just as she based the old judge in *Clock Without Hands* on Tennessee's Grandpa Dakin. "She loved life passionately and, even when in dire stress, always managed to survive somehow. When her husband killed himself, they lived in an old rectory outside Paris. Reeves had a tree all picked out and two lengths of rope, insisting they hang themselves together. 'All right, I can no longer fight with you,' sighed Carson, 'but first let's have some wine.' They stopped at a tavern, Carson stole out the back door, got a bus ride back to Paris, and never saw him alive again. There were only two great female writers—Carson and Jane Bowles—both so vulnerable, and so mad. The human body cannot hold that much talent. It has to explode. All the charming people I've ever known are a little bit mad. I am very suspicious of people who appear to be outwardly happy all the time and have always regarded them as somewhat simpleminded."

At the corner of St. Ann and Royal he is almost hit by a bus named Desire. "Sad, sad," he shakes his head, "it replaced the old streetcar years ago. You know I took quite a bit of poetic license in that play. If you follow the instructions in the play and take that streetcar, it never went to a place called Elysian Fields, and even if it did, you wouldn't be in the Quarter anymore. I used it because I liked the name Elysian Fields." Past the gumbo shops and windows filled with fig preserves, past the boarded-up horse stables, across Bourbon Street, where, even at midday, the sound of Dixieland jazz lifts toward the Louisiana sky where clouds never touch. "I wrote the first draft of *Camino Real* in that house," he says, or, "Victor, take a picture of me in front of old

Andrew Jackson's statue covered with pigeon shit." He is feeling his oats.

Just behind the Morning Call, where Tennessee spent many early hours in the foggy predawn of New Orleans drinking black coffee with chicory to wash out hangovers, stands the old streetcar named Desire which operated on the streets of the city from 1903 to 1935. The squat little man standing in front of the iron railing that protects it from invaders doesn't seem to know its motor has stopped running and its electrical wires have long been disconnected. Tears appear in his eyes. "Come on, baby, let's eat," he says suddenly, breaking the mood as he scurries from the site. "I'm so hungry I could eat moose pie."

He sips a vermouth cassis at the bar of Brennan's, served by darkies who look like they just stepped off an Uncle Ben's rice box. "How you, Mr. Wi'yums," they grin. A wild, electrified woman flies at him with intense determination in her eyes, nearly knocking him off his barstool. She is Mrs. Irving Stone, whose husband is in town promoting a new book. "Mr. Williams, I just want to tell you we are on a cross-country tour"—she unfolds a series of eighteen plane tickets, each one representing a different city, and throws them across his chest, causing him to spill his vermouth cassis on his blue jump suit—"and this ticket right here says New Orleans, which wasn't on the trip, but I told them I don't care if it isn't a book town, I don't care if people don't read books there, it's so much fun. I only love two men in the world—Lawrence Durrell and Tennessee Williams." She throws her arms around him, gives him a wet kiss and flees to her table, where she is joined by her husband, who does *not* come over and tell Tennessee Williams he is one of the two greatest men in the world.

"Who *is* that woman?" growls Tennessee. "And who is Irving Stone? I hope he doesn't come over too, because I don't ever remember reading anything he ever wrote. What did he write?"

"He wrote a book about Michelangelo and a book about Andrew Jackson and a book about Vincent Van Gogh and now he's got a new book about Sigmund Freud. . . ."

Tennessee rolls his eyebrows. "Hmmm . . . can't think of any original characters, eh?"

Our table is ready. People are staring at the world's most famous

playwright with a young man in a tightfitting Tom Jones jump suit.
"After lunch," announces Big Daddy, "we are going to purchase you
a conservative blue suit, Victor. If you are to continue to be my
secretary, you'd better start looking the part. These red Santa Claus
suits you wear are fine for Key West, but they don't go over at the
Edwardian Room of the Plaza hotel."

"Can I have a shoulder bag, too?" asks Victor.

Tennessee rolls his eyes toward heaven and strokes his beard,
grinning a jack-o'-lantern smirk. "No need to gild the lily." He lets out
a scream of laughter.

Tennessee studies his menu. "I'd like to order a Waldorf salad, but
my doctor won't let me eat nuts. He didn't say anything about
cannibalism, however. Hehhehhehhehheehee. Although I'm sure it's
very bad for the cholesterol." He settles for grits and grillades, a veal
dish served with red-eye gravy. A waiter with a rather large behind
passes the table. Tennessee reaches out and pinches it. The waiter
hurls around, his fists doubled. "What the . . . oh, it's *you*, Mr.
Williams . . . what are you doing in town?"

Tennessee looks innocent-guilty, like a choirboy who has just been
caught sneaking a bullfrog into the collection plate. "We ah heah fo'
Holy Week," he says, exploding with laughter. The waiter leaves,
laughing too, and rubbing his derrière. "Don't you think I should
become an actor? I am sixty years old, nobody in the world has a
voice like mine, and with my new beard, I could play a lot of
grotesque, decadent old Sydney Greenstreet parts. I'm a great ham,
ya know, and a notorious publicity hound. When I was in London
recently doing a poetry reading, Pier Paolo Pasolini, the Italian
director, came up to me afterward and said, 'You know, Mr. Williams,
you're really an actor!' and I said, 'Okay, got any parts for me?' It's
much more fun than writing for the screen. I once spent several
months under contract to MGM in 1943, making $250 a week, and I
didn't write a goddamn thing except a thing for Lana Turner called
Marriage is a Private Affair. It wasn't bad, but I was writing for a *real*
actress and Miss Lana Turner could not say the lines, so they finally
told me they couldn't use my script because it was simply beyond her
abilities. When I saw the picture, they only kept two of my lines. Then
they asked me to write a movie for Margaret O'Brien and I refused. I
loathe and detest child actors. Can you imagine Tennessee Williams

writing for Margaret O'Brien? It would be ludicrous. Later, when I did
the screenplay for *Senso,* Luchino Visconti used his old standby,
some hack woman he keeps around, to rewrite my script and when I
finally saw *that* one, only one scene of mine was left—a scene in a
bedroom with two people waking up in a bed. There was a line that
went, 'There's always a sound in a room when you wake,' and
Visconti had a fly buzzing around. Of course, that's not what I meant
at all. When I wake up I always start belching. There's always that
sound of getting rid of the poisons from the night before. I've never
had any success writing for the screen unless it is a film script of one
of my own plays.

"I might as well be an actor. I just paid my income tax for last year.
I paid $65,000 and I didn't write a damn thing. Somebody is
screwing me! Nobody ever tells me anything. I didn't even know
Summer and Smoke was being done as an opera until someone in
St. Louis wrote me about it. I don't think anyone wants to encourage
me at all." His voice mounts hysterically and people from
surrounding tables turn around to stare. Uplifted eyebrows turn into
knowing smiles when they recognize the speaker. Tennessee settles
down to his red gravy, dipping it up in hearty spoonfuls, forgetting his
outburst like a hen in a barnyard whose feathers soften once again
after being knocked off her nest. "Anyway, I've made a great deal of
money during my life and I don't know where most of it has gone. I
own an apartment building here in New Awlyuns called the Patio
Pool Apartments which is inhabited by more than its share of dykes.
Last time I was here, I walked into the courtyard and screamed, 'All
right, all dykes—*out!*' There was a great banging of shutters. Property
is an awful hassle, ya know. You have to pay for the eviction of
undesirable tenants. Actually, I've always had a great relationship
with dykes. They don't frighten me at all. Some of my best friends
are dykes. One is a notorious lesbian in the Quarter who draws
people's pictures in front of the St. Louis Cathedral for a dollah."
There is an enormous rustle of summer organza as solid silver forks
go clattering into the china plates.

Another waiter passes with a tray of hot bananas foster. "He looks
just like Marlon Brando. I first met him in 1947, when I was casting
Streetcar. I had very little money at the time and was living simply in
a broken-down house near Provincetown. I had a houseful of people,

the plumbing was flooded and someone had blown the light fuse.
Someone said a kid named Brando was down on the beach and
looked good. He arrived at dusk, wearing Levi's, took one look at the
confusion around him, and set to work. First he stuck his hand into
the overflowing toilet bowl and unclogged the drain, then he tackled
the fuses. Within an hour, everything worked. You'd think he had
spent his entire antecedent life repairing drains. Then he read the
script aloud, just as he played it. It was the most magnificent reading I
ever heard and he had the part immediately. He stayed the night,
slept curled up with an old quilt in the center of the floor.

"I have never indulged in any sexual encounter with any actor who
ever appeared in one of my works, although there was *one* quite
famous one who tried. I was at the roulette table in San Juan once
when a waiter delivered a crystal goblet filled with cold milk. It was
from a young actor who had sought me out to read for a part. He
looked like a Midwestern basketball player and seemed totally
unsuitable, but he read well and later got the part. He tried to follow
me to my room to consummate the arrangement and I said, 'That
won't be necessary—the part is yours because you read superbly!'
Actors are such children. I am always very shy with them. I was so ill
for years I don't remember anything about my opening nights; I was
too drunk to know where I was. Estelle Parsons, however, was quite
brilliant in *The Seven Descents of Myrtle*, but the poor thing had no
help. José Quintero didn't direct her properly, so everything that
happened onstage was her own invention. The film version of that
play was perfectly disastrous. Gore Vidal wrote it, he said, out of
friendship for me. Baby, with friends like that. . . . I have not had
good relations with Sidney Lumet. He directed that flop as well as
The Fugitive Kind, which was so dark and murky it looked like
everyone was drowning in chocolate syrup. And Brando and Anna
Magnani engaged in a clash of egos never before equaled. And I also
didn't understand why Joanne Woodward had to be so dirty all the
time. I also hated *Cat on a Hot Tin Roof*, although it made a lot of
money for me. Elizabeth Taylor is not what I had in mind at all for
Maggie the Cat. Maureen Stapleton I think is an absolute genius and
one of the total innocents of the world, you know. Very self-
destructive. She's a genius because her talent doesn't seem to come
from anywhere. It just comes out of her fingertips and her toes and

her kneecaps. And I loved Vivien Leigh. And Kim Stanley. Another
case of too much talent to fit one body. Once she came running up
to me at a party and began to beat me on the chest, which was not
good at all for my breast cancer, ya know, and screamed at me, 'How
could you write that dreadful play?' I never did find out which play
she was talking about. The last time I saw her I gave a party for her in
my rooms at the Plaza and she came three hours late. She walked in
just as everyone was packing up to leave, all wrapped in swaddling
black draperies, and sweating in the face. The next day she called up
and apologized sweetly for her behavior, asking if there was anything
she could do for me and I said, 'Baby, I'm out of Nembutal and I
cannot sleep,' and she telephoned her pharmacy and they delivered
by special messenger a whole supply of Nembutal, which got me
through the next week and a half. I adore her. She has never been
closely associated with my plays, but we understand each other. A
kook likes a kook, baby. She once played Blanche DuBois in
Houston, but nobody told me about it until too late and I never saw
her in it. I think she would be the best Blanche DuBois in the world.
The worst Blanche DuBois in the world was poor Tallulah, although I
must say she was amusing. I'm sure that attack on Blanche DuBois
being a drag queen started when Tallulah played her. When she
came down to Florida she would say, 'I'm going to take a suppository
and do not become alarmed at anything that might happen. I will
soon become incoherent and leave the room, but let the party
continue.' Then she would turn into a zombie and pass out in the
middle of the floor. I don't think anyone ever realized how
desperately ill poor Tallulah was. By the time she opened in Milk
Train in New York, she was beyond all help and her voice had given
out completely. She could no longer project beyond the first row and
I was no help at all because I was desperately ill myself at the time.
Tallulah always blamed the failure of that play on Tony Richardson
and the goddamn Chinese gongs, but most of it was my fault because
I allowed people to do whatever they liked with my plays then. I'm
much more protective now."

And so it goes, the wine flowing into the talk, with Tennessee
Williams never running out of stories, anecdotes, philosophical
observations, on a lazy afternoon in New Orleans. It is possible to
think twice before taking him home to dinner (he once stood up at

one of New Orleans' most distinguished tables and announced he
was an octoroon just to clear the room), but it is difficult to dislike
him. How can you dislike an honest man who wears his trump cards
on his sleeve like an epaulet? He stands like a tiny troll in the
revealing sunlight outside the restaurant, not at all resembling a man
who writes plays about incest, rape, cannibalism, homosexuality and
rape, trying to say good-bye nicely so as not to hurt anyone, his voice
a furry caterpillar, sinuous and warm, wriggling into all kinds of boozy
shapes. "I must hurry now before the store closes to buy young
Victor his new suit. I saw a notice in *The Village Voice* last week," he
says from nowhere, "advertising exotic massages administered in a
bubble bath. Victor, make a note of that so I can try it on my next
visit; the only thing I've never done is take heroin, because that's the
end, baby. Pills and booze are a slow means to an end, but heroin is
the end itself."

A Jesus freak selling religious pamphlets stops him.

"What're you pushing, baby?" he says. "I'm selling the word of
God in a book called *As It Is,* which teaches you self-acceptance."
Tennessee rolls his eyes, tugging on his beard with glee. "I could use
some of *that,*" he chuckles. He pays the Jesus freak five dollars and
says over his shoulder, "The hippie movement is becoming quite
profitable, I *see.*" The Jesus freak gives him the peace sign, stuffing
the fiver into his dirty jeans.

Tennessee enters a curio shop selling rare antiques, manuscripts
and maps of buried pirate treasure. He is complaining about the ring
he bought that morning. "It's not Victorian enough. I only look good
in Victorian jewelry. I lost three diamonds in the ocean near Key
West. I lose all my jewels swimming. But this is not Victorian enough.
I think I'll give it to young Victor, here." Young Victor is preoccupied
with a drawing of a skull. A trompe l'oeil: on closer inspection, the
skull becomes a woman looking into an oval mirror. It is called
Vanity.

"Can I buy it, Tom?" asks Victor gently. Only Tennessee's closest
friends call him Tom.

"Absolutely not," he cries, visibly upset by the skull. "I will not
have it in my house. It's all about death and I cannot stand anything
around me that reminds me of death."

Gentleness, kindness, mixed with madness and contradiction—

conflicting traits that define the man, occurring in uneasy rhythmic patterns. Outside the shop, he is merry once more. You don't know whether to laugh or humor him. A man of shifting contrasts, like watermarks on a desert horizon.

I say farewell at the edge of the Quarter. "Ya know, I'll be all right. They've left me for dead, but I'll survive." He searches the Tiffany-lamp sky of New Orleans, looking for carrion birds perhaps, always nearby in his shadowy mind, waiting to dive. Then his face breaks into a reassuring grin and he is the mischievous imp once more, tapping his foot on the corner of Royal and Canal in a blue denim jump suit, blue tennis shoes and a long gray overcoat. "I told my friend Gore Vidal, I said, 'Gore, baby, I slept through the Sixties,' and my friend Gore, he said, 'You didn't miss a thing!'"

Meeting with Tennessee Williams
Jeanne Fayard/1971

From *Tennessee Williams* (Paris: Éditions Seghers, 1972), 130-135. © 1972 by Jeanne Fayard. Reprinted by permission. Trans. Marlene J. Devlin.

With a deep tan, a thick beard, and slow, even nonchalant gestures, Tennessee Williams does not seem to be a man tortured by conflicts. There is great charm and gentleness in his voice, and a very great simplicity. Reputed to be very secretive and timid, always preoccupied, fleeing mundane conversations and social gatherings, Williams takes refuge in a life of wandering and nocturnal excursions. Only the typewriter, placed in front of the window, seems the stable element, the permanent sanctuary. Tennessee Williams appears to be the opposite of the confident writer: he mistrusts his style and questions himself about his characters. Above all, his conversation is marked by great bursts of explosive and infectious laughter, and suddenly, with a faraway look, he continues to talk but seems to be pursuing an eternal dialogue with himself, out loud. Then he returns with a story whose humor contrasts with the seriousness of his reflections. He is a man of contradictions in whom laughter and gaity seem to mask a profound anguish.

TW: I loved the set and the entire production of *Sweet Bird of Youth*. Edwige Feuillère is marvelous! And Françoise Sagan's translation is very poetic; she has refined all that was heavy in my text. I am trying more and more to reach a classic and poetic style.

The critics? No, I don't want to read them, I work instead.

I live with my characters. They are more real than I am. They are more I than I am. My work is the only way of realizing myself.

JF: Throughout your work, one finds the same kind of characters, first women: Laura, Blanche, Alma . . . then men: Val, Sebastian, Shannon.

TW: Yes, they are not the same, but there are resemblances among them.

JF: Your work, it seems to me, is a quest of the androgynous.

TW: Exactly.

Hannah? She had to pass through the tunnel of despair. She is a Blanche purified of confusion and sensuality. She is nearly detached from life. She feels for others. She accepts everything from others. Val? He is still trapped in his corruption and engaged in his struggle to maintain his integrity and purity. He is in a sense more moving because of this struggle.

JF: Val is a very complex character; he gives to each one what they demand: Carol (his body), Eva (his spirit), Lady (body and spirit).

TW: But these fragmented personalities are not reconciled. There is still a duality.

A duality not reconciled.

I love these lines of Hart Crane which I recite often and used as the epigraph for *Streetcar*:

> And so it was I entered the broken world
> To trace the visionary company of love, its voice
> An instant in the wind (I know not whither hurled)
> But not for long to hold each desperate choice.

They are magnificent lines! Hart Crane! "The Broken Tower." It was his last poem. He killed himself at the age of 33. A fantastic man! He could have lived . . . but you know that they did not even acknowledge receiving his poems, this magazine where he had sent them. He thought that he was a failed artist; it was the only thing he had written during his trip to Mexico; then he drowned himself.

JF: Yes, poets sometimes need a little success, not too much . . . but a little just the same!

TW: They don't have so much need of succeeding as of being reassured, to the extent that they really believe in the worth of their work. Money helps when one gets old. But one can be young without money.

JF: Hannah was initiated into oriental philosophies; did they attract you?

TW: Yes, although I have never studied them.

I have traveled in the Orient and spoken with Buddhist monks. I was in Singapore one day and I visited the House of the Dead where they were having a great ceremony. There were people drinking, laughing, orchestras, a banquet. Someone had just died. It was a liberation from body and suffering.

JF: The last step?

TW: Oh! I believe that all adult life is a preparation for that.

JF: Your work is marked by corruption and yet it is very pure.

TW: It is always a struggle to achieve cathartic purity. As in life. In each one's life there is a struggle to purify oneself, at least with the Puritans. I am a decadent Puritan. Hannah is right. One should attain her level. . . But I don't think that I can. She is alone, but she says that she is prepared to face it.

Shannon? He has not achieved his quest. He will never finish it. He will never accept himself except through drink. He will work out a compromise with the widow Faulk and will become reasonable. But he will always be "Black Irish," a victim of drink and sex. He will have to immerse himself in these to resolve the conflicts.

These divided characters reappear constantly in my work: Val, Shannon, Blanche, Alma. . . Sebastian? He is completely enslaved by his baser nature and this is what destroys him. His death is a ritualistic death, symbolic. And when he fails, when he is unable to write his poem that summer, then he is completely lost. He was a little more decadent than the others.

JF: Or less aware of his decadence? Is purity awareness in the midst of evil?

TW: You mean, is purity something that one practices, a discipline; I think so—but not really. Yes, to remain aware but keep a feeling of repulsion.

JF: And of compassion; there is much of it in your work.

TW: Yes, that's what they tell me and I believe it. But my gravest problem as a writer is to not repeat myself constantly—with these divided people, their struggle. . .

JF: Doesn't Christopher Flanders [*The Milktrain Doesn't Stop Here Anymore*—Editor] mark an evolution; he is an angel of death?

TW: He really didn't have depth. I didn't understand him myself. That's finally why the play didn't work. I was very ill and depressed at the time. I understood the old woman Goforth, but one can never know if Christopher is really a good man who comforts dying women, if he is sincerely devoted to them, and if he really wants to help them endure their agony. I wanted to make him deliberately ambiguous, but I think that I made him too ambiguous.

JF: It seems to me that he confused transcendental truth which he is seeking with a maternal need that he feels to protect elderly women. His god is a maternal god and not a masculine one.

TW: I never saw it like that.

JF: It's only my impression and I could be wrong!

TW: It's also possible that you're right. (He noted the word "Motherly" on a piece of paper.) You know, when one writes and the unconscious has as much importance as it does for me, one really doesn't know what he is saying.

Val? He is very hurt when he discovers that Lady used him as a stud to satisfy her sexual needs. He is at first disappointed but finally reconciles himself to this idea because it is part of his nature.

JF: Val, Sebastian . . . are studs; they are also the ones who give the most spiritually; isn't that a contradiction?

TW: The classic stallion gives a lot whether or not he has the intention!

Chance Wayne? He is the same kind of stud. But that's not what he wanted to be. It was not his choice. He went too far into his corruption. The Princess? At the end she is so preoccupied with her comeback that she is almost hysterical. But you know that her comeback will only be another disillusionment. She didn't have a big enough heart. And he had insulted her. She has been a monster for too long. And so someone had to lose. Chance is used in a symbolic manner. It is a ritualistic death, a metaphor. He had to be real to be important. You cannot use a character as a dramatic symbol if he is not first real for you. I didn't discover his real value until the end.

JF: Blanche doesn't know her real nature.

TW: Yes, she says, "I don't tell truth, I tell what *ought* to be truth." She lives in a fairyland. That's why she goes mad. There is no sure refuge in a fairyland. Not for long, in any case. In her heart, she is pure. Sensual, but pure.

JF: What is purity for you?

JF: Perhaps what I'm still searching for. I continue to search for it and for reconciliation with death.

JF: What is true innocence?

TW: Living from day to day.

I like life, even if it is not always agreeable, but I know of no other alternative. I have not yet reconciled myself to death. I can't imagine how to achieve that. Death is inevitable. The greatest trick in life is learning to accept that.

JF: Because it's the only thing that one does alone?

TW: Yes, people attend the dead but in reality one is alone.

JF: Is the quest for the androgynous for you the reconciliation of opposites?

TW: In a sense, yes . . . But is it a step from *being* to *non-being*? Because *non-being* is *non-being*, it seems to me, the end of existence. It's the greatest step that one can take. People wait for death, but in fact, most do not desire it, they prefer it.

JF: By non-being, you mean the absence of pleasure. . .

TW: It is the absence of intensity which is so saddening.

JF: In fact, the myth of the androgynous should not be the renunciation of being, but heightened being?

TW: Yes, but the androgynous is a myth, as you say, an ideal! You can seek it but never find it. However, the androgynous is the truest human being. And if it's a myth, where does that leave us?

Paris, 3 October 1971

A Talk about Life and Style with Tennessee Williams
Jim Gaines/1972

From *Saturday Review,* 29 April 1972, 25-29. © 1972 by Saturday Review Magazine Co. Reprinted by permission.

It was Easter Monday in New York City, and several theater critics seized the occasion to declare that the reputation of Tennessee Williams—a reputation generally believed to be somewhat ghostly these days—had been resurrected.

The playwright cared little for the metaphor; but he had reason to be pleased that his new play, *Small Craft Warnings,* a melancholy study of a group of characters gathered in a Southern California bar, was received with genuine enthusiasm. One critic praised the play for its "seedy honesty," and Clive Barnes wrote in *The New York Times:* "I suspect it may survive better than some of the much-touted products of his salad years." The sixty-one-year-old Williams had not received that sort of praise from the New York critics in more than a decade—not since *Night of the Iguana* opened on Broadway to highly favorable reviews in 1961.

Even before the critics rendered their judgments, however, I was prepared to admire the play. Indeed, I have long regarded Tennessee Williams as something of a national treasure—one of those rare literary artists whose work springs from a passionate desire to "tell all" about himself and his world.

Accordingly, I arranged to visit the playwright at his home in Key West three weeks before the opening of *Small Craft Warnings.* I was not interested in attempting yet another of the psychoanalytic dissections that have been written about him in recent years. I wanted to learn what I could about the master's work habits, creative technique, past influences, and aspirations for the future. . . .

On the first evening of my visit, the playwright took me and some

213

of his friends to a local restaurant famed for its turtle steak. We heard an account, eerily reminiscent of *Suddenly Last Summer,* of the slaughtering of sea turtles—how they are impaled on large hooks and the meat is carved out of the shell by a man renowned for his quick facility with the butcher knife. Williams also told of a one-winged sea gull named Pete and a local pelican whose gular pouch had been mutilated, both of which creatures depended for food "on the kindness of strangers." All of this was accompanied by the sound of a group of senior citizens lifting frail choruses of "Smile, Smile, Smile" and other old favorites.

A race riot had broken out the day before, and after dinner Williams wanted to visit the scene. Outside, the night was shot through by the flashing lights of police cars and the sound of sirens converging on the scene of more violence downtown. The restauranteur told us that someone had just been shot in the local pool hall. Williams was finally persuaded not to visit the riot area but to return to the safety of his home.

The next morning, after he had taken his regular swim in the pool, Williams wrapped himself in a yellow beach towel, lowered himself onto a chaise lounge, and tilted his face toward the sun. As we talked, he sipped a glass of red wine. I asked him how he got himself started working every morning.

"Well, now it's a habit. When I get up, all I'm interested in is work. I have my coffee alone; I don't want anybody around. I go into the studio, and I work. I've read the stories about Hemingway sharpening twenty pencils every morning to get himself started, but I don't believe them. I take a martini in with me. The hours in the studio are the high point of my day. They're what my day is for, you know? The rest is just passing time as agreeably as possible. But the writing is the challenge and excitement of the day."

Does he use diagrams to keep characters or the story line in focus?

"Nah. It shocked me to learn that F. Scott Fitzgerald used diagrams. The only time I attempted it was with *Stairs to the Roof.* I pinned up a little schedule on the balcony of the rooming house where I lived in the old slave quarter of New Orleans. It said, you know, 'tomorrow scene three' and 'then discover stairs to the roof' or whatever it was. I worked with a schedule because I was desperately poor at the moment, and I hoped it would help me cut down the time."

Does he have a clear focus on characters and story line when he starts to work on a play?

"Noo. I *see* somebody, you know? Like I saw Blanche sitting in a chair with the moonlight coming through a window onto her. My first idea for the title was 'Blanche's Chair in the Moon.' But I only wrote one scene then. She was waiting for Mitch, and he wasn't showing up. That was as far as I got then; it was December of 1944. I felt *Streetcar* so intensely that it terrified me. I couldn't work for several months I was so terrified. I said, 'I can't cope with it; I can't carry this off.' I didn't go back to it until 1947, when I was in New Orleans, after I had written *Summer and Smoke.* Then I went back to it, and it wrote itself, just like that. I finished it here in Key West in the La Concha Hotel. It took me by storm. Blanche was so dynamic, she possessed me. I got that out very quickly.

"You see, I don't work from the beginning to the end of a play. Usually, I have a vision of the most dramatic scene, the central scene, and then I work around it for the approach and the denouement, you know? Like in *Small Craft Warnings,* I first saw Leona remembering her beautiful brother and the violin piece he used to play. Not that I kept that scene completely intact. In fact, I'd like to trim that scene down now, take out some of the repetition and get some more detail in. I think she should interrupt her lyric speech at some point and scream something like: 'They *told* me he hung out in the Greyhound's men's room. Arrested! What filthy lies people tell! He was just too weak.' You know, to break it up. Then go back to the lyricism.

"I think that subconsciously I know the story line before I start to work, but I have to go through many drafts before I know for sure. It comes out, it emerges like an apparition out of the mists."

Has he ever felt in the course of his work that "something inside" was taking over?

"Only about three or four days out of a year. It's like, you know, something transcendental, and those are the days when you really write the play. Technically you're working on it every day, but those few days each year are the times you write, you know, with expansion, with great, great freedom. It's like something inside yourself, a possession."

He told me he thought the character Miss Alma in *Summer and Smoke* was the most fully developed of any in his plays. I then asked him which he considered the most healthy, the most integrated.

"Well, I think that Leona in *Small Craft Warnings* is a fully integrated woman, you know? She is the first really whole woman I have ever created and my first wholly triumphant character. She is truly devoted to life, however lonely—whether it be with a stud like Bill or some young faggot she takes under her wing because he reminds her of her brother.

"I think the character I like most is Miss Alma, though. You know, she really had the greatest struggle. It seemed that Blanche had really solved her problems. She had certainly expiated the death of her husband already through her continual orgy with those boys of the army camp. But she was an hysteric, on a collision course with some terrible thing in her that Stanley brought to a head. I think Alma was certainly the more triumphant of the two, though Blanche was perhaps the more feeling. You see, Alma went through the same thing that I went through—from puritanical shackles to, well, complete profligacy."

He laughed. I asked him what he really meant by "profligacy," and his expression became grave. "Freedom," he said. "Liberation from taboos. I don't make any kind of sex dirty except sadism."

Has he ever created a character so large as to be unmanageable?

"Well, I was so delighted with Stanley Kowalski that I could hardly hold him within bounds. And Big Daddy Pollitt [in *Cat on a Hot Tin Roof*] was hard to contain. I loved writing for Big Daddy. Kazan [who directed the play on Broadway] insisted that he come back in for the third act, but I had nothing for him to say, so I had him tell a joke."

Because Elia Kazan had some strong reservations about the ending of the play, Williams extensively rewrote the third act. The new version was so different from the original that both third acts now appear whenever the play is published. I wondered how Williams felt about that rewrite now.

"I still prefer the one that I wrote first. But the thing is, I worked longer on the third act as Kazan wanted it, and, consequently, it is texturally the better written of the two, the more fullbodied. You see,

the other was just in second draft, while the one I wrote under his
scrutiny was in fourth or fifth draft. But still I think I prefer the original
ending, though I doubt that the play would have been successful with
it.

"You know, on the surface, I didn't resent his making me change it
so much, but it was like a deep psychic violation. I was very disturbed
after that experience with *Cat.* In fact, I couldn't write for several
months after that. I went to Rome and simply could not write.
Kazan's the only one I would do it for, though. He is a man of such
enormous talent. He did make the difference between success and
failure in a lot of cases, you know. He is a man of great vitality and
great directorial talent, which, I think, are also apparent in his own
writing.

"It was thrilling to work with him. He wanted me vitally involved in
every rehearsal. He never said, 'Go away for a week while I'm
blocking.' He was always pleased to see me there. He would say,
'Tennessee, come up here. Now how would you do this? Show us
how you would do it.' I remember he had me doing the old lady with
the tin flowers in *Streetcar.*"

I knew Williams often revised his plays during production, and I
wanted to know whether he felt his work was improved in the
process.

"Yes, ultimately, although the second or third drafts may not be as
good as the first. When you get into the fourth or fifth, you begin to
see what you've done wrong and go back more to the first and yet
retain some of the improvements. It's really only on the fourth or fifth
time over that you can incorporate the best of the lot. I think I do
some of my best writing when a play is in production. The
imminence and the excitement of the opening, you know, are a great
spur to the activity of writing."

Does he approve of the films that have been made of his plays?

"Very few of them. I like *Baby Doll,* which I wrote. And I like
Streetcar, which I wrote and Kazan directed. The rest are the work of
Hollywood 'pros.'"

He told me he considered his best writing to be in his short stories
and one-act plays. I asked which were his favorites.

"Oh, I loved 'Three Players of a Summer Game' and 'Rubio y
Morena' and 'Two on a Party.' And I think that the first half of 'Desire

and the Black Masseur' is very good. Of the short plays, I think I like best 'The Unsatisfactory Supper,' 'Something Unspoken,' 'Auto-Da-Fé,' and '27 Wagons Full of Cotton.'"

How has his writing changed over the years? What is he getting at in his latest work?

He laughed at the question. "I think I've fought what they call withdrawing action from an early peak act." Then he raised his wine glass and began combing through his beard.

"I've certainly grown less naturalistic, in the Sixties very much less. I think that I'm growing into a more direct form, one that fits people and societies going a bit mad, you know? I believe that a new form, if I continue to work in the theater, will come out of it. I shall certainly never work in a long play form for Broadway again. I want to do something quite different. I'm very interested in the presentational form of theater, where everything is very free and different, where you have total license. I wouldn't even mind having a young collaborator now on a thing or two."

He told me he usually does not talk about work in progress, but then, paradoxically, said that his latest project is very exciting.

"I'm writing something about the whore of Babylon. Babylon is Now, the contemporary world. I place it, arbitrarily perhaps, near Place Pigalle in Paris. Really, this whore is very funny." Williams began to giggle as he talked about her. "She is a compulsive eater. She is constantly eating, and her chambermaid is starving. And this poor chambermaid keeps coming in and saying, 'I see you are having a good deal to eat today.' Anyway, the chambermaid keeps mentioning all the hors d'oeuvres the whore has had—this, that, and the other, you know—and the whore keeps saying, 'Oh, yes—edible, very.' It's called Edible, Very, and Bubu de Montparnasse is one of the characters. An American tourist comes in and can't get it up. Nixon comes in at one point, too, and she receives him. Then at the end, the whore gets involved with the chambermaid, who tells her, 'Madam, your creditors are at the door,' and she says, 'Oh, back to bed.' This is after a long lyrical monologue that takes place as dawn is breaking." Williams was laughing uproariously. "Yes, I shall enjoy writing that. And I want to get a young collaborator because this whole thing is just a charade."

What effect does growing older have on his work? Does he find his power increased or diminished?

"Well, you know, as you grow older your powers diminish somewhat. At sixty-one you do not expect your powers to increase, you know, unless you're crazy. Perceptions become somewhat more acute, but what are perceptions without powerful expression? The power of a writer is very closely related to sexuality, sexual power. Not that I have lost my sexual power. No, that is very persistent. But there is a decline of sexual security, of mental assurance, you know?

"Also, well, I no longer feel that my hat is in the ring. You know, it used to be a terrible bit of competition. I would be at the Music Box, and Inge would be at the Morosco. I didn't truly respect his work. Now I could be on the same block as Edward Albee and wish him luck. Now I could even wish Inge luck. I've done what I can, and what is left for me to do is just sort of codas for my work. Something might work out, but that's a matter of speculation.

"You know, the press is very anxious to call *Small Craft Warnings* my comeback, but I don't see it that way. I wish they could just take it in stride. I'm not trying to come back to Broadway; I wouldn't even if they wanted me to. I'm just continuing to do what I've always done, and that is writing plays. I can't do anything else."

I said I had observed a younger following for his plays than in past years and asked whether he had any idea why this should be so.

"Don't you think it's probably that I've never stopped having to fight for existence? I think it is that each play expresses a struggle to survive and be liberated. The young people dig that, I think, and recognize it when they see it. I think they also recognize a revolt against 'square' values."

I asked whether the problems that led to his nervous breakdown and hospitalization two years ago were still with him.

"No, there's been a great change. In the bin I came so close to death that I realized I had to take care of my life, that I valued it. And I do value it. I'm going to take care of it as long as it's, you know, necessary. Certainly I don't want to wind up in an intensive care unit with all kinds of tubes stuck in me. I wouldn't allow that, and I don't think that's going to happen. I feel relatively well. I have no pains of any noticeable sort. I just came too close to death in the hospital."

We talked about his experience with psychoanalysis, and I asked him whether he concurs with the opinion of most psychiatrists that the creative impulse is a kind of neurosis.

"It's possible, but it's also a therapeutic measure, don't you think? I believe that writing is a purification of that which is sick in the person. I've always found a total release in writing, and it's always been the only cure for me. I've tried psychoanalysis several times, and it gave a little immediate help at a time of crisis, but it was no long-term solution. Only the act of creation has been long term for me.

"Psychoanalysis confirmed certain insights that I had. It enabled me to get over my hatred of my father and to look upon the family situation dispassionately and clearly, to see my father more as a victim than a tyrant. He had just died a year or two before—just after *Baby Doll* came out as a film. The last picture I have of him is from the Knoxville paper; it shows him standing under the marquee, saying, 'I see nothing wrong with this picture.'" Tennessee laughed in his special way—more like a squeak than a guffaw. Then, more quietly, he said, "He wasn't really a redneck; he wasn't against the blacks. He was a man of violent temper, but still he was totally honest."

Does Hemingway's oft-quoted remark that a writer is at his best when he is in love apply to Williams? He flung his head back operatically and almost sang his reply.

"Oh, yes! It lifts you so high. Yes, my best work was always done when I was deeply in love. There's a great balance between the work and the love, you know? But for me it's always had to be love. I've had, you know, one-night stands, but they were rarely of any consequence and usually ended badly or in embarrassment. I think that love can occur on a single occasion, you know, when it happens to be some transcendentally beautiful experience. But this is rare. Usually, it is something that happens over a period of time."

Did he think, then, that a writer's training had to be more experiential or sensual than intellectual?

"Not exactly. I'd say it would be difficult to train a writer intellectually. A lot of writers don't go to college these days, you know, and not going doesn't seem to hurt them. But I think it helped me to go to college. I was forced to read the literature of the theater, and I read it all. This was at the University of Iowa's drama department. I remember I took a course in comparative literature under a German teacher—wonderful old man. The first semester he taught something I dug—I think it was Joyce—and the second semester he put us on to Goethe. The material was so badly translated that I just said, 'This man is a bore.' Not that directly, of course, but he threw a book at me he was so furious. Of course, Goethe could not have been a bore in his original language. The professor gave me an A-plus the first semester and a D-minus the second.

"Chekhov, of course, was a tremendous influence on me. I began to read Chekhov in depth when I was twenty-four and living in Memphis. I got his short stories from the library, and I had never before come in contact with anything so penetrating, so beautiful. Later I read his plays.

"D. H. Lawrence was influential, I think, but it was merely that I felt an identification with his view of life. I don't think he influenced my writing. I just felt we were getting at the same thing—a belief in the purity of sensual life, the purity and the beauty of it. There was a touch of mysticism in him, too. Perhaps more than just a touch.

"The first time I wanted to become a playwright was when I saw Alla Nazimova in *Ghosts* from the peanut gallery of the American Theater in St. Louis. She was so shatteringly powerful that I couldn't stay in my seat. I had to get up and walk around. It was then that I decided I wanted to write for the theater."

Williams said he thought that writers were really not very different from other people.

"Writing is a form of release that many people are denied, you know? I have met many people who were not writers who had the sensibility of writers, and I've felt that they were easier to be with. I don't think of writers as being easy to be with, because they are under continual tension. I think that to become a writer one has to compensate for something in one's nature, compensate for it or purify it, however you want to put it. I usually find it happiest to live with creative people—whether they be actors or poets or just people who have a great gift for life. That in itself is a creative thing."

Does he think that the writer in America who wants to be well known or well read or even just published has to compromise himself in one way or another?

"He's much better off if he compromises not at all, providing he has talent and something to say. People like Genet never compromised. William Burroughs never compromised. Paul Bowles never compromised. I think the best contemporary writer was Paul Bowles's wife, Jane Bowles. I think her collected works are just about the single greatest American contribution to letters. She has a perception of a kind that I haven't found in any other writer. She's written only one play, but I think it is a masterpiece—*In the Summer House*. I call the gazebo in my back yard the Jane Bowles' Summer House, you know.

"Of course, I've always been most interested in the southern writers. I think Flannery O'Connor is a superb artist. Carson McCullers at her best was also a great writer—a fine sensibility unfortunately stricken by strokes too early to fulfill her potential.

"I think Hemingway was unquestionably the greatest. I think *Islands in the Stream* is his most important work, epic in scope. You know, I was not inclined to like his wife, Miss Mary, until I had read *Islands* and realized that she had risked the possibility of being hit by a great deal of flack of the sort thrown up against an artist who had always invited that kind of flack—you know, that beautiful declaration of his love for a man at the end. They say he was 'often inebriated' when he wrote it, but if you like Hemingway the man, here you get the man more truly than in any other work. I admired above all his poet's feelings for words. And here, finally, whether or not he intended to, he told the complete truth. For that reason, it is his greatest work. I like all of it."

I asked him if he has any recurring dreams.

"Flying dreams, yes, but I haven't had one in some months. Last night I dreamed that I had been projected three thousand years into the future in some kind of laboratory experiment. I turned into a gray vapor that was in a state of levitation. I was with some other impersonal character; we were levitating together. I was told that I would live to be ninety in this transmogrification. But that wasn't very satisfactory to me, because I was just this piece of gray vapor rising in the mist."

How does he evaluate himself as a literary figure?

"Once I said to someone, 'I think I'm a minor artist who has somehow managed to create two or three major works. I'm not sure which they are.' But I see no reason for a writer to attempt an assessment of his own work; he's probably a pretty unreliable judge. I'd gladly settle for a term such as 'special.'"

Playboy Interview: Tennessee Williams

C. Robert Jennings/1973

From *Playboy*, April 1973, 69-84. ©1973 by *Playboy*. Reprinted by special permission of Playboy Magazine, Inc.

In the past two years, Williams has returned to work with a vengeance—no longer seeking success, he says, only a respectable kind of acceptance. Unburdening himself of doctors, lawyers and managing agents, he has fairly exploded with new ideas, new plays, poetry and short stories. . . . To explore the tortured inner landscape of this shy, scared man who, despite his resurgence, still considers himself a failed artist, *Playboy* sent freelancer C. Robert Jennings to interview him in New York and New Orleans, two of Williams' three adopted homes. (The third is Key West.)

Jennings reports: "Tennessee Williams was directly responsible for my first and lastingest love: the theater. What passed for my adolescence was just peaking when I saw *Streetcar*—five times—on Broadway and became riveted to the theater for life. Yet I confess that my awe of the playwright had been diminished by his toxic visions and affectations of the past decade. This, curiously, served me well when I went into this assignment: I found the man and the whomped-up myth to be very different, indeed. I came to see that this was not, as Truman Capote had told me, a 'rather dumb man' with a once-flaming talent, nor even the publicity nut that recently he seemed to have become, but a highly private and complex human being with his poetic if not his personal madness under control. He was at once introverted, thin-skinned, humanistic, obdurate, suspicious and vindictive; as cunning, tough, and ageless as a crocodile. At first blush, he was disconcertingly crotchety, self-dramatizing, arch, with some of the subhuman idiosyncrasies of the self-made star *manqué* on the hard comeback trail, a lame phoenix rising unsteadily from bitter ash. In the grimmer reaches of his paranoia, he harbors ancient grievances, like a long-wounded wife. But I came to know that Williams holds with Gide's warning: 'Do not understand me too quickly.'

"I met him in New York after the final performance of his little motet of a play, *Small Craft Warnings,* which was made notable by his own quite believable performance as a hard-drinking, down-at-the-heels doctor in a seedy Southern California beach bar. Backstage, we were introduced by his new manager, Bill Barnes of International Famous Agency, and Williams greeted me warmly. He is short but oddly handsome. As the only character in the play who wore the same clothes offstage as on—white linen suit and white panama hat, a gold cross on his chest—he was the first to arrive at the closing-night cast party. Noting his unease, I began talking about his play in general and his performance in particular, and I asked him if he was a ham. He looked at me with malevolence and flashed: 'And who are *you?*' Then to Barnes: 'Who *is* this?' Bristling, I countered: 'I'm the guy who just crossed a continent to see you, with your OK. We just met.' 'Mmm,' he muttered and wandered uncertainly away.

"As it was already my second day in the city, I assumed that he would get his act together in time to hold our first interview session, which was to have been at dinner, after the party. That turned out to be one of my wilder assumptions. He was so unglued over everyone's tardiness that he dismissed the nonparty as "poorly organized" and sulked out into the muggy Manhattan night with a beautiful Botticelli boy poet, without saying goodbye to anyone. Later I made the tactical error of having a drink with his producer at the bar of the same beanery in which he was dining with three young men, including the poet. Though we were several leagues out of earshot, he accused me the next day of spying on him. Moreover, he seemed convinced that *Playboy* was out to 'get homosexuals.' With two friends in tow, he was 45 minutes late for our first lunch and made no apology. We were seated at one of the tables favored by the fabled Algonquin Round Table, but Williams turned his back to the room with: 'I don't want to be on display, I'm in a death sweat.'

"Knowing that he drinks mostly wine, I asked if he'd like a cold dry white. Without looking up from the menu, he snapped, 'I think that all depends on what we're eating, don't you?' With which he ordered, all ruffles and flourishes, a Pouilly-Fuissé and chicken pancakes with white meat. When the waiter explained that the meat was mixed, Williams became slightly hysterical and, his noisy drawl turning heads at adjoining tables, said: 'Well, you just have the chef make it all white for *me*.' When I heard that his sister Rose, long confined to a mental hospital in Ossining, New York, was dining with him at the Plaza, I asked if I might meet her, if only for a minute. He was aghast, rolled his eyes skyward and said: 'Good God, man, you can't be serious.' When later he changed his mind, I had changed mine, too, and he professed to be 'highly disappointed' that I failed to show up. 'She looked so pretty,' he said ruefully. And so it went, achingly.

"Until my third day in New York, just as I was about to split the scene, when I managed somehow to engage his confidence. Though still paranoid, he suddenly dropped his guard and became warm, open, courtly, hospitable, funny—and piteously vulnerable. He never spoke off the record. For Williams, having virtually stripped himself naked in his work, no longer has anything to hide. He is an open wound. He not only asked me up to his suite at the Hotel Elysée, fittingly shabby-genteel and haunted by the ghost of the great Tallulah Bankhead, who had lived there for many years (as had Ethel Barrymore before her), but he invited me to fly to New Orleans with him. There he would seek a respite from his writing, rewriting and acting labors, and I would be talking to an '*exhausted* old man.' Besides, he added, only his French Quarter apartment had a handsome young houseboy named Victor who 'looks like a young Gore Vidal,' its own veranda and a huge, full-lipped bust of Lord Byron 'that I always kiss good night—he's very sympathetic.'

"We were driven by chauffeured limousine to the airport and, when the agent informed Williams that, although he carried a first-class ticket, he had been misbooked in tourist, he flared once more and demanded to see the boss. When another airline agent politely asked for his autograph, he refused. Once in the air, he ordered a vodka martini and, dismayed at the paltry size of it, ordered several more. Relaxed at last, he abruptly changed his manner yet again and, then and for the next six days, gave of himself (and others) intimately, unsparingly and, for the most part, graciously, revealing more, he averred, than he had in his completed but still unpublished, highly personal memoirs—for which Doubleday advanced him $50,000. His ramblings, whether lucid or manic, were almost always accompanied by giggles or a loud, mad cackle. He also gave equal time to the many people who stopped him on the street, one of whom went on at such length and so boringly about a play that I intervened, then said to Williams: 'That is the price of fame.' Said he: 'The price is too high, baby.'"

Playboy: Why did you walk out on our first appointment?

Williams: Because I'm blind in one eye and I thought you were Bill Buckley—you *do* look a bit like him—and I can't stand Bill Buckley. I met his wife at a party once and I was drunk enough to think she was beautiful. At the same party, I was confronted by this creature, George Plimpton, who did three interviews with me for the *Paris Review* and took three days of my time for each one and printed nothing. He said he lost them, but of course I don't believe it. When he was introduced at the party, I said, "Fortunately, Mr. Plimpton is so much taller than I, and I am so drunk, at least I don't have to look at his face, I need only look at his shirt front."

Playboy: If you stayed at that party, what made you decide to leave the closing-night party for *Small Craft Warnings*—before it began?

Williams: I thought it would be sad, and it would be better without me. The night before we closed, in the part of the play where someone asks Doc how it went at Treasure Island when he returns from performing an abortion there, I blurted out, "Not as bad as it will go at the New Theater next week if they bring in Nelly Coward!" [Williams' play closed to make room for the musical revue *Oh Coward!*—Ed.] They should have kept it running; it was just building. It wasn't Doc, the part I played, but Quentin, the homosexual, with whom I identified. You see, *Confessional,* upon which *Small Craft Warnings* was based, was written in 1967, and during that period I was under so much sedation that I couldn't feel any surprise, and

there seemed to be an increasing sameness and brutality in my
personal relations. My life was one as close to oblivion as I could
make it. Like Quentin, I had quite lost the capacity for astonishment,
and the lack of variation and surprise in sexual relations spreads into
other areas of sensibility. Quentin's long speech [about being an
aging homosexual—Ed.] was the very *heart* of my life, you know?
Though, of course, Quentin's sexual aberration was never mine—I
would never reject a person because he returned my touch, you
know? I *love* being touched.

Playboy: Do you now feel capable of astonishment and surprise—
in every area?

Williams: Oh, yes, yes. Except my physical energy is low. I don't
feel psychologically jaded; I'm just a little enervated from the effort of
acting, you know? We received a funny cable from some theater
manager in Australia, who said, "We have been approached about
Mr. Williams' touring Australia in *Small Craft Warnings*. We are fully
acquainted with Mr. Williams' abilities as a playwright, but we know
nothing about his abilities as an actor. Can you give us some
information?" My agent said, "How shall I reply to them?" I said,
"Just say forget it, man." I want to see kangaroos, but not that bad.

Playboy: Besides Quentin, with what other characters of yours do
you identify?

Williams: All of them—that is my gift. Alma of *Summer and
Smoke* is my favorite—because I came out so late and so did Alma,
and she had the greatest struggle, you know? Blanche in *Streetcar*
was at it like knives from the time of the death of her husband,
fucking those soldiers at camp. She had to expiate for feeling
responsible for killing him. When he told her about his relations with
an older man, she called him disgusting; then she just went out and
solved her problems with a continuous orgy. *I* didn't even masturbate
until I was 27. I only had spontaneous orgasms and wet dreams. But
I was never frigid like Miss Alma, not even now, when I most need it.
But Miss Alma grew up in the shadow of the rectory, and so did I.
Her love was intense but too late. Her man fell in love with someone
else and Miss Alma turned to a life of profligacy. I've been profligate,
but, being a puritan, I naturally tend to exaggerate guilt. But I'm not a
typical homosexual. I can identify completely with Blanche—we are
both hysterics—with Alma and even with Stanley, though I did have

trouble with some of the butch characters. If you understand schizophrenics, I'm not really a *dual* creature; but I can understand the tenderness of women and the lust and libido of the male, which are, unfortunately, too seldom combined in women. That's why I seek out the androgynous, so I can get both. I couldn't have raped Blanche, as Stanley did. I've never raped anybody in my life. I've *been* raped, yes, by a goddamn Mexican, and I screamed like a banshee and couldn't sit for a week. And once a handsome beachboy, very powerful, swam up on a raft, and he raped me in his beach shack. I had a very attractive ass and people kept wanting to *fuck* me that way, but I can't stand it. I'm not built for it and I have no anal eroticism.

Playboy: What do you mean by seeking out the androgynous?

Williams: I mean I'm only attracted to androgynous males, like Garbo. Ha! After a few drinks, I can't distinguish between the two. I find women much more interesting than men, but I'm afraid to try to fuck women now. I find sexual *excitement* in women, but I can't complete the act with them. By completing the act I don't mean oral copulation. I'm just as anxious to feel a woman's ass and embrace and kiss her and enter her as I am a boy.

Playboy: Why are you afraid to go through with it?

Williams: Because women aren't as likely as the androgynous male to give you sexual reassurance. With a boy who has the androgynous quality in spirit, like a poet, the thing is more spiritual. I need that. And the other, too; I always want my member to enter the body of the sexual partner. I'm an aggressive person, I want to give, and I think it should be reciprocal. It's wonderful when they do and *you* do—let's face it.

Playboy: But isn't that somewhat contradictory—

Williams: I *am* contradictory, baby.

Playboy: What we mean is that women can certainly reciprocate as well as men, be equally spiritual, and there is the obvious physiological advantage.

Williams: Unfortunately, I cannot combine the two. Until I was 28, I was attracted to girls, but after that I fell in love with a man and felt it was better for me as a writer, for it meant *freedom*. If I were saddled with a wife and family to support—and I'd have had several wives by this time—it'd be disastrous. Oh, I'm very lucky that I've *had* women in my life, as I can write about both sexes equally well. I've loved them very deeply, but I'm shy of women sexually. I'm shy of *men* sexually. I'm very moral. I think it's most likely I'll go back to a woman in the end. Women have always been my deepest emotional root; anyone who's read my writings knows that. But I've never had any feeling of sexual security—except with my longtime secretary Frank Merlo, who served me as I had to be served. He both loved and hated me for it. I've always been terrified of impotence, even when I was very young, and Frank and Bette cured me of it.

Playboy: Bette?

Williams: Bette was the only woman with whom I ever had a fully realized sexual affair. We were at the University of Iowa together. It lasted three and a half months—and then I found that androgynous boys could give me more. And as an artist, I was better off with a boy because I couldn't *afford* a girl. But at bottom, it doesn't make a goddamn bit of difference who you go to bed with, as long as there's love. I can't get it up without love. Sex is so much an integral part of my work that I must talk about it—but sex isn't the center of my life. Love is a great deal if you can get it, but my work is everything.

Playboy: Did you ever have any kind of sexual contact with another woman?

Williams: Yes. My great female love was a girl named Hazel from St. Louis. But she was frigid. She'd make me count to ten before she'd let me kiss her; we were both 11 when we met and we were sweethearts until she was in college. She said, "Tom, we're much too young to think about these things." But I constantly thought about sex. In fact, the first time I had a spontaneous ejaculation was when I put my arm around Hazel on a river boat in St. Louis. She had on a sleeveless dress and I put my arm about her and stroked her bare shoulder and I had on white-flannel pants and I *came,* and we couldn't go on dancing. She didn't say anything about it. She was such a dear girl, but I couldn't be as close to her as she needed me to be. I can be a bitch. I was busy with someone else, and so I failed her. I was wise to her—her frigidity, her need—but I couldn't admit her to my life again. Hazel and I both went on pills and liquor. She married another man but killed herself when she was still very young.

Playboy: When was your first homosexual encounter?

Williams: In college I was deeply in love with my roommate, "Green Eyes," but neither of us knew what to do about it. If he came to my bed, I'd say, "What do you want?" I was so puritanical I wouldn't permit him to kiss me. But he could just touch my arm and I'd come. Nothing planned, just spontaneous orgasms. The only sex we were exposed to was with dreadful old whores with cunts like diseased orchids. But my first real encounter was in New Orleans at a New Year's Eve party during World War Two. A very handsome paratrooper climbed up to my grilled veranda and said, "Come down to my place," and I did, and he said, "Would you like a sunlamp treatment?" and I said, "Fine," and I got under one and he proceeded to do me. That was my coming out and I enjoyed it.

Playboy: Is that how you lost your virginity—or did you really make it with Bette?

Williams: Oh, Bette and I really did it. I was in my late 20s—a shockingly advanced age. I wasn't very virile, I was just terribly oversexed, baby, and terribly repressed. As I said, I had had orgasms before, but not through penetration of another person's body. And I never masturbated until one year before I lost my virginity. I didn't know what such a thing *was*. Well, I'd heard of it, but it never occurred to me to practice it.

Playboy: Was there a moment in your life when you decided to commit yourself to one sex or the other?

Williams: No, no. I never thought much in those terms, and I still don't. I'm either in love or not in love. Oh, I've had casual adventures, yes. But, as I said, I don't think there can be truly satisfactory sex without love, even if it's only a one-night stand.

Playboy: Do you consider yourself promiscuous?

Williams: Decidedly not. I feel right now I'm trying to meet my work, and I don't have energy for both work and sex at the moment. I see you don't believe that statement. Well, I have many people spending the night with me, because I *like* a companion at night; the people at the Hotel Elysée in New York think I'm terrible. But I go mad at night. I can't be alone, because I have this fear of *dying* alone. But they're usually there just for the ceremony of the dropping of the sleeping pill. Every night I take a hot bath and I have a massage if there's someone around who's any good at it.

Playboy: Still, could you live and work long without sex?

Williams: I don't *want* to live without sex. I need to be touched and held and embraced. I need human contact. I need sexual contact. But at my age, one becomes terrified of impotence. I no longer feel I have the power I had. The problem is to find a partner who won't demand it of you but will offer it when the time is suitable. A really gifted sexual partner can give you complete potency if he wants to—or can deprive you of it totally. So many people just like to tease, you know. Age bothers me only in this area; at my age, one never knows whether one is being used as an easy mark or if there is a true response. But I do know that I shall never cease to be sensual—even on my deathbed. If the doctor is young and handsome, I shall draw him into my arms.

Playboy: Isn't it true that until 1970, you never talked openly about your homosexuality?

Williams: That's right. David Frost had me on his show and asked me pointblank if I were homosexual. I was very embarrassed. I said, "I cover the waterfront." He called a station break, mercifully, and I said, "I should think you *would*." And the audience gave me an ovation. Then Rex Reed went into the subject in *Esquire*. But the *Atlantic* piece upset me the most. This man came to Key West as a guest, but he stayed to eavesdrop on the terribly vulnerable privacy of a man struggling to recover from a long breakdown—*me*. It was malicious, distorted and libelous by venomous implication. I became socially ostracized in Key West. People drove past my house screaming, "Faggot!"

But I don't care what anyone knows about me anymore. I just don't give a shit, which gives me a new sense of freedom. I have a reputation for immorality, but *I* know that I'm the most goddamn fucking puritan that ever was. And I'll *never* give up my house in Key West. Key West once had the most beautiful people I've ever met in my life, mostly blacks—before Howard Johnson and Ramada Inns arrived. When the two races integrate, we shall have the most physically and spiritually beautiful race in the world, but it will take at least 150 years. Key West is still the favorite of my three homes. I want to die there.

Playboy: Are you afraid of death?

Williams: Who isn't? I've almost died so many times, but I didn't die because I didn't really want to. I don't think I shall die while I'm happy. I think I can delay death. I don't spend much time thinking about it, though. I've even become rather accustomed to those panicky little heart attacks that I have at times. I've had them most of my life, and how many of them were strictly of nervous origin, I don't know. Of course, if a person with a bad heart gets too agitated, that could trigger an attack, so you have to avoid such circumstances. I have always suffered from claustrophobia and fear of suffocation. It's why I travel first-class. And for a long time, I couldn't walk down a street unless I could see a bar—not because I wanted a drink but because I wanted the security of knowing it was there.

I think a lot of my work has dealt with death. I have a preoccupation at times with death and a preoccupation with sensuality—well, with a number of things. I wouldn't say that death is my main theme. Loneliness is. But I do find it difficult to accustom myself to the death of friends. Unfortunately, most of my close friends are dead. I have a few surviving ones, but not many. I've lost most of them in the last few years, you know? Frank, Diana Barrymore, Carson McCullers, all the doomed people. We did seem to flock together, didn't we?

Playboy: Have you striven consciously for a kind of immortality, as some writers do?

Williams: Oh, heavens, I've never given it a thought. I just don't want to be a total has-been during my lifetime. That's what I try to avoid, mostly by hard work, baby.

Playboy: You said you'd almost died many times. How?

Williams: I can't understand why anyone would give a damn about the sex life or the sicknesses of a tired old man.

Playboy: For one thing, you're not just any old man; you're not even old. For another, both may be organic to your work.

Williams: Oh, all right, then. The Sixties were the worst time for me. At the beginning of one play, *Camino Real*, I quoted Dante: "In the middle of the journey of our life, I came to myself in a dark wood where the straight way was lost." I didn't know then what a prophet I was. The Sixties were no good for me even from the beginning, from *Night of the Iguana* on; everything went to pieces for me. I told Gore Vidal that I didn't remember a thing about the Sixties—that I thought I had *slept* through them. And he said, "Don't worry, you didn't miss a thing." First Frank was taken sick and I didn't know it. It was a harrowing illness and it manifested itself in erratic behavior. I think he went on hard-core-drug stuff, and you try to hide that, you know.

Frank was probably the greatest person I've ever known. He died so nobly. It was 1963 and we had a small apartment on East 65th Street. He was entering the terminal stage of lung cancer, and I moved into the study and he took the master bedroom. Fortunately, I had this huge sofa, which I slept on quite comfortably, except that I would hear him all night being racked with his cough and I would keep wanting to go in there and see if he were all right. I was so afraid he would hemorrhage like my grandmother. She died of a hemorrhage. But I couldn't, because he kept his door locked. He didn't want anyone near him. He was like a cat—they withdraw when they're dying. Well, Frank did not die alone, though *Atlantic* said I was so frightened of death that I deserted him on his deathbed, which is a malicious lie that infuriated me. Frank was very happy to have me there. But the only person he wanted in the room with him was little Gigi, our sprightly bull terrier, and in the morning they would emerge from the bedroom and she would trot at his heels. And they would sit side by side watching television. She would pretend to be watching, too.

I was with Frank the day of his death. The poor boy was put in a ward with patients who had just had brain-cancer operations, brain-tumor operations, and if you've ever seen people who've just had that operation, they're appalling to look at, you know. Their mouths are unnaturally swollen, their eyes are popping, they're sort of vegetables. And I begged him to go to a private room. I said, "Frank, you mustn't be surrounded with this," and he said, "How could it matter to me now?" And then he pointed to little cups of bloody sputum all along his bedside table. He knew he was going to go. But finally they *did* move him to a private room and he was down there gasping for breath. It seemed to me to be at least half an hour before they brought his oxygen to him; hospitals can be so callous. He never voiced any complaint. He never said, "I'm so frightened." But he wouldn't stay in bed. He kept getting up and staggering over to a chair. He'd sit in the chair a minute and then he'd stagger back to the bed. I asked him, "Frank, why won't you stay in one place?" He said, "I'm just so restless today, I've had so many visitors." I said,

"Frank, would you like me to go?" And he said, "Oh, no, I'm used to *you.*" And then he died.

Playboy: The press always referred to Frank as your secretary. What was your true relationship?

Williams: Once, when I was working on a screenplay in Hollywood, Jack Warner said to Frank, "And what do *you* do?" Without a moment's hesitation, he said, in his quiet way, "I *sleep* with Mr. Williams." Frank would also put me down like a prize shit when I deserved it, and I often did. One loved him for it. He taught me life. He was my great male lover.

Playboy: Did your decline begin with his death?

Williams: That wasn't the beginning, no. My professional decline began after *Iguana.* As a matter of fact, I never got a good review after 1961. I suppose it might make an interesting story to say that my breakdown was related to one person's death, but it's not true. I was broken as much by repeated failures in the theater as by Frank's death. Everything went wrong. My life—private and professional— and ultimately my mind broke. But it came back—I trust it's *partly* back. I must say, I still have periods of hysterical behavior, but then I always have had. I do think I'm in my right mind now. I feel no pain anymore, just morning sickness.

Playboy: You mentioned bad reviews. Are you particularly sensitive to criticism of your work?

Williams: Reviews can be devastating to me. A barrage of bad reviews contributed enormously to my demoralization. The plays weren't that bad—*Slapstick Tragedy* and *Kingdom of Earth* and *In the Bar of a Tokyo Hotel* and *The Seven Descents of Myrtle* and *The Milk Train Doesn't Stop Here Anymore,* in which Hermione Baddeley got fabulous reviews. I don't think the play worked out sufficiently well, but I've seen *worse* plays do much better. Walter Kerr dismissed *Gnädiges Fräulein* in one line. He said, "Mr. Williams should not attempt black comedy." I'd never *heard* of black comedy, though I'd been writing it all my life.

During that period, I was abandoned by friends to a large extent. People ceased to think of me as an existing person. I was, you know, a sort of apparition. I was only interested in work and I had just *three* sexual experiences in four years, which I think was certainly unhealthy. I'm sure I was more depressed than I was aware of being, but when you're under sedation constantly, except when you're working, then things don't bother you terribly. A depression, you know, can easily be obscured by drugs. I think most people who take drugs are covering up depression.

Playboy: What finally precipitated your breakdown? Was the critical disaster of *In the Bar of a Tokyo Hotel* in 1969 the last straw?

Williams: Yes. *Time,* which is usually kind to me, said it was more deserving of a coroner's report than a review. I was not amused. The reviewers were intolerant of my attempt to write in a freer way. *Life* said I was finished, and its obituary was reproduced in *The New York Times.* I ran off to Japan with Anne Meacham, who starred in the play, to escape the brutality of the critics. But I couldn't escape. I began washing the pills down with liquor and I just went out of my mind. I took sedation every night, and every morning I took something related to speed, so that I could still write. Finally I returned to Key West, and one morning I was preparing coffee at the stove and I was staggering about from the synergistic effect of the pills and liquor, you know. I was falling a great deal in the Sixties. Anyway, I got the boiling coffee off the stove and then I fell and it spilled all over my right shoulder—I was naked—and it gave me very severe burns.

It's almost the last thing I remember before they committed me to the loony bin, except when I was in a doctor's office and he was bandaging my shoulder. And the next thing I knew, my brother Dakin was in town and we were at the airport; and next I was in the basement of the house in St. Louis with a bottle and Dakin had brought me a typewriter and I couldn't hit any of the right keys, and I told him the typewriter was no good and he said, "Tom, you really must check into the hospital *now."* And I said, "No, I've decided not to. I'll be all right; I'll go back to Key West." So there was a great deal of discussion about *that,* you know.

But finally I conceded that I would go to the hospital, provided they would send an ambulance for me. Well, Mother said this was ridiculous—it would just alarm the neighbors—and so it turned out that my brother drove me over. I spent one day there in a very deluxe ward watching television programs. I was so demented that all the programs seemed to be directed personally at *me*—isn't that fantastic? Even Shirley Booth's little program, *Hazel*. I thought Shirley was making veiled innuendoes about me, and then all of a sudden my brother came in grinning with a bunch of flowers and some crayon pictures drawn by his children, and in came Momma, and I said, "I'm leaving here at once." And they said, "Oh, no, Tom. In fact, you're being transferred to another section." And I said, "Oh, no I'm not." So I rushed into the closet and somehow got into my clothes and I rushed down into an elevator and noticed a horrible intern—sort of an albino creature, you know—towering over me, and every time I pressed the DOWN button, he would shove the doors open with this great arm of his. I just couldn't escape. And so finally I ran back to my room and I said, "You must get me out of this nuthouse." I was panicky. And my mother sort of pretended to be having a faint. She said, "Oh, some smelling salts, please," and was going into a swoon, a *Southern* swoon.

By this time, my mind was quite clear. The shock of the situation had cleared my senses and so I started toward the door again, thinking I would go down the fire escape or something, and there was this *goon* squad with a wheelchair and they pushed me to the violent ward. I had my little flight bag, containing my pills and my liquor, with me and the last thing I remember is their snatching it from me as I was wheeled into the violent ward. The rest was just a series of wild hallucinations until, I don't know how much later, I woke up and my brother was there and he said, "They say you nearly died. By the way, did you know you had a silent coronary?" I had had three heart attacks while I was having convulsions. I don't know why it was necessary to tell me, but then, Dakin acts by obscure impulses. It's hard to hate him, though; he has a great deal of humor and I think he's one of the great eccentrics of our time.

Anyway, my incarceration in the bin was nothing less than an attempt at legal assassination. I've never cracked up again—I'm too *scared* to. I'm *never* going back to the bin. A physician there loathed me and refused to attend me. He was one of the most evil men I've ever known, a monster. The idea of *not* seeing a patient who had brain convulsions and a coronary is shocking. Eventually, I came under the care of three neurologists who were supposed to be eminent but weren't. Undue risks were taken with my life; I lost 30 pounds and nearly died. Well, that was the end of my long death wish. Now I want to live. That's the main trouble with Key West: I can't get a doctor there. Last year I fell into a fish pond and cut my back and broke a rib and no doctor would see me for a *week*. I had to call my doctor in New Orleans. He said, "Take two aspirins," and I said, "I'm allergic to aspirin!" But I had a fever and took them anyway and I was soon cured.

Playboy: Last year a story was published that you had breast cancer and had gone to Bangkok to die. What was that all about?

Williams: If I were going to die, I would have been in Rome. I didn't have cancer, I had an old gynecomastia, a swelling in the breast that comes from the liver, from having too much to drink. Of course, I've imagined I've had cancer for 20 years. But that was all *shit*. A military surgeon in Bangkok completely removed the swelling. I have large pectoral muscles from swimming all my life, so it wasn't easy—in fact, it was quite painful, as the anesthesia wore off before he had finished. He said, "Don't worry about your chest, worry about your fucking liver." So I've cut down to drinking mostly wine, with an infrequent vodka martini and a little rum in my tea.

Playboy: What's your latest malady, real or imagined?

Williams: Well, last summer I had to leave the play when I got thrown from a horse in Montauk. I was riding with a young surfer and we kept *leaping* over arroyos in the woods. A horse is something I should stay off of because of a chronic hemorrhoid condition. Anyway, after falling I developed a thrombosis *and* gangrene. The pain was affecting my heart because of my chronic cardiac condition. Everything *about* me is chronic. Bill Barnes, my agent, booked me into Doctors Hospital and got me the best doctors available. He was like Florence Nightingale. They told me they had to operate. I knew that I was *doomed*, of course, all those surgeons in their dreadful green gowns. The 15 minutes before I went under were the longest of my life. And while I was there, I got hooked on Demerol. I *love* it, but it didn't kill the pain. Anyway, I recovered and I went straight back into *Small Craft Warnings*.

Playboy: How did you happen to make the switch of agents to Barnes from the formidable Audrey Wood, who had represented you from the first?

Williams: That is a very touchy subject, because, for one thing, she and Bill are still good friends. I suppose the last straw was when

Two Character Play, the one I've rewritten as *Out Cry,* was about to go on in Chicago, in July 1971. Audrey left the day before the play opened, and she wasn't too private in the way she left. There were even rumors that I had attacked her. A Chicago newsman who hates me said I was beating her and I had threatened to jump out the window. An actress friend compounded it by saying to me, "You may not betray confidences, but you do betray friends." But Audrey's behavior was atrocious. She has the sympathy of the theater establishment, but they don't know the facts.

Playboy: What *are* the facts?

Williams: I only said to her, "You've never wanted this play to succeed." And she simply walked out on me. I was just having my usual opening-night nerves.

Playboy: Why did you change the title of the play to *Out Cry?*

Williams: It fits so perfectly. I had to *cry out,* and I did. It's the only possible title. At one point, the actress cries out, "Out, out, human out cry." It's about two people who are afraid to go out. "To play with fear is to play with fire," one of them says, and the other replies, "No, fear is worse. . . ." It's a history of what I went through in the Sixties transmuted into the predicament of a brother and a sister. But in its earlier versions, people were either bored with it or didn't know what it was all about. Claudia Cassidy came out of retirement to review it and she *loved* it, and that kept it running. I think *Out Cry* is my most beautiful play since *Streetcar,* and I've never stopped working on it. I think it's a major work. I don't know whether or not it will be *received* as one. It is a *cri de coeur,* but then all creative work, all *life,* in a sense, is a *cri de coeur.* But the critics will say I am excessively personal and I pity myself.

Playboy: Can't you forget about the critics?

Williams: I've forgotten about them, baby. I wish they'd forget about me.

Playboy: It's clear that you haven't. And certainly they won't.

Williams: Umm, I suppose. I hope I'll never become one of those querulous old writers who go after critics. I shall never answer them. It does no good to criticize the critics. But it's true that sometimes I think they are out to get me; it's an American syndrome. They knock you down with all the ammunition they've got, and they've got plenty. They've got all that power. They pretend they don't, but they

know they do, and they love it. *Everybody* loves power. They want to
try to judge you on traditional form when you're trying to move to
something freer, like presentational theater, when you depart from
realism and put style on the presentation itself—as Tom O'Horgan
does so well. The critics still want me to be a poetic realist, and I
never was. All my *great* characters are larger than life, not realistic. In
order to capture the quality of life in two and a half hours, everything
has to be concentrated, intensified. You must catch life in moments of
crisis, moments of electric confrontation. In reality, life is very *slow.*
Onstage, you have only from 8:40 to 11:05 to get a lifetime of living
across.

But the personal criticism of me is no better than the criticism of my
plays. Some members of the press are still virulently against the
outspokenly sensual person. I shall not name them, but they are
significantly influential. One of them said I wasn't the sort of person
one would take to dinner—that I didn't mind telling people I was an
octoroon. Ho! I had just announced to some stuffy, small-minded
people that I was an octoroon and I hoped they didn't mind. But I'm
not white trash; one of my ancestors on my father's side was a scout
for the Choctaw and Cherokee. Fortunately, there are also a great
many people who don't think of me as a bum; a lot of them think of
me as Tennessee Ernie Ford!

Playboy: How does your public image differ from the private
person?

Williams: I think the theater public has an image of me that has
very little relation to the truth. I think that I come on very open and
corn-pone and hearty and all that, but I'm really a very private
person—in a profession where privacy cannot be practiced very
easily. But I must say this is a little hypocritical, because I really don't
like to practice privacy now. I enjoy being a public figure, more or
less. I like people recognizing me and saying hello to me on the
street, as they do since I've taken up acting. I think I would miss
it if people suddenly didn't know me or talk about me. And I don't
mean getting the right table in the right restaurant, either; I don't
go to Sardi's because I'm always so afraid they'll send me upstairs.
And Elaine's seats me only out of sheer compassion for my
condition.

Playboy: You are certainly more visible now than you used to be.

Some critics have said that you seem to be implicitly begging for mercy, in a rash of newspaper and TV interviews.

Williams: I have simply emerged, after that long period of deep depression when I didn't care if I was alive or dead. I am living again and I am glad to be alive and I've been happy to go on TV or *anything.* I suspect it has always been an instinctive thing with me, when being interviewed, to ham it up and be fairly outrageous in order to provide good copy. Why? I have a need to convince the world that I still exist and to make this fact a matter of public interest and amusement. I'm such a ham, you know. Kim Stanley once said to me, "There are actors and there are hams, baby, and I hope you know what *you* are." I could be a screen actor if the part fit me. My appearance on the Oscar show last year was by invitation of the Academy, and I was delighted to attend. I wanted to get the point across that I haven't forgotten what it feels like to receive a public award, one that's presented to you by the official arbiters of excellence in that field of creative work in which you serve.

Playboy: Did you have George C. Scott in mind when you said you didn't understand how certain artists of truly pre-eminent power can deny their admirers the pleasure of expressing that admiration?

Williams: Certainly. But also, I said I understand his conscientious reluctance to make of himself a public endorsement of the dangerous principle of competition, especially when he is, sometimes justifiably, skeptical of the values and methods by which winners are selected.

Playboy: We understand you had to cut your Oscar address extensively before presenting it.

Williams: It was much too long. Have you ever known a Southerner who wasn't long-winded? I mean, a Southerner not afflicted with terminal asthma?

Playboy: What were your feelings about Charlie Chaplin's appearance that night?

Williams: I think he exhibited that forgiveness and that proud humility of spirit that characterize only the greatest of original and lasting artists, by returning to the locality that once chose to exile him, to receive so graciously an apology so long delayed for so petty an offense, based on ludicrous assumptions. I would call his gesture one of those rare and beautiful things that still can and do occur in the human heart.

Playboy: Over the years, you've spent some time in Hollywood. How did you first land there?

Williams: In 1943, I was ushering at Broadway's Strand Theater for $17 a week. The attraction was *Casablanca* and for several months I was able to catch Dooley Wilson singing *As Time Goes By*. Anyway, one day Audrey Wood informed me I had been sold to MGM for the unheard-of sum of $250 a week. But I had to write a screenplay based on a dreadful novel for Miss Lana Turner—who couldn't act her way out of her form-fitting cashmeres. The producer, Pandro Berman, came back at me with the script and said, "She can't understand such literate dialog," although I had avoided any language that was at all eclectic. They used exactly two lines of mine. Then they asked me to do a screenplay for Margaret O'Brien and I threw in the sponge. Margaret *O'Brien!* I'm *allergic* to child actors and I said, I can't possibly write for her for *any* amount of money. For the next six months, even when I wasn't working, I'd go in once a week just to collect my pay check. I'd never *seen* such money, and I was able to live on half of it and bank the rest. I rather enjoyed it, and I was able to write *The Glass Menagerie* then.

Playboy: Who were your friends in Hollywood?

Williams: My oldest friend on the Coast is Christopher Isherwood; I met Thomas Mann through him. Gavin Lambert is another old friend out there. But Mae West is the only movie star I went out of my way to meet. I just wanted to pay my respects. I told her that she was one of the three greatest talents ever to come out of the movies, the other two being W. C. Fields and Chaplin. She said, "Umm, well, I don't know about Fields."

Playboy: Your own plays and movies have been filled with beautiful and famous people. Did any of them become friends, or were they important to your life in any way?

Williams: I was always very shy with actors. They all liked Frank very much, however, and he formed a sort of bond between me and the actors, made it easier for us to have contact. I see Michael York and his wife, Pat; Michael is a charming, charming young man, but to me his importance is that of a great actor. Maureen Stapleton became a good friend; she is a genius. I saw Gerry Page the other day and she looked a *mess*; she's let herself go so and her house was a rat's nest. People like Brando and Paul Newman I merely saw after performances when I dropped in to congratulate them in their dressing rooms. When I'm in Rome, I see Anna Magnani.

Playboy: She was once quoted as saying she wanted to marry you.

Williams: Well, she was saved. I don't think she ever really thought she was in any danger of it. Besides, I like delicate breasts.

Playboy: Do you have any other favorites?

Williams: I'm always after Maggie Leighton to star in my plays; she can do anything. And I loved Vivien Leigh. She had this *grace*. Then there was Tallulah: She was never dull, but she could be tiring. It's too bad she destroyed herself so quickly. But one could never accuse her of sweetness, exactly. When they revived *Streetcar*, she pissed on my play. She said to me, looking like a frightened animal, "I'm afraid it wasn't the greatest Blanche you've ever seen." I said, "No, in fact, it was the *worst*." She just nodded her head very sadly. All the drag queens were out there screaming; she was a riot. But she did quite an amazing job of controlling the faggots; whenever there were lines they'd scream at, she'd draw herself up and try to shut them off. Being a natural camp, it was difficult for her to cut down on it, but she did try. In any case, being at bottom too much of a lady, she wasn't right for the part. For Blanche, an actress has got to be a bit of a *bum*. And during the second production of *Milk Train*, Tallulah no longer had enough strength to project her voice. It was her last appearance on Broadway.

When she visited me in Key West, she raved over Leonzia, my cook, and asked if she might go back to the kitchen, thank her and tell her I didn't deserve her. She said, "Oh, you divine treasure, I've never tasted such divine food in my life, you beautiful creature, you're too great to be *here*." Then she came back into the room and said, "That goddamn cook is the ugliest nigger God ever put guts into." Then she would announce that she was going to take a suppository and, whatever it was, she would just turn into a zombie and pass out on the floor.

Playboy: Did you ever have an affair with any of these stars?

Williams: I'm not about to allow myself to be turned on by my actors sexually, because it would interfere with the professional thing. I don't approve of a playwright or a director or a producer using actors as sexual objects. I've been to bed with the assistant stage manager, yes, but that was long before he *became* assistant stage manager. I'm overly puritanical in this respect. I realize that many directors have gotten fabulous performances out of actors because they've slept with them.

Playboy: Which of the films that have been based on your works did you like best?

Williams: I liked *A Streetcar Named Desire* and I liked *Baby Doll*, both of which I wrote for the screen. I also liked *The Roman Spring of Mrs. Stone*, from my novel, and *Sweet Bird of Youth*, which was probably better than the play. Though *Glass Menagerie* may be my best play, *Cat on a Hot Tin Roof* is still my favorite. But I hated the movie. I don't think the movie had the *purity* of the play. It was jazzed up, hoked up a bit. I OKed Burl Ives after he read one line, but Elizabeth Taylor was never my idea of Maggie the Cat.

Playboy: It's been said that you had an extremely hard time writing *Streetcar*, that it "possessed" you.

Williams: I worked on it on and off for three years or more. I thought it was too *big* for the theater. Its subjects had not been dealt with before. It was Blanche, this lascivious, demonic woman, who possessed me. *Streetcar* contained just about everything but sadism—which is about the only form of sex of which I disapprove. Cruelty may be the only sin. The rape of Blanche was not sadistic, however, but a natural male retaliation. Stanley said of Blanche, "We've had this date with each other from the beginning!" and he meant it. He had to prove his dominance over this woman in the only way he knew how.

Playboy: Richard Harris once said he thought that all the great performances Brando might have given after *Streetcar* were buried in the files of his psychiatrist—a judgment that has fortunately since been disproved. But do you feel that psychiatry can dissipate the creative impulse?

Williams: Potentially, it's possible. I never saw any decline in the quality of Brando's acting, but I thought he was terribly ill-advised in his choice of certain screen vehicles that were not worthy of his great talent.

Playboy: Have you ever been in psychoanalysis?

Williams: I've gone to analysts only at periods when it was absolutely necessary, and they *did* help me. I don't feel they've hurt my work; after all, you spend 50 minutes just rambling away about anything to them. Writers are paranoid, because they're living two lives—their creative life, which they are most protective of, and their life as a human being. They have to protect *both* lives. I put a premium on the creative life. One risks one's personal life in order to work, and when one cannot work, or when one expects total failure, there is a crisis. In one such crisis, I went to Dr. Lawrence Kubie, who said I'd written nothing but violent melodramas because of the violence of the times. He told me to break up with Frank, whom I suspected was a heroin addict. Kubie thought I should be heterosexual. He was a *strict* Freudian. He was a divine man, but I wouldn't break up with Frank, of course, so I broke up with Kubie. Besides, if I got rid of my demons, I'd lose my angels.

There are times in your life, though, when you reach such a peak of crisis that you *have* to go to a shrink. But even he can't finally solve it. He just gets you through it. Kubie would imitate my father and scream at me—to break the doors down, you know. What he gave me was not forgettable. I actually learned to respect my father, and now that he's dead, I love the old son of a bitch. But I wouldn't get within a mile of a shrink now, if I could help it. I don't even think I'll have another nervous breakdown. I'll become hysterical, but I won't crack. It's a good release to be hysterical—like having an orgasm.

Playboy: Why do you feel you won't have another breakdown, after so many in the past?

Williams: Because I don't allow myself to feel constant disappointment anymore. I don't hate myself habitually. I try to recognize my limitations and to content myself with what I'm able to do. It's all very banal: I order my coffee and juice and it comes immediately and then I go straight to the typewriter and don't stop until noon. I usually have several things going at once; I can switch to anything.

Playboy: Have any other writers exerted a special influence on your work?

Williams: The only ones of which I am conscious are Chekhov and D.H. Lawrence. I greatly admire Rimbaud and I love Rilke. Gide always seemed a bit prissy to me. Proust I admire enormously, but he wasn't an influence. Hemingway was, without any question, the greatest; he had a poet's feeling for words, economy. Fitzgerald's early books I thought were shit—I couldn't finish *Gatsby*—but I read *Tender Is the Night* several times. There are very few writers I can stand; isn't that awful? But I'm mad about Jane Bowles and Joan Didion and, of course, I like the Southern writers, Flannery O'Connor and Carson McCullers, a very dear friend who was the only person I could ever write in the same room with. We used to read Hart Crane's poems to each other. Miss Didion's first novel, *Run River*, is good writing, but it begins with a murder and I'm always suspicious of anything that begins with a murder. It's like beginning a novel with fucking your mother—where do you go from that? So I never finished it. But I think *Play It As It Lays* is masterful.

Playboy: What about your friends Gore Vidal and Truman Capote?

Williams; Friends? Baby, with friends like that. . . . Once I was about to go to Ischia with Truman and his good friend Jack Dunphy, who's a *much* better writer than Truman; his *Friends and Vague Lovers* is a better book than anything Truman could *ever dream* of writing. Anyway, Truman said to me, "Anne Jackson tells me that when Margo Jones was directing *Summer and Smoke*, she said, 'Baby, we're doing a play by a dying man. We've got to give it all we've got.'" So I didn't go to Ischia with him. Gore and I were friendly until *Two Sisters* came out; he said that with the passage of time, I had gone mad.

Playboy: Do you think that trucking around with the Beautiful People, as Capote does, harms one's work?

Williams: No, I don't think it harms it at all. I think that very likely, in Truman's case, it enhances his work. Like Proust, he might find these people a source of creative stimulation. And he says nothing about these people that isn't humanly interesting. Some of them have tremendous charm and cultivation.

Playboy: Would you like to live as he does?

Williams: No, I've never wanted a house in Beverly Hills or in Palm Springs, like Truman. I've never wanted to live on the piazza, like Gore. I've never wanted a big villa, never wanted a yacht. I've never wanted a Cadillac. In fact, I don't want any car at all. I used to get panicky on the California freeways. I always carried a little flask with me and, if I forgot it, I would go into panic. When I need a car, I rent a car.

Oh, there are certain things necessary for me. I travel around a great deal and I arrive exhausted. I need someone to help me with my luggage, and my agent sees that I have someone to meet me. It's not so much a matter of luxury as it is making it possible to get around. I like certain fine restaurants like Galatoire's and the Plaza because I can take my sister there and they know her and they are acquainted with all her little idiosyncrasies, like sometimes she will receive the Coca-Cola she ordered and she will say, "Oh, mercy, this Coke has gin in it." And they laugh. They don't mind at all. She'll make me taste it and I'll say, "I'm sure it has no gin, Rose," and she'll drink it. She's terrified of alcoholic spirits; my mother *drilled* it into her, you know, that they were wicked.

Playboy: Didn't you once write an essay saying that success and security were a kind of death to an artist?

Williams: Yes, after *Glass Menagerie*, which made me an instant celebrity, I just shut out the world and came to suspect everyone in it, including myself, of hypocrisy. Though I think I am less inclined to hypocrisy than anyone I know. I think hypocrisy is something imposed upon all of us. Maybe it's just exercise of a certain propriety. I wouldn't call it wearing a mask so much as, upon occasion, one must just behave in a manner that is not precisely instinctual. But my public self, that artifice of mirrors, has ceased to exist and I have learned that the heart of man, his body and his brain are forged in a white-hot furnace for the purpose of conflict. That struggle for me is creation. Luxury is the wolf at the door and its fangs are the vanities and conceits germinated by success. When an artist learns this, he knows where the dangers lie. Without deprivation and struggle, there is no salvation and I am just a sword cutting daisies.

Playboy: Aren't you making the job of creation tougher for yourself by spending so much time eating in posh places with stylish people and drinking more than one should drink?

Williams: No, I think I'm making it easier. After some four hours of work every morning seven days a week, you try to spend the rest of your time as pleasantly as possible. I swim at the New York Athletic Club, which I'm not too fond of—or perhaps they're not very fond of me; they gave me hell on the gay thing. If I were a *duck,* I'd be swimming in Central Park. In New Orleans and Key West, I have my own pools. But I feel very depressed if I don't work during the day, *every* day.

Playboy: Being a Catholic, do you take time out for Mass or confession?

Williams: I would *love* confessionals if I could get up at that time, but *writing* is a confessional, and I feel that I confess everything in these interviews. What is there left to say? My brother Dakin had me converted to Catholicism when he thought I was dying; it did me no harm. I've always been very religious; I was religious as an Episcopalian and I'm still religious as a Catholic, although I do not subscribe to a great many of the things you are supposed to subscribe to, like the belief in individual immortality. Nor in the infallibility of Popes. I think Popes are among the most fallible people on earth, so this is heresy, isn't it? And yet I *love* the poetry of the Church. I love to go into either a high Anglican service or a Roman Catholic service. And I love to receive communion, but I'm usually working Sunday morning—so I take communion at funerals.

Playboy: Is your Catholicism unconventional in any other respects?

Williams: Well, I wouldn't care for extreme unction at my death, because if they came at you with it, you'd know that you'd had it. And I believe in contraception of every kind. Anybody who doesn't oppose the population explosion is out of his mind. Overpopulation ruins the ecology of all life. Any candidate who will not admit he's for abortion is frightened. I think a politician should say *only* what he believes and not equivocate, as McGovern tried to do.

Playboy: You supported McGovern, didn't you?

Williams: Yes, I was one of the few people outside Massachusetts who thought that Nixon didn't have a chance. This horrid war has eroded the whole fabric of American life, incontestably. The destruction in America of the ideal of beauty is one of the most apparent and depressing things of all and devolves on the man who's ruling this country. I think that when you prosecute an immoral war for so many years—a war that is disgraceful in that it pits such a powerful nation against such a pitifully underprivileged people—then morality is destroyed for the whole country. And that is why I was so strongly for McGovern. I wish that I could have been of some service.

I am bored with movements, however. The gay libs' public displays are so vulgar they defeat their purpose. When women invade a stag bar, it's ridiculous. Fantastic transvestites in open convertibles making absolute asses of themselves are only hurting their cause—ridiculing homosexuality. I've never belonged to any party, but I think there will eventually have to be some form of socialism in this country, with its size and numbers and variety. I had lunch with Yevtushenko at the Plaza and he said that I would be a millionaire in Russia and I said, "I'd rather be poor in America, baby." He had been to see *Small Craft Warnings* and he said that I had put only 30 percent of my talent into that play and I said, "Isn't it remarkable that I put *that* much into it?" The bill for lunch ran into three pages. There was barely room to sign it. I told him, "You're a capitalist *pig.*"

Playboy: You're pretty well off yourself, aren't you?

Williams: Everybody coaxes me into talking about how wealthy I am. My royalties mostly come from abroad, foreign productions, you know, and they add up. I have houses, too, and a considerable amount of stocks. I don't even know their value, though, so I don't know my worth precisely. But it's not as much as President Nixon's, who lists his property alone as $800,000. When I asked my lawyer what my estate amounts to, she said the exact amount of money is not what you're worth, it's your work.

Playboy: Speaking of which, you said recently that you regard yourself as a failed artist, that you don't think you could ever do another major play, that what is left is just a sort of coda for your work. Why?

Williams: I've had moments of depression in which I've said such things, no doubt. But *Out Cry* is a major play, as I've said. This morning I wrote the best fucking scene since 1961, baby. And I shall write stories, I suppose, as long as I see and feel them. I tend to *see* and *hear* my plays and stories before I write them; I hear the mad music of my characters. But I don't think any piece of work is ever what one wishes it to be, or that one's completed works ever fulfill one's potential.

Playboy: What do you feel are your greatest gifts—and your greatest limitations?

Williams: I'm strongest on characterization, dialog, use of language. And I do have a sense of what is theater, I believe. Oh, but weaknesses, I have so *many*. When we were first reading *Sweet Bird*, I jumped up and said, "Stop it at once. It's dreadfully overwritten." If things are powerfully directed and acted, however, the purple writing becomes true. My greatest weaknesses are structural. And I overdo symbols; they're the natural language of drama, but I use them excessively. I'm also inclined to be overly introspective, but I don't know how to avoid it. I am an introspective person. I don't like writing that doesn't come deeply from the person, isn't deeply revealing *of* the person.

Playboy: When your life story is filmed from the memoirs you've written, who will play Tennessee Williams?

Williams: Let me see, who's the handsomest young actor around? Michael York? Marjoe is quite charming—he has everything Billy Graham doesn't. Victor, my houseboy in New Orleans, breaks my heart—isn't he beautiful?—but he can't act.

Playboy: So we're back to sex. Do you believe that, in the final analysis, a man follows his phallus?

Williams: I hope not, baby. I hope he follows his heart, his frightened heart.

Interview with Tennessee Williams
Cecil Brown/1974

From *Partisan Review,* 45 (1978), 276-305. ©1978 by *Partisan Review.* Reprinted by permission.

The street Tennessee lives on in Key West—Duncan—is as narrow as an alley. When the cab finally clumped to a stop in front of a white conch house with a picket fence, the cabdriver said, "So, this is where Tennessee Williams lives? Most people on the island like him, but I don't." The reporter asked why not. The cabdriver answered that he didn't know, he just didn't.

The gate needed a hinge so it dragged an arc like windshield wipers make on a foggy morning. The playwright opened the door in his bedroom slippers, his lips parting with a broad smile. Tennessee's face is very impressive, aged with deep corrugations and a brilliant smile that exfoliates and spreads over the entire face like a laughing flower. His voice is sonorous, with a protracted southern accent. "Well, you know," he said as he led the way into the living room, "I don't know if I have anything to say, hahaha!"

On the Dick Cavett show some months back he displayed his New Orleans home to the public. New Orleans is his front room, but the Florida Keys is where he works. Beside the typewriter in his study was a copy of Rilke's *Duino Elegies,* a fan which once belonged to Hart Crane, and a picture of D.H. Lawrence hung on the wall.

Int.: You have a new play coming out? *Red Devil Battery Sign?*

Williams: Yes. The casting is not complete. And the financial backing is not secure. I don't usually write expensive plays. It cost about thirty thousand dollars to revive *Cat On A Hot Tin Roof,* for example. This new play will cost three hundred and fifty thousand. I hope to have the casting and production deal closed by the middle of

February. If they don't have the production deal ready by then, I'm
going to publish the play as I have written it, and then I'm going to
leave a codicil in my will that it cannot be changed. Because when
you die, they do that sometimes. They try to rewrite your work.

Int.: What else was happening in New York? See any movies?

Williams: Saw *Chinatown.*

Int.: Did you like it?

Williams: Oh yes. There was an element in it I love very much.
Corruptibility. I didn't like Fay Dunaway being shot like that in the
end. I think Polanski is hung up on blood. There are very few
sensational crimes committed in America for which the true culprits
have been found. Very few. I'm not sure Charles Manson is the real
culprit. I wasn't sure when I was watching *In Cold Blood* last night
that those two boys were the real killers. I'm not certain that Truman
(Capote) believes it either. I don't trust the law. I think they are more
interested in looking good in the public's eye by catching just
somebody.

Int.: But Manson admitted he did it, didn't he?

Williams: Oh, well, he wasn't even there. He was accused of
controlling these people by ocular power—that's ridiculous. Even
Sirhan Sirhan and Oswald are not, I don't think, the real culprits. The
law has an image of itself as an efficient prosecutor. I think there is
something back of "that," and something back of "that" and
something back of *"that."*

Int.: Aren't you paranoid?

Williams: Perhaps, but I think we should be skeptical. We are
living in some terrible times. Do you remember Dorothy Kilgallen?
She was the only person that interviewed Jack Ruby and before she
printed that interview she died very mysteriously. Now, they say she
died of an overdose of pills and liquor. I've met her on several
occasions and I never noticed any signs of inebriation and I know
these signs very well. Look at Martha Mitchell. Hahaha! Martha
wants to be a lady! (He roars with laughter now.) Anyway, she claims
that Governor Wallace told her that Nixon was involved in the
assassination of Kennedy. Well, nobody has heard of Martha Mitchell
since. (He chuckles.) Yes, baby, we live in some frightening times.
But you're too young to get scared, and I'm too old.

Int.: Were you frightened when you were thirty?

Williams: When I was thirty I was very frightened. But conspiracies have been going on since the beginning of time. Big money is behind it.

Int.: The character of Chance Wayne which Paul Newman played in *Sweet Bird of Youth*—was that based on somebody you knew?

Williams: I imagined it. It was a character who spoke for something in all of us. Chance Wayne was very impressed by success, but you know, hahaha! It doesn't take that much imagination to discover that kind of character.

Int.: How did you get along with Paul Newman?

Williams: I never had a real conversation with Newman. He just didn't like me. I'd go to his dressing room and say hello. We just never got to know each other, I guess. I do think that he is a liberal—whatever that means. He supports the right causes, but I don't think he'd lay his life on the line for a cause. He's not like Marlon Brando, who is inscrutable. Although I hardly know him as well as Newman, I felt there was a deep person behind him, an inscrutable person.

Int.: Newman seems to be gifted with youth, like Dorian Gray.

Williams: Oh, he's much tougher than Dorian Gray, who was a romantic figure out of old soft-headed Oscar Wilde's imagination. Wilde was a great wit but a sentimentalist. I have a great definition of sentimentalist! A sentimentalist is somebody who will not cross the English Channel to avoid going to Reading Jail. Shit, you don't learn anything in jail! There is nothing I want to learn in jail!

Int.: Don't you think "The Ballad of Reading Gaol" was worth it? Or "De Profundis"?

Williams: No! Any fool would have crossed the Channel! But the Irish are a strange lot, aren't they? You just can't win against those establishment people. Wilde should have known that. He didn't have a chance! Not on those grounds. (He roars with savage laughter.) Wilde was the biggest fool of his time! He was a wit and a fool at once, and it was this paradox that made him an important figure. But his letters are his greatest work, his masterpiece, just as D.H. Lawrence's letters are his best work. Lawrence had a very intense view of life. Sometimes this intensity can keep you from the emotion itself, keep you from inside of the feeling, you know. Sometimes when I feel very intense about somebody it makes me impotent, I get terrified.

Int.: Is sex a big part of your life now?

Williams: Occasionally I want sex, but it's not an obsession the way it used to be. Fortunately, I've passed the time—hahaha!—in my life when I concerned myself too much with those matters! I occasionally want sex but I don't let it bother me. I find it useful to my work.

Int.: You put it in your work?

Williams: Yes, I don't need all that activity anymore.

Int.: How did you come to write a play about D.H. Lawrence?

Williams: I went to Taos, New Mexico, in 1939 to meet all the people who knew him. His wife, Frieda, especially made a deep impression on me. I started writing the end of a long play about Lawrence. The short play *I Rise in Flame, Cried the Phoenix* is the end of a much longer play I had in mind, but when I got to New York my agent said, "Nobody is interested in Lawrence! Don't waste your time on that." So, I dropped it, which was a shame because I could have made a wonderful play out of D.H. Lawrence's life. So, I wrote instead, *Battle of Angels* which was my first professional failure.

Int.: Why was it a failure?

Williams: They closed it almost as soon as they opened it. I think I once described it as a play with intense religiosity and hysterical sexuality coexisting in one person. The audience didn't like it, the critics said it was dirty, and at least one official said that I should have been run out of town for having written it.

Int.: What was the outcome of all this?

Williams: I was given a hundred dollars and told to go somewhere and rewrite it. I came here to Key West. That was in 1941.

Int.: Was D. H. Lawrence an ass-man?

Williams: I don't think he was physically well enough, do you? But I don't think, like some of his biographers, that he was impotent.

Int.: You have a brother. What's he like?

Williams: My brother is a nut. He's running for senator—*again!* Hahaha! He won't run for the House of Representatives, that's not good enough for him. Only the Senate will do. He advertises himself—hahaha!—as "Tennessee Williams's brother!"

Int.: What is his political status now?

Williams: Oh, he's still a lawyer. He converted me to Catholicism, but then turned right around and had me put in a loony bin!

Int.: When was that?

Williams: I was in it for about three months in 1969 around Christmas time. My brother *put* me away. I couldn't write anything there. They wouldn't give me anything to write with. They even took away my glasses. The doctor Max Jacobson gave me some speed, but it wasn't entirely his fault. You were supposed to give up drinking, but I wouldn't give up drinking. When I got out it was all right except that I'd had a coronary and three convulsions in one day. I was somewhat damaged, hahaha! (He laughs convulsively.) After I got out I wrote many things. It didn't stop me from writing. I rewrote *Out Cry* around 1970, around that time, after my deep depression.

Int.: What's your opinion about that play now? It was not very well received. *The New York Times* was bothered by the lack of humor and the hermaphroditic nature of the two characters, feeling that this two-character play was actually a one-character boring monologue.

Williams: I think it's my best play since *Streetcar Named Desire*. But they (critics) don't understand it, but they will one day.

Int.: What does it have that your other plays do not? What's so great about it?

Williams: It's a very personal play. It's my own human outcry. The style is different too.

Int.: Was it the change in your writing style that caused the deep depression?

Williams: This depression had to do with a sudden reversal in my writing, yes, and also perhaps more particularly with the death of the person I had lived with for fourteen years, Frank Merlo. Almost immediately after his death, the depression came on. There's a brief period of shock in which you feel almost nothing.

Int.: Frank Merlo probably had more influence on your life than any other person—outside your family?

Williams: Frank had a great influence on my life as an artist. After his death there was a drastic change in my style of writing.

Int.: What was Frank like?

Williams: Frank was a very beautiful person. When he died of lung cancer, he was very young. He was operated on nine months before he died. When he had x-rays they discovered this cancer and operated on it at Memorial Hospital, but they couldn't remove it because it was too close to his heart. They called me and said that he had six months to live. Nobody told him. How could you tell him? (He pauses. There is great sadness in his voice as he continues as if mesmerized by the story itself.) He didn't know until he could hardly breathe and began bringing up blood. By that time he must have known. He must have known that I knew. But he never said anything. I visited him every day. That's what made me so mad about the *Atlantic* piece because they said that I was so terrified of death that I wouldn't visit my best friend when he was dying. I was with him every day. I mean it wasn't easy. He was very brave, though. It didn't frighten me as much as it numbed me. The shock—then I realized all of a sudden that I was lost. I didn't know how to handle my life then.

Int.: Did he in any way anticipate the shock that was going to come to you?

Williams: Probably. In retrospect, I think that Frank should have been told, for I think that people can make an adjustment, not a happy adjustment, but they can make some kind of psychological adjustment. So that when the terminal, the really terminal state comes, it's not so horrible. You usually have several good months, you know, reasonably good months between the diagnosis and the time you become really sick. He died in Memorial Hospital in New York, which I don't recommend. They weren't kind. They've become very callous, you know, they've seen so much death. He was a very healthy man but he smoked four packs of cigarettes a day. He was almost a chain smoker. I was with him the last day. He went to sleep so I left the room. A few hours later I was told that he died. I think that he realized he was going to die that night. When I came to his hospital room he pointed to these little paper cups full of blood. Just pointed to them. He could talk, but he didn't say anything, just silently pointed to them.

Int.: After Frank's death, you went to the loony bin, and after the loony bin you came out with a confirmed new style of writing.

Williams: Yes.

Int.: Are you fascinated by madness?

Williams: Somewhat fascinated. I saw *One Flew Over the Cuckoo's Nest* and I thought it was appallingly bad. It had absolutely no pertinence to the subject matter.

Int.: Madness and comedy—do you associate these two?

Williams: Real madness is very terrible. It's hard to treat with humor.

Int.: But you were never afraid of going mad yourself?

Williams: The tragic condition is terrible. I think that most of us are a a little mad. After all, we have to try to make an entity out of all our predecessors, all the fragments of previous being that went into our beings—to make a composite unit out of it. It's almost impossible. We are bound to be somewhat divided and split. I think all of us are. Who knows (speaking almost to himself), who knows what it takes to make a civilized self.

Int.: What was your father like?

Williams: My father was a man who would not express his feelings freely, you know. I'm sure he had feelings. He'd gone up to see *The Glass Menagerie* in Chicago; he was deeply impressed that it was sold out! They had to put a chair up in the aisle, a folding chair. He was very impressed. My pa and I never had an articulated relationship. We used to drive into work every day from the suburbs, all the way down close to the waterfront in St. Louis. I used to try to think of something to say to him. I would compose about three sentences in my mind, hahaha! But he didn't go to that much trouble. I could hardly bring out the three sentences. I would say something like "the smog is heavy today," or "the traffic is bad," you know, and to each one he would grunt in some disparaging way: "What's this son-of-a-bitch trying to talk to me for." In retrospect I don't think he was that bad. I think he wanted to talk too. But we were just so tongue tied with each other.

Int.: Did he have any idea who you were going to be? Did he encourage you or did he think it peculiar that you persisted in writing poems?

Williams: He didn't discourage me, and he didn't encourage me. His sister was my greatest proponent as a poet because on the Williams side we are related to Sidney Lanier, the Civil War poet who wrote "Song of the Chattahoochee" and "The Marshes of Glynn"— that's his best work. Yes, his sister was impressed by my writing poetry. But my father, he only liked two things of mine, *Baby Doll* and a short poem called "Kitchen Door Blues." (Tennessee throws his head back and recites the poem in a very beautiful, deep resonant voice.)

My old lady died of a common cold.
She smoked cigars and was 90 years old.
She was thin as a paper with the ribs of a kite,
and she blew out the kitchen door one night.
Now, I'm no younger'n the old lady was
When she lost gravitation and I smoke cigars
I get sort of peaked an' I look kinda pore,
So for God's sake, lock that kitchen door!

Hahaha. He used to read that out loud, he liked that.

Int.: And he liked *Baby Doll?*

Williams: Oh yes, he defended *Baby Doll*. In the last picture I have of him, taken by some Knoxville newspaper, he is standing under the marquee of the movie house, pointing at the title of the picture "Baby Doll" and the caption was "I don't see anything wrong with this picture." hahahaha!

Int.: That was as far as he got? Huh? (laughter)

Williams: Who knows, he was not one who would say. I think he loved me. I was named for his father, you know. He didn't like the fact that I was a sissy. He used to call me Miss Nancy.

Int.: Were you a sissy?

Williams: I was! I didn't do the things he thought I should be doing. He thought in the summer I should get a job like other boys; he didn't understand why I was so shy. Well, my mother made me these things and I think he did too.

Int.: Was she protective of you?

Williams: She was totally protective and he was overly the opposite. He would come slamming drunk in the house and say, "Well, Tom, did you get a job today?" I would hear him all the way up on the avenue.

I don't put my father down. Because if I had ever appealed to him for money I guess he would have given it to me.

Int.: Did he have money?

Williams: Adequate, adequate. He spent an awful lot on girls, hahaha, and liquor and poker.

Int.: Did you know that?

Williams: I knew it, yah, my mother knew it.

Int.: You were good in ROTC?

Williams: Yes. Well, I think I have a natural talent for shooting. I think it's my family heritage to shoot good, you know, because (hahahaha) the Williamses were all in the war—I would never go in the war, but I just naturally inherited a gift maybe for shooting, not that I ever exercised it. But . . . Clark Mills, he's one of the sweetest people I've ever known. We used to work together. He would work on poetry and I would work on plays in St. Louis in the basement of his home. . . .

Int.: You were nineteen or twenty then?

Williams: No, no. I was older than that. Let's see . . . how old was I? I was in the shoe business—my father took me out of college (University of Missouri) after three years because I flunked ROTC which he respected highly (hahaha) which I couldn't make.

Int.: Is that one of the reasons why he thought you were a sissy?

Williams: Yes, one of them. There had always been a great military tradition in the Williams family. He quit college to go into the Spanish-American War so it was a great shock to him that I couldn't pass ROTC. But I did learn to shoot good.

Int.: Your sister had one of the first prefrontal lobotomies in the country. Did the writing of *Glass Menagerie* help you to express some of your feeling toward your familial situation and your sister's condition?

Williams: Oh, yes. Especially toward my sister, but it's even expressed in a short story called "Portrait of a Girl in Glass."

Not very long after that I lost my job at the warehouse. I was fired for writing a poem on the lid of a shoe-box. I left Saint Louis and took to moving around. The cities swept about me like dead leaves, leaves that were brightly colored but torn away from the branches. My nature changed. I grew to be firm and sufficient.

In five years' time I had nearly forgotten home. I had to forget it, I couldn't carry it with me. But once in a while, usually in a strange town before I have found companions, the shell of deliberate hardness is broken through. A door comes softly and irresistibly open. I hear the tired old music my unknown father left in the place he abandoned as faithlessly as I. I see the faint and sorrowful radiance of the glass, hundreds of little transparent pieces of it in very delicate colors. I hold my breath, for if my sister's face appears among them—the night is hers!

Williams: Is that the end of the story or the play?

Int.: End of the story.

Williams: My sister did ask a question—we were dressing a Christmas tree—it was the first time I realized that she was mentally off base. She said, "do stars really have five points?" I didn't put that into the play, but I think it's in the short story. I'd have to read it over because it's so long since I've written it. I just remember my sister making that remark.

Int.: Was Nonno in *Night of the Iguana* based on your grandfather?

Williams: "Nonno" means grandfather in Italian. Yes. It was an affectionate portrait of my grandfather. Who, however, was not as mercenary as the old man in the play, who was always saying to his daughter, "what's the take, Hannah?" I thought he was a touching compliment to old age.

Int.: You seemed not only to have used art as a way of re-creating your own identity, as all great artists do, but to have re-created your family too, casting their limitations in a more sympathetic light.

Williams: Yes, I don't think I would have been the poet I am without that anguished familial situation. Therefore I don't think we should busy ourselves for the sufferings of our familial relationships because they do charge us, you know, with a certain dynamism; and if we're really creative people, we release it in our work. I've yet to meet a writer of consequence who did not have a difficult familial background if you explored it. Of course, a lot of people never turned out to be creative at all because they had terrible familial backgrounds; they just crack or break.

Int.: Let's talk about two friends of yours, "Coroydon" and Donald Windham.

Williams: When did you hear about "Coroydon?"

Int.: Is it true that you asked him to live with you and caused him to leave three million dollars?

Williams: He did live with me for a while.

Int.: What about the three millions and the Lady in England that you forced him to leave?

Williams: No, that's ridiculous. Where do you get these ridiculous stories?

Int.: You called him down and gave him a check for five thousand dollars and said, "I've changed my mind, please excuse me."

Williams: That was during the sixties, but the truth of the matter is that this particular lady, who was in her eighties, she and her daughter had decided to dismiss him because of his drinking habit. But, you know, people make up all kinds of stories about me.

Int.: What about Donald Windham? Your long friendship with him is so impressive.

Williams: Donald Windham and I have much the same heritage, you know, I love that man, as a friend.

Int.: But you were never lovers?

Williams: Never, never. The first night I met him, he was the most beautiful boy I'd ever seen, and I was introduced to him by Harold Vinal, a poetry editor, one of the first people I met in New York. He brought me over to this apartment, this pad, on Fifty-Second Street, which was called "Swing Alley" or "Jazz Alley" or something in those days. He had a little walk-up, a cold water flat so we went over there and I was enchanted by Windham's appearance, by his face and we started dancing to the music from the place below and I kissed him and this Indian boy came up to me and said, "you'd better cool that" or something to that effect, "his lover doesn't like it." So it stopped right there. I've always been very scrupulous in those matters. I don't like to intrude in love relationships.

Int.: A Foul-Mouthed Gossip has it that you used your plays for a casting couch.

Williams: There is no truth to those rumors. I have always kept my professional work in the theater free of my love life. In the first place, I regard theater too seriously to compromise it with sex scenes. I am not very promiscuous. I am a sensual person, however; I think the artist has to be a sensual person. I certainly don't indulge in seduction with actors. My friendship with Donald became a very beautiful friendship that has endured, that could have endured indefinitely.

Int.: You saw that it would be better to leave the good things the good things?

Williams: Neither of us made any decisions; things just intruded. Our lives just drifted apart; I don't know if they will ever come back together again, but I regard things that were perfect once as remaining perfect always. Sometimes it would be a mistake to try to put it back together—you discover so many differences that didn't exist, but it's better to keep it preserved in the amber (hahaha), except he knows that I love him.

Int.: You were described by Donald Windham as being extremely diligent when you were young.

Williams: Yes.

Int.: And at the end of the day you had worked very hard and then you would cruise and he said he cruised with you.

Williams: He did indeed. Our youth was rather proper, to the extent we could make it so. Ha!Ha!Ha!

Int.: He said that you were very handsome, very good-looking, and you had a cataract in your walled eye which you corrected when you got money.

Williams: It didn't quite correct it; it's still walled and my eyes are still very sensitive.

Int.: Why do magazines create these stories about you? The sensational stories about your sex life? Do you play up that sort of thing?

Williams: Those stories are spurious. These interviewers ignore everything of a serious nature and just play up an event and exaggerate anything they can find that is of an embarrassing nature. That isn't good. That's embarrassing for my family; I have a family—I have a mother who reads—her eyesight is better than mine. My sister is exposed to reports of these stories even though she's a mental invalid. She's very alert and she gets these reports. My brother is trying to make it in politics, you know, these things are very harmful to him; they are embarrassing to me. For instance, in New Orleans I got to use the athletic club; if too much shit gets around about me, I ain't gonna be welcomed there, you know. I notice the way I'm received at hotels, you know, and at restaurants, I can't afford to play up to that sort of thing.

Int.: But don't you use the principle of exaggeration in your work?

Williams: My work, yes. I can do that, I don't mind doing that.

Int.: Do you find it's poetic justice that an artist has to be hounded by inaccuracies as a result of his creative exaggeration?

Williams: I don't think he should be, no. I think that a lot of artists are not. In France, Genet is not and in America, Henry Miller is not. It seems to be an American form, an American thing to do that. There are a great number of eccentric people in England. And they're not put down as they are in America. People are more tolerant of eccentricity in England, where it is a tradition. If I had my preferred place to live it would be England, but they would have to push it down a little towards the South, you know?

Int.: In art you exaggerate in order to create emphasis.

Williams: I exaggerate because I don't like to write realistically; it doesn't interest me very much.

Int.: But you don't think the public has the same desire not to deal with things realistically or factually when they deal with you?

Williams: Well they got to more or less because there are plenty of things that are eccentric about me: I'm wall-eyed, I'm this, that and the other.

Int.: Do you ever feel that your experience can never be ordinary? That whenever you have an ordinary experience, your great imaginative gift immediately turns it into something more fantastic?

Williams: I think I have a fairly clear conception of the world I live in.

Int.: Are you at all bitter about the way society treats its artists in America or the way society treats itself?

Williams: I don't waste time on that, it doesn't do me any good—that business doesn't help me, it only depresses me—little punks in this world. I hurt when I'm depressed. I am aware of it, yes, you know; I'm gonna do what I can to correct it—but what can I do, you know.

Int.: Did you think at any point in your life you encouraged rumors about yourself?

Williams: Oh sometimes you get the "Oh fuck it all" attitude. I knew an old lady who wore dentures and she was a lady poet, a rather eccentric sweet old thing, and she climbed up the hill to write her poems. The Muse didn't visit her, and she said, "Oh dash it all" and threw everything away. . . . She didn't realize that she threw her dentures away too ha, ha, ha! She went to a party several days later and somebody said tactfully, "why Louise, why I notice you've had some extractions lately." He he he! Poor thing had thrown her dentures away and hadn't realized it. He he he he! You can find anything in art that is equally fantastic. You see, art is compressed and there has to be exaggeration in art form to catch the outrageousness of reality, because art has less time in which to capture it, you see; you have a whole, you have a wide stretch of time for the outrageousness to exist in life. But in an art form, no, it has to be within a compressed space of time—of course, some people write realistic short stories and so they don't try to capture the outrageousness of reality. Sometimes the truth is more accessible when you ignore realism, because when you see things in a somewhat exaggerated form you capture more of the true essence of life. The exaggeration gets closer to the essence. This essence of life is really very grotesque and gothic. To get to it you've got to do what may strike some people as distortion.

Int.: What is the value in realistic short stories?

Williams: I've never discovered it except in the case of a few great writers, like Stephen Crane and Hemingway.

Int.: Even Hemingway had exaggeration.

Williams: I think William Faulkner certainly did, like in "A Rose For Emily."

Int.: How would you describe your writing style?

Williams: I don't write in the stripped, bare style that one often encounters nowadays. I can write in a style that's so simple you wouldn't believe it. But that style doesn't suit me. Actually, I write in several different styles, but the ideal style is the conversational. I can't write without cadence. I have to hear the sound first.

Int.: Does your state of mind affect the plays as you write them?

Williams: Yes, it does, completely. I don't follow a conscious, intellectual framework when I write. I discover the play as I write it, and it usually takes a year and a half to two to finish it. These young kids today knock them out so fast! It's very enviable. I don't know how they do it.

Int.: Yes, but they don't knock out great ones.

Williams: I don't know about that. I never really know *when* I have a play. I just hope. It's maybe two years later I'll realize how good a play is.

Int.: How do you begin a play?

Williams: I begin it—you don't really want to know that, do you? Hahaha! I don't want you to examine the methods of my work too closely because it will make my writing self-conscious; I just don't like to scrutinize them that closely.

Int.: So you allow yourself a lot of latitude in terms of what your play is going to be?

Williams: Oh, yes. Any little thing in mind of somebody, a word, something someone says or something—anything certainly, some German name, an innuendo, and I usually work in an exploratory draft and then I have a good idea of what I'm doing. Then I write a second draft and usually a third and sometimes I've written maybe six or seven. There is no such thing as a process of doing writing.

Int.: When you deal with symbols like that you're not aware of . . .

Williams: Of it being a process? I don't plan what I do, it happens. I read over each day's work, then I become more conscious of what I'm doing with it, you know, what direction it should go in.

Int.: Are you ever conscious of what impact a play might have on the public?

Williams: Never at all. The public is so under-educable.

Int.: That includes critics?

Williams: Well, certainly critics. They can praise to high heavens an inferior work and make absolutely merciless ridicule of something much superior. So, how can you possibly predict which way they are going to jump. Sometimes it seems quite arbitrary. There are one or two who have a certain point of view to which they adhere, like Walter Kerr. I think he's the most brilliant in the sense of writing; he and Harold Clurman write the most brilliantly *written* criticism. They have certain biases and Mr. Kerr is convinced for some reason that I cannot write very well about male characters. He's right to this extent, that the feminine sensibility is more usable to me as a writer.

Int.: Why?

Williams: Just is.

Int.: Because the feminine sense is closer to the artist's sense?

Williams: I think it is closer to art, yes, but I think I have, especially in my play *Red Devil Battery Sign*, created a very very intense readable male character, that is equal in force to the female character. Brick (in *Cat*) is a very very delicately drawn character, he just didn't have as many lines but he was not a superficially drawn character. Stanley was pretty primitive and primordial in his instincts, but in many ways defensible. He was reacting with an animal's instinct to protect its own, its own terrain from invasion, by that element that he could not comprehend, which happened to be Blanche. Shannon was a more complete sympathetic male. Shannon was a very complex male, at least I think so.

Int.: Nothing expresses the essence of religious man better than the characterization of Shannon, the Episcopal minister, who knelt with one of his young, attractive female followers and found himself in the reclining position. Was it his despair that made Shannon so real to us?

Williams: He was torn between belief and disbelief, between sexuality and guilt. Yes, it's been sometime since *Iguana* and I don't recall all the details of Shannon. I just know he was a pretty well-drawn character.

Int.: When you say that the feminine sense is closer to the artistic principle does that have anything to do with your own sexuality?

Williams: I think the sensibility of the kind we're discussing can exist in a person totally celibate.

Int.: As in Hannah?

Williams: Yes. Well, you'll call me the Artful Dodger now. After you have written and published this piece we'll have a real conversation. (hahahaha)

Int.: What are you hiding from?

Williams: Right now, man, this is Watergate. I'm not about to have any incriminating tapes. (hahaha)

Int.: I think you're doing fine, though, you know. Would you comment on the intellectual conflict between Jews and Blacks?

Williams: Stay clear of anything racist. I was talking to an Irish journalist in Chicago at the Chicago Athletic Club and they granted me the free use of the pool. I was there for *Out Cry*. So, I said, "Oh, you're Irish, aren't you?" I said, "Well, the Blacks and the Irish are my two favorite people," and it infuriated him because I put Black first. He gave me a bad write-up. (hahaha) So, I've discovered now that one must think no race. I am crazy about the Blacks. And I must say I know people who ask, "Why don't you write about the Blacks?" I said because I would be presumptuous; you know, I don't know the Blacks that way.

I am terribly involved in the Black movement because I think it is the most horrible thing (racism). I think that the White people in America, southern and northern equally—even more northern—have exercised the most dreadful injustices, historically, and even now, discrimination, and not just in terms of jobs. No, that's not where it's at. No, and I wouldn't blame any Black man for looking at me and saying, "There's a red-neck honky," and that he hates me.

I can tell you, in my lifetime, I'm sixty-three, I have noticed a great improvement on both sides, but more on the side of Blacks. I think the Blacks, with great valiance, are fighting their way up and out. But, it's taking too fucking long, isn't it? I mean, after all, one wants it *now* and not in some remote future. It reached its most terrible crisis in the prison riot, don't you think?

Int.: You have many parallels between your life and Hart Crane's: dominant father who disliked poetry; an overprotective mother; tortured, gifted son-poet. . . .

Williams: Yes, I have a codicil in my will that when I die I am to be pushed off a ship where Crane went down. (He takes the fan off the wall.) Hart Crane's mother sent me his fan.

Int.: Is Hart Crane one of the better American poets?

Williams: I think at least since Whitman and at his best I think he is better than Whitman. I don't know any American poet that is equal to him.

Int.: What about Emily Dickinson, did she have some of his qualities?

Williams: Oh, she was very constricted in form, don't you think? Obviously form. She's wonderful, but it's a pity that she was so constricted in form; there's no variety in it.

Int.: She didn't seem to be a self-conscious poet where it seemed that Hart Crane was dealing with some of the self-consciousness of his own life and maybe the life that was forced upon him.

Williams: Oh, I think Emily Dickinson was a more private person.

Hart Crane was the opposite of private; I think he splashed his life all over (hahaha), he spilled it like blood, but I don't think he had any choice.

Int.: What's the first thing that struck you about Hart Crane's life the first time you read him?

Williams: Oh, the beauty of the poetry, the intensity and the beauty of the torturer.

Int.: Did you find the diction difficult?

Williams: At first, yes. I had to read it repeatedly and then it became quite lucid to me, quite clear. I liked the broken rhythm, so unlike Emily Dickinson, you know, whose rhythm is da-da-da-da-da you know, poor thing—her thoughts, her imagination were so fabulous but there was such a monotony in her rhythms.

Int.: Crane had a jazz rhythm to him.

Williams: He did indeed. I loved the broken rhythm. I don't have that, I can't get that jazz rhythm, you know, in writing because I like cadence, but I don't like iambic pentameter. I was in my early twenties. The rhythm I always have you know, I can't escape from cadence because it's too ingrained in that. I can't write without cadence, I wish I could, because I know people writing right now who are not confined to cadenced speech, but I'm hooked on cadence. I have to hear the sound.

Int.: The other influences on your life: who are some of the other poets, who are some of the other people?

Williams: Poets, you know there are very few good poets. Elizabeth Bishop, I knew her in Key West, she's one of the greatest poets in America; Marianne Moore, she's a great poet. Yes, a great gallantry and humor. Of course, I don't find her comparable to Crane. No, a spinster likes to write about the intricate construction of a spider, you know, the spots on an antelope; you see, it can be beautiful, but it isn't like a man eviscerating himself beautifully, you know, like Crane—it doesn't hit me that way—of course to some people it does. I think Wallace Stevens is an excellent poet. You know, he was an executive in a Hartford, Connecticut, insurance company. And how you can combine that with being a great poet I don't know, but he did. He was a great poet.

Int.: William Carlos Williams was also a doctor.

Williams: I understand that he was a great poet but I never could read his poetry with much empathy. I've read some of his plays you know, and I like them, but the poetry, never, maybe I haven't exposed myself to it sufficiently.

Int.: Were you particularly fond of reading Shakespeare as a dramatist?

Williams: I began to read him when I was a child. My grandfather had all of Shakespeare's works and I read them all by the time I was ten, and my favorite was *Titus Andronicus* where the queen of the Goths eats two children; they're baked in a pie and she eats them. I liked that. So as a child of ten, I was interested in blood and guts Shakespeare. I don't think I was yet impressed by the great writings or poems.

Int.: Yes, that play is supposed to be his least mature work.

Williams: Some people say that he didn't even write it. It's ridiculous. Have you ever read the goddamn thing? It's the most ridiculous thing. Now, my friend Professor Oliver Evans saw that play and said it was a masterpiece, so I read it over again, well now, I could see it could be presented as a masterpiece, you know, if you are willing to accept all this Gothic horror, you know, but it seemed to me also the theater of the ridiculous.

Int.: And the theater of the absurd.

Williams: Yeah, on paper it seemed that way because of the Gothic elements in it; the boys raped Lavinia and cut her tongue out and cut off her hands so she could neither speak nor write the accusation against them. And the father kills Lavinia because she's been raped, after she witnessed the Queen of the Goths, Tamora, eating her sons baked in a pie; well it's one of the most ridiculous plays ever written.

Int.: The interesting thing about *Titus* is Aaron, the Moor who has a baby with the queen. Aaron takes the Black baby with him and he says, "This is my child and I will very probably die with this child." And the son of the queen runs in and says to him, "You have, villain, undone our mother!"

Williams: "You have undone our mother!"

Int.: And Aaron says, "I beg your pardon, I have done thy mother."

Williams: Oh no! That's Shakespeare—that humor is Shakespeare. That's pure Shakespeare!

Int.: And that comes to be, of course, the model for *Othello*.

Williams: Yeah, Othello is Shakespeare's greatest play, in my opinion, don't you think so? The dynamics of that play are so believable, so intense and the language is so beautiful—that and *Macbeth*. I prefer it to *Hamlet*, although the language of *Hamlet* is superb and the soliloquies are matchless, still I do not understand *Hamlet*, really. I think the closet scene, the scene between Hamlet and his mother, Gertrude, may be the greatest scene Shakespeare ever wrote, but still as a whole, I don't dig it—psychologically I can't groove on it. What happens at the end of all this dueling, and the poison and all that? It doesn't have the inevitability of, the purity of line as *Othello* has, or *Macbeth*. I really couldn't tell you what *Hamlet* is about. They say it's about indecision, the weakness of indecision, I've heard of that before, that's no explanation. Maybe I've never read it properly or seen it performed properly, maybe I'd get more out of it.

Int.: The feeling I get—

Williams: Is what?

Int.: Is that it's a self-conscious, intellectual play.

Williams: I don't think the "To be or not to be" speech in *Hamlet* is as great as the "tomorrow, tomorrow," speech from *Macbeth*. (Now Tennessee throws his head back and begins to recite the "Tomorrow" speech in the most resonant, musical, deep cello-voice.)

> Tomorrow and tomorrow and tomorrow
> Creeps in this petty pace from day to day
> To the last syllable of recorded time
> And all our yesterdays have lighted fools
> The way to dusty death. Out, out, brief candle!
> Life's but a walking shadow; a poor player
> That struts and frets his hour upon the stage; and then is heard no more.
> It is a tale told by an idiot, full of sound and fury
> signifying nothing.

That's a greater soliloquy than any in *Hamlet*, I think. And then to put out the light! Put out the light! Isn't that a great soliloquy? Has it ever been settled who Shakespeare was?

Int.: I tend to think that he was one person.

Williams: I think he was Shakespeare. I think it's all a lot of bullshit this question who he was.

Int.: They say he was not very conscious of his genius in his works and he seemed not to care about immortality.

Williams: I think he cared a great deal about keeping his company going (hahaha), don't you? And writing the best he could for it; sure, that was the question.

Int.: He seems to have been very successful too, from all evidence.

Williams: Was he successful? I don't suppose he was.

Int.: Financially respectable.

Williams: I don't think he was, was he? I don't think he lived with great luxury.

Int.: He had enough money to buy a knighthood.

Williams: Did he buy a knighthood?

Int.: He bought one for his father.

Williams: For his father, I didn't know that. When my grandfather took me to Europe we visited Stratford—I saw what was said to be his grave and various other reliquary things but I didn't hear he bought a knighthood for his father. What was the use of that, was the father living or what?

Int.: Yeah, apparently it was a matter of status.

Williams: Oh, how awful, but he was never called Sir William Shakespeare. Wasn't he sort of middle-class as most good writers are?

Int.: Bourgeoisie?

Williams: Bourgeoisie. Very few come out of the upper class, the so-called upper class.

Int.: The upper class always looks down on the creative arts because they change the status quo.

Williams: I don't know any upper-class writers. Except I knew the Sitwells. I guess you'd call them upper-class writers. They were said to be Plantagenets, hahaha! I'd say that's pretty upper class. I liked them, they were so upper class they were good! They were appealing, you know. I remember meeting them. Edith was weighted down with all these jewels. She did write well, but it was not my kind of thing.

Int.: What about Virginia Woolf and by the way, what do you think of James Joyce?

Williams: Virginia Woolf, I could never read her. I liked James Joyce. I love *Ulysses*. I didn't like *Finnegans Wake*. I didn't like it where he went into a transmutation of words. Went on and on forever! I don't like to work over reading, do you? I just like to enjoy. I suppose I could try to read that again, but the only profit I felt when I first read it was the Anna Livia Plurabelle passage; wash women exchanging conversation while they washed clothes.

Int.: Don't you think that in *Finnegans Wake* Joyce used rhythm and cadence to untie meanings?

Williams: Oh, the Irish can't escape that cadence either, you know. Lord, how they do love it! William Butler Yeats was a great poet.

Int.: He would have loved your work because he finally discovered that conversational rhythm of yours only in his last poems and in that wonderful play, *Purgatory*.

Williams: I never read it.

Int.: It is beautiful, beautiful music.

Williams: Should I read it?

Int.: Yes, I think that's his best play.

Williams: One of my favorite poems is "Sailing to Byzantium." Was that his early period or late period?

Int.: I'm not an authority but I think it was his middle period because he wrote several poems on that theme but he only perfected it in "Sailing to Byzantium."

Williams: I thought that was his greatest poem.

An aged man is but a paltry thing,
A tattered coat upon a stick.
That is no country for old men, the young
In one another's arms, birds in the trees:

That's really a beautiful poem. When I get drunk I love to read poetry.

Int.: The sound, the cadence of it—

Williams: Yes, lulls you—

Int.: Do you write much poetry now?

Williams: Not as much as I used to; I find it's just as easy to incorporate it into the plays.

Int.: I love your reading on that record of your narrative poem, "Yellow Bird."

Williams: Oh, that. Do you know I improvised a lot of that as I read it. Faye Dunaway's crazy about it, and every time I see her she plays it for me. She plays the record and says she's determined to make a movie of it. I don't like to read my plays. I like to see them performed well once in a while.

Int.: What does a good actor do when he performs?

Williams: That's what I'm trying to find: I'm looking for a good actor. I can't get Marlon Brando.

Int.: You have a part for him?

Williams: Yes. There are other good actors. There are plenty of them. But I've got to find one that's right by January or February 'cause after that I'm going to write a codicil to my will again. It cannot be changed.

Int.: The play cannot be changed?

Williams: Yeah, because if I should die, they'd do that; they'd get somebody to rewrite it, and it means too much to me. I'm waiting only to the middle of February and if they haven't found the right actor by then it's going to be sealed.

Int.: You're writing a new play now?

Williams: Oh, I'm just writing little plays now, plays that involve dancing, mime and dancing.

Int.: It seemed to be more poetical, less conflicted than *Cat* and *Streetcar*.

Williams: You know, I got tired of long plays; I don't want to sit three hours and listen to these long, long plays. I know that I can say what I have to say in an hour or fifteen minutes.

Int.: Do you still read the Greeks?

Williams: I used to read the Greeks when I was young, but I can't read them anymore. One can't write a tragedy today without putting humor into it. There has to be humor in it now; it's so hard for people to take tragedy seriously because people are so wary now. I have seen few tragedies that were successful without humor in them.

Int.: What about this new play?

Williams: *Red Devil Battery Sign?* It's the best thing I've written in a long time. It's a tragic love story with a great deal of music. It takes place in Dallas, Texas, and the hero is the leader of a band of Mariachis. They sing between each scene and sometimes during the scenes and dancing too—it's an expensive thing to put on.

Int.: Are you getting into a new form?

Williams: Yes, a new form. I think my new plays reflect new attitudes. I hope they do.

Int.: What are some of the new attitudes you think might be reflected in your new plays?

Williams: You got me! hahaha! I remain a romanticist and a sensualist and a lover of God and a believer. What else good can I say about myself (hahaha), I got a lot of bad things in me; I ain't about to tell you, though.

Int.: What is the basis for a metaphor of cannibalism in "Desire and the Black Masseur" and *Suddenly Last Summer*?

Williams: Man devours man in a metaphorical sense. He feeds upon his fellow creatures, without the excuse of animals. Animals actually do it for survival, out of hunger. Man, however, is doing it out of, I think, a religious capacity. I use that metaphor to express my repulsion with this characteristic of man, the way people use each other without conscience.

Int.: The violent images you found in *Titus Andronicus,* when you were reading it as a kid, did you ever imagine you would create images like that, like the image of a man being eaten by boys in *Suddenly Last Summer*?

Williams: I don't think it's as awful as that thing in *Titus Andronicus,* do you?

Int.: I think it's more civilized.

Williams: It's more metaphorical, isn't it. It horrified me, the film; Sam Spiegel made the mistake of inviting me to a private screening of it in his apartment and I walked out in the middle of it. I was so offended by the literal approach because the play was metaphorical; it was a sort of poem, I thought—I loved Katharine Hepburn in it but I didn't like the film, to be honest. The American Film Theater should have done *Suddenly Last Summer.* Then they would have caught it with Anne Meacham, Robert Lansing, Hortense Alden. It would have been beautiful. It was a play that should not have been made into a film at that period.

Int.: How did you sell the rights?

Williams: I sold them over the phone myself. Sam Spiegel, he called me up and he said, "I'll give you $50,000 and 20% of the profits." I thought that was a good deal so I said okay. We didn't go through any agent that time. And do you know he paid me all those profits as far as I can tell. As far as I know he was perfectly honest with me.

Int.: What did the terms of the profits come to?

Williams: Don't know, it was quite a bit.

Int.: Do you still get residuals from those films?

Williams: Occasionally.

Int.: The *Cat* opened again on Broadway and it's doing very well. What changes have they made in it?

Williams: I made some changes in the end, not as much as I anticipated.

Int.: I heard Elizabeth Ashley is very good in it. Is she as good as Elizabeth Taylor?

Williams: She is brilliant in it. Liz Taylor is no actress. She was a personality. She was better than usual because she looked so beautiful; she was directed by Richard Brooks who's a wonderful director except that at the end he cheats on the material, sweetens it up and makes it all hunky-dory. Even in *Streetcar* they softened up the end a little bit; they made Stella decide never to sleep with Stanley again which is a total contradiction to the meaning of the play; he does, the meaning of the play is that he does go on with her. And Richard Brooks wrote a fabulous screenplay of *Sweet Bird of Youth* but he did the same fucking thing. He had a happy end to it. He had Heavenly and Chance go on together, which is a contradiction to the meaning of the play.

Int.: Did you ever intend to write any more screen plays?

Williams: Those experiences had discouraged me from the whole thing. I felt that if one didn't have control the work would ultimately, inevitably lose its truth.

Int.: Film is not one of your favorite forms as a writer?

Williams: I love to go to the movies now and I think they've improved vastly, but I would never write a screenplay again unless I knew I had real control over the script.

Int.: You're never interested in directing anything?

Williams: Oh, it's too complicated, too technical and too exhausting, no I couldn't do it.

Int.: Do you think the cinema industry and filmmakers will suffer from the lack of great talent such as yours in the cinema?

Williams: It seems to me that they've got a lot of good talent around, you know. They seem to have talents particularly suited to cinema. The stage was always where I got my working model.

Int.: What was it that made you so successful as a writer for the stage?

Williams: I think I have a curious combination of traits that are viable on the screen and on the stage. Joe DiMaggio came up in an elevator in a Chicago hotel: He said, "You're Mr. Williams, aren't you?" He said, "I want to congratulate you, you're selling the best thing in the world." I said, "What are you talking about?" He said, "Sex." Hahaha! That's an over simplification, isn't it? Hahahaha. But, I liked it. That was a long time ago.

Int.: Because sex is closer to the truth?

Williams: Ya, I can see a lot of things by putting sex in it. I don't have trouble doing it, putting sex in it; I like it, you know. It seems very beautiful to me to write sex into plays.

Int.: What are some of your other qualities?

Williams: I have a sense of drama, a seventh sense, I think I do. I like dramatic confrontation.

Int.: To express ideas or to express feelings?

Williams: Feelings, mostly. I've been reading the diary of Vlasilov Nijinsky, the early diary in St. Moritz when he was going mad. He keeps saying "I am a man of feeling, my wife thinks!" (laughter) I think people with a slight tendency toward madness are more inclined to feel, you know. And, I think a tendency toward it, not total madness, but a tendency toward it, is very adaptable to the stage. Strindberg found that out.

Int.: He wasn't mad, but slightly mad?

Williams: Yes, because you know you get like that, you really hit out and the audience likes it. They like the madness in you hitting out. It is the most beautiful thing that Vlasilov Nijinsky wrote; he said a lot of profoundly true things, of course, some of them were mad too.

Int.: Is Blanche mad or does she just give in to the situation of her being mad?

Williams: I think she's broken at the end.

Int.: Which is not the same thing?

Williams: She had personal, great strength and personal vulnerability that was finally broken.

Int.: The madness becomes a metaphor to express that.

Williams: Yes.

Int.: To be taken away.

Williams: Yes. I think it was the only solution for her to go away, to be taken away or to go away. She was not adaptable to the circumstances as they were, that the world had imposed on her. She was a sacrificial victim, you know; she was metaphorical as a sacrificial victim of society.

Int.: There's great wit in her, too.

Williams: Oh quite funny, she's funny.

Int.: She fights with incredible stamina.

Williams: Yes, she fights to the end. She's a tiger, extreme tigers are destroyed, not defeated.

Int.: She had some of the nature of a great poet too.

Williams: Not a great poet; she had had some good speeches but she was eloquent in the way that maybe southern ladies are, you know. I always thought she had her comic side, her little vanities, and her little white lies, but when it came down to the nitty-gritty she wasn't a liar. She told the truth when she had to. But, she was broken on the rock of the world; I find her a sympathetic character, but I also find Stanley sympathetic. (laughter)

Int.: Yes, that made a great drama because there was a great conflict there.

Williams: You have to understand both sides.

Int.: In these new plays do you still try to strike at the audience, do you still try to shock them?

Williams: I don't think I'm the tiger I used to be. Hahaha. I'm trying to deal with them differently.

Int.: I'm very curious about these new short stories too because the *Eight Women* is the expression of the femininity.

Williams: Several sides of one, yes. Oh, I should think women are getting very funny and touching, don't you?

Int.: What is it that makes them so attractive?

Williams: I don't find men funny; they don't amuse me much. Why is that? I don't understand why!

Int.: Maybe because we're men.

Williams: They just don't make me laugh, they just don't amuse me as much. Women are closer to life really, they're more naked, more like naked life.

Int.: You mean they are not afraid? as men are?

Williams: They are closer to life, it seems to me. I may be mistaken, it seems to me that men bury themselves in businesses and moneymaking, competition and that sort of thing; women seem to me organically closer to love which is where life is, where it began, where it is.

Int.: You're not pessimistic about death are you?

Williams: Baby, I'm not scared of death, I don't think so. I have that normal, you know, apprehension, but I'm accustomed to the fact that my heart skips beats, especially when I drop my Nembutal at night. I know in about 10 minutes it's gonna stop palpitating. But, it don't alarm me like it used to. There's been a lot of talk about me having cancer—I ain't got cancer! Because I have taken *every* possible test. And if doctors want you to know you have cancer, they'll tell you; and I've got a doctor in New York who's older than me and I've pounded my fist on the table and I said, "I know I must have cancer!" and he said, "Mr. Williams, you are making me angry, I can't say you've got cancer, you've abused your liver, yes, but you haven't got cancer."

Int.: Did you go to China once to an acupuncturist?

Williams: No, I went to Bangkok because I had a swelling under my left tit here.

Int.: You thought you had breast cancer?

Williams: Yes, and this cardiologist in New Orleans, I came back from Europe and on the trip back by boat, I discovered this little swelling here, and he said, "Well, breast cancer is very unusual in men" and he said, "but, rare, unusual things can happen." I said, "Well, you don't have to tell me *that!*" He said, "I would advise you to postpone this trip to the Orient and have an immediate operation on this swelling." I was with Professor Evans and he said, "Oh, it's not necessary at all, I know the King's surgeon in Thailand." He wanted to get back there, and he said, "He can certainly perform an operation on Mr. Williams if it is really necessary," so we went there. Well he knew a *military* surgeon who had never met any member of the royal family and he operated on my left breast. He operated under local anesthesia, I didn't even have a hospital room reserved, operated in a little clinic, and well, he cut it out and I had what they called a genical masty, which is a swelling that men of my age get when they, you know, have abused their livers, and it stayed this way since 1970; it hasn't changed any. So, he said the pathological report was not malignant. I have a little scar tissue, that's all.

Int.: Are you a hypochondriac at all?

Williams: Oh yes, I've always been a hypochondriac; I wouldn't say it bothered me much.

Int.: Do you think about money much now?

Williams: No. I think I manage my money well. I own property in New Orleans and Coconut Grove. I could live on that. Insecurity is very bad when you are old. Like Maggie in *Cat* says, "You can be young without money, but you can't be old without it." hahaha! She says, "Either you got to be young, or older with money!" She's just telling it like it is!

Int.: Do you still have to go to backers for money for your plays?

Williams: Baby, you still have to go to them to get money. Still, there are some people who are patrons of the arts, people who care very deeply about theater. The Rockefellers gave me a few hundred dollars to get started. Of course, my big hits came along when you could still get movie sales—can't get them anymore. I am waiting for the big one, you know; to see if the backers will come up with the money for this production. The play has to be produced soon. When they know the conditions, they goddam better produce it hahaha! They all know it's money.

Int.: It's money for them?

Williams: They know it's money. I know it's something else; I don't need money. I got more money than time.

Int.: You used to say it the other way around.

Williams: Yah, I got more money than time and that don't mean I'm rich! But they're going to find out, they're going to find out.

Int.: (Seeing a picture of a young man leaning in a corner.) "Who is that?"

Williams: "Oh, that's Frank Merlo—if only he had been an

actor—he wasn't an actor but he could stand in a barroom and
brawl!" Tennessee laughed.

That evening the reporter was introduced to the Lady Maria St.
Just, a very attractive, elegant woman, a Russian by birth and English
aristocrat by marriage. Out in the garden, the marble table was set for
four. A candle flickered under the warm breath of the tropical breeze.
Maria had cooked the veal and Tennessee made the turnips with his
special sauce, a mixture of vinegar and tarragon. When we are all at
the table, it's an album cover picture.

"I know this is not the subject of a polite conversation," Tennessee
said, "but I have heard that women can reproduce independently of
men." "Oh, you mean, like chickens," the Lady exclaimed with
complete credulity as she served Tennessee's plate, having carefully
removed the dry chops. "I don't like the dry ones," he complained,
"I can't eat the dry ones." "No, Tennessee, this is not a dry one," the
Lady said. "Good." The playwright continued . . . "that women can
still biologically, produce independently of men, but all the offspring
will be female and that eventually the whole world would be
women." Having completed this prologue which is a setup, a big
soap bubble of fantasy, he leans back in his chair, his eyes wet with
laughter. The Lady, fingering a Greek Cross, said, "But Tennessee,
how is that possible?" "Somebody told me that," he laughed, "but I
don't believe anything I hear anyway." I said, "Tennessee, who told
you that? Sounds like the Foul Mouthed Gossiper." "What's that?
Gossip?—Oh, yeah, yes! Gossip! Women's Lib, perhaps?" he
chuckled.

His regular speaking voice is sophisticated, European, Southern,
relaxed, conversational tone, brilliantly phrased—danceable. It's also
his writing voice which he calls cadence. In this voice, sound and
meaning are holding hands like lovers, all of his serious opinions are
presented in this voice. On the second level chuckling indicates
improbability. Finally, to indicate the folly of life, he throws his head
back and roars.

"They had me address a Women's Lib Group—Women's Gay Lib
Alternative, whatever *that* means! There are many Lib groups, you
know, but this was a very rough group. A splinter group. They
seduced me into coming by writing a very beautiful letter and I

accepted. Bill Barnes, my agent, said, "I'd better go with you." So, we went. We were the only men admitted to this meeting, and they looked like they were all trying to appear as *truck-drivers* ("Sailors," I added encouragingly, Tennessee cracking up on cue) and I was *trapped* but Billie sat near the door—so he could get out, hehehe! I told them that neither sex is completely one sex, that we have vestigials of the other sex. Men have, you know, nipples, which are no longer any use to them. And so, with the female, who has vestigial counterparts of a male penis! What an awful uproar went up among these girls! I didn't think I'd get out of there alive! It was near riot!" He threw his head back and roared with laughter.

The most important event in Tennessee Williams' life was when he realized how his weaknesses were to be his strengths. A cruel father frustrated his hopes of romance with a girl whom he wanted to attend college with, but the strict father felt the girl would distract from his son's studies. So, Tom went to a different college. Then, the father took him out of that one in his third year to work in his shoe concern. Tennessee turned this into a strength: he disciplined himself, hammering on his typewriter after work into daybreak. Finally after two years of this he went back to college, this time to the University of Iowa, where he graduated at age twenty-seven. Then, he moved to the Latin Quarter of New Orleans, the Greenwich Village and Berkeley of its time, known affectionately as "sin city," a world far from what his father would ever admit to. Tennessee never returned to Mississippi or St. Louis to live, although he traveled everywhere else in the world, Taos, New Mexico, California, and New York when he was still poor, and Europe and Indonesia when he became rich. His choice of where he lives—New Orleans and Key West—are expressive of the folly and fantasy in the southern temperament, which he loves so well. His captivating charm is due to his having to make peace with two extremes of a man possessed by a very sensual nature and a memory of a guilt-ridden past hovered over by a cruel, inhibiting and ruthless father. He used art to remake his familial and personal shortcomings into one of the strongest personalities in America.

"Yevtushenko is a very charming man, but not very diplomatic," Tennessee said in his serious voice. "He saw my play *Small Craft Warnings* and we met for lunch the next day. He said to me,

'Tennessee, you have only put thirty percent of yourself into that play. I am not alone in this opinion. Everyone around me is saying the same thing.' I said to him—hahaha—isn't it fortunate that I have thirty percent *left*! Hahaha!"

What about Solzhenitsyn?"

I have only read *Cancer Ward*. It lacks poetry, you know," he paused, "but I would like to translate Chekhov some day." This evening's conversation took a serious turn as Tennessee got on the subject of contemporary playwriting and playwrights. "The whole of a play is exaggerated," he said, "but Harold Pinter has solved that in his last play. The one about two women and a man. Maria, what's the name of that play. We saw it together. It's Pinter's last play." "Have you met him?" I asked. "Yes, I met Pinter and he is a lovely man. We agreed that Jane Bowles is a great prose writer. Her novel, *Two Serious Ladies,* is my favorite. I like "A Day in the Opening" as the best of her short stories. And she wrote a very beautiful play called *In the Summer House.* She died about a year ago and was about ten years younger than myself. But I like Pinter, he has a very elusive style. . ." "A very understated style, isn't it?" Maria said. "Pinter gets all his points by understatement; Tennessee gets his by overstatement. In Pinter you get very little but in Tennessee you get a lot. You know what I mean?" Maria explained to me.

In *Out Cry* the metaphor for the theater is the theater itself and therefore "the door and the wall," as Tallulah said, "are real, even though the play may not be." The players in *Out Cry* perform their "two character play" to a pretend audience. Thus, to the dialogue between the lyric and the realist theater, Tennessee adds a few lines: Plays don't have to be realistic for another reason; reality no longer enchants us with its pain. As Felice says, "Even pain has a limit." Reality can no longer pose a threat to a man because even pain has a limit. Reality can no longer pose a threat to a man because it is only one of the guises of *existence*. Imagination is just as valid to existence as is reality. Hence, Tennessee's new emphasis is now not on conflict, but mime and dance.

There are two images of Tennessee we should keep in mind, one as a poor starving young poet and the other one of a rich young poet. In the first, he is literally starving in some little town in Florida, the name's not important. Anyway, he finally lands a job as a teletype operator, but the guy working with him is a nut, just out of the asylum. Tennessee has the graveyard shift with the nut. The nut tells beautiful stories, and Tennessee is amused. He loves crazy people, then and now. He's had a lot of experience with it. Everything is going along fine until the boss warns him about his inefficiency. The employer practically gets on his knees, "Please, Williams, don't make me fire you in times like these when there just aren't any men around!" But one day, the lunatic and the poet botch a teletype message and the boss has to let the poet go, but retains the service of the lunatic. Tennessee beat it back to New York where he got a job in a hotel as a bell boy.

In the other image he is rich. He is the darling of the literary scene in New York, London, Rome, wherever he goes. At the end of an announcement of a new play by Tennessee Williams would usually be attached notes like this: "Tomorrow, after having read the notices, the author will be off for Italy, Spain, North Africa, Greece and Ceylon. He does not plan to return until next winter."

Between these two images, Tennessee has chosen the best from both worlds. He has been famous and wealthy a long time, but he has known poverty. Now his life is simple, almost without desire. His philosophy is epicurean: each man takes care of his own garden, leave God out of it. His consensus of life: "Self-pity is the worst emotion there is, next to deliberate unkindness."

After dinner Maria delighted us with a story about an Irishman, Pat, whose friend got his head cut off by the British. "And so, Pat had to go and identify his friend," she said, "and when the head of his friend was held up"—she lifted her arms high overhead—"'is this your friend,' the British asked him, holding the head up, 'No' says Pat, 'he wasn't that tall.'"

There was a silence. Time indeed seemed suspended. Tennessee looked very quiet in this last picture I have of him. Then he said, "Power is an embarrassing thing to have. I never wanted power, except power over myself." Then he pushed himself back from the table, as if to take all of his life and his work into better perspective. "It's nice, you know, to have a simple life. I want to love and that can be it," he said, looking up at me, "You know what I mean?"

Tennessee Williams
Charles Ruas/1975

From *Conversations with American Writers* (New York: Alfred A. Knopf, 1985), 75-90. © 1984 by Charles Ruas. Reprinted by permission.

The living room of Tennessee Williams's New York apartment at the Elysée Hotel had that impersonal elegance of white walls and white French furniture. The few mementos, such as framed photographs and books scattered around the rooms, only heightened the impression of transience. By contrast, Tennessee Williams, relaxed in casual dress on the sofa, was welcoming and smiling with contentment about his recently published memoirs.

His secretary, Joe Uecker, who maintained their schedule, had refreshments prepared on the coffee table. Tennessee introduced me to his sister, Rose, a petite woman, powdered and rouged and wearing a red tulle dress and bolero jacket. She smiled sweetly and sat with a drink, watching us as we talked—she would doze, wake up, take another drink, and then doze off again. Tennessee spoke to her as to a child, which seemed his customary way. He explained that Rose always visited him from upstate New York when he was staying in town.

Tennessee Williams entered the conversation with good-humored curiosity and spoke in a drawling nasal Southern twang. His mood was mercurial, at once laughing and anxious, stoical and sentimental, kindly and caustic. As he became more relaxed with each drink, he was more confiding, laughing at himself and the folly of the world. Only fatigue put an end to the conversation.

TW: I'm quite through with the kind of play that established my early and popular reputation. I am doing a different thing, which is altogether my own, not influenced at all by other playwrights at home or abroad, or by other schools of theatre. My thing is what it always was, to express my world and experience of it in whatever form seems suitable to the material.

CR: Were you conscious of this change, or was it something you experienced and understood in retrospect?

TW: My plays in the 1940s and 1950s were relatively conventional in their construction, because my mind was relatively balanced. You see, the dreadful period of almost clinical depression had not set in yet. But as my life became more desperate I had to change the style, because the conventional pattern of a play no longer could contain that kind of frenzy.

CR: Was it the pressures of your success or the attacks by the critics that brought on this crisis?

TW: It was the sudden change as much as anything. The public and the critics were both favorable for quite a while. That's usually the case with a playwright in America who breaks through at all. From about *Menagerie* through *Cat* I had only one or two failures, such as *Camino Real*, which was a commercial failure. Later it was recognized as an artistic success. It was too broad a canvas to work on, and neither I nor the director seemed to realize that it was really a romantic pageant. I'm hoping that in the opera we're making of it now, for production next year, the pageant quality will come through more clearly.

CR: Your love for that play continually comes up.

TW: Oh, yes, because it has such a free form, and I love that. I like breaking out of the conventional forms. Now, *Red Devil Battery Sign* is a return to the conventional pattern but with a most volatile subject matter.

CR: What other work failed?

TW: *Period of Adjustment*, although we thought it was going to be my most popular play. I called it a comedy. It really wasn't a comedy. It was funny, yes. So is *Streetcar* funny. Blanche is a scream in that thing. I would laugh like hell when I wrote both of them. But *Period of Adjustment* isn't. I began to go into areas of my own head which were not easily communicable to a large audience, but now are beginning to be.

CR: When did you begin to feel that you were losing your command over the theatre?

TW: With plays like *Camino Real*, which I thought most surely would be recognized for eloquence of language and certain passages but was simply dismissed by the critics, just laughed at. I remember in Philadelphia I was very angry on opening night. Great blocks of people would get up and start walking out, and I would get in the aisle and try to turn them back into their seats. I'd scream and peg things at them.

CR: Is there a critic or any criticism that you've found pertinent to your writing?

TW: I think the best thing you can do about the critics is never say a word. In the end you have the last say, and they know it. They can close your play, but if it has vitality it will be done again. Sooner or later they will accept it.

CR: But as a leading playwright, surely you were prepared for the worst as well as the best.

TW: It didn't surprise me, to tell you the truth. It's the pattern in America. A writer has a period of success, and then there is something instinctive in the critical world; they create a figure which is somewhat larger than its actual size, and then they start trying to cut it down to what they think is its actual size. Sometimes they diminish it to the vanishing point.

CR: Did you write *Glass Menagerie* while working the graveyard shift at a factory in St. Louis?

TW: Well, no. A lot of people think I wrote *The Glass Menagerie* while I was employed by MGM. This is not true. I didn't write for films for more than three weeks. I was given the assignment of writing a film for Lana Turner—*Marriage Is a Private Affair*, it was called. The producer happened to have an attachment of a romantic nature to the lady, but he was realistic about her abilities as an actress. He would keep saying, "Oh, this is beautiful stuff, Mr. Williams, but she can't say it. She doesn't know how to read it. Now, why don't you just forget all about this Hollywood business, this screenwriting business, and just go out to Santa Monica. We're obliged to pay you two hundred forty dollars a week, so just come in and collect your check, go back out to Santa Monica Beach, and do your own work," he said, "because your own work is good." I saved enough money so that I could spend a summer free of harassment, and free of occupation, in Provincetown. I wrote *The Glass Menagerie* there, and also in the law school dormitory at Harvard, because I had a friend there.

CR: Perhaps I'll write the dorm suggesting they put up a plaque. Was that your first success as a playwright?

TW: Success is such a false word, really. I think perhaps Andy Warhol can define it: "Success is what sells," isn't it?

CR: It must give you some satisfaction to know that your plays are part of the international repertory.

TW: Yes, but as I said, they are usually the ones that were successful, the earlier ones. I get a good many letters from people who appreciate my work, but I don't get very good notices.

CR: Which play marks the transition in your writing?

TW: Let's say that the work has become darker. It began to become darker in the sixties and it became so dark that people find it painful. Now we're in a particularly escapist period. People want lighter and lighter things, and my work continues to get darker. *Camino Real* was a real departure from convention, yes, but *Suddenly Last Summer* was the first work that reflected the emotional trauma, that of my life, very deeply.

CR: The play introduces psychoanalysis to investigate the pathology beneath these privileged lives.

TW: Yes, quite true. I think mainly through the *tour de force* performance by Anne Meacham and Hortense Alden they broke through to the public, got the response to esoteric material on opening night.

CR: It's also the play that gives a definition of God.

TW: These people were total sybarites, creatures with no social conscience whatsoever, and consequently they're godless. They would conceive of God as being the predatory birds killing the newly hatched turtles. They would think that was the face of God. God exists in our understanding of each other, and in our acts based upon our understanding. This is what the doctor does at the end, when he accepts the girl's story. Now, Sebastian's death is treated realistically on the screen, which was deplorable. Actually, cannibalism was simply a dramatic metaphor. It's never been accepted as such because people have seen the picture and not the play.

CR: All of your plays were made into films. It's in *The Milk Train*

Doesn't Stop Here Anymore that you have a central character who
lives by sexually exploiting others.

TW: *Milk Train* is going to be recognized as an important film,
some say, because it was much better written than the play version. It
was somewhat damaged in the end by the foolish act of the man
tossing a big diamond into the ocean. That wasn't in the script.

CR: I didn't know that you had written the screenplay.

TW: I wrote the screenplay. But I didn't write that scene, because
the ambiguity is supposed to exist: there's the element of the con
man in him, but there's also an element of the mystic. He has made a
career out of attending very old women to the door but, I think, with
real concern for them.

CR: The metaphor of cannibalism in *Suddenly Last Summer* is sex
as one person consuming another.

TW: I think it's as old as time, as old as human history. I think
people have always paid for the sexual favors of the younger. I'm
very grateful that my sexual appetites are waning and that I look
more for companionship now than for sexual excitement. I'm not free
of Eros, but Eros may be free of me. There's a lot of comedy in that
when you don't have to be heavy about it.

CR: Which play, then, establishes your changed viewpoint?

TW: I think it became pretty dark in *In the Bar of a Tokyo Hotel*
and *A Slapstick Tragedy. The Gnädiges Fräulein* has a gothic quality
to it, a grotesque comedy that was incomprehensible to people. They
didn't even see the humor in it. They just saw what fears they have.
Everyone has the fears that are expressed in these plays—death,
confinement, and deprivation.

CR: Your characters have become isolated. Are they beyond
forming relationships, or are they autonomous, if that's possible?

TW: There are people who are by nature autonomous, in that they
are incapable of relating to other people. They do on the surface, but
there's no inner commitment to another person, or other people, or
to society.

CR: But that's a prevalent attitude nowadays.

TW: There's a particular withdrawal I've noticed in the seventies
from social commitment, of feeling any responsibility to the society in
which you live, and the time in which you live. I find it boring as hell.
One of my best lines is "There's no such thing as an inescapable

corner with two people in it." You have escaped into the other person, from your solitary self.

CR: In these plays, you present characters talking about themselves.

TW: Yes, people trying to be comprehended by other people, and talking almost compulsively about themselves. I find myself doing that. I become very garrulous about myself if I have an audience.

CR: On stage, in *Small Craft Warnings, Out Cry,* in *Tokyo Hotel* . . .

TW: Everybody is talking about himself. Actually, I think that's a fault. I saw a play in London that impressed me enormously, Harold Pinter's *No Man's Land.* The four characters—each had a scene in which he was the principal talker. There was a good interchange among them, although there was no real communication. One of the points he makes is that although they talk a great deal, and deliver long soliloquies, they don't really reach each other.

CR: Whereas your characters do, however briefly.

TW: Sometimes they do. I hope they do. Perhaps I'm a little less dark in my view of life than Pinter, although he writes more amusingly. He's very funny.

CR: *Out Cry* is an example of why you feel your later plays are misstaged. [New York: Lyceum Theatre, 1 March 1973—Editor]

TW: I had a number of references to sunflowers in the script; they had these huge projections of sunflowers on the back wall. They weren't necessary, unfortunately. I don't blame it on the gentleman who designed the set, because he was encouraged in this. Everything had to be literally shown. If they were in prison, there had to be bars, or trapped figures projected in huge size on the cyclorama of the set. It was put together by Mr. Peter Glenville, the director. He arbitrarily took out whatever he thought he wanted from all the versions. I had practically nothing to do with it. For instance, Genevieve Bujold came down from Canada twice to read for the part of the girl. I was not permitted to hear her. She would have been perfect opposite Michael York.

CR: Ordinarily, you rewrite your plays for each production?

TW: I rewrite more than most people.

CR: How many versions of *Out Cry* have there been?

TW: The first version was the one in London in '67. To tell you the truth, I was in no condition to notice much going on. I behaved abominably. I was introduced to the director and I said, "You know, plays have to be directed." To the designer I said, "Was that a set?" Well, I've had much happier experiences.

CR: You felt you were giving them what they deserved?

TW: No, I don't think so. I think a playwright should try to keep his cool under all circumstances. Even with Mr. Merrick—that's the acid test.

CR: Was the play rewritten for the Chicago production in '71?

TW: The text of the Chicago production was close to the current text, but it was not edited, it was not cut. One of the great improvements now is that the play has been reduced to its proper size. Between a third and a fourth has been cut out.

CR: Was it Mr. Glenville who re-edited the play for performance in New York?

TW: I'm being slightly unfair, because he did consult me to some extent about it. But I was so overawed by the prospect of having a Broadway production for this little play that I just let him go ahead. Things only got a bit uptight when we were on the road. I felt that I was not being allowed to cut and revise as I should. The time seemed wasted.

CR: It's surprising how the text of a play seems to have an autonomous existence.

TW: Autonomous existence apart from the writer?

CR: Yes, the way directors cut, change, and shape the text.

TW: Well, I'll tell you. People associate my name with successes. I've had a succession of failures. You have no idea of how it reduces your power. You have less and less say when you are dealing with people who are dominating and aggressive. You have less and less control over your productions.

CR: Are producers drawn to your plays chiefly because your earlier works were guaranteed box-office hits?

TW: I think that my new work is just baffling to them. They read it, and something intrigues them perhaps. Then, when they try to stage it, it eludes them.

CR: What do you think of experimental theatre groups which do not rely on the text for the performance?

TW: There's a great subtlety in interpretation by the director and the performers when they work as an ensemble with an exquisite sense of what each of them wanted, what they were working towards. There's a unity there, a concept.

CR: Even though you are a Broadway playwright, are you interested in experimental productions for your new plays?

TW: I find that my great happiness in the theatre now is not on Broadway, but off-Broadway and off-off-Broadway. There's not the financial responsibility hanging over your head. You don't feel there's three hundred sixty thousand dollars riding on something that you've written. I don't think that the money thing should be there at all, but it is there. That's what the producers are thinking about: "OK, we're making money here in Boston, but will we be making it in Washington for seven weeks?" Considerations of that nature impinge too much. I will never write for Broadway again. Except I made this one commitment to myself, which was to complete the play in which Anthony Quinn was so brilliant, *The Red Devil Battery Sign*. Quinn couldn't work off-Broadway. Certain big stars just can't work off-Broadway. A limousine has to pick them up and take them to the theatre, wait there all during the performance, and take them back to their Park Avenue hotel. That's part of their life style they cannot abandon because they feel they will be abandoning the prestige.

CR: You stated to the press that you felt that the demise of *Red Devil* before reaching Broadway was politically motivated.

TW: We had four producers. Bob Colby wanted to bring it in, but the other two sided with Merrick and decided not to bring it in, despite the fact that we were doing good business. [Boston: Shubert Theater, 18-28 June 1975—Editor] But they did me a favor. I am glad this is on tape because I am going to say it: it made me so angry when they closed that I said, "God damn it, I'm going to show them I can write a fine play out of this." I worked like hell on it, and it is a fine play now, and it has a strong straight story line. I used every trick of the craft I've learned to hold an audience. I've used sex—that's not a trick because I'm naturally sensual and like sexual scenes. The emphasis is no longer on sexuality. The emphasis now is on the inexorable story of two doomed people. He is doomed by a malignant growth on the brain, which is coming back after an operation. She is going to be faithful to her early heritage and testify before Congress in the McCarthy hearings. She has decoded documents in her possession which are seized when her godfather is murdered. The whole thing goes towards an inevitable conclusion.

CR: The events are set during the McCarthy hearings. Which aspect of that witch hunt did you find most upsetting?

TW: It's the moral decay of America, which really began with the Korean War, way before the Kennedy assassination. The main reason we were involved in Vietnam was so two hundred billion dollars worth of equipment could be destroyed and would have to be bought again. We're the death merchants of the world, this once great and beautiful democracy. People think I'm a communist [for saying this], but I hate all bureaucracy, all isms. I'm a revolutionary only in the sense that I want to see us escape from this sort of trap.

CR: Yet in your plays, many of your characters express a painful class consciousness rather than a social consciousness.

TW: All my plays have a social conscience. I don't think that any play, any playwright, or any work of art is going to make any difference in the course of history. History is inexorable in its flow, and I think the flow of history is towards some form of social upheaval. I'm giving you my viewpoint. I'm not stating fact, I'm telling you what I feel, what I intuit. Our country got into trouble when it ceased to be able to exist within its own frontiers. When it had to expand onto other continents, that was the beginning of our moral collapse.

CR: Do you see the possibility of change?

TW: I have a positive view of the future. I think we're going to go through almost total destruction, but not quite. I think we'll stop just short of it.

CR: What form of government do you foresee for this country? Is there a model you have in mind?

TW: I think England is fast approaching some kind of socialism, but they will retain their monarchy. They should, because a monarchy is an ornament. I met Princess Margaret recently at a party when some drunken Southern lady pushed me into a loveseat next to her. She said, "You two sit down and have a good giggle together." Princess Margaret was so startled, but so was I. I'm always impressed by the beauty of behavior of people trained in a certain way. The monarchy sets an example of good breeding and good manners for a whole nation. I believe that society can rectify any inequities without the shattering of gentle behavior. I find myself violating my own principles at times. It makes me angry when I'm forced to get angry.

CR: Is it the moral code attached to that behavior which you value?

TW: The moral way is the way of survival now. They become identical.

CR: Your characters fear social degradation. Is that the effect of the Depression? In your *Memoirs* you mention trying to join the WPA writers' project.

TW: In those days you had to prove your family was destitute or they wouldn't let you on. I had no way of proving that my father was destitute, because he was a sales manager of a branch of a big shoe company. He wouldn't give me a penny. Nevertheless, I wasn't eligible.

CR: Did that awaken a political awareness?

TW: Oh, I was a socialist from the time I started working for a shoe company. That will do it *every* time. Sixty-five dollars a month. Surrounded by all these lathes, my God!

CR: You write about Hart Crane, who influenced your own poetry.

TW: I never met Hart Crane. I read of his death in 1932, when he jumped off the stern of a ship called the *Esmeralda*. It was twenty-four hours north of Havana, and in my will there is a codicil that I should be buried at sea as close as possible to the point where he jumped overboard, because I had a great reverence for Hart Crane as an artist.

CR: In your *Memoirs* you've said that *In the Bar of a Tokyo Hotel* is the first full statement of your darker vision.

TW: That was the last play I wrote before I had my overdiscussed breakdown. You see, I was in a deep depression from 1963 till the breakdown occurred in 1969. At the time of *In the Bar of a Tokyo Hotel* I was just approaching the collapse. The producers, a very nice couple named Marks, were visiting in Key West, and I was seeing them daily. I didn't know they were in town. I was working slowly out of my own conscious mind. The one thing I rewrote during my confinement is *Tokyo Hotel*.

CR: What was your interpretation of the play?

TW: The theme of creation. I think the couple, the artist and his wife in that play, were two sides of one person. One side was a man driven mad by the passion to create, which was frustrated, and the woman, as he described her, was a compulsive bitch.

CR: What kind of changes did you make?

TW: Textual changes. I tried to remove some of the hysteria from the painter's talk about his work.

CR: Those are some of your most eloquent passages.

TW: I think the most beautiful passages were those of the woman. I also like the scene just before his death when he says, "One of those diaphanous August afternoons . . ." The music of the language is what I like.

CR: I found the description of the creative process beautiful.

TW: Of course that doesn't impress me because I'm so familiar with it. I was going through a bad time corresponding to what the painter was going through. But do you know who I thought I was writing about? Jackson Pollock, not myself. Tony Smith, a dear friend of mine, was also a close friend of Pollock's, and I knew towards the end that Jackson Pollock was crawling around naked on the floor with a spray gun, just spraying canvas and just streaking it over the canvas with his fingers.

CR: As the painter in *Tokyo Hotel* strips himself and nails the canvas to the floor. Were you aware of the suicidal drive in Pollock?

TW: Yes, yes. I realized that when he drove his car into a tree accidentally, but drunkenly. These things are not accidental. I know because I did the same thing with a car in Italy after a violent quarrel with a lover. I just filled a Thermos with martinis and I drove faster and faster, drinking the whole Thermos bottle. A truck came out of a side road and I just turned slightly, but I didn't control the car, and wrapped it around a tree. Well, this is a form of suicide. My typewriter flew out of the back seat and hit me on the head. It was amazing that I survived. I had a concussion. When I came to, I was surrounded by all these Italian farm people, *contadini*, they call them. Each had a little glass in his hand and was shaking like this. They thought I was dead.

CR: I wanted to ask you your thoughts on writer's block, and the idea of a writer having said all that he has to say, in the manner of E. M. Forster.

TW: All writers have periods of block, and some of them are blocked permanently. It seems to me around age forty-five it occurs, and it may be just a matter of their running out of material. They've said what they have to say. I've been blocked myself. The cause of it was a time of depleted energy after I had completed a piece of work. I just didn't have the strength to go on. The thing to do is rest, to take time off and let the energy rebuild. The desire to create is one of the strongest urges a human spirit can contain. It will always break through, I think.

CR: Aside from your plays and film scripts, you have written novels, poetry, as well as your *Memoirs*, so it's difficult to think of you as having any sort of block.

TW: Oh, I have, though, continually. I could have written much more and much better if I had not always been afraid of my inabilities to write. But I've learned to live with it. It's a bit late to start worrying that I won't be able to write at sixty-five. I haven't written half enough.

"Life Is a Black Joke"
Lothar Schmidt-Mühlisch/1975

From *Die Welt* [West Berlin], 29 December 1975, 13. Trans.
Kathryn Wright Brady.

America's literary world is divided: just last summer, the high priest of
New York critics, Clive Barnes, announced "the great comeback of
Tennessee Williams," and a few weeks ago in the *Sunday Times*
[(sic) New York *Sunday News*, 19 October 1975, 3—Editor] the
skeptical question was raised, "Does his future lie behind him?" The
author himself is seeking his own confirmation, his own rehabilitation.
The first part of his *Memoirs*—he even includes a graphic description
of his sex life—has kindled quite lively discussions. In San Francisco
preparations are under way for the premiere performance of a
comedy. And in the "English Theatre" in Vienna, the curtain will rise
tonight on the world premiere of the new version of his play, *The Red
Devil Battery Sign*, which was a complete failure in its first version in
Boston some time ago.

In the lobby of Vienna's Hotel Imperial, where an abundance of
gold and mahogany disguises the vanished glory of the former
Danube monarchy, the small, delicate man stands out only because
of his light brown, narrow-waisted fur jacket. Surprisingly, this
Tennessee Williams is—at least outwardly—far removed from the
neurotic bundle of nerves that one might imagine him to be. He is
excessively cordial, immediately personal, and unafraid of questions,
although he hates interviews. His only stipulation: "Let's have a drink
first."

But his cheerfulness is a bit deceptive. Tennessee Williams, 64, has,
after all, not without reason escaped to the Danube for his premiere
performance. "I would like to try some things out. And I have no
desire to allow myself to be torn apart by American critics because of
that." His next remark sounds even more reflective. "You Europeans
love your artists more; you forgive them for not always being

consistently good." For a man like Tennessee Williams, such indulgence seems to be critical. Gradually, one begins to grasp the ambiguity his plays touch on: the existence of sensitivity in the merciless harshness of America's success-oriented society. Williams himself says, "I can't live without writing. And in my writing I always reveal myself; my plays actually deal only with me. Believe me, to be a writer—that's a cruel profession."

And that, according to his own account, contributed significantly to his plunge into the deepest crisis of his life at the end of the sixties. With alcohol and stimulants he kept himself at his writing desk. His nerves failed. "And then I faced the decision whether I wanted to continue to live or not. I came to the simple realization: Life—that means simply continuing without any intellectual or spiritual justification."

Yet there is more to it than this. Doesn't the apparent fatalism conceal a longing? What then was the crisis actually all about? Williams answers only after long reflection. "It was the contradiction between two sides of my nature: between gentleness and violence, between tenderness and harshness." The crisis of an author which one is so ready to attribute to his neuroses reveals itself to be the ancient dualism of Western drama: love and destruction.

Did one side win? Williams shrugs his shoulders. "Things change very little." Has he again found his identity in society? "The problems of society, which in the forties and fifties were also my problems, have obviously not been solved. In the sixties they only then appeared to dissipate. Many people believed in political, social solutions. But I have the impression that a change is taking place now. In this sense, one could perhaps say that I will again find my identity in society."

His favorite place to live (and therefore to work) is on his small island off the coast of Florida. "There I have light and peace." The other apartments in New Orleans, San Francisco, and New York serve more practical purposes. New York is for business. So the work goes on. Does he, like the *Sunday Times* [sic], see his future already behind him? He laughs. "At 64, one naturally has the greatest part of his life behind him. But as an author, I can't say that. I just continue working, regardless of what comes of it. I believe, for example, that my new play, the *Red Devil* in its current version, belongs with *A*

Streetcar Named Desire, The Glass Menagerie, Camino Real, and
Cat on a Hot Tin Roof as one of my five best plays. It is, incidentally,
a political play."

That, of course, raises the question of whether the crisis didn't after
all bring about a change in Tennessee Williams' creative work. He
doesn't deny that but attributes it to the fact that the nature of the
questions has changed. "For the first time in my life I gained a
genuine relationship to the social conditions of the world. I always
had the same problems as the people in my plays: no connection to
the outside world. I was trapped within myself. That problem, at
least, was solved in the crisis of the late sixties, which one should
certainly not take to mean that I suddenly became a sociological
author. But my main characters now have a political dimension to the
extent that they no longer act blindly out of themselves, but rather are
aware of the effect of their actions."

And Williams also views that personally. "I believe that society can
identify again with my current problems." He explains now more
clearly what has actually changed. "The relationship of people to
each other, the need to escape from loneliness, the problem in all its
aspects—all that of course has its social and political dimensions.
These relationships which I earlier did not see in this way, I now
portray in my new plays."

Has he then become an optimist? He rejects that idea almost
fatalistically. "I have already said that a person must simply continue.
For me only that is realistic."

Still, America seems to be discovering her Tennessee Williams
anew. In Washington, New York, and Los Angeles, five of his works
are being performed this season and, for the most part, play to full
houses. But for Williams himself, the kind of success his new works
will have is perhaps more important. His rediscovered self-confidence
is still not so strong that a new crisis is not possible. "Life is a black
joke," he says ironically to characterize his outlook. And the man
who loves Mozart and Wagner is more in need of his comeback than
he himself will admit. So in Vienna, it should be decided whether
America's most important living playwright will once more be able
effectively to enrich today's dramatic production.

Orpheus Holds His Own: William Burroughs Talks with Tennessee Williams

James Grauerholz/1977

From the *Village Voice*, 16 May 1977, 44-45. © 1977 by the *Village Voice*. Reprinted by permission.

Although they were both born in St. Louis within three years of each other, William Burroughs did not meet Tennessee Williams until 1960, when they were briefly introduced at a table in the Cafe de Paris in Tangiers, by Paul and Jane Bowles. Burroughs had read and admired Williams's short stories, and later in the '60s Tennessee was known to quote at length from Burroughs's *Naked Lunch*. But despite their mutual acquaintances (including the Bowleses and the painter Brion Gysin), they were not to meet again until 1975, at a gathering of the American Academy of Arts and Letters. Their first conversation of any length took place at a party after a Burroughs reading at Notre Dame University earlier this year, and there they talked and carried on like old friends.

Tennessee's new play, *Vieux Carré*, opens tonight on Broadway. Burroughs and I attended a preview two Saturdays ago. The next day we visited him at the Hotel Elysée, where he has maintained a spacious flat on the 12th floor for some time. It was late afternoon, and as I arrived, a few minutes after Burroughs, they were already seated at the opposite ends of a sofa. Tennessee seemed chipper; he got up to show us a pastel gouache he had just completed on his terrace that morning. Two bottles of wine arrived, and Burroughs and Williams resumed their talk.

Burroughs: When someone asks me to what extent my work is autobiographical, I say, "Every word is autobiographical, and every word is fiction." Now what would your answer be on that question?

Williams: My answer is that every word is autobiographical and no word is autobiographical. You can't do creative work and adhere to facts. For instance, in my new play there is a boy who is living in a house that I lived in, and undergoing some of the experiences that I underwent as a young writer. But his personality is totally different from mine. He talks quite differently from the way that I talk, so I say the play is not autobiographical. And yet the events in the house did actually take place.

Burroughs: All of them?

Williams: There are two characters in it, a boy and a girl, whom I knew later in another house, not in that one. But all the others were there at 722 Toulouse Street, in 1939.

Burroughs: What has happened to that building?

Williams: Still there, it's vacant now. Just as the boy says at the end of the play: "This house is empty now . . . they're disappearing—going . . ."

Burroughs: That's a strange time-pocket, the French Quarter.

Williams: Yeah. I did go there first in 1939. I did have a lot of those experiences then, but I did not leave there with a wealthy old sponsor. [As The Young Writer does in *Vieux Carré*] I don't know why I put that in, wishful thinking . . . I lived there with a clarinet player, broke as I was. And I had to pick squabs for a living on the West Coast—but that's another play.

Burroughs: What about the character of the landlady?

Williams: She was like that. She wasn't named Mrs. Wire, but she was very much like that. She poured the boiling water through the cracks in the roof, on a photographer downstairs. I think he was a famous one, named Clarence Laughlin. He did give very rowdy parties, which outraged her—maybe because she wasn't invited.

Burroughs: Well, she was certainly magnificent in the play— Sylvia Sidney.

Williams: She *is* magnificent. I think she's one of our great, great actresses.

Burroughs: One thing I would like to comment on, about the play, is the recreation of the past—nostalgia, if you will. It came through more there than it does in a film with all the devices of Hollywood. Of course, the stage sets were spectacular, but it interested me because at times I really felt the period. But then they

try something like *The Great Gatsby*, and there's not a whiff of the
'20s in it.

Williams: You remember the '20s?

Burroughs: Oh heavens, yes.

Williams: I only ask because there are few people living who do
. . . That's the sad thing about growing old, isn't it—you learn you
are confronted with loneliness. . . .

Burroughs: One of the many.

Williams: Yes, one of the many—that's the worst, yes.

Burroughs: After all, if there wasn't age, there wouldn't be any
youth, remember.

Williams: I'm never satisfied to look back on youth, though . . .
not that I ever had much youth.

Burroughs: Writers don't, as a rule. . . . Would you say this play
was an expansion of the short story, "The Angel in the Alcove"?

Williams: Oh yes. At first I thought it was a big mistake to transfer
a story of mood—you know, mostly mood and nostalgia—to the
stage; that it would seem insubstantial. But now we are running the
two plays together, you know?

Burroughs: What is it, two and a half hours? I didn't have the
feeling that it was too long.

Williams: I have plays of mine that seem to go on forever. . . .
You know, actors are not well treated, unless they're stars.

Burroughs: They lead a hard life. Hitchcock always had a very
low opinion of actors.

Williams: I have a high opinion of actors—of their intelligence, I
mean. I think they're smarter than they're reputed to be. Capote says
they're all fools—but I think they're brighter than him . . . oh, he's
going to sue me again! [*laugh*] You know he sued me for $5 million;
I've never been so flattered. [*laughter*] I merely expressed some
disbelief that he would descend to such a literary level, as a last
installment of *Answered Prayers*. I think these things are so silly . . .
because who wants to spend all that time in a courtroom, or on court
fees? It's the lawyers who get the money, not the plaintiff or the
defendant. But I'll tell you, Truman's a great self-publicist. He's quite
a theatrical personality, he is.

Burroughs: He is indeed. . . . Where did you write this play?

Williams: I wrote *Vieux Carré* on a ship called the Oronza. My agent booked me out, after a play called *Out Cry*—some people called it *Out Rage*; in its longest form it *was* rather an outrage, of tedium. So I happened to be going to California to see Faye Dunaway play Blanche DuBois opposite Jon Voight [Los Angeles: Ahmanson Theater, 28 March 1973—Editor], so I said, "I want to get away. I want to get a *long* way away." My agent booked me onto this Cherry Blossom Cruise—it turned out to be a *geriatric* cruise. Everybody on it was 80 or over, and they had huge stabilizers to keep the ship from rocking. You know? The great pleasure in ocean travel is the *rocking*, the *motion*. . . . The sea underneath you. Well, this ship was utterly motionless, and yet these old people were breaking hips right and left. The doctor's office was always full of them. And three died before we hit Yokohama.

Burroughs: Any burials at sea?

Williams: I was told there were secret ones at midnight, yes. And when we arrived at Yokohama, the Japanese customs officials grinned; they said, "How many this time?" Meaning, how many had been collected by the Reaper? And we said, "Only three we know for sure." He said, "Usually it's double that many before they reach Yokohama." Heh heh heh. We jumped ship at Yokohama, although we were booked on a round-the-world pass. I doubt if there were any passengers left living by the time they completed their trip. There was nothing to do on the Oronza but play bridge or write. And I do love bridge, but I was kicked out of every bridge game, I was so incompetent. I learned how to play bridge in a psychiatric ward. My brother tried to teach me how to play chess in the psychiatric ward, but I couldn't learn.

Burroughs: I notice you don't drink hard liquor?

Williams: I allow myself one drink a day of hard liquor. While I'm working. Otherwise, I do drink wine. Because I really prefer wine, it's not much of a deprivation.

Burroughs: That story of "The Angel in the Alcove" was written quite a while ago, wasn't it?

Williams: Oh God, yes. Must have been the '50s. . . . [October 1943—Editor]

Burroughs: Paul Bowles had a first edition of that book of stories. [*One Arm and Other Stories*, 1948—Editor] I remember I borrowed his copy to read. I was on junk at the time and I dripped blood all over it, and Paul was furious. [laughter] It should be quite a collector's item—first edition, and with my blood all over it.

Williams: Do you ever take drugs at all anymore?

Burroughs: No, not that kind. No, I don't have a habit or anything like that.

Williams: I've always wanted to go on opium. I did try it in Bangkok. I was traveling with a professor friend of mine, and he had been in the habit of occasionally dissolving a bit of—you know, it comes in little long black sticks—dissolving it in the tea, and drinking it. And he was angry at me, or confused mentally, I don't know which—and so I called him one morning, as he'd gotten me this long black stick of opium, and I said, "Paul, what do I do with it?" And he said, "Just put it in the tea." So I put the whole stick in the tea. I nearly died of an OD, of course. I was puking green as your jacket, you know? And sicker than 10 dogs all that day. I called in a Siamese doctor. He said, "You should be *dead.*" I said, "I feel as though if I weren't walking or stumbling about, I would be." I've always said I wanted to write under the drug, you know, like Cocteau did—all of a sudden, my head seemed like a balloon and it seemed to go right up to the ceiling. . . . Do you ever take goof balls?

Burroughs: Ummm, I have, of course, yes. But, I'm not an aficionado. You know, De Quincey reports that Coleridge had to hire somebody to keep him out of drug stores, and then he fired him the next day when the man attempted to obey his instructions. He told him, "Do you know that men have been known to drop down dead for the timely want of opium?" Very funny indeed.

Williams: It's all a big joke. Maybe a black joke, but it's a big joke. And if they told me the play was closing tonight, I'd go "Ha haaa!"

Burroughs: Tennessee, have you written film scripts?

Williams: Yes, I've written one called *One Arm,* which has been floating around, I don't know where it is. I wrote it one summer while I was taking Dr. Max Jacobson's shots. I did some of my best writing while taking those shots. I had incredible vitality under them. And I got way ahead of myself as a writer, you know? And into another dimension. I never enjoyed writing like that. You've never written on any kind of speed, have you Bill?

Burroughs: Well no, I'm not a speed man at all.

Williams: I am a downer man.

Burroughs: I don't like either one very much.

Williams: Speed is wonderful, while I was young enough to take it; but you don't like either one, now? You don't need any kind of artificial stimulant?

Burroughs: Ummm, well, you know . . . of course, cannabis in any form is—

Williams: Cannabis has the opposite effect on me. But I think Paul finds it very helpful—Paul Bowles. But I have tried it; *nothing.* Just stonewalled me.

Burroughs: Did you do any work on the screenplay of *Suddenly Last Summer?*

Williams: Thank God, no. In fact, when I first saw it I walked out on it, begging Mr. Vidal's pardon. But, he *did* a wonderful workmanlike job, yes. . . . The person who fucked it up, if you'll excuse my language, was Joe Mankiewicz. I wrote the play, but you know—the play was an *allegory,* and consisted mainly of two monologues.

Burroughs: What did you feel about the film?

Williams: I walked out. Sam Spiegel, the producer, gave a private showing of it at a big party, and I just got up and walked out. When you began to see Mrs. Venable, and it became so realistic, with the boys chasing up the hill—I thought it was a travesty. It was about how people devour each other in an *allegorical* sense. But that's what a character says in one of my stories: "All art is an indiscretion, all life is a scandal." [*laughter*] It's possible to make it that. Taylor Mead succeeds, at least . . . I come close. [*laughter*] I hate *politesse,* don't you, Bill? I don't like people who play it too close to the vest— especially when there isn't too much of it left. I intend to *enjoy* what little there is. We're having a very literary discussion, aren't we? [*hearty laugh*] I avoid talking about writing. Don't you, Bill?

Burroughs: Yes, to some extent. But I don't go as far as the English do. You know this English bit of never talking about anything that means anything to anybody . . . I remember Graham Greene saying, "Of course, Evelyn Waugh was a very good friend of mine, but we never talked about writing!"

Williams: There's something very private about writing, don't you think? Somehow it's better, talking about one's most intimate sexual practices—you know—than talking about writing. And yet it's what I think we writers, we live for: writing. It's what we live for, and yet we can't discuss it with any freedom. It's very sad. . . . Anyway, I'm leaving America, more or less for good. Going to England first.

Burroughs: For good or for bad. . . .

Williams: Well, when I get to Bangkok it may be for bad, I don't know—[*laughter*] And after I get through with this play in London, I should go to Vienna. I love Vienna in the summer. I love sitting out in the wine gardens.

Burroughs: I was there in 1936. Remember the Romanische Baden?

Williams: The Roman Baths, I went to them . . . they're lovely, too.

Burroughs: Right near where the Prater used to be.

Williams: I've ridden on that ferris wheel in the park.

Burroughs: Me, too.

Williams: The one that was used so beautifully in *The Third Man*. I first went to Vienna in, it must have been 1949 or '50. I went alone . . . oh, but you can't be lonely in Vienna, you know. Not in summer. [pause] I'm just coming out with a new book of poems, *Androgyne, Mon Amour*. They're not as good as the first ones, naturally. But, there's one, or two or three . . .

Burroughs: I did some *I Ching* with this poetry this afternoon.

Williams: What is *I Ching*?

Burroughs: Well, you know—like the *Book of Changes*. You open it at random, pick a phrase out, write it down, then shift them around and hook them up.

Williams: Oh, I would love that! You might come up with something better, that way.

Burroughs: Yes, it is interesting.

Williams: Would you like to hear a poem about a junky?

Burroughs: Yes.

Williams: All right. This was during my depression period. [reading]:

"I met an apparition, and so did she.
She was as lovely as ever and even more fragile than
        ever and her eyes
were blind-looking.

I found myself able to think and speak a little.

'What have you been doing lately?'

Indifferently she said: 'When you take pills around the clock what you do is try to get money to pay the drugstore.'"

This lady was the mistress of a famous man who threw her over; she died of liquor and pills.

Burroughs: Deadly combination. Because as you know, the alcohol potentiates the toxicity.

Williams: I think it's most remarkable that you avoided any commitment to drugs, you know? Except cannabis. And you're strong enough to control it. I'm strong enough to control anything I take. . . .

Burroughs: Old Aleister Crowley, plagiarizing from Hassan i Sabbah, said: " 'Do what thou wilt' is the whole of the Law."

Williams: Regarding drugs, you mean.

Burroughs: Regarding anything . . . And then Hassan i Sabbah's last words were: "Nothing is true; everything is permitted." In other words, everything is permitted because nothing is true. If you see everything as illusion, then everything is permitted. The last words of Hassan i Sabbah, the Old Man of the Mountain, the Master of the Assassins. And this was given a slightly different twist, but it's the same statement as Aleister Crowley's, "Do what you want to do is the whole of the Law."

Williams: Provided you want to do the right thing, yes.

Burroughs: Ah, but if you really want to do it, then it's the right thing. That's the point.

Williams: Isn't that an amoralist point of view?

Burroughs: Completely . . . completely.

Williams: I don't believe you're an amoralist.

Burroughs: Oh yes.

Williams: You *do* believe it?

Burroughs: Well, I do what I can. . . .

Williams: I don't think it's true.

Burroughs: We were both brought up in the Bible belt; but it's obvious that what you want to do is, of course, eventually what you *will* do, anyway. Sooner or later.

Williams: I think we all die, sooner or later. I prefer to postpone the event.

Burroughs: Yes, there is that consideration.

Williams: I'm in no hurry. But one doesn't choose it. I've always been terrified of death.

Burroughs: Well . . . why?

Williams: I'm not sure. I say that, and yet I'm not sure. How about you?

Burroughs: Well, as I say, I don't know. Someone asked me about death, and I said, "How do you know you're not dead already?"

Roundtable: Tennessee Williams, Craig Anderson, and T.E. Kalem Talk about *Creve Coeur*

Ira J. Bilowit/1979

From *New York Theatre Review*, March 1979, 14-18.

Bilowit: I wonder if we could start with Tennessee telling us about the genesis of *Creve Coeur.*

Williams: I wrote this play in San Francisco about three years ago, I guess. It was a long one-act at the time. Maybe it should have remained that way. We still hope to cut a lot out. I hope everyone working on it will cooperate, because what this play primarily needs is cutting. What most plays need is cutting.

Out Cry was deplorably long. That's what was most damaging to it. When I wrote it in 1967, I was so crazy I didn't know where I was. When you're really crazy you do some of your best work, you know.

Anderson: My best work is always when I'm crazy, when I'm nervous and upset.

Kalem: Everyone in the theatre is crazy.

Williams: But you (Craig) appear to be so sane. You scare me out of my mind.

Kalem: But did *Creve Coeur* start with an image? Was there a scene?

Williams: No, no. Nothing ever starts with me except having to write every morning . . .

Kalem: Well what about *Iguana*?

Williams: You write a few lines . . . oh yes. It was the image of the iguana. We caught that iguana, really, in Acupulco somewhere in the summer of 1940.

Bilowit: Craig, when did you first read or get hold of *Creve Coeur*?

Anderson: Oh let's see. It must have been . . . when? Tennessee? I think it was in March.

Williams: I remember we had the first reading way uptown somewhere.

Anderson: Tennessee had given the play to a director, and the director had brought the play to me.

Williams: I'd given the play to Bill Barnes, actually . . .

Anderson: That's right, it came through Tennessee's agent. I was looking for a project for the Spoleto festival. And I thought there was no better way to celebrate the Spoleto festival in Charleston, South Carolina, than with the premiere of a new Tennessee Williams play. Tennessee and I got together, and liked each other, and we decided to give it a try down there. So we put the project together at that time, in March, and went into rehearsal and performed it in May and June down in Charleston.

Bilowit: Was the version of the play that you saw a full length play?

Anderson: No. We did not have an intermission originally. We expanded it to a full-length. It's a short full-length, in any case.

Williams: It must be shorter, too, I think.

Kalem: You're going to try to do it without an intermission?

Williams: Oh, we'll keep the interval. I like to go out and get a little white wine.

Bilowit: Other than the fact that it's a Tennessee Williams play, what specifically attracted you . . . ?

Anderson: Oh, the women. Tennessee's women are always so fascinating. Here he's written a play about four women only, and it's about four women without men, and about their dealings without men. Each one of them has this sort of yearning relationship, whether it's vicarious or whether it's an actual experience. It's lovely to watch Tennessee's women deal by themselves, without any influence of men in their lives.

Williams: Oh, the men's influence is in their lives all right. I mean, take Peg Murray now, her character's very influenced by her brother Buddy. And Shirley Knight is certainly very influenced by T. Ralph Ellis, the school principal.

Anderson: But the men never show up though—which is the wonderful concept about the play!

Williams: Oh, yes, they don't appear on stage.

Anderson: We feel like we know them all very well, but they're dealing with their men without the men being there. The strong attraction to the play that I had originally revolved around how this is going to be resolved, how are we going to find out about it? As Tennessee grew with the play and it became more developed, that problem became more and more fascinating. And the women are the most beautiful characterizations. This play is simply lovely in the way that the three women vie for each other's favor at different times.

Bilowit: Did you go to Charleston and work on the script there, or was it all in advance?

Williams: We started revisions in Charleston, yes.

Bilowit: And in the production there, were there things that you felt didn't work?

Williams: I got bored with the second half. That's the part I hope to get cut still further.

Bilowit: What didn't you like about it?

Williams: Well, I got bored with it.

Kalem: When I saw it in Charleston, I had some reservations. To mention the plus thing of course, I feel that the element of compassion—which is always deeply present in Tennessee's work— was very obviously present in this, and made it possible to overlook certain things. I thought the use of language was not the equal of the kind of language that Tennessee has used . . . can use. On the other hand, he has his signature, his voice. All the great playwrights have a specific voice.

I believe Tennessee Williams is not only our greatest playwright, he is the world's greatest living playwright. That's on the basis of the total body of work. We don't expect people like Joe Namath to go on forever, but we expect our artists to go forever. We expect them to keep surpassing themselves. I think that's an intolerable burden. I think that drama is a very intense art form—it eats up a great deal of intensity in the man who does it. And I wonder, sometimes, for how many years one can do it. Tennessee certainly has done it for a very long time. And the principal works are permanent works. The inevitability of a great work of art is that you cannot imagine the time when it didn't exist. You can't imagine a time when *Streetcar* didn't exist, when Blanche DuBois wasn't with us, when Stanley Kowalski wasn't with us . . . A great gift of Tennessee's is the gift of creating character. They impress themselves, they become part of your memory bank. And, in fact, you judge other characters by them, you judge people in real life by them. No one would have said about Adlai Stevenson that he had a Hamlet complex, except that we know Hamlet. To get back to this particular play, I think that one difficulty I had, for instance, was in believing that the Shirley Knight character could have presumed so much on such a brief relationship with this one socialite school principal. Do you feel that people do do that?

Williams: Oh, yes. I think that the thing you'll find with pretensions is that they're way, way out of reality.

Kalem: Way out of reality. And of course she's in a kind of a "Last Chance Saloon" situation, right?

Williams: Well, she devoted her youth, and a lot of it, to this musical prodigy who's afflicted with premature ejaculation, not likely to be cured.

Kalem: I recall now that I wasn't entirely aware of the background nature of the lives of the women who were presented. Somehow or other whatever they said, and whatever was said about them, didn't complete the picture for me, in an in-depth kind of way. I think also that Tennessee was doing something he wouldn't have done, let's say earlier on, and that's describing the characters through a certain narration instead of rendering them. That is, making the things happen before your eyes, through the force of imagery. I think the time can come when a writer says, "If I'm telling you this, it's true." But that is not necessarily . . .

Williams: Oh, I never tell myself that. No, no. I say exposition is the death of drama. You can't have long expository speeches unless, as you say, they are replete with a sort of lyrical imagery that will make them whole. But if I had put lyricism into the mouths of any one of those characters, it would have been out of character, it wouldn't have rung true.

Kalem: All right, I recognize that aspect of it.

Williams: It has certain self-limiting aspects to it.

Kalem: In other words, they were not suitable for arias, as you'd call them.

Williams: No, there's nobody who could speak an aria among those characters. Though there are *touches* of lyricism now—it couldn't go before.

Kalem: Do you find in a play like this that one character particularly captures your attention? I won't say runs away with the action, but that you care more about one character than another? Or identify more, if that's what one does?

Williams: I found all of the ladies equally fascinating. Almost equally fascinating. I was sitting in front of a lady last night, two ladies, and they were saying, "Oh, that Williams. He's always disparaging women." What do they mean by that?

Kalem: I can't begin to grasp that. I think quite the reverse. There ought to be a society of American actresses that gives you a medal—a special medal!

Williams: I've always thought that I dealt with them sympathetically.

Kalem: Well, I would have to agree with you on that. I don't see that . . .

Williams: I deal with all characters as graciously as possible. I mean, Shannon, in *Iguana*, was certainly not a morally admirable person, yet you understood him and felt compassion for him.

Bilowit: Craig, what were your feelings about the production that you did at the Spoletto? Were there shortcomings? Things that you feel should have been changed and are now being worked on?

Anderson: Tennessee and I had some conversations during the production in Spoletto and afterwards. Our feelings were sort of similar in that we felt a need to have more of a punch in the second act. The second act seemed to dissipate, rather than build climactically. What we've been doing in the work here at the Hudson Guild production is to try and build the second act into a kind of climax.

The final five minutes of the play is stunning because it does, of course, bring us full circle all the way around with the Shirley Knight character. But the beginning parts of the second act were somehow similar in style to the first act. Tennessee has changed it. The first act is almost farcical. And the second act changes the mood from farce into, in my opinion, complete realism. They do sit down and they talk eye-to-eye about the problem, and the sensitivity of the characters comes out of that. I think in the Charleston production, the first act was quite farcical and the second act seemed to blend into farce also, rather than reaching that extra sensitivity. Now we've got two different styles for the two different acts, and they work very well together. The audiences in previews so far have been responding overwhelmingly to the play, and I think it is because of that change. The characters are stronger, too. The characters, I think, have more definition.

Tennessee is a rewrite specialist. Every time he needs to write a little more, he writes fifty pages. It's nice, because he gives the director and himself the opportunity of cutting away later on until it's down to the bare bone of what's there and what needs to stay. That's what we're in the process of going through right now.

Bilowit: Tennessee said that he would like to cut a lot that is there now. Do you agree?

Anderson: Absolutely. Absolutely. There's information which is overstated somewhat. The only way to learn about that, of course, is to put it in front of an audience and find out when they get nervous, when they feel that they've got that information. I think in a lot of Tennessee's plays there's a lot of information which he withholds from the audience—for the audience to interpret for themselves. And only by cutting are we going to get to that point with this particular play. We're almost there with it now.

Bilowit: You have the same director, and three of the four actresses are the same . . . ?

Anderson: We have two. Charlotte Moore and Shirley Knight are with us. Peg Murray is now doing Jan Miner's part, and Jane Lowry is playing the upstairs German lady.

Bilowit: Do the new actresses change the character in any way?

Anderson: A lot. I think a lot. A whole different interpretation. I think the character of Bodey will go down in Tennessee Williams' history as a fascinating woman whom a lot of ladies are going to want to play for years and years to come. This particular performance by Peg Murray is very different than the one Jan Miner gave. They're both different types, they're both very good.

Bilowit: You mean texture, and character . . . ?

Anderson: Absolutely. In my opinion, this is a chamber play. It's a small slice of what's going on in the lives of these people. I think in

Charleston we had a large production in a big theatre. It's nice now to shrink it back down to the intimacy of the Hudson Guild Theatre, and watch all the nuances being flushed out. Because the actors at the Hudson Guild Theatre, or any of your small, off-off-Broadway theatres in town, are really forced to "be" the characters rather than to "act" them. When you "act" in the Hudson Guild Theatre, you get caught. I mean you can't do it. You've got to become those people. And that's where this play belongs. It doesn't belong with people "acting" and becoming big. It belongs in the smallness of the characters. We're flushing those out right now, and the detail is fascinating.

Kalem: I think there are certain plays that lose when they move from small theatres to Broadway.

Williams: Oh, the St. James Theatre. When they tried to do *Streetcar* in the St. James—I hated that. [4 October 1973—Editor] I thought that Lois Nettleton was not right as Blanche. I went out at intermission and didn't want to go back there again.

Kalem: You never usually say those things. You're very gracious to the actresses, actually. I know even when you have different views, you rarely express them in public.

Williams: She just wasn't Blanche. She just wasn't distinct.

Kalem: Talking again about the second act, I thought that you didn't have a sufficient element of surprise. Once *we* knew that *Bodey* knew that this chap had turned her down, and Bodey had hidden the Sunday paper, then the audience was sort of "in" on it—and we knew that basically the outcome would be rather sad.

Williams: I wish she didn't say anything. That's one thing I want to cut.

Bilowit: Could we talk about the relationship of this play to your other plays? Other than the fact that they all have great women, is there some direct relationship that you feel?

Williams: I think this play is quite separate from my other work. It's almost a different genre. It is not realism. The true note, the key note of the play is struck by Charlotte Moore. You could hardly say that she's realistic. Now, Jan Miner was far less realistic; she was gothic, you know. Then you have Peg Murray, who's a fine actress, but she's playing it too much like a lady, you know. She's not giving it that rough, massive, craggy, gothic quality that Jan had. And her wig must go . . . Bodey wouldn't have hair like that. Jan's hair came down, oh my God, a wonderful dramatic effect. It gave a wonderful craggy, gothic quality to her. She fleshed out the play just by her appearance. I'd written the part for Maureen Stapleton. She heard it read aloud, and she said, "Oh, that other part. She's got all the goodies," meaning the Shirley Knight part. I don't think that's true.

Kalem: Actresses always think that way. Actors don't.

Bilowit: Ted, do you see any relationship between this play and the others?

Kalem: Only in the sense that there is an over-all relationship. He's the laureate of the violated heart. That's the thing that recurs, time and again, in his plays. His patriot of gratuitous cruelty which occurs [sic]. I don't know how you feel about the sort of quasi-lesbian character.

Williams: There is no lesbianism involved. Not even the faintest suggestion.

Kalem: I see. But she does seem to enter into a real struggle for the possession of the Shirley Knight character . . . she and Bodey?

Williams: She loves nephews and nieces. She knows now that the thing with T. Ralph Ellis is not going to work out. And she wants desperately to get Shirley to settle for her brother Buddy, her twin brother.

Kalem: Yes, that's what Bodey wants. But the other lady . . .

Williams: Oh, Charlotte Moore. She is older and she . . .

Kalem: She sort of struggles with Bodey for possession of . . .

Williams: No, it should be quite clear to you. She's not physically . . .

Kalem: Well, let's forget physical. Isn't there a tug-of-war there?

Williams: Oh, there's a tug-of-war. Charlotte Moore's character wants to advance herself socially by moving into an exclusive place to gain a sort of entrance. And it's too expensive for her. She tries to get all she can out of poor Shirley Knight, to swing the deal.

Kalem: Loneliness, of course, is again an abiding theme.

Williams: Loneliness is the main theme.

Kalem: How to cope with it. And I think we could go through all the works and find this.

Bilowit: Craig, you also feel that all the characters are singular and new?

Williams: I'm not saying that all the characters are singular and new, but the style of the play is singular.

Anderson: However, as Ted says, despite the style of the play being unusual for Tennessee, it still does beckon Tennessee's signature. And that has to do, I think, with a lot of the language of the play. When these characters speak and I close my eyes in the theatre, I can't think of any other playwright writing that language or having those characters talk that way. It simply must be a Tennessee Williams play, I say to myself. And that I find in his other works, of course, that that signature is involved. Again, it's loneliness of people. Tennessee, what about the point of these ladies trying to climb up the social ladder, and the economic ladder, trying to better themselves?

Williams: Oh, in St. Louis that's enormously important. St. Louis is a very very materialistic city. Unless you have the right address, you're in trouble, socially. Also, the size and the kind of car you drive is more important than who your grandfather was.

Anderson: The play, Ira, has nuances of that in it also, because it's basically about two lower-middle-class, would you say, ladies?

Williams: Well, Bodey certainly is . . . she's an aristocrat of the heart. She thinks she's important aristocracy. As for the Shirley Knight character, she's not at all like Blanche, she's rather scatterbrained. She is amusingly foolish. Blanche was really rather bright and witty.

Kalem: There's another recurring characteristic which is present in this play—valor.

Williams: Valor, yes. Valor. When she knows the romance has failed on her, she does accept what is awful. She says to Miss Gluck, "Now Sophie. We just have to go on. That's all life seems to offer or demand, just go on."

Anderson: Which is what a lot of your plays are about in the final analysis.

Williams: She goes right on to Creve Coeur.

Kalem: We all must go on.

Williams: Exactly. *Cat* was about that.

Kalem: Well, also that subtle interplay that Beckett has somewhere. That is, the feeling that you can't go on, and the feeling that you must go on. It isn't just "I'm going to go on." It's the realization of how close you are to not being able to go on. Then you simply will yourself to go on, recognizing, among other things, that the alternative is not living.

Williams: Yes. I have a friend in San Francisco who's deliberately courting this alternative. I don't know what the hell to do about it.

Bilowit: Would you like to move this play somewhere else as you've had others moved?

Anderson: Absolutely. Tennessee's plays, once they're refined and they're ready, deserve that all audiences see them. And I regret at Hudson Guild that we don't have enough space for the people that already want to see this play. We sold out a day and a half after the tickets went on sale. So we're completely sold out as it is. I regret that we can't have more people come to see Tennessee's works. So, yes, obviously the point is to try and get more people in to see them, and the only way of doing that is to transfer it to a larger theatre.

Kalem: Well, the thing that remains is for Tennessee to receive the Nobel prize. Every year the American *Pen* says name a candidate and we'll send it to the committee in Stockholm, and every year I write *Tennessee Williams*. I hope that more people are doing that. I think it's unconscionable that Eugene O'Neill should have been the only American playwright to receive the Nobel prize.

Williams: I could use that money, you know. It's increased, hasn't it? How much is it now?

Kalem: Close to $150,000, I think.

Williams: My God. I could retire on it.

Kalem: You'll never retire.

Williams: I mean I could stop having productions. I *couldn't* stop writing.

Bard of Duncan Street: Scene Four

John Hicks/1979

From *Florida Magazine, The Orlando Sentinel,* 29 July 1979, 18-19. © 1979 by *The Orlando Sentinel.* Reprinted by permission.

Printed below is the concluding part of a lengthy essay-interview cast in quasi-dramatic form. Earlier scenes summarize familiar biographical-bibliographical data and set the Key West stage. Emphasis falls upon Williams' assault (with friend Dotson Rader) by four or five young men on Duval Street in late January 1979. On the whole, Williams abhorred the publicity and thought the episode blown out of proportion. It was not, as some thought, the first shot in a local war between gays and straights. The episode is alluded to in Scene Four.—Editor

Time ticks on toward the bewitching hour in the house on Duncan Street. **Tennessee** *talks of the theater, of celebrated people he has known and hasn't known, of people he admires or doesn't admire, homosexuality and other things.*

Serious theater is ailing on Broadway, is struggling for life off-Broadway, and is alive and well in the provinces, in the assessment of Tennessee Williams. "I think Edward Albee was quite correct when he described Broadway as being like the Strip at Las Vegas. They're some wonderful shows on it—if you just want a show.

"*Ain't Misbehavin'* is one of the most charming musical dancing shows I've ever seen; Bob Fosse's *Dancin'* was wonderful, but that is not theater to me. Aside from *Gin Game*, I doubt very much if there's been much serious theater on Broadway in the last two years."

The best drama, he says, is being done in regional theaters, an environment that he enjoys. "I like an intimate theater. A regional theater usually isn't too large. They have excellent equipment." And the people involved are more enthusiastic, and the critics "not as jaded."

Critics. Williams has been engaged in something of a declared war with them for a long time. Following the Duval Street incident, he joked, "Maybe they weren't punks at all, but New York drama critics."

New York critics, he says, have a "fixed image of you—which is usually hostile—in their minds when they go to see your work." Regional critics "give you an even break, and the same is true of London. London has the most brilliant critics of all the English-speaking theater."

Not that Williams acknowledges many brilliant playwrights for those critics to brilliantly criticize. Looking back momentarily, he bows respectfully toward Eugene O'Neill, the American master whose work he most enjoys. Then, he speaks of Edward Albee as "indisputably the best" present-day American playwright and England's Harold Pinter as "the greatest living contemporary playwright."

But his aspect darkens when he reaches the name of Tom Stoppard, whose *Night and Day* currently is a hit in London and which will move onto these shores later this year.

"I'm trying to read *Travesties*," Williams says. "I think this man, who has an intellectual following in the theater, I find him a charlatan. He's not funny. He's an intellectual poseur. I hate to say bad things about a fellow playwright—but this man's not in my opinion a playwright. I don't mind going on record in that opinion. . .

"*Travesties* was produced by the Royal Shakespeare Company. Yet, I find it unreadable. It's not over my head. I have yet to encounter a work in the theater that was over my head and, believe me, I'm not an intellectual."

But, while he cools to Stoppard, he warms to those who bring plays to life. "I like all great actors," he says, ranking Sir John Gielgud and Sir Ralph Richardson at the top of the list.

"I think John Gielgud is the greatest living actor, not (Sir Laurence) Olivier," Williams says, an opinion likely to startle some. Gielgud and Richardson have earned their dear nearness to the heart of Tennessee Williams, in part, because "being stage actors, I value them more highly than I do any screen actor."

The stage craft of Donald Madden, Stacy Keach and Michael

Moriarty has impressed him, but he laments a scarcity of serious roles for men.

"Great women favorites of mine are Irene Worth, who was American born but who has acted principally in England, Geraldine Page, Maureen Stapleton, Jessica Tandy. I found myself very impressed by Sandy Dennis on the West Coast when I went to see her perform in *The Eccentricities of a Nightingale*." [Long Beach Theatre Festival, 14 February 1979—Editor]

Jane Fonda also has his admiration. "I think she's a marvelous, pretty influence for liberalism in the United States." He once tried to tell her so.

"In the 1960s, I discovered she was staying at the Chelsea Hotel in New York, and I called her. I wanted to tell her how much I admired her. Well, the voice answering the telephone was Jane's voice, but she didn't admit she was Jane Fonda. She said, 'Thank you, I will pass on that message to her.'"

He eventually met the owner of the voice at an Academy Awards affair, he says.

And, then, there is Brando.

"I never understood Brando, as a person nor as an actor. I think he could have had a great stage career. He should have continued on the stage and done movies now and then for the money. . .

"He did some masterful stuff, *Last Tango in Paris*, but too much of the stuff he did was below his quality as an actor. Oh, I thought he was superb in *The Godfather*. He approaches his work very, very seriously whatever he does. That's why I wish he had given more of himself to the stage. But he was too restless, didn't want to spend a year and a half in one play. . .

"You know, he's gained a great deal of weight. But, now, he could be magnificent in certain roles just as Orson Welles could be. . . Brando's face is still marvelous. . .

"I think in his interviews he used to tell the truth. He said he realized he needed a lot of money for security in later years and the best way for him to get it was through the films."

In the past, motion pictures based on his plays have left Williams with mixed emotions, but his current attitude toward the cinema is favorable. "Right now, I think I wouldn't mind writing for the screen because the screen has become much more sophisticated than most of the stage around New York. And there's nothing that's really taboo anymore on the screen. . .

His screen-watching at the moment is pretty much restricted to old movies on television. He hasn't much use for the regular programming, but he did become absorbed in the recent TV rendition of John Dean's book *Blind Ambition*.

"I found the acting riveting, the story very, very powerful. I want to read the book now."

In a 1976 essay, "Selected Memories of the Glorious Bird and the Golden Age", Gore Vidal wrote of Williams, the Glorious Bird of the title, "The Bird seldom reads a book and the only history he knows is his own; he depends, finally, on a romantic genius to get him through life." [*New York Review of Books*, 5 February 1976, 13-18—Editor]

Williams finds that amusing. "I read enormously. Gore Vidal says I don't read at all. I'm afraid that's only because I don't read Gore Vidal's books except when he writes essays. He writes brilliant essays." He laughs. "Occasionally, I read a novel of his."

Those he has read more closely include William Faulkner ("a very, very honest man . . . a Southern gentleman"), Joan Didion, Muriel Spark, and the German author Peter Handke.

Handke's writing, Williams says, is "oblique, elusive, enormously evocative." Laughter. "Now, I'm sounding like a goddamn intellectual! But these are the terms I would use, and provocative. Subtle, in other words."

He loves "all good poets," among them Hart Crane, of course, T.S. Eliot, John Crowe Ransom and Marianne Moore.

Though Key West is renowned as the city of Ernest Hemingway, Papa had left town by the time Williams arrived on the scene. "I only met him for one afternoon and that was in Havana at a bar-restaurant called the Floridita. We had a nice friendly conversation, and he gave me a letter of introduction to Fidel Castro. I was with the English critic Kenneth Tynan, and he gave us both the letter, and we met Fidel Castro."

Williams never met Scott and Zelda Fitzgerald, the subjects of his "ghost play," but says that he feels akin to Zelda, burned to death in a North Carolina asylum fire in 1948, eight years after her husband died.

In *Clothes for a Summer Hotel*, Zelda and Scott have a spectral meeting on the lawn of the sanitarium the day following Zelda's death. "Not only the Fitzgeralds are there, but the scene changes, through whatever stage magic that I can bring to bear, to the middle and late '20s in the south of France. . .

"I think that Zelda has as much talent as her husband did. It's true she was schizophrenic, but, very often schizophrenic people can write beautifully. And she did write a beautiful book called *Save Me the Waltz* . . . There are passages in it that have a brilliancy that Fitzgerald was unequal to."

Zelda's novel is autobiographical, and Fitzgerald was angry with her for writing it because he felt that "it invaded his own material" for *Tender Is the Night*, Williams says. "Well, his material was Zelda's life! Naturally she felt she was entitled to write about her life."

Sad laughter.

Ghost play. So much of Williams' life seems a ghost play acted out by unseen presences, memories, whispers of the past: the grandparents Dakin, Miss Rose, Frank Merlo, the specter of homosexuality—considerably subdued from the one that haunts the pages of *Memoirs*.

"Strangely enough it was not I who first announced that I was homosexual. It was a news magazine. Not that I was ever embarrassed particularly by it. I lived a fairly respectable life with one man for 14 years, and I've never been a promiscuous person or a person who has used his sexual tastes in a way that I thought was wanton or an exploitation of other people.

"I never felt much conscious guilt about it. I think that society has imposed upon homosexuals a feeling of guilt that makes them somewhat neurotic, that makes all of us somewhat neurotic. Right now, I don't think too much about it because, at 68, it is no longer a paramount issue in one's daily or nightly life."

He ponders a growing militancy among some gays, the recent rioting in San Francisco after former city official Dan White was convicted on relatively minor charges of voluntary manslaughter in the shooting deaths of Mayor George Moscone and Supervisor Harvey Milk, a homosexual.

"I think the gay population of San Francisco was quite rightly outraged. Of course, I don't believe they expressed it properly in

burning police cars, creating a riot. . . I'm afraid that militant
movements of any kind often use the wrong tactics."

A quiet plea for reason from a man whose life effort has been
spent transmuting—to use a Williams' word—madness into meaning,
a man whose business is communicating, who believes "there have
been few occasions on which I felt that I couldn't reach the
audience."

Tennessee Williams continues to extend his hand, and his
understanding.

He did not die in the 1960s; he moved onto a new plane of
existence. Nor has he fallen beneath the fists of Key West punks in
the 1970s. He continues moving, and if not physically immortal, at
least marches to the rhythm of the Dylan Thomas verse that
introduces *Cat on a Hot Tin Roof:*

And you, my father, there on the sad height,
Curse, bless, me now with your fierce tears, I pray.
Do not go gentle into that good night.
Rage, rage against the dying of the light!

And he seems to request no more than Chance Wayne in *Sweet
Bird of Youth:* "I don't ask for your pity, but just for your
understanding—not even that—no. Just for your recognition of me in
you, and the enemy, time, in us all."

He dreams a long-time dream of bringing Miss Rose to Key West to
live. Miss Rose whose care, he notes in *Memoirs,* "is probably the
best thing I've done with my life, besides a few bits of work."

Dreaming. "I think with the proper companion she needn't be kept
in a sanitarium any longer, and I hope she will settle down. She's
very happy where she is. She makes the best of it. She's been very
brave about everything she's been through."

Bravery. "After all," he wrote in *Memoirs,* "high station in life is
earned by the gallantry with which appalling experiences are survived
with grace."

Love. "My sister and I have continued to be close. You see, we
haven't allowed our closeness to dissolve over the years. . . She is
now a woman of 70, although she looks 10 years younger . . . She

has very beautiful eyes and she's kept her figure very beautifully. Her reflexes are quicker than mine. . .

"It's a great thing to feel that you're loved and cared for. That is very necessary to me, and my sister retains that ability to care."

Darkness, warm and serene, closes about the conversation. Somewhere to the east, Aurora rolls the sun along the ocean's back, moving toward her accustomed rendezvous. Tennessee Williams, upon his rattan throne, contemplates tomorrow.

"I think," he purrs in wine-rich tones, "I must always have someone in my life who I feel is at least concerned about me to some degree."

There is a tone of loneliness here, an echo of Val Xavier, perhaps: " . . . we're under a life-long sentence to solitary confinement inside our own lonely skins for as long as we live on this earth!"

Or of forsaken Alma Winemiller in *Summer and Smoke:* "Oh, what a lovely, lovely solitaire! But solitaire is such a wrong name for it. Solitaire means single and this means *two*! It's blinding, Nellie! Why it . . . hurts my eyes!"

How many millions of someones there must be in the world who have longed to return across the footlights the concern that Williams has shown for humankind. But, even if there were none. . .

"I think the most important thing to me is the creative activity. And there is a fear that I will not work well, and there is the great joy at the same time when the work is starting and I *am* working well. Or, if not, at least when I am working and I have the end in sight and I know where I am headed."

There is a profound hush filled with a million unspoken but deeply felt thoughts, thoughts waiting to be heard, understood and interpreted by the poet. Not for himself alone but for everyone in this world who depends on the kindness of strangers. Everyone.

The Art of Theatre V: Tennessee Williams
Dotson Rader/1981

From *The Paris Review*, 81 (Fall 1981), 145-185. Reprinted in *Writers at Work: The Paris Review Interviews*, Sixth Series, ed. George Plimpton (New York: Viking Press, 1984), 75-121. © 1984 by The Paris Review, Inc. Reprinted by permission of Viking Penguin Inc.

The Paris Review interview with Tennessee Williams took place over several weeks, first in Chicago, and then in New York.

In Chicago, Williams was hard at work on the production of a new play being done at the Goodman Theater. It is a humorous and moving work called *A House Not Meant To Stand*, the title referring to the state of American civilization at present. I interviewed Williams in his suite at the Radisson Hotel on North Michigan Avenue in Chicago. . . . He was tanned, having spent most of the winter at his home in Key West, Florida. He looked ten years younger than his age. He was in an unusually happy mood, in part because the play was going well, but also because he had around him a number of close friends, among them Jane Smith, the actress and widow of artist Tony Smith. . . .

Three weeks later, after flying to Key West from Chicago, Williams came to New York. While he keeps an apartment in the city, he rarely uses it. Instead, as has been his habit for many years, he stayed at the Hotel Elysée on East 54th Street. . . . I completed the interview with Tennessee Williams in his suite at the Elysée. . . . Williams very much dislikes talking about his work and the process through which he creates his art. But in New York, on that dreary, gray day, he was open to it and told me what he could about how he writes.

The Genesis of Writing

I was a born writer, I think. Yes, I think that I was. At least when I had
this curious disease affecting my heart at the age of eight. I was more
or less bedridden for half a year. My mother exaggerated the cause.
She said I swallowed my tonsils! Years later, when I had the *Time*
cover story [9 March 1962—Editor], and she was quoted, doctors
looked it up and said, "A medical impossibility!"

But I do think there was a night when I nearly died, or possibly *did*
die. I had a strange, mystical feeling as if I were seeing a golden light.
Elizabeth Taylor had the same experience. But I survived that night.
That was a turning point, and I gradually pulled out of it. But I was
never the same physically. It changed my entire personality. I'd been
an aggressive tomboy until that illness. I used to beat up all the kids
on the block. I used to confiscate their marbles, snatch them up!

Then that illness came upon me, and my personality changed. I
became a shut-in. I think my mother encouraged me to be more of a
shut-in than I needed to be. Anyway, I took to playing solitary games,
amusing myself. I don't mean masturbation. I mean I began to live an
intensely imaginative life. And it persisted that way. That's how I
turned into a writer, I guess. By the age of twelve, I started writing.

Mother and Miss Rose

My mother—everyone calls her Miss Edwina—was essentially more
psychotic than my sister Rose. Mother was put away once, you know.
She was put away long before she was old, in the early part of the
decade of the Fifties. I was on St. Thomas in the Virgin Islands, and
she called me up.

"Tom, guess where I am?" she said.

"Why, Mother, aren't you at home?"

"No, Tom, they put me away!"

She was living alone, and I guess her fantasies got the best of her.
She thought the blacks were planning an uprising in St. Louis, and
they were exchanging signals by rattling the garbage pails. She called
the family doctor over to tell him about these threatening aspects of
life, and he took her right to the bug house! So I left St. Thomas and
sprung her.

Later, when I was in St. Louis, the phone rang and she picked it up. There was no one at the other end. After a while, she said, "*I know who you are! I'm here waiting! Unafraid!*"

Mother chose to have Rose's lobotomy done. My father didn't want it. In fact, he cried. It's the only time I saw him cry. He was in a state of sorrow when he learned that the operation had been performed.

I was at the University of Iowa, and they just wrote me what happened. I didn't know anything about the operation. I'd never heard of a lobotomy. Mother was saying that it was bound to be a great success. Now, of course, it's been exposed as a very bad procedure that isn't practiced anymore. But it didn't embitter me against my mother. It saddened me a great deal because my sister and I cared for each other. I cared for her more than I did my mother. But it didn't embitter me against Miss Edwina. No, I just thought she was an almost criminally foolish woman.

Why was the operation performed? Well, Miss Rose expressed herself with great eloquence, but she said things that shocked Mother. I remember when I went to visit her at Farmington, where the state sanitarium was. Rose loved to shock Mother. She had great inner resentment towards her, because Mother had imposed this monolithic puritanism on her during adolescence. Rose said, "Mother, you know we girls at All Saints College, we used to abuse ourselves with altar candles we stole from the chapel." And Mother screamed like a peacock! She rushed to the head doctor, and she said, "Do anything, *anything* to shut her up!" Just like Mrs. Venable, you know, except that Mother wasn't as cruel as Mrs. Venable, poor bitch. Whatever Mother did, she didn't know what she was doing.

She was terrified of sex. She used to scream every time she had sex with my father. And we children were terrified. We'd run out in the streets and the neighbors would take us in.

A year or so before Mother died, she believed she had a horse living with her in her room. She didn't like its presence at all, and she complained bitterly about this imaginary horse that moved into the place with her. She'd always wanted a horse as a child. And now that she finally had one, she didn't like it one bit.

At the end, she changed her name. Miss Edwina dropped the "a" from her name and became Edwin Williams. That's how she signed herself. It's strange to have a mother who at ninety-four decides to call herself Edwin.

Miss Rose smokes too much. She enters a restaurant and asks, "How many packs of Chesterfields do you have? *I'll take them all!*" Or she'll ask in a store, "How many bars of Ivory soap do you have? That all you got? Well, I need at least twenty!"

One night Rose went with me to Mrs. Murray Crane's as a dinner guest. She had a huge reticule with her. Do you know what that is? It's a huge embroidered bag. Rose was very sly, as schizophrenics often are. All during dinner, after each course, or even while people were eating, she would turn to Mrs. Crane, this stately dowager to her right, and say, "Have a cigarette, dear?" And Mrs. Crane would reply, "Oh, I don't smoke, Miss Williams. I do not smoke! And I fear that you're smoking too *much*, Miss Williams!"

Well, Miss Rose took umbrage at that. So after dinner she excused herself. There were four or five lavatories in this duplex apartment, and Rose was gone for a *remarkably* long time. When she came back her reticule was absolutely packed like Santa Claus' bag. She'd cleared the house completely out of soap and toilet paper! It was the biggest haul since the James Brothers. Needless to say, we didn't get a return engagement there.

She's very nervous, you know. When she was in Key West while you were there, she was trying not to smoke so she tried to keep herself busy. She took it upon herself to water all the trees and plants, and there are a great many. Rose would take a glass of water from the house, water a plant with it, return and fill the glass, and go out again, all day long. I find that touching, how she tries to occupy her time.

She has curious misapprehensions about things. Richard Zoerink was so kind to her. They would go walking in Key West along the water. He'd buy her an ice cream cone, something she loves. One day, I asked Rose where she'd been that afternoon, and she said that she and Richard had taken a walk along the Mediterranean Sea, and she enjoyed the view of Italy. Lovely Miss Rose. She thinks she's Queen of England, you know. She once signed a photograph of herself to me, "Rose of England."

I love her, you know. For a person like Rose who spent many years in a state asylum, as she had to do before I got any money, living is constantly a defensive existence. The stubbornness, the saying "No!" flatly to things is almost an instinctive response. If I say to Rose, "Don't you think it's time for you to get some rest?" her instinct is just to say "No!"

Once in Key West some people dropped by, and they began telling some very bawdy jokes. Rose didn't approve. So she got up and stood in a corner with her hands clasped in prayer. My cousin Stell, who was taking care of her, said, "Rose, why are you standing like that?"

Rose replied, "I'm praying for their redemption!"

Success

It all began for me in Chicago in 1944. I've had some of the happiest times of my life here. We were in Chicago for three and a half months with *The Glass Menagerie*. We opened in late December, and played until mid-March. And I had a lovely time. I knew a lot of university students, you know?

So I associate the success of *Menagerie* with the Chicago critics Claudia Cassidy and Ashton Stevens. They really put it over. The opening night audience had never seen this kind of theater before, and their response was puzzlement. And I suppose the play would have died here if Claudia Cassidy and Ashton Stevens hadn't kept pushing and pushing and pushing. They compared Laurette Taylor to Duse, which was a good comparison, I think. Miss Cassidy is very elderly now, but her mind's as sharp as a whistle!

Menagerie got to New York in 1945. It was sold out three and a half months before it opened. People would stop off in New York to see it because they knew it was a new kind of theater, and they knew about Laurette's incredible performance, though the rest of the cast was pretty run-of-the-mill.

The sudden success? Oh, it was terrible! I just didn't like it. If you study photographs taken of me the morning after the huge reception it got in New York, you'll see I was very depressed.

I'd had one eye operation, and I went into the hospital for another one I needed. Lying in the hospital, unable to move for several days, people came over and read to me, and I recovered some sense of reality.

Then, after *Menagerie*, I went to Mexico and had a marvelously happy time. I went alone. Leonard Bernstein was there. He introduced me to Winchell Mount, who gave weekly Saturday night dances. All male. And I learned how to follow! I was the belle of the ball because I could always dance well, but I gave up that career for writing.

Before the success of *Menagerie* I'd reached the very, very bottom. I would have died without the money. I couldn't have gone on any further, baby, without money when suddenly, *providentially, The Glass Menagerie* made it when I was thirty-four. I couldn't have gone on with these hand-to-mouth jobs, these jobs for which I had no aptitude, like waiting on tables, running elevators, and even being a teletype operator. None of this stuff was anything I could have held for long. I started writing at twelve, as I said. By the time I was in my late teens I was writing every day, I guess, even after I was in the shoe business for three years. I wrecked my health, what there was of it. I drank black coffee so much, so I could stay up nearly all night and write, that it exhausted me physically and nervously. So if I suddenly hadn't had this dispensation from Providence with *Menagerie*, I couldn't have made it for another year, I don't think.

Where Plays Come From

The process by which the idea for a play comes to me has always been something I really couldn't pinpoint. A play just seems to materialize, like an apparition it gets clearer and clearer and clearer. It's very vague at first, as in the case of *Streetcar*, which came after *Menagerie*. I simply had the vision of a woman in her late youth. She was sitting in a chair all alone by a window with the moonlight streaming in on her desolate face, and she'd been stood up by the man she planned to marry.

I believe I was thinking of my sister because she was madly in love with some young man at the International Shoe Company who paid her court. He was extremely handsome, and she was profoundly in love with him. Whenever the phone would ring, she'd nearly faint. She'd think it was he calling for a date, you know? They saw each other every other night, and then one time he just didn't call anymore. That was when Rose first began to go into a mental decline. From that vision *Streetcar* evolved. I called it at the time, *Blanche's Chair in the Moon*, which is a very bad title. But it was from that image, you know, of a woman sitting by a window that *Streetcar* came to me.

Of course, the young man who courted my sister was nothing like Stanley. He was a young executive from an Ivy League school. He had every apparent advantage. It was during the Depression years, however, and he was extremely ambitious. My father had an executive position at the time with the shoe company, and the young man had thought perhaps a marriage to Rose would be to his advantage. Then, unfortunately, my father was involved in a terrible scandal and nearly lost his job. At any rate, he was no longer a candidate for the Board of Directors. He had his ear bit off in a poker fight! It had to be restored. They had to take cartilage from his ribs, and skin off his ass, and they reproduced something that looked like a small cauliflower attached to the side of his head! So any time anybody would get into the elevator with my father, he'd scowl, and people would start giggling. That was when the young man stopped calling on Rose. He knew the giggling had gone too far and gotten into the newspapers.

The idea for *The Glass Menagerie* came very slowly, much more slowly than *Streetcar* for example. I think I worked on *Menagerie* longer than any other play. I didn't think it'd ever be produced. I wasn't writing it for that purpose. I wrote it first as a short story called "Portrait of a Girl in Glass," which is, I believe, one of my best stories. I guess *Menagerie* grew out of the intense emotions I felt seeing my sister's mind begin to go.

Influences

What writers influenced me as a young man? *Chekhov!*

As a dramatist? Chekhov!

As a story writer? Chekhov!

D.H. Lawrence, too, for his spirit, of course, for his understanding of sexuality, of life in general.

Effects

When I write I don't aim to shock people, and I'm surprised when I do. But I don't think that anything that occurs in life should be omitted from art, though the artist should present it in a fashion that is artistic and not ugly.

I set out to tell the truth. And sometimes the *truth* is shocking.

Looking Back

I now look back at periods of my life, and I think, Was that really *me*? Was I doing those things? I don't feel any continuity in my life. It is as if my life were segments that are separate and do not connect. From one period to another it has all happened behind the curtain of work. And I just peek out from behind the curtain now and then and find myself on totally different terrain.

The first period was from the age of eleven until I left the university and went into the shoe business. I was madly in love with a girl named Hazel who was frigid. And that period in my life was marked by extreme shyness. I couldn't look at people in the face without blushing. In high school, I couldn't verbally answer questions. I could only give written answers. I couldn't produce my voice. It sounded like grunting, you know? *That* shy. I supposed it was caused by an unconscious clash in me between my sexual drives and the puritanism imposed by my mother, and the great fear my father inspired in me. He was a terrifying man. He was so unhappy that he couldn't help but be tyrannical at home. That was one period.

The next period was happy. It was after I came out in the gay world. I didn't think of it as coming out. I thought of it as a new world, a world in which I seemed to fit for the first time, and where life was full of adventure that satisfied the libido. I felt comfortable at last. And that was a happy time, but *The Glass Menagerie* ended that period and new problems developed with success.

From then through the Sixties, because even during the Sixties I was working more or less steadily, that was another period different from the rest. But at the end of the Sixties I ended up in the bug-house because I violated Dr. Max Jacobson's instructions not to drink when I took the speed injections. Toward the end, this combination produced paranoia and affected my memory and my health. When I went to New York, I couldn't remember having met my producers before, although they'd had daily meetings with me in Key West.

Finally, after Anne Meacham and I fled to Tokyo after the terrible reception of *In the Bar of a Tokyo Hotel*, I became more and more ill. I had to be assisted up stairs. When I returned home alone to Key West I was *very* ill. They were building a new kitchen on my house, and the stove was in the patio. It was still operating there while the builders worked. I was stumbling around with a Silex pan, totally disoriented, trying to get it on the stove. And I just sat down on the stove! It was an electric stove, and I inflicted third degree burns on my body! I think Marion Vaccaro called by brother, and Dakin came down to Key West. He called Audrey Wood, and she said, "Well, put him in a hospital." But she didn't bother to say which one.

Dakin, thinking I was going to die anyway, I was in such terrible condition, had me immediately converted to Roman Catholicism so I'd be saved from hell, and then he just threw me into Barnes Hospital (St. Louis), right into the psychiatric ward, which was *incredibly* awful. They suddenly snatched away *every* pill I had! The injections went too. So I blacked out. It was cold turkey, baby. They tell me I had three brain convulsions in the course of one long day, and a coronary. How I survived, I don't know. I think there were homicidal intentions at work there. I was in that place for three and a half months. The first month I was in the violent ward, although I was not violent. I was terrified and I crouched in a corner trying to read. The patients would have terrible fights over the one television set. Someone would put on the news, and another patient would jump up, yelling, and turn on cartoons. No wonder they were violent.

Christianity

I was born a Catholic, really. I'm a Catholic by nature. My grandfather was an English Catholic (Anglican), very, very high church. He was higher church than the Pope. However, my "conversion" to the Catholic church was rather a joke because it occurred while I was taking Dr. Jacobson's miracle shots. I couldn't learn anything about the tenets of the Roman Catholic church, which are ridiculous anyway. I just loved the beauty of the ritual in the Mass. But Dakin found a Jesuit father who was very lovely and all, and he said, "Mr. Williams is not in a condition to learn anything. I'll give him extreme unction and just pronounce him a Catholic."

I was held up in the Roman Catholic church, with people supporting me on both sides, and I was declared a Catholic. What do you think of that? Does that make me a Catholic? No, I was whatever I was before.

And yet my work is full of Christian symbols. Deeply, deeply Christian. But it's the image of Christ, His beauty and purity, and His teachings, yes . . . but I've never subscribed to the idea that life as we know it, what we're living now, is resumed after our death. No. I think we're absorbed back into, what do they call it? The eternal flux? The eternal shit, that's what I was thinking.

Poetry

I'm a poet. And then I put the poetry in the drama. I put it in short stories, and I put it in the plays. Poetry's poetry. It doesn't have to be called a poem, you know.

Young Writers

If they're meant to be writers, they will write. There's nothing that can stop them. It may kill them. They may not be able to stand the terrible indignities, humiliations, privations, shocks that attend the life of an American writer. They may not. Yet they may have some sense of humor about it, and manage to survive.

Writing

When I write, everything is visual, as brilliantly as if it were on a lit stage. And I talk out the lines as I write.

When I was in Rome, my landlady thought I was demented. She told Frank (Merlo), "Oh, Mr. Williams has lost his mind! He stalks about the room talking out loud!"

Frank said, "Oh, he's just writing." She didn't understand *that*.

Rewriting

In writing a play, I can get started on the wrong tangent, go off somewhere and then have to make great deletions and begin over, not *all* the way over, but just back to where I went off on that particular tangent. This is particularly true of the surrealist play that

I'm currently writing. I'm dedicating it to the memory of Joe Orton. *The Everlasting Ticket* it's called. It's about the poet laureate of Three Mile Island. I'm in the third revision of *Ticket* at the moment.

I do an enormous amount of rewriting. And when I finally let a play go, when I know it's complete and as it should be, is when I see a production of it that satisfies me. Of course, even when *I'm* satisfied with a production, the critics are not, usually. In New York especially. The critics feel I'm basically anarchistic, and dangerous as a writer.

Audience

I don't have an audience in mind when I write. I'm writing mainly for myself. After a long devotion to playwriting I have a good inner ear. I know pretty well how a thing is going to sound on the stage, and how it will play. I write to satisfy this inner ear and its perceptions. That's the audience I write for.

Directors

Sometimes I write for someone specifically in mind. You know, I always used to write for (Elia) Kazan, although he no longer works as a director. What made him a great director was that he had an infinite understanding of people on an incredible level.

At one point Kazan and José Quintero were rather equal in talent. That was when Quintero began at the Circle in the Square downtown and did things like *Summer and Smoke* and *A Long Day's Journey Into Night*. Those early things. Then he took heavily to drink.

He was living at a very fashionable address, the penthouse apartment at 1 Fifth Avenue. I remember walking with Quintero out on the terrace. I said to him, "Why are you killing yourself like this with liquor? Because you are, you know. You're drinking much too heavily." He always liked me very much. He was an extremely kind and sweet person. He said, "I know. I know. It's just that all of a sudden I got all this attention, and it made me self-conscious. It scared me. I didn't know how my work was *done*. I simply worked through intuition. Then suddenly it seemed to me as if secrets of mine were being exposed." And so he drank excessively, and now he can't drink at all.

During *The Seven Descents of Myrtle*, as they called it, although it

was actually *Kingdom of Earth*, Quintero was drinking so heavily that
Estelle Parsons said she couldn't take direction from him. David
Merrick was producing, and he came to town. He said, "I have to fire
this man. He's destroying the play." And I said, "Mr. Merrick, if you
fire poor José I'm going to withdraw the play." So he let it come in.

You know, in those days David Merrick was a lovely man. He's
been around the bend some since, but he was so nice in those days.
We both went to Washington University. We were in the same drama
class, I believe. In the Sixties he used to come to my apartment at the
Mayfair when I wouldn't go out ever. He came over there to tell me
he wanted to do *Kingdom of Earth*. And I just slurred something in
reply. That's how I talked in those days. He said, "It's a very funny
play!" And I went *grrrowwww* . . . I didn't give a shit whether he put
it on or not, or whether I lived through the night.

Titles

Sometimes I'll come up with a title that doesn't sound good in itself,
but it's the only title that really fits the meaning of the play. Like *A
House Not Meant To Stand* isn't a beautiful title. But the house it
refers to in the play is in a terrible state of disrepair, virtually leaking
rain water everywhere. That house, and therefore the title, is a
metaphor for society in our times. And, of course, the critics don't
like that sort of thing, nor do they dare to openly approve of it. They
know who butters their bread.

Some titles come from dialogue as I write a play, or from the
setting itself. Some come from poetry I've read. When I need a title
I'll usually reread the poetry of Hart Crane. I take a copy of Crane's
work with me when I travel. A phrase will catch my eye and seem
right for what I'm writing. But there's no system to it. Sometimes a
line from the play will serve as its title. I often change titles a number
of times until I find one that seems right.

There is a Catholic church in Key West named "Mary, Star of the
Sea." That would make a lovely title for a play.

Line Changes

Performers can be enormously valuable in suggesting line changes in
a play, I mean if they're intelligent performers. For instance,

Geraldine Page. She's very intelligent, and she's a genius at acting. Being a genius at acting, and being intelligent aren't always the same thing. She'd suggest line changes. She'd say, "I find this line difficult to read." I think most of her suggestions were good, although she's not a writer. So I'd make the changes to satisfy her. I often do that with actors, if they're intelligent and care about the play.

Marlon Brando

Brando came up to the Cape when I was there. There was no point in discovering him, it was so obvious. I never saw such raw talent in an individual, except for Laurette Taylor, whose talent was hardly raw. Then, before he was famous, Brando was a gentle, lovely guy, a man of extraordinary beauty when I first met him. He was very natural and helpful. He repaired the plumbing that had gone on the whack, and he repaired the lights that had gone off. And then he just sat calmly down and began to read. After five minutes, Margo Jones, who was staying with us, said, "Oh, this is the greatest reading I've ever heard, even in *Texas!*" And that's how he was cast in *Streetcar*.

Warren Beatty

I didn't know of Warren's work, and I thought the role in *The Roman Spring of Mrs. Stone* should be played by a Latin-type since the role's a Roman gigolo. I happened to be in Puerto Rico with Marion Vaccaro, you know, the banana queen? She and I were gambling. She was playing blackjack, and I was playing roulette. All of a sudden a waiter came up to me with a little glass of milk, on a silver platter, and said, "A gentleman has sent this to you." I said, "I don't appreciate this kind of sarcasm!" So I went on playing roulette.

After I'd lost the amount of money I allow myself to lose, I started to leave. And there standing grinning at the door was Warren Beatty.

"Tennessee, I've come to read for you," he said. He was very young then, a really handsome boy.

I said, "But why, Warren? You're not the type to play a Roman gigolo."

And he said, "I'm going to read with an accent, and without it. I've come all the way from Hollywood to read for you."

"Well, that's lovely of you." And Marion and I went to his room, and he read fabulously. With an accent, and without.

Warren has no embarrassment about anything. Whenever he sees me he always embraces me. What an affectionate, warm, lovely man. I've found actors to be lovely people, although there are a few of them who have been otherwise.

Audrey Wood

Ever since my split with Audrey Wood [his longtime agent] there's been a holding pattern. I think she's the dominant figure in this. I think she has stock in the concern, ICM, and she won't allow anything to happen until I'm dead, baby.

Why did I break with her? I didn't. Just the usual thing happened. An opening night. My nerves always go like spitfire then. We had a very good first preview (of *The Two Character Play*). The second preview we had a bunch of old, sour dames. They didn't get anything, and they hated it. It enraged me. I always lose my mind slightly when I get angry. Audrey was used to this. It happened time and time again. It shouldn't have surprised her at all. And I just turned to her after the performance and said, "You must have been pleased by this audience," because she hadn't been pleased by the enthusiastic, younger audience the night before. She got angry, and left town immediately with the greatest amount of publicity. And I realized that she had neglected me so totally during my seven years of terrible depression that any kind of professional relationship with her was no longer tenable.

I don't hold grudges. So when I encountered her some time later in the Algonquin Hotel, I stretched out my hand to touch hers. There was no way of avoiding her. She hissed like a snake! and drew back her hands as if I were a leper. Well, since then I know this woman hates me! She'd lost interest in me. I don't think you should lose interest in a person who is in deep depression. That's when your interest and concern should be most, if you're a true friend. [For Audrey Wood's reflection on this episode, see *Represented by Audrey Wood* (New York: Doubleday, 1981), 202—Editor.]

And I think I had a great deal to do with making her career. She'd only sold *Room Service* to the Marx Brothers before I came

along and got her Bill Inge and Carson McCullers and . . . this
sounds bitter, and I hold no animosity toward people. I hope I don't.

Best Friends

Carson McCullers and Jane Bowles were my best friends as writers. I
think if poor Carson had not suffered this very early stroke when
she'd barely turned thirty, she would have been the greatest
American writer. She had recurrent illnesses, of course, each
diminishing her power. It was a tragic thing to watch. It went on for
ten years. I met her in Nantucket. I'd written her a fan letter about
The Member of the Wedding, I thought it was so lovely. I knew
cousins of hers. And at my invitation, she came to the island to be my
guest. Such an enchanting person! This was the last year before she
had a stroke, the year Carson lived at 31 Pine Street in Nantucket
with Pancho and me.

My other great writer friend, Jane Bowles, I first met in Acapulco in
the summer of 1940, after I'd broken up with Kip. I took a trip to
Mexico on one of these share-the-expense plan tours. I went down
with a Mexican boy who'd married an American hooker, you know?
He met her at the World's Fair. The poor girl was terrified. She was a
sweet girl, but she was a hooker and he didn't know it. And she'd
come to my room at night and tell me they were having terrible
problems sexually. I think he was gay, you know, because all the
other men in the car were. That's a pretty good indication! She said
she wasn't getting any sex, and she thought I'd provide her with
some.

I said, "I'm afraid, honey, it's not quite what I do anymore because,
frankly, I'm homosexual."

"Oh, that's all right," she said, "I know female hygiene is a lot
more complicated!" God, I thought that was a funny answer!

Apparently, their marriage worked out somehow. I left some of my
gear in the trunk of the car, and several years later after I'd become
known, after *The Glass Menagerie*, she shipped it all back to me with
a very lovely note.

It was that summer in Mexico when I met Jane Bowles. I knew she
was there with Paul. Poor Paul was always sick. He couldn't eat
anything in Mexico. But there's very little in Mexico you *can* eat, at

least not in those days. They were such a charmingly odd couple, I loved them both. Jane produced such a small body of work, but it was tremendous work. And Paul's work? I guess it's about as good as anything is now.

Frank Merlo

I met Frankie by accident at the Atlantic House in Provincetown one summer, the summer of 1947 when I was finishing *Streetcar*. I was in the Atlantic House, and Pancho was there, Margo Jones, and Joanna Albers. We were all living in a cottage. Stella Brooks was singing at the Atlantic House, and I'd gone out on the porch at the Atlantic House to breathe the fresh air and the lovely sea mist coming in. And Frankie came out behind me, and leaned against the balcony, and I observed that beautifully sculptured body in Levis, you know? I was rather bold, as I am at certain moments. And I just said, "Would you like to take a drive?" He grinned, and said yes. He'd come there with John LaTouche, you know, the songwriter.

So we drove out to the beach and made love. It was ecstatic, even though it was in the sand.

I didn't see him again until accidentally I ran into him in a delicatessen on Third Avenue. I was living in an apartment designed by Tony Smith on East 58th Street. Frankie was with a young war buddy of his. And I said, "Why Frank!" And he said, "Hi, Tenn." I said, "Why haven't you called me?" And he replied, "I read about your great success, and I didn't want to seem like I was trying to hop on the bandwagon."

He and his buddy came home with me to this lovely apartment. And Frankie just stayed on. He was so close to life! I was never that close, you know. He gave me the connection to day-to-day and night-to-night living. To reality. He tied me down to earth. And I had that for fourteen years, until he died. And that was the happy period of my adult life.

Travel

I'm restless. I like traveling. When Frank Merlo was living, he being Sicilian, we spent four or five, sometimes six months out of the year in Rome.

I was once asked why I travel so much, and I said, "Because it's harder to hit a moving target!"

The Competition

I don't compete with Eugene O'Neill or anyone else. My work is totally in its own category. It's more esoteric than anyone else's, except Joe Orton's. And I don't compete with Joe Orton. I love him too much.[1]

Eugene O'Neill

Now O'Neill is not as good a playwright as, for instance, Albee. I don't think he's even as good as Lanford Wilson. I could give you quite a list.

I liked O'Neill's writing. He had a great spirit, and a great sense of drama, yes. But most of all it was his spirit, his *passion*, that moved me. And when *The Iceman Cometh* opened to very bad notices, very mixed notices at best in New York, I wrote him a letter. I said, in reading your play, at first I found it too long, then I gradually realized that its length, and the ponderosity of it, are what gave it a lot of its power. I was deeply moved by it, finally.

He wrote me a very nice reply and said he was always deeply depressed after an opening and that he appreciated my letter particularly. But that letter has disappeared like most of my letters.

Liquor

O'Neill had a terrible problem with alcohol. Most writers do. American writers nearly all have problems with alcohol because there's a great deal of tension involved in writing, you know that. And it's all right up to a certain age, and then you begin to need a little nervous support that you get from drinking. Now my drinking has to be moderate. Just look at the liver spots I've got on me!

Opening Nights

On opening nights in the old days, when I really could drink—I can't drink heavily now because of this pancreatitis I developed from over-

[1]Among his plays are *What the Butler Saw*; *Entertaining Mr. Sloane*; *Loot*; and *Funeral Games*. In 1967, Joe Orton was murdered in his sleep by his longtime lover Kenneth Halliwell. Later that night Halliwell committed suicide. Joe Orton was thirty-five at the time of his death.

drinking—but when I *could* drink, on opening nights I'd either have a flask on me and keep myself drunk and stand at attention in the theater, or else I'd dart out to the nearest bar and sit there until nearly before the curtain came down and then I'd head back into the theater.

Now I take openings much more calmly. If they're giving a good performance, and they usually do on opening night, I just sit and enjoy it. After the curtain, I take a red-eye flight out of town. I have a car waiting for me with the luggage in it, and scoot out to LaGuardia or Kennedy and take the red-eye to Key West.

Key West

It's delightful. When I first went there in 1941 it was still more delightful than it is now. I have one-quarter of a city block there now, you know. A swimming pool. My studio with a skylight. I have a little guest house in the form of a ship's cabin, with a double-decker bunk in it. And I have my gazebo, the Jane Bowles Summer House. Everything I need for a life. It's a charming, comfortable place.

Habits of Work

In Key West I get up just before daybreak, as a rule. I like being completely alone in the house in the kitchen when I have my coffee and ruminate on what I'm going to work on. I usually have two or three pieces of work going at the same time, and then I decide which to work on that day.

I go to my studio. I usually have some wine there. And then I carefully go over what I wrote the day before. You see, baby, after a glass or two of wine I'm inclined to extravagance. I'm inclined to excesses because I drink while I'm writing, so I'll blue pencil a lot the next day. Then I sit down, and I begin to write.

My work is *emotionally* autobiographical. It has no relationship to the actual events of my life, but it reflects the emotional currents of my life. I try to work every day because you have no refuge but writing. When you're going through a period of unhappiness, a broken love affair, the death of someone you love, or some other disorder in your life, then you have no refuge but writing. However, when depression comes on of a near clinical nature, then you're paralyzed even at work. Immediately after the death of Frank Merlo, I was paralyzed, unable to write, and it wasn't until I began taking the speed shots that I came out of it. Then I was able to work like a demon. Could you live without writing, baby? I couldn't.

Because it's so important, if my work is interrupted I'm like a raging tiger. It angers me so. You see, I have to reach a high emotional pitch in order to work if the scene is dramatic.

I've heard that Norman Mailer has said that a playwright only writes in short bursts of inspiration while a novelist has to write six or seven hours a day. Bull! Now Mr. Mailer is more involved in the novel form, and I'm more involved in the play form. In the play form I work steadily and hard. If a play grips me I'll continue to work on it until I reach a point where I can no longer decide what to do with it. Then I'll discontinue work on it.

Drugs

There was a very lovely young guy at New Directions named Robert MacGregor, who's dead now. He'd been a patient of Dr. Max Jacobson. He only took little pills that Jacobson gave him. I was in a state of such profound depression that he thought anything was worth trying, so he took me to Jacobson. It was through this Robert MacGregor that I had those three years of Jacobson shots that he mailed to me in the various parts of the country.

I did find Max Jacobson's shots marvelously stimulating to me as a writer. And during those last three years of the Sixties, before my collapse, I did some of my best writing. People don't know it yet, but I did.

My collapse was related to the fact that I continued to drink while taking the shots. I was not supposed to. I had a bad heart. Dr. Max Jacobson never listened to my heart. Never took my pulse. Never took my blood pressure. He would just look at me. He was really sort of an alchemist. He would look at me for a long time. He had all these little vials in front of him. He'd take a drop from one, and a drop from another, and then look at me again, and take another drop or two. . . . Of course, the primary element was speed. And after I had a shot, I'd get into a taxi and my heart would begin to pound,

and I'd immediately have to have a drink or I wouldn't be able to get
home. I'd have died in the cab otherwise.

On Being Single

I think it made it possible for me to practice my profession as a writer.
You know what happened to poor Norman Mailer. One wife after
another, and all that alimony. I've been spared all that. I give people
money, yes. But I couldn't have afforded alimony, not to all those
wives. I would've had to behead them! Being single made it possible
for me to work.

Homosexuality

I never found it necessary to deal with it in my work. It was never a
preoccupation of mine, except in my intimate, private life. In my
work, I've had a great affinity with the female psyche. Her
personality, her emotions, what she suffers and feels. People who say
I create transvestite women are full of shit. Frankly. Just vicious shit.
Personally, I like women more than men. They respond to me more
than men do, and they always have. The people who have loved me,
the ratio of women to men is about five to one, I would say.

  I know there's a right wing backlash against homosexuals. But at
the age of seventy I no longer consider it a matter of primary
concern. Not that I want anything bad to happen to other
homosexuals. God knows, enough has.

  I always thought homosexual writers were in the minority of
writers. Nobody's yet made a correct census of the actual number of
homosexuals in the population of America. And they never will be
able to because there are still too many closets, some of them rather
securely locked. And it's also still dangerous to be openly
homosexual.

Cruising

I enjoyed cruising, more for Donald Windham's company, than for
the pick-ups that were made. After all, pick-ups are just pick-ups. But
Windham was a delightful friend to be with. I always realized that he
had a streak of bitchery in him. And that's why my letters to him had
a great deal of malicious humor in them. I knew he liked that. And

since I was writing to a person who enjoyed that sort of thing I tried
to amuse him with those things. Of course, I didn't know he was
collecting my letters! And I didn't know I was signing away the
copyright. I'm happy the letters were published because they're
beautiful, I think. I'm very unhappy that he may have shut down
London Magazine with that lawsuit.[2]

There used to be a place in Times Square called the Crossroads
Tavern, right near a place called Diamond Jim Brady's. The place
was closing down, and on this occasion these big, drunk sailors came
and picked us up. We didn't pick *them* up. I wasn't attracted to them.
I didn't want to, and I felt really uneasy about the situation. But
Windham was always attracted to rough sailor types.

As it happened Windham was staying at the Claridge Hotel, which
doesn't exist now in the Times Square area. He had been living with
a painter, Paul Cadmus. He was occupying a room with Paul
Cadmus, and it was through Paul Cadmus that he met Sandy
Campbell.[3] It had been inconvenient for Cadmus to have Donald
Windham at his place one night, and so he'd gotten him a room at
the Claridge. And Donald had taken the two sailors and me into
Claridge's.

I got more and more suspicious because in the lobby the sailors
said, "We'll go up the elevator, and you wait ten minutes, and we'll
meet you in the corridor. . . ." Or something like that. It seemed
suspicious, but I was a little high, and so was Donald.

We got up to the room, and it was really a bestial occurrence. I
hated every minute of it. Finally, after they ripped the phones out of
the wall, they stood me against a wall with a switchblade knife while
they beat Windham, knocking a tooth out, blackening both his eyes,
beating him almost to death. I kept saying, "Oh, don't do that, don't
hit him anymore! He's *tubercular!*"

Then they said, "Now it's your turn!" So they stood poor, bloody
Windham against the wall while they beat me nearly to death. I had a

---

[2]When Donald Windham published *Tennessee Williams' Letters to Donald Windham:
1940-1965* (Holt, Rinehart, and Winston, New York, 1977), Dotson Rader wrote an essay for
London Magazine reviewing the letters. The piece was critical of Windham. Mr. Windham
responded with a lawsuit, later settled out of court.
[3]Sandy Campbell is Windham's friend and companion.

concussion from the beating. Next thing I knew I was at the
emergency Red Cross station at the YMCA where I lived.

Kip

Kip was very honest, and I loved him and I think he loved me. He
was a draft-dodger from Canada. He had a passion to be a dancer,
and he knew he couldn't if he went into the war. It'd be too late, he
felt, when it was over, for him to study dancing. You see, he was a
boy of twenty-one or twenty-two when the war happened.

I've written a play called Something Cloudy, Something Clear
about Kip. The setting is very important in this play. It involves a
bleached, unfurnished beach shack in which the writer, who
represents me, but is called August, is working on a portable
typewriter supported by an old crate. He sleeps on a mattress on the
floor. Alongside that set is the floor of another beach house shack
that's been blown away in a hurricane. This floor, however, forms a
platform on which Kip used to dance, practicing dancing to my
Victrola. The subtitle of the play is The Silver Victrola.

I prefer the title Something Cloudy, Something Clear because it
refers to my eyes. My left eye was cloudy then because it was
developing a cataract. But my right eye was clear. It was like the two
sides of my nature. The side that was obsessively homosexual,
compulsively interested in sexuality. And the side that in those days
was gentle and understanding and contemplative. So it's a pertinent
title.

Now this play is written from the vantage point of 1979, about a
boy I loved and who is now dead. The author (August) knows it's
1979. He knows Kip is dead, and that the girl whom Kip dances with
is dead. I've invented the girl. Occasionally during the play the author
onstage will make references that puzzle the boy, Kip, and the girl.
But the author is the only one who realizes that it's really forty years
later, and the boy and girl are dead, and he survives, still he survives.
It happened in the summer of 1940, and it's a very lyrical play,
probably the most lyrical play I've done in a very long while.

Kip died at the age of twenty-six. It was just after I completed my
professionally abortive connection with MGM. The phone rang one
day and an hysterical lady said, "Kip has ten days to live." A year

before I had been told that Kip had been successfully operated on for a benign brain tumor.

He was at the Polyclinic Hospital near Times Square. You know how love bursts back into your heart when you hear of the loved one's dying.

As I entered Kip's room he was being spoon-fed by a nurse: a dessert of sugary apricots. He had never looked more beautiful. Kip's mind seemed as clear as his Slavic blue eyes.

We spoke a while. Then I rose and reached for his hand and he couldn't find mine, I had to find his.

After Kip died his brother sent me, from Canada, snapshots of Kip posing for a sculptor and they remained in my wallet some twenty years. They disappeared mysteriously in the Sixties. Well, Kip lives on in my leftover heart.

Hemingway and Fitzgerald

Hemingway had a remarkable interest in and understanding of homosexuality, for a man who wasn't a homosexual. I think both Hemingway and Fitzgerald had elements of homosexuality in them. I make quite a bit of that in my rewrite of *Clothes for a Summer Hotel.*

Have you ever read "A Simple Enquiry" by Hemingway? Well, it's about an Italian officer in the Alps during the First World War. And he's of course deprived of female companionship. He has an orderly, a very attractive young orderly. He desires the orderly. And he asks the boy, rather bluntly, "Are you interested in girls?" The boy panics for a moment, and says, "Oh, yes, I'm engaged to be married." And the boy goes out of the room, and the Italian officer says, "I wonder if that little sonofabitch was lying?"

The final line in Hemingway's *Islands in the Stream* is one man saying I love you to another. It didn't mean they'd had homosexual relations, although Gertrude Stein intimated that Hemingway had. But does it matter? I don't think it matters.

You know what he said about Fitzgerald? Hemingway said that, "Fitzgerald was pretty. He had a mouth that troubled you when you first met him, and troubled you more later."

Fitzgerald played the female lead in the Princeton Triangle Club, and there's a picture of him as a woman that's more feminine than

any woman could look. Fitzgerald never had an affair with anybody
but his wife. There was Sheila Graham at the end, but did he sleep
with her? I doubt it. Anyway, I don't think the sexuality of writers is all
that interesting. It has no effect, I can tell you that. In very few
instances does it have any effect on their ability to portray either sex.
I am able to write of men as well as women, and I always project
myself through whichever sex I'm writing about.

Fidel Castro

I met Castro only once, and that was through Hemingway. The time I
met Hemingway was the time I met Castro. I was in Havana during
the first year of Castro's regime. Castro would have remained a friend
of the United States except for that bastard John Foster Dulles who
had this phobia about anything revolutionary. He apparently thought
that Mr. Batista—a sadist who tortured students to death—was great
fun.

I met Hemingway through Kenneth Tynan at the restaurant
Floridita in Havana. Hemingway and I had a very pleasant meeting.
He gave us both a letter of introduction to Castro. Hemingway said
this was a good revolution. And if Mr. Dulles hadn't alienated Castro,
it might have been.

Castro was a gentleman. An educated man. He introduced me to
all the Cuban cabinet. We'd been waiting three hours on the steps for
this emergency cabinet meeting to end. When he introduced us, he
turned to me and said, "Oh, that *cat!*" and winked. He meant *Cat on
a Hot Tin Roof*, of course. I found that very engaging.

John F. Kennedy

I met President Kennedy through Gore Vidal, at the family estate in
Palm Beach before he was President. And then I met him at the
White House where he gave a great dinner party for André Malraux
and invited all the literary people, the theater people.

John Kennedy was a great gentleman, a really good, gentle man.
On the way to see him we were caught in terrible traffic. Gore Vidal
isn't a particularly good driver, though he's a good writer at times. So
we were an hour late for lunch with Mr. Kennedy, and he acted as if
we were on time. His manners were so impeccable, and Jackie was a

tremendous charmer, and still is, I presume, although I haven't seen her in a long time.

The Carter White House

The first time I went there was some occasion when the film industry was being honored. At that time the Carters had not yet adjusted themselves to entertaining. He's rather abstemious, Mr. Carter, which is the one major fault I found with him. We were only allowed to have one very small glass of what was purported to be a California chablis. I downed my glass in one swallow, and then tried to figure out how to get some more. All there was was wine. No hard liquor. Nothing. But you could only have one glass. So I got ahold of Sam Spiegel, who is a very portly gentleman, and I said, "Sam, will you stand in front of the table and slip me another glass of wine surreptitiously?" So I hid behind Sam, and he snuck me several small glasses which helped to get me through the evening.

Later, when I went to the White House, the Carters had begun serving champagne. But they never did get around to hard liquor.

I think Jimmy Carter was a great humanitarian, and his second term might have been wonderful compared to what we got. I thought his human rights concern was right, and I am sorry that our government had abandoned it.

I don't think the big money people wanted Mr. Carter back in. He wasn't pliable enough.

Jane Wyman

Jane Wyman was in the movie of *The Glass Menagerie*. She married Ronald Reagan. The no-nose girl married the no-brain man!

Hollywood

Most of my films were subjected to excessive censorship. Which is one of the reasons why I might be interested in seeing *Streetcar* done again as a film by Sidney Lumet, now that Kazan has stopped directing. But I'd have to have a great Stanley, and the only person they've mentioned so far is Sylvester Stallone, and so I'm not paying much attention to this project of remaking *Streetcar* until there's a suitable Stanley, and a really great actress to play Blanche.

In the 1940s I had a glorious time in Hollywood because I was fired almost at once from the project I was working on and they had to continue to pay me. That was in my contract. For six months they had to pay me $250 a week. This was in 1943 when $250 was equivalent to about $1000 now, I would guess. They had to pay me whether I had an assignment or not.

First they put me on *Marriage Is a Private Affair* for Lana Turner. Well, they expressed great delight with my dialogue, and I think it was good. But they said, "You give Miss Turner too many multi-syllable words!" So I said, "Well, some words *do* contain more than one syllable!" And Pandro Berman, who loved me very much—Lana Turner just happened to be his girlfriend at the time—he said to me, "Tennessee, Lana can tackle two syllables, but I'm afraid if you go into three you're taxing her vocabulary!"

Then they asked me if I'd like to write a screenplay for a child star, one named Margaret O'Brien. I said, "I'd sooner shoot myself!" By that time I knew I'd get the $250 regardless.

So I lived out in Santa Monica and had a ball until the money ran out.

Elizabeth Taylor

Monty Clift was one of the great tragedies among actors, even more than Marilyn Monroe, I believe. One of the loveliest things about Elizabeth Taylor was her exceptional kindness to him. Many women were very kind to him. Katharine Hepburn. But Elizabeth particularly. She's a very dear person. She's the opposite of her public image. She's not a bitch, even though her life has been a very hell. Thirty-one operations, I believe. Pain and pain. She's so delicate, fragile really.

I saw her in Fort Lauderdale at the opening of Lillian Hellman's *The Little Foxes*, and she held that stage as if she'd always been a stage actress. But she has a little deficiency of humor. I knew she would catch it. I hoped she would. And she opened so well in Washington that I think she must have caught the humor.

I know you think Lillian Hellman's a somewhat limited playwright. But *Hellman* doesn't think so, does she? No! After the opening, when I saw Liz Taylor could act on stage, there was a huge party,

with great imported champagne, the works! The director was seated
next to me at my table. He said he had to get up and call Hellman.

I said, "Well, tell her I want a piece of her royalties!"

So he gave her the message, and came back to the table grinning.
"Hellman said to tell you the check is in the mail!"

She's a funny woman, and a skillful playwright. Several of her
plays are enormously skillful. . . . I've heard she has emphysema.
Who *isn't* sick! They're all sick and dying!

William Inge

Bill Inge was a tragic person. *Tragic.* The critics treated him very
cruelly. They're brutal. I always thought he wrote two wonderful
plays. *Come Back Little Sheba* was a brilliant play. That's when I
introduced him to Audrey Wood. And then he wrote a play in which
a kid kills his mother, an enormously brilliant work. *Natural Affection,*
or something like that.

I met him in St. Louis. I came back there during the run of
Menagerie in Chicago, and he interviewed me for a paper called the
St. Louis *Star-Times.* He was the drama and music critic for it. He
entertained me quite a bit the week I was there. We became friends.

At the end of his life, Barbara Baxley, with whom he attempted to
have a heterosexual affair, and who was very, very fond of him,
called me and said that Inge was in a desperate situation in
California. "He's sleeping with lots of barbiturates under his mattress.
He only gets up to drink, and then he goes back to bed."

I said, "He's on a suicide course."

She said, "I know it. He commits himself voluntarily, and then lets
himself out the next day."

"Who's he with?"

"His sister," she said. "I want you to call his sister and tell her that
she's got to commit him."

So after consulting Maureen Stapleton, who said I should, I did call
his sister and she said, "Yes, that's just how it is." She was talking in a
whisper. I said, "I can hardly hear you. Why are you whispering like
that?"

She answered, "Because I never know whether he's up or down."

I said, "Just listen then. Get him into a hospital. Don't have him commit himself. *You* commit him. Otherwise he's going to kill himself."

Well, a month later in Rome I read a headline in the Rome *Daily American* that Bill Inge was dead. [10 June 1973—Editor] He had asphyxiated himself by running the motor on his car in a closed garage.

Fitzgerald, Hemingway, Hart Crane, Inge . . . oh, the debris! The *wreckage!* Toward the end of an American writer's life it's just dreadful. Hemingway's last years were a nightmare. He tried to walk into the propeller of a plane. Fitzgerald's end was not much better, although it was less dramatic. . . . Once they become known, everybody wants a piece of them.

Christopher Isherwood

I met him in the Forties in California. At the time he was into Vedanta, an Eastern religious thing. He was living in a monastery. They had periods of silence and meditation, you know. The night I met him, through a letter from Lincoln Kirstein, I arrived during one of these silent periods. The monk who opened the door handed me a pencil and paper to write what my business was and who I'd come to see. I wrote "Christopher Isherwood," and they regarded me with considerable suspicion from that point on.

In this big room in the monastery, everyone was sitting in . . . what do they call it? The lotus position? Including Christopher. All strictly observing the vow of silence. I didn't dig the scene.

I suddenly made some reference out loud about the Krishna. I didn't know who the hell he was, I was only trying to break the silence. Christopher got up, and wrote on a piece of paper, "I'll call you tomorrow." He was very polite, and he took me to the door.

He's a superb writer, and I haven't a clue why he went through this period in a monastery. I think it was a period of unhappiness in his life. I think his love affair with Bill Caskie was breaking up, or had broken up, and he had not yet found Don Bachardy. He was intensely lonely. So he went into this monastery that had this vow of silence and poverty.

I found Chris terribly attractive, not so much in a sexual way, but as

a person. Charismatic. Brilliant. And one of the greatest gentlemen
I've known. So, being attracted to him, I declared myself.

Then I found out that another one of the vows they took in this
place was sexual abstinence! Christopher said to me, "Tennessee, it's
perfectly all right if I submit *passively* to oral intercourse, but I cannot
perform it. I'd be breaking the vow!" I howled with laughter, and so
did he. Then we cemented our friendship.

Yevtushenko

What's happened to him? Is he still in favor with the Soviets?

When he was last in the States he asked me to have lunch with
him. He ordered bottles of Chateau Lafite Rothschild. And the bill
was so tremendous it occupied three pages! I was stuck with it, of
course. I told him he was a fucking capitalist pig!

He was accompanied by this very fat gourmand of a translator who
didn't translate anything. Yevtushenko spoke perfect English and he
understood English perfectly. And the alleged translator didn't
understand a damn thing except how to eat and drink like a rich
capitalist!

I've heard a lot of people speak against Yevtushenko. I don't know
how far he can be trusted, but he's charming in his way. If you can
afford it.

Truman Capote

I met Truman in 1948, I guess. He'd just published *Other Voices,
Other Rooms*. I thought he was quite cute, slim, with this marvelously
witty, slightly malicious tongue. I got mad at him after awhile. He said
something cruel about Frankie. Frank Merlo, Jack Dunphy, who was
Truman's friend, and I, we were all travelling in my Buick Roadmaster
convertible. We'd gotten as far as Naples. At a waterfront restaurant
in Naples he said something quite cruel, and I said I'm not going on
to Ischia with this man. After a couple of days, Frankie talked me into
it. And we went anyway.

I never disliked Truman after that, I just realize that he has this
impulse to be catty at times. I think it's because he's a little guy who's
been picked on a lot, especially when he was growing up. You know,
Truman makes the mistake of claiming he was born in New Orleans,

and giving interviews, even points out the house he was born in. Everyone knows he was born in Huntsville, Alabama. Everyone in Huntsville claims him. They all know it, it's registered.

Now why does he do such things? I think it's because the poor little man likes mystery, likes to confuse people about himself. Well, Truman's a mythologist, baby, you know that. That's a polite way of saying he does fabricate. I love him too much to say he's a liar. That's part of his profession.

My Funniest Adventure

I was alone in Miami. Frank (Merlo) hadn't arrived yet from New York. I was staying in Miami until he got there and took me to Key West.

It was night, and I was lonely. I walked out onto Biscayne Boulevard. There's a park along there. This young vagrant was lolling on a bench. I think he was mentally retarded, poor child. I struck up a conversation with him. He seemed not too bright, but personable. I said I was alone, would he like to accompany me to my hotel? He said he would. Well, once he got under a street light I saw he'd never be able to go through a hotel lobby because his clothes were so dilapidated. So I suggested that we go out by the pool where I had a cabana.

We got out there, and he suddenly jerked my wallet out of my pocket. I had only seven dollars in it, though. Then he tried to get my wrist watch off. I had a very simple clasp upon it, but he couldn't manage to get it unclasped. Finally he gave up on that. I wasn't frightened at all for some reason. I was wearing a ring with three diamonds and he couldn't get that off either. It was a tight fit. So I said, "Now this is a very silly situation. I've got hundreds of dollars upstairs in my room. You sit down here and rest, and I'll be down in a little while with a large sum of money for you." I'd realized by this time that he was a moron.

Well, I went back to my room in the hotel, locked the door, and went to bed. And at half hour intervals all night, the phone would ring and he'd say, "I'm still waiting!" I finally said, "Baby, go see a doctor. You really think I was coming back down with a hundred dollars for you?" I liked the poor kid by that time.

It's the funniest adventure I ever had. "I'm still waiting!" He might still be.

Humor

You know, with advancing age I find humor more and more interesting. Black humor, especially. My present play, the one I'm working on (*The Everlasting Ticket*), I call a Gothic comedy. My humor is Gothic in theater. I make some serious, even tragic observations about society, but I make them through the medium of comedy.

The Rich

My feeling about the rich is not anger, really, but a feeling that they are emotionally restricted. They live in a very narrow, artificial world, like the world of Gloria Vanderbilt, who can be very unpleasant, you know. Or the Oscar de la Rentas, who are the most shocking of all. They are the Madame du Barrys of our time! You mention Oscar de la Renta to me and I turn purple with rage. They are basically very common people, you know. I know where he's from and how he started, and I know all about where she's from, too. Now they think they're the best thing since the invention of the wheel. I find them an outrageous symptom of our society, the shallowness and superficiality, the lack and fear of any depth that characterizes this age, this decade. It appalls me.

The Sixties were a decade of great vitality. The civil rights movement, the movement against war and imperialism. When I said to Gore Vidal "I slept through the Sixties" I was making a bad joke. I was intensely aware of what was going on. Even in the violent ward I read the newspapers avidly. Then we had brave young people fighting against privilege and injustice. Now we have the de la Rentas.

Today's College Kids

They aren't noticeable now. They seem to be totally reactionary, like the rich. The ones I've met rarely seem different from their parents in attitudes and values.

In the Sixties, or even the early Seventies, the kids I met seemed to be in revolt against the mores and social ideas of their parents. It may just be an illusion of mine, but it seems today that the children are frightened of deviating from their parents' way of life and thought. The ME-ME-ME Generation. Selfishness. A complete lack of interest in what's happening in the world. No interest in what's going on in El Salvador, this military junta supported by our government that rushes its troops into villages, pulls the peasants out and slaughters them! American kids don't care. In Guatemala, four hundred people a day being slaughtered, although no one mentions it much. Honduras. Don't they care, this generation? We know why Allende was assassinated, and how and why. All Latin America is in strife, and the ME-ME-ME Generation doesn't appear to care.

The Sixties were intensely alive! We were really progressing towards a workable, just society. But then Nixon came along, and everything fell back into its old routine of plutocracy.

Lectures

I don't give formal lectures, although they call them that. I just give formal readings. Once I went to the University of Tennessee in Knoxville with a prepared lecture. When I got there I discovered I'd left the lecture at home. So I had to get up on stage and improvise, which infuriated the professors. They were outraged! Knoxville, like other academic places, is very reactionary.

The State of the Culture

Literature has taken a back seat to the television, don't you think? It really has. We don't have a culture anymore that favors the creation of writers, or supports them very well. I mean, serious artists. On Broadway, what they want are cheap comedies and musicals and revivals. It's nearly impossible to get serious work even produced, and then it's lucky to have a run of a week. They knocked Albee's *Lolita* down horribly. I've never read such cruel reviews. But I felt it was a mistake for Albee to do adaptations. He's brilliant doing his own original work. But even so, I think there's a way of expressing one's critical displeasures with a play without being quite so hard, quite so cruel. The critics are literally killing writers.

Regrets

Oh God, yes, baby! But I can't think about them now. So many things to regret. But there are, I believe, so very *few* things that one can change in one's life. There are very few acts of volition. I don't believe in individual guilt. I don't think people are responsible for what they do. We are products of circumstances that determine what we do. That's why I think capital punishment's an outrage. But then the population growth and the growth of crime have become so enormous there aren't enough prisons to put people in. Prisons. Killing. Yet I don't believe in individual guilt at all, and sometimes I wonder whether I even believe in collective guilt. And yet I do believe that the intelligent person, the moral individual, must avoid evil and cruelty and dishonesties. One can try to pursue a path of virtue. That remains to us, I hope.

The Nobel Prize

I'll tell you why I think I haven't gotten it.

I'd heard I'd been nominated for it several times in the Fifties. But then suddenly a scandal happened. This lady, I call her the crepe de Chine Gypsy, went to Stockholm. And she lured me to Stockholm by telling me she was living in a charming little hotel near the waterfront, and that I would have my own suite with a private entrance. And that I would have a fantastic time, if you know what I mean—I was at the height of my fame then—she used my name as an excuse to get all the people around that she'd wanted to meet but had no way of meeting. She later turned out to be a dominatrix! Well, she had all the press there. She was like a field marshal! "You over that way! You over there! You do not approach Mr. Williams until I give you the signal!" Barking out orders. Oh, it was just terrifying. The next morning the newspapers all came out saying Mr. Williams arrived in Stockholm preceded by a very powerful press agent! And my agent in Scandinavia, Lars Schmidt, who married Ingrid Bergman, said, "You know, you've been nominated for the Nobel Prize but now it's finished." The scandal was so awful, the press having been abused, and they associated me with this awful woman.

Well, after all, one doesn't *have* to get it. It'd be nice because it's a lot of money, isn't it? I could use that, if I could get it.

Current Work

I've been busy with the production of the new play, *A House Not Meant To Stand*. The production of a play is for me an event that eclipses everything else, even turning seventy. I love the Goodman Theater, and I'm going to work with them again. We're already making plans to move this play on to the main stage, and to do *Something Cloudy, Something Clear*, about the summer when I met Kip on the Cape, though I've added other characters besides Kip and me.

And I've got an important play, *In Masks Outrageous and Austere*. It's a line of Eleanor Wylie's, from a poem by her. It goes like this: "In masks outrageous and austere / the years go by in single file; / Yet none has merited my fear, / and none has quite escaped my smile."

It happens to fit the play, which has a great deal of poetry in it and yet at the same time the situation is bizarre as hell. It's about the richest woman on earth. Babe Foxworth is her name. She doesn't know where she is. She's been abducted to Canada, on the east coast. But they don't know where they are. A village has been constructed like a movie set to deceive them. Everything is done to confine and deceive them while her husband is being investigated. Babe is really an admirable person, besides her hypersexuality, though that can be admirable. I think it is! It's a torture to her because she's married to a gay husband who's brought along his boyfriends. I think it's an extremely funny play.

Advice To Young Playwrights

What shouldn't you do if you're a young playwright? *Don't bore the audience!* I mean, even if you have to resort to totally arbitrary killing on stage, or pointless gunfire, at least it'll catch their attention and keep them awake. Just keep the thing going any way you can.

The Money People

Do you know what the most difficult aspect of playwriting is? I'll tell you. *It's dealing with the money people.* The commercial end of it is

the most appalling part. The demands for changes and rewrites don't
bother me if they're made by the director, and I think they're
intelligent demands. But when the money people get into the act,
you're in trouble.

My Most Difficult Play

I think *Clothes for a Summer Hotel* was the most difficult play to
write, of all my plays. Because of the documentation I had to do. I
had to spend four or five months reading everything there is about
Fitzgerald and Zelda. There's a huge amount of material. Finally,
when it was written I had to cut an hour out of the play on the road.
José Quintero was in very fragile health, and after every opening, he
had to flee. So I had to do it without any help or advice from
anybody. To cut an hour out of it. And then I had to start rewriting it.
The scene the critics objected to most violently was that between
Hemingway and Fitzgerald. But that's an integral part of the play
because each was a central figure in the life of the other. I thought the
confrontation between them indispensable. Now I've rewritten the
play again, and I've built up that scene, not so much in length of
playing time, but in content, making it more pointed.

Zelda Fitzgerald

Zelda's one great love affair was with this French aviator. It was her
first infidelity to Scott, and probably her only one. It was aggressive
because she was being liberated by infidelity from this very
possessive love that Scott had for her. And for the first time she was
experiencing erotic ecstasy. She'd never experienced that with Scott.
She used to complain to poor Scott that he was sexually inadequate.

She frightened the aviator by the violence of her reactions. She
went around the bend because of him. She tried to kill herself,
swallowing the contents of a bottle of morphine or something. The
aviator was frightened away.

Zelda was also terribly anti-Semitic, like most Southern women,
and a touch of it goes into the play (*Clothes*). I think I just couldn't
leave it out and do a true portrait of her. I have her make a single
anti-Semitic remark in the play, which is about Sheila Graham whose
real name is Lili Sheil.

In the theater you hardly dare use the word Jew, and it's really a detriment to a very fine people that they're so frightened of any criticism whatsoever, although after the Holocaust they certainly have reason to be frightened. I have no feelings of anti-Semitism, but those feelings do exist in other people, and it's difficult to present a picture of the world as it truly is without on occasion allowing a voice to those sentiments.

Children

I'm very happy I never had any children. There have been too many instances of extreme eccentricity and even lunacy in my family on all four sides for me to want to have children. I think it's fortunate I never did.

Rose, Dakin, and I are the last of two direct blood lines, the Dakin family, and the Williams. And all three of us are childless.

Handling Loneliness

It's not easy. I have a few close friends, though. And you can get by with a few. And as for sex? I don't feel I require it that much anymore. I miss having a companion very much. I'll never be without someone with me, although it'll just be someone who is fond of me and takes care of me, but it won't be a sexual thing anymore.

Death

Everyone's afraid of it, but I'm no more than most, I suppose. I'm beginning to reconcile myself to it. I'm *not* reconciled to dying before my work is finished, though. I have a very strong will. There were occasions in the last years or so when I might have gone out. But my will forces me to go on because I've got unfinished work.

Index

A

Academy of Motion Picture Arts and Sciences, 241
Actor's Workshop (San Francisco), 117
Ain't Misbehavin', 318
Albee, Edward, 95, 99, 120, 125, 131, 137, 189, 190, 219, 318, 319, 341
Albers, Joanna, 340
Alden, Hortense, 154, 274, 287
Allende, Salvador, 356
All My Sons (Miller), 65
Alpha Tau Omega, 6, 170
American Academy of Arts and Letters, 299
American Film Theater, 274
American National Theatre, 24
American Pen, 317
Anderson, Judith, 178
Anderson, Robert, 34
Angry Silence, The, 73
Anouilh, Jean, 99
Answered Prayers (Capote), 301
Arabian Nights, The, 17
Aria da Capo (Millay), 22
Ashley, Elizabeth, 275
Atkinson, Brooks, 189
Atlantic Monthly, 147, 188, 194, 232, 234
Auden, W.H., 22

B

Bachardy, Don, 352
Baddeley, Hermione, 117, 196, 235
"Ballad of Reading Gaol, The" (Wilde), 253
Bankhead, Tallulah, 117, 122, 154, 184, 196, 205, 226, 243, 282
Barnes, Bill, 225, 238, 281, 309
Barnes, Clive, 136, 213, 296
Barretts of Wimpole Street, The, 114
Barrymore, Diana, 86, 233
Barrymore, Ethel, 226

Batista, Fulgencio, 348
Baxley, Barbara, 351
"Beat the Devil" (Capote), 177
Beatty, Warren, 337
Beckett, Samuel, 95, 98, 120, 137, 316
Bel Geddes, Barbara, 165
Bergman, Ingrid, 357
Berlin, Irving, 186
Berman, Pandro, 242, 350
Bernstein, Leonard, 330
Best Man, The (Vidal), 70
Bishop, Elizabeth, 268
Blind Ambition (Dean), 321
Blues, the, 92-93
Bogart, Humphrey, 177
Book of Changes, 305
Booth, Shirley, 237
Boston, 7, 10, 18, 25, 193, 296
Bowden, Charles, 109
Bowles, Jane, 159, 167, 200, 222, 246, 299, 339-40
Bowles, Paul, 93, 167, 222, 282, 299, 302-3, 304, 339-40
Brandeis University, 108
Brando, Marlon, 42, 52, 119, 203-4, 242, 244, 253, 273, 320, 337
Breen, Robert, 20, 22, 23
Britneva, Maria (Lady Maria St Juste), 155-56, 280-83 passim
Broadway, 3, 5, 6, 12, 21, 23, 25, 26, 27, 31, 33, 34, 36, 37, 45, 47, 51, 52, 56, 66, 84, 93, 95-96, 101, 108, 136, 156, 157-58, 165, 213, 218, 219, 275, 290-91, 299, 314, 318, 329, 356; Off-Broadway, 27, 52, 56, 61, 66, 84, 85, 93, 96, 99, 101-2, 165, 291, 314
"Broken Tower, The" (Crane), 209
Brooks, Richard, 275
Brooks, Stella, 340
Buckley, Tom, 147, 232
Buckley, William, 227

Bujold, Genevieve, 289
Burch, Dr. George, 186
Burroughs, William, 222, 299
Burton, Richard, 195
Bus Stop (Inge), 34

C

Cadmus, Paul, 345
Campbell, Sandy M., 345
Campbell, Victor Herbert, 185-206 *passim*,
     226, 250, 252
Cancer Ward (Solzhenitsyn), 282
Cantor, Arthur, 151
Capote, Joe, 177
Capote, Nina, 177
Capote, Truman, 155, 156, 177, 198-99,
     224, 246, 301, 353-54
Caretaker, The (Pinter), 95, 98
Carter, Jimmy, 349
Caskie, Bill, 352
Cassidy, Claudia, 193, 239, 329
Castro, Fidel, 321, 348
Cavett, Dick, 251
Chaplin, Charlie, 241, 242
Chekhov, Anton, 28, 85, 114, 131, 221,
     245, 282, 331
Cherry Orchard, The (Chekhov), 71
Chicago, 6, 18, 26, 78, 83, 85, 86, 93,
     109, 193, 239, 257, 266, 325, 329
Chinatown (Polanski), 252
Clark, Dane, 104
Clift, Montgomery, 154, 350
Clock Without Hands (McCullers), 200
Clurman, Harold, 42, 46, 265
Cocteau, Jean, 303
Colby, Bob, 291
Coleridge, Samuel Taylor, 303
Colton, John, 164
Come Back Little Sheba (Inge), 351
Conflagration (Mishima), 73(film)
Cooper, Gary, 25
Cornell, Katharine, 114
Corsaro, Frank, 97
Crane, Hart, 20, 23, 199, 209, 246, 251,
     267-68, 293, 321
Crane, Stephen, 264
Crawford, Cheryl, 22, 33
Crowley, Aleister, 306
Curtains (Tynan), 88

D

Dakin, Rosina Otte (grandmother of TW),
     57-58, 234, 322

Dakin, the Reverend Walter Edwin (grand-
     father of TW), 5, 39, 44, 57, 87, 127,
     153, 163, 166-67, 169, 200, 260, 322,
     333
Dancin' (Fosse), 318
Dante, 233
David Frost Show, the, 198, 232
Davis, Bette, 97, 101, 165, 193
"Day in the Opening, A" (Jane Bowles),
     282
Dean, John, 321
Dear Ruth, 20
Death of a Salesman (Miller), 33, 65, 66
de la Renta, Oscar, 355
Dennis, Sandy, 320
"De Profundis" (Wilde), 253
De Quincey, Thomas, 303
Diary of Anaïs Nin, The, 131
Dickinson, Emily, 267-68
Didion, Joan, 246, 321
DiMaggio, Joe, 276
Dirksen, Everett M., 132, 184
Dorian Gray (Wilde), 253
Doubleday, 227
Dowling, Eddie, 6, 14-15, 27, 107
Drama Critics Circle Award, 12, 18, 25, 34,
     47, 108, 109
Dramatists Guild, 151
"Dream of Tennessee Williams, A" (New-
     love), 147, 195
Duino Elegies (Rilke), 251
Dulles, John Foster, 348
Dunaway, Faye, 252, 273, 302
Dunphy, Jack, 246, 353
Durrell, Lawrence, 201
Duse, 329

E

Eliot, T.S., 22, 321
Entertaining Mr. Sloane (Orton), 341
Esquire, 148, 194-95, 232
Evans, Maurice, 3
Evans, Oliver, 156, 158, 269, 278-79
Existentialism, 121

F

Fadiman, William, 11
Farther Off From Heaven (Inge), 21
Faulkner, Henry, 168
Faulkner, William, 95, 120-21, 128, 155,
     264, 321
Federal Theatre Project, 23

Ferlinghetti, Lawrence, 134
Feuillère, Edwige, 208
Fields, W.C., 242
Finnegans Wake (Joyce), 272
Fitzgerald, F. Scott, 214, 246, 321-22, 347-48, 352, 359
Fitzgerald, Zelda, 321-22, 359
Five Young Poets (Laughlin), 7
Fonda, Jane, 320
Ford, Tennessee Ernie, 240
Forster, E.M., 294
Fosse, Bob, 318
Freud, 119, 129, 201, 245
Friends and Vague Lovers (Dunphy), 246
Frost, David, 198, 232
Funeral Games (Orton), 341

G

Garbo, Greta, 61, 166, 195, 229
Gassner, John, 7
Gelber, Jack, 95, 98
Genet, Jean, 222, 263
Get Away, Old Man (Saroyan), 15
Getty, J. Paul, 156
Ghosts (Ibsen), 114, 221
Gide, André, 25, 198, 225, 245
Gielgud, Sir John, 319
Gin Game, The, 318
Giraudoux, Jean, 99
Glavin, Bill, 139, 171, 172, 173
Glenvill, Peter, 289, 290
Godfather, The, 320 (film)
Goethe, 221
Graham, Billy, 250
Graham, Sheila, 348, 359. See Lili Sheil.
Great Gatsby, The (Fitzgerald), 246, 301
Greek tragedy, 76-77, 273
Greene, Graham, 304
Grizzard, George, 108
Group Theatre, 7
Gysin, Brion, 299

H

Hagen, Uta, 89
Hall, Willis, 62
Halliwell, Kenneth, 341
Hamlet (Shakespeare), 270
Hancock, John, 117
Handke, Peter, 321
Harris, Julie, 154, 165
Harris, Richard, 244
Harvey, 20

Hassan i Sabbah, 306
Havana, 348
Havoc, June, 152
Haydon, Julie, 6
Hayes, Helen, 165-66
Hellman, Lillian, 350-51
Hemingway, Ernest, 121, 155, 167, 214, 220, 222, 245-46, 264, 321, 347-48, 352, 359
Hemingway, Mary, 222
Hepburn, Katharine, 154, 274, 350
Herlihy, James Leo, 187
Hill, George Roy, 66
Hingle, Pat, 108
Hiroshima, Mon Amour, 77
Hitchcock, Alfred, 301
Hollywood, 3, 8, 10, 36, 71, 102, 117, 166, 196, 217, 242, 286, 350
Hopkins, Miriam, 3, 7, 18, 193
Horney, Karen, 119
Hunter, Tab, 117, 196
Hutchins, Robert Maynard, 94

I

I Am Curious, 137
I Ching, 305
Iceman Cometh, The (O'Neill), 341
In Cold Blood, 252(film)
Inge, William, 21, 34, 219, 339, 351-52
International Creative Management (ICM), 338
International Famous Agency, 225
In the Summer House (Jane Bowles), 167, 222, 282
Ionesco, Eugène, 99
Iowa, University of, 4, 6, 7, 17, 220-21, 230, 281, 327
Isherwood, Christopher, 163, 242, 352-53
Islands in the Stream (Hemingway), 222, 347
Ives, Burl, 244

J

Jackson, Anne, 246
Jacobson, Max, 120, 148, 255, 303, 332, 333, 343
John Birch Society, 90
Jones, Jennifer, 177
Jones, Margo, 11, 21, 22, 29, 246, 337, 340
Jonson, Ben, 21
Joyce, James, 221, 272

K

Kazan, Elia, 26, 31, 33, 36, 41, 44, 52, 59, 64-68 passim, 88, 92, 99-100, 101, 104, 119, 122-23, 154, 159, 216-17, 335, 349
Keach, Stacy, 319
Kennedy, Jacqueline, 348-49
Kennedy, John F., 252, 292, 348
Kerr, Walter, 136, 189, 235, 265
Key West, 35, 36, 38, 47, 66, 105, 109-10, 131, 137, 147, 148, 149, 153, 158, 159, 161, 162, 166-67, 172, 173, 178, 182, 186, 187-88, 189, 193-94, 202, 213-14, 215, 232, 236, 238, 243, 251, 254, 268, 293, 297, 318, 321, 323, 325, 328, 329, 333, 342
Kiernan, Kip, 339, 346-47, 358
Kilgallen, Dorothy, 252
Kirstein, Lincoln, 352
Knight, Shirley, 309-16 passim
Kopit, Arthur, 99
Kramer, Hazel, 332
Kubie, Lawrence, 169, 245
Kupcinet, Irv, 93

L

Lambert, Gavin, 242
Lanier, Sidney, 6, 95, 257
Lansing, Robert, 274
Last of the Southern Winds, The (Loovis), 166, 182
Last Tango in Paris, 320
LaTouche, John, 340
Laughlin, Clarence, 300
Laughlin, James, 7, 29
Laurette, 66
Laurie, Piper, 108
Lawrence, D.H., 4, 36, 85, 221, 245, 251, 253, 254, 331
Lawrence, Frieda, 254
Lee, Gypsy Rose, 159
Le Gallienne, Eva, 22
Leigh, Vivien, 165, 205, 243
Leighton, Margaret, 82, 83, 97, 101, 158, 165, 243
Liebling, Bill, 151
Life, 157, 190, 236
Little Foxes, The (Hellman), 350
Little, Stuart W., 151
Loggia, Robert, 42
Lolita (Albee adaptation), 356
London, 27, 62, 77, 95, 110, 155
London Magazine, 345

Long and the Short and the Tall, The (Hall), 62
Long Day's Journey Into Night (O'Neill), 40, 335
Loot (Orton), 341
Loovis, David, 161, 162, 170, 172, 181-82
Lorca, Garcia, 28
Lorre, Peter, 177
"Love, Love, Love" (Vidal), 72-73
Lowry, Jane, 313
Lumet, Sidney, 119, 204, 349
Lyndon, Andrew, 161, 163, 172-83 passim

M

Macbeth (Shakespeare), 270
MacGregor, Robert, 343
Machiz, Herbert, 101
MacLeish, Archibald, 22
Madden, Donald, 135, 319
Magnani, Anna, 36, 42, 47, 62, 110, 119, 165, 192, 204, 243
Mailer, Norman, 343, 344
Malraux, André, 348
Mankiewicz, Joe, 304
Mann, Thomas, 242
Manson, Charles, 252
Marjoe, 250
Marlowe, Christopher, 21
Marriage Is a Private Affair, 202, 286, 350
"Marshes of Glynn, The" (Lanier), 257
Marx Brothers, 338
McCarthy, Joseph, 132, 291
McCullers, Carson, 89, 94, 107-8, 155, 156-57, 168, 186, 199-200, 222, 233, 246, 339
McCullers, Reeves, 199, 200
McGee, Leoncia, 172, 243
McGhee, Brownie, 92
McGovern, George, 248
McGrath, Leueen, 109
Meacham, Anne, 135, 157, 165, 173, 190, 236, 274, 287, 333
Mead, Taylor, 304
Member of the Wedding, The (McCullers), 156, 199, 339
Merlo, Frank, 155, 171, 188, 191, 230, 233-35, 242, 245, 255-56, 279-80, 322, 334, 340, 343, 353, 354
Merrick, David, 290, 291, 336
Merton, Thomas, 134
Metro-Goldwyn-Mayer, 8, 11, 166, 202, 242, 286, 346
Mexico, 85, 118, 330, 339-40

Michelangelo, 201
Milk, Harvey, 322
Millay, Edna St. Vincent, 22
Miller, Arthur, 26, 65, 88, 100, 120
Miller, Henry, 263
Mills, Clark, 7, 259
Miner, Jan, 313, 314-15
Mishima, Yukio, 73
Mississippi, 3, 4, 5, 6, 9, 12, 16-17, 46, 79, 87, 169
Missouri, University of, 7, 17, 259
Mitchell, Martha, 252
Monroe, Marilyn, 350
Moore, Charlotte, 313, 314, 315
Moore, Marianne, 268, 321
Moriarty, Michael, 319-32
Morley, Robert, 177
Morris, Newbold, 20
Moscone, George, 322
Mount, Winchell, 330
Murray, Peg, 309, 313, 314-15
Myra Breckinridge (Vidal), 186

N

Naked Lunch (Burroughs), 299
Nathan, George Jean, 14-15
National Theatre Conference, 23
Natural Affection (Inge), 351
Nazimova, 114, 221
Nettleton, Lois, 314
New Directions, 7, 29, 343
Newlove, Donald, 147
Newman, Paul, 242, 253
New Mexico, 4, 254
New Orleans, 4, 8, 29, 48, 150, 151, 152, 159, 166, 173, 185, 188, 189, 192, 194, 197-98, 200-1, 203, 226, 231, 251, 262, 279, 281, 297, 300, 353-54
New School of Social Research (New York), 7
New Wave writers, 95, 98-99
New York, 6, 7, 9, 11, 26, 29, 35, 38, 43, 45, 47, 50, 59, 69, 78, 97, 102, 107, 109-10, 131, 137, 154, 169, 187, 252, 261, 297, 325, 329, 335
New York Herald Tribune, 12
New York Times, 115-16, 162, 190, 195, 213
Night and Day (Stoppard), 319
Nijinsky, Vlasilov, 276
Nin, Anaïs, 131, 192
Nixon, Richard M., 132, 218, 248, 249, 252, 356

Nobel Prize, 317, 357
No Man's Land (Pinter), 289
North, the, 43, 48

O

O'Brien, Margaret, 202, 242, 350
O'Connor, Flannery, 94, 222, 246
O'Horgan, Tom, 240
Olivier, Sir Laurence, 319
O'Neal, Patrick, 97, 101
One Flew Over the Cuckoo's Nest, 257(film)
O'Neill, Eugene, 3, 40, 61, 63, 114, 317, 319, 341
Orton, Joe, 335, 341
Osborne, John, 62, 95, 99
Oswald, Lee Harvey, 252
Othello (Shakespeare), 270
Other Voices, Other Rooms (Capote), 353
Outward Bound, 30

P

Page, Geraldine, 82-83, 89, 165, 242, 320, 337
Pancho, 339, 340
Paris Review, 123, 227, 325
Parsons, Estelle, 204, 336
Partisan Review, 72
Part of a Long Story, 62
Pasolini, Pier Paolo, 202
Paul Slickey (Osborne), 62
Pinter, Harold, 95, 98, 99, 282, 289, 319
Play It As It Lays (Didion), 246
Playmakers, The (Little and Cantor), 151
Plimpton, George, 123, 227, 325
Poetry: A Magazine of Verse, 7
Polanski, Roman, 252
Pollock, Jackson, 294
Porterfield, Bob, 20, 22, 23
Producers Theater, 42
Proust, Marcel, 31, 245, 246
Pulitzer Prize, 34, 45, 47, 64, 108, 192
Purgatory (Yeats), 272

Q

Quinn, Anthony, 291
Quintero, José, 66-67, 204, 335-36, 359

R

Rader, Dotson, 318, 345

Ransom, John Crowe, 321
Ray, Johnny, 33
Reagan, Ronald, 349
Reed, Rex, 232
Reid, Kate, 109
Repertory Theatre (New Orleans), 152
Represented by Audrey Wood (Wood and
    Wilk), 338
Richard II (Shakespeare), 189
Richardson, Sir Ralph, 319
Richardson, Tony, 205
Riggs, Lynn, 21
Rilke, Rainer Maria, 245, 251
Rimbaud, Arthur, 245
Rockefeller Foundation, 11, 151, 166, 194,
    279
Rome, 35, 36, 47, 110, 131, 137, 155-56,
    187, 217, 238
Room Service, 338
"Rose for Emily, A" (Faulkner), 264
Ruby, Jack, 252
Run River (Didion), 246

S

Sagan, Françoise, 208
"Sailing to Byzantium" (Yeats), 272
San Francisco, 322-23
Saroyan, William, 15, 26, 27, 28
Sartre, Jean Paul, 121
Save Me the Waltz (Zelda Fitzgerald), 322
Schmidlapp, Horace, 22
Schmidt, Lars, 357
Schneider, Alan, 109
Schwartz, Delmore, 22
Scott, George C., 241
"Selected Memories of the Glorious Bird
    and the Golden Age" (Vidal), 321
Selznick, Irene, 52
Senso (Visconti), 203
Seventies, the, 288, 355-56
Sevier, John (Williams' ancestor), 5
Shakespeare, 21, 23, 74, 76, 114, 269-71
Shanghai Gesture, The (Colton), 164
Shaw, George Bernard, 3
Sheil, Lili, 359. *See* Sheila Graham.
Sidney, Sylvia, 300
"Simple Enquiry, A" (Hemingway), 347
Sirhan, Sirhan, 252
Sitwell, Edith, 271
Sixties, the, 148, 185, 190, 196, 207, 218,
    233, 236, 239, 261, 287, 297, 298, 320,
    332, 336, 343, 355-56
Skin of Our Teeth, The (Wilder), 33

Smith, Jane, 325
Smith, Tony, 294, 325
Snyder, Gary, 134
Solzhenitsyn, Aleksandr, 282
"Song of the Chattahoochee" (Lanier), 6,
    257
Southern writing, 73-75, 94-95, 128, 199,
    222, 246, 321
South, the, 5, 11, 16, 43-49 *passim*, 73-75,
    94-95, 132, 199, 359
Spark, Muriel, 321
Spellman, Francis Cardinal, 43, 57
Spiegel, Sam, 154, 274-75, 304, 349
Spoleto Festival (Charleston, SC), 309
Stallone, Sylvester, 349
Stanley, Kim, 205, 241
Stapleton, Maureen, 42, 89, 108, 165,
    204-5, 242, 315, 320, 351
Stein, Gertrude, 347
Steinbecks, the John, 67
Stevens, Ashton, 329
Stevens, Wallace, 268
Stevenson, Adlai, 311
St. Louis, 4, 5, 6, 10, 12, 13, 17, 79-80,
    113, 142, 143, 149, 154, 162, 169, 173,
    199, 203, 221, 230, 236, 257, 259, 299,
    316, 326-27, 351
Stone, Irving, 201
Stone, Mrs. Irving, 201
Stoppard, Tom, 319
Story, 7
Strindberg, August, 72, 131, 276

T

Tandy, Jessica, 89, 154, 165, 320
Taylor, Elizabeth, 86, 120, 154, 204, 244,
    275, 326, 350
Taylor, Laurette, 6, 18, 23, 27, 165, 199,
    329, 337
Tea and Sympathy (Anderson), 34
Tender Is the Night (Fitzgerald), 246, 322
Terry, Sonny, 92
Theatre '47 (Dallas), 21, 29
Theatre Guild, 3, 7, 9, 18, 25, 166, 193
Theatre of the Absurd, 109, 118, 269
Thirties, the, 194
Thomas, Dylan, 323
Thurber, James, 193
Time, 93-94, 157, 163, 236, 326
Titus Andronicus (Shakespeare), 269, 274
To Have and Have Not (Hemingway), 167
Travesties (Stoppard), 319
Turner, Lana, 11, 202, 242, 286, 350

Twenties, the, 301
Two Serious Ladies (Jane Bowles), 282
Two Sisters (Vidal), 185-86, 246
Tynan, Kenneth, 82, 88, 155, 321, 348

U

Uecker, Joe, 284
Ulysses (Joyce), 272
Untermeyer, Louis, 22
U.S. Public Theatre Foundation, 24

V

Vaccaro, Marion Black, 333, 337
Vanderbilt, Gloria, 355
Vidal, Gore, 70, 72, 148, 155-56, 185-86,
    204, 207, 226, 233, 246, 304, 321, 348,
    355
View From the Bridge, A (Miller), 100
Village Voice, 206
Vinal, Harold, 261
Visconti, Luchino, 159, 203
Voight, Jon, 302

W

Wallace, George, 252
Warner, Jack, 235
Warren, Robert Penn, 95
Washington University, 4, 7, 17, 336
Watergate, 266
Watts, Richard, 54
Waugh, Evelyn, 304
Way of Chuang Tzu, The (Merton), 134
Webster, John, 21
Webster, Margaret, 3, 18, 22, 25
Welles, Orson, 320
Welty, Eudora, 94
West, Mae, 242
What the Butler Saw (Orton), 341
White, Dan, 322
Whitman, Walt, 20, 267
Who's Afraid of Virginia Woolf? (Albee), 189
Wilde, Oscar, 253
Wilder, Thornton, 33
Wilk, Max, 338
Williams, Cornelius Coffin (father of TW), 5,
    6, 126, 153, 169, 188, 220, 245,
    257-59, 281, 327, 331, 332
Williams, Dakin (brother of TW), 149,

172-76 passim, 184, 194, 236-37, 248,
    254-55, 322, 333, 360
Williams, Edwina Dakin (mother of TW), 5,
    6, 89, 116, 126, 127, 142, 143, 149,
    153, 161-62, 169, 176, 188, 236-37,
    247, 258-59, 262, 326-28
Williams, Isabel (aunt of TW), 153, 159,
    257
Williams, John Sharp (Williams' ancestor), 9
Williams, Rose Isabel (sister of TW), 87, 89,
    116, 146, 153-54, 162, 176-77 (Rose
    Isabel Williams Foundation), 187, 188,
    197, 200, 226, 247, 259-60, 262, 284,
    322, 323-24, 326-29, 330-31, 360
Williams, Tennessee (Thomas Lanier Wil-
    liams):
  Life: childhood and adolescence, 3, 5,
    12, 16-17, 46, 79-80, 87, 104, 112-13,
    127-28, 129, 142-43, 153, 169, 230,
    258, 326, 332; drugs, 114, 130, 144,
    148-49, 172, 185, 191, 205, 206, 255,
    303-4, 306, 343-44; education, 4, 7, 17,
    170-71, 220-21, 230, 231, 259, 281;
    family relations, 10, 12, 16, 79, 87, 110,
    162, 169, 176-77, 327; homosexuality,
    146, 159, 169-71, 181, 189, 198,
    228-32, 248, 249, 280, 322-23, 330,
    332, 339, 340, 344-47, 352-53, 354-55;
    illness, 51, 60, 105, 113, 135, 137-38,
    143, 144-45, 147, 148-49, 162-64,
    173-76, 184-85, 186-88, 190, 191, 196,
    197, 219, 236-38, 255, 278-79, 293-94,
    297, 326, 332-33, 343-44; psycho-
    analysis, 50-52, 54-55, 110, 115, 119,
    152, 169, 187, 220, 244-45; religion,
    57-58, 72, 109, 127, 137, 140-41,
    149-50, 168-69, 195, 206, 248, 255,
    333-34; social values, 5, 15, 57, 81, 90,
    92, 128-29, 131-33, 146, 248-49, 252,
    266-67, 292-93, 297-98, 322-23,
    355-57, 359-60
  Works: All in One, 36; American Blues,
    7; Androgyne, Mon Amour, 305; And
    Tell Sad Stories of the Deaths of Queens,
    189; "Angel in the Alcove, The," 301,
    302 (see Vieux Carré); "Auto-Da-Fé,"
    218; Baby Doll, 43, 44, 45, 54, 57, 119,
    217, 220, 244, 258 (see 27 Wagons Full
    of Cotton); Battle of Angels, 3, 4, 5, 7,
    9-10, 18, 25, 27, 28, 36, 42, 84, 166,
    193, 254 (see Orpheus Descending and
    The Fugitive Kind); Blanche's Chair in the
    Moon, 215, 331 (see A Streetcar Named
    Desire); Blue Mountain Ballads, 93;
    Camino Real, 27, 30-33, 36, 66, 67,

91-92, 118, 120, 134, 142, 175, 200, 233, 285, 286, 287, 298; *Candles to the Sun*, 7; *Cat on a Hot Tin Roof*, 34-35, 36, 37, 39, 40, 41, 45-46, 52, 54, 66, 72 (film), 86, 88, 92, 117, 119 (film), 130, 154 (film), 155, 164, 204 (film), 216-17, 244 (film), 251, 266, 273, 275, 279, 285, 298, 316, 323, 348; *Clothes for a Summer Hotel*, 321-22, 347, 359; *Creve Coeur*, 308-17 *passim*; "Desire and the Black Masseur," 217-18, 274; *Eccentricities of a Nightingale, The*, 320 (*see Summer and Smoke*); *Edible, Very*, 218; *Eight Women (Eight Mortal Ladies Possessed: A Book of Stories)*, 277; *Enemy: Time, The*, 59 (*see Sweet Bird of Youth*); *Everlasting Ticket, The*, 335, 355; *Fugitive Kind, The*, 7 (play); 68 (film), 204 (film) (*see Battle of Angels* and *Orpheus Descending*); *Garden District*, 50, 56, 57 (*see* "Something Unspoken" and *Suddenly Last Summer*); *Glass Menagerie, The*, 6, 9, 10, 12, 13-15, 18, 20, 25, 26, 28, 29, 34, 36, 38, 39, 47, 70 (film), 80-82, 87, 105, 107, 108, 115, 117, 122, 154 (film), 156, 165-66, 168, 188, 194, 196, 242, 244, 247, 257, 259, 285, 286-87, 298, 329-30, 331, 332, 339, 349 (film), 351 (*see* "Portrait of a Girl in Glass"); "Gnädiges Fräulein, The," 116, 165, 235, 288 (*see Slapstick Tragedy* and "The Mutilated"); *Hang It Loose*, 195; *Hide and Seek*, 36; *Hi-Point Over a Cavern*, 142 (*see Period of Adjustment*); *House Not Meant to Stand, A*, 325, 336, 358; *I Can't Imagine Tomorrow*, 136; "Ice-Blue Wind, The," 179; *I Never Get Dressed 'Til After Dark on Sunday*, 178 (*see Vieux Carré*); *In Masks Outrageous and Austere*, 358; *In the Bar of a Tokyo Hotel*, 134, 135-37, 139, 157, 163, 172, 190, 235, 236, 288, 289, 293-94, 333; *I Rise in Flame, Cried the Phoenix*, 254; *Kingdom of Earth*, 163, 235, 335 (*see The Seven Descents of Myrtle*); "Kitchen Door Blues," 258; *Knightly Quest, The*, 123; *Memoirs*, 227, 250, 284, 293, 295, 296, 322, 323-24; *Milk Train Doesn't Stop Here Anymore*, 117, 119, 163, 195, 196, 205, 210-11, 235, 243, 287-88 (film); "Mutilated, The," 165 (*see Slapstick Tragedy* and "The Gnädiges Fräulein); *Night of the Iguana, The*, 78, 80-82, 83-87, 93, 97-98, 100, 101, 104, 109, 118, 153,

157, 158, 168 (film), 193, 200, 209, 210, 213, 233, 235, 260, 266, 312; *Now and at the Hour of Our Death*, 138; *One Arm*, 158 (screenplay), 303 (screenplay); *One Arm and Other Stories*, 302-3; *Orpheus Descending*, 36, 38, 42, 45, 46, 47, 51, 52, 55, 68, 84, 86, 104, 108-9, 119, 128, 136, 150, 169, 209, 211, 324 (*see Battle of Angels* and *The Fugitive Kind*); *Out Cry*, 239, 249, 255, 266, 282, 289-90, 302, 308 (*see The Two-Character Play*); *Period of Adjustment*, 62, 64, 66, 67, 104, 117, 141, 142, 285 (*see Hi-Point Over a Cavern*); "Portrait of a Girl in Glass," 259-60, 331 (*see The Glass Menagerie*); *Recluse and His Guest, A*, 138; *Rectangle with Hooks, A*, 138; *Red Devil Battery Sign, The*, 251, 266, 273-74, 285, 291-92, 296, 297-98; *Roman Spring of Mrs. Stone, The*, 61, 67-68, 244 (film), 337 (film); *Rose Tattoo, The*, 36, 38, 42, 47, 54, 89, 117, 125, 135; "Rubio y Morena," 217; *Seven Descents of Myrtle, The*, 204, 235, 335-36 (*see Kingdom of Earth*); *Silver Victrola, The*, 346 (*see Something Cloudy, Something Clear*); *Slapstick Tragedy*, 109, 120, 126, 163, 235, 288 (*see* "The Gnädiges Fräulein" and "The Mutilated"); *Small Craft Warnings*, 213, 215, 216, 219, 225, 227-28, 238, 249, 281-82, 289; *Something Cloudy, Something Clear*, 346, 358 (*see The Silver Victrola*); "Something Unspoken," 52, 218 (*see Garden District* and *Suddenly Last Summer*); *Stairs to the Roof*, 5, 10, 32, 214-15; *Streetcar Named Desire, A*, 25-29 *passim*, 33, 35, 36, 38, 45, 47, 52, 54, 64, 66, 71 (film), 80-82, 84, 86, 110-22 *passim*, 152, 153-54, 159, 173, 189, 197, 200, 203-4, 205, 209, 211, 215, 216, 217 (film), 224, 228-29, 239, 243, 244 (film), 255, 266, 273, 275 (film), 276-77, 285, 297-98, 302, 310-11, 314, 316, 330-31, 337, 340, 349 (film) (*see Blanche's Chair in the Moon*); *Suddenly Last Summer*, 50, 52, 69-70 (film), 74, 86, 101, 118, 146, 154 (film), 210, 214, 274, 287, 288, 304 (film), 327 (*see Garden District* and "Something Unspoken"); *Summer and Smoke*, 29, 36, 38, 66, 82-83, 84, 89, 108, 156, 199, 203, 215, 216, 228, 246, 324, 335 (*see The Eccentricities of a Nightingale*); *Sweet Bird of Youth*, 52-53,

59, 60, 62, 66, 89, 103, 136, 154 (film), 159, 165, 208, 211, 244 (film), 250, 253 (film), 275 (film), 323 (*see The Enemy: Time*); *Tennessee Williams' Letters to Donald Windham, 1940-1965*, 344-45; "Three Players of a Summer Game," 138, 217; *27 Wagons Full of Cotton*, 36, 218 (*see Baby Doll*); *Two-Character Play, The*, 158, 164-65, 179, 193, 239, 338 (*see Out Cry*); "Two on a Party," 217; *Unsatisfactory Supper, The*, 218; *Vieux Carré*, 299, 300-2 (*see I Never Get Dressed 'Til After Dark on Sunday*); "What's Next on the Agenda, Mr. Williams?" 179-80; *Will Mr. Merriwether Return from Memphis?* 138; "Yellow Bird, The," 78 (Caedmon recording), 273 (Caedmon recording); *You Touched Me* (with Donald Windham), 21, 36, 39.

Writing: apprenticeship, 4-5, 7-8, 10-11, 17-18, 28-29, 48, 112-14, 143-44, 150-52, 166-67, 193-94, 202-3, 242, 281, 286-87, 293, 300, 326; critics, 41, 51-52, 56-57, 61-62, 66-67, 83-85, 93-94, 96, 108-9, 117-18, 119, 130, 136-37, 157-58, 164-65, 189-90, 193, 208, 213, 219, 235-36, 239-41, 255, 263, 265, 285-86, 296-97, 319, 335, 356; dramaturgy, 28, 31-33, 41, 52-53, 59-61, 65, 66, 67, 88, 98-99, 103, 108, 117-18, 123, 125, 128-29, 196-98, 214-15, 216-17, 218, 240, 249-50, 264-65, 273-74, 277, 282, 285, 294, 300, 304, 308, 311-12, 314-15, 316, 330-31, 334-35, 341, 358; film adaptations, 67-68, 69-72, 119-20, 154, 203-4, 217, 244, 274-76, 287-88, 303, 304, 320-21, 349-50; habits of work, 11, 26, 28, 31, 47, 62, 104-6, 111, 114-15, 117-18, 121-22, 124, 129-30, 152, 154-55, 195-96, 214-16, 265, 295; production, 26, 48, 60, 62, 64-68 *passim*, 83-85, 88, 95-96, 101-2, 117, 122-23, 154, 193, 217, 279, 289-91, 308-17 *passim*, 318-19, 335-36, 336-38, 341-42, 342-43, 358; southern temper, 11, 16, 43-49 *passim*, 94, 241; themes, 14, 28, 32, 37, 39-40, 42, 45, 50-51, 55-56, 59, 61, 67, 71, 77, 82-83, 90-92, 103-4, 110-11, 116-17, 118-19, 128, 142, 145-46, 150, 210-12, 216, 233, 244, 257, 274, 276-77, 287-89, 291-92, 293-94, 304, 316
Williams, William Carlos, 268-69
Wilson, Lanford, 341
Windham, Donald, 36, 39, 260, 261-62, 344-46
Wolfe, Thomas, 25
Wood, Audrey, 29, 115, 149, 151-52, 164-65, 166, 188-89, 190, 194, 238, 242, 333, 338-39, 351
Woodward, Joanne, 204
Woolf, Virginia, 272
Worth, Irene, 320
Wylie, Eleanor, 358
Wyman, Jane, 349

Y

Yeats, William Butler, 272
Yevtushenko, Yevgeny, 249, 281-82, 353
York, Michael, 242, 250, 289
Young, John, 161, 171-72, 176, 177, 181, 182
Young, Stark, 189
Yurka, Blanche, 22

Z

Zoerink, Richard, 328